Afro-Marxist
Regimes

Afro-Marxist Regimes

Ideology and Public Policy

edited by
Edmond J. Keller
&
Donald Rothchild

Lynne Rienner Publishers • Boulder & London

Cover design by Douglas B. Hecox

Published in the United States of America in 1987 by
Lynne Rienner Publishers, Inc.
948 North Street, Boulder, Colorado 80302

and in the United Kingdom by
Lynne Rienner Publishers, Inc.
3 Henrietta Street, Covent Garden, London WC2E 8LU

Library of Congress Cataloging–in–Publication Data

Afro–Marxist regimes.

 Proceedings of a conference held in Santa Barbara,
Calif., From Dec. 6-8, 1985.
 Bibliography: p.
 Includes index.
 1. Ethiopia—Politics and government—1974– —
Congresses. 2. Mozambique—Politics and government—
1975– —Congresses. 3. Angola—Politics and
government—1975– —Congresses. 4. Zimbabwe—
Politics and government—1980– —Congresses.
5. Socialism—Africa, Sub–Saharan—Case studies—
Congresses. 6. Africa, Sub–Saharan—Foreign
relations—United States—Case studies—Congresses.
7. United States—Foreign relations—Africa,
Sub–Saharan—Case studies—Congresses. 8. Africa,
Sub–Saharan—Foreign relations—Soviet Union—
Case studies—Congresses. 9. Soviet Union—Foreign
relations—Africa, Sub–Saharan—Case studies—
Congresses. I. Keller, Edmond J., 1942–   .
II. Rothchild, Donald S.
JQ3752.A38 1987   321.9'2'0967   87–16776
ISBN 0–931477–90–5 (lib. bdg.)
ISBN 1–55587–100–3 (pbk.)

Printed and bound in the United States of America

The paper used in this publication meets the
requirements of the American National Standard
for Permanence of Paper for Printed Library
Materials Z39.48–1984. ⊗

Life continues in those who continue the revolution...A Luta Continua!
—Samora Moises Machel

This book is dedicated to
the legacy and memory of
Samora Moises Machel
29 September 1933–19 October 1986

Contents

List of Tables   ix

Preface   xi

1   Afro-Marxist Regimes   *Edmond J. Keller*   1

Part 1   Ideology and State Power Consolidation

2   State Power Consolidation in Ethiopia   *Marina Ottaway*   25

3   State Power Consolidation in Mozambique
     Herbert Howe and Marina Ottaway   43

4   The People's Republic of Angola:
     A Radical Vision Frustrated   *John A. Marcum*   67

5   State Power Consolidation in Zimbabwe:
     Party and Ideological Development   *Masipula Sithole*   85

Part 2   Public Policy and Policymaking in Afro-Marxist Regimes

6   Development and Counterdevelopment Strategies
     in Mozambique   *John S. Saul*   109

7   The Political Economy of Development in Ethiopia
     Dessalegn Rahmato   155

viii   Contents

8   The Angolan Economy: A History of Contradictions
     Gillian Gunn   181

9   Afro-Marxism in a Market Economy:
     Public Policy in Zimbabwe
     Michael Bratton and Stephen Burgess   199

**Part 3 International Influences on the Policymaking
          of Afro-Marxist Regimes**

10   Soviet Influence on Afro-Marxist Regimes:
     Ethiopia and Mozambique   *L. Adele Jinadu*   225

11   South Africa and Afro-Marxism: Pretoria's Relations
     with Mozambique and Angola in Regional Perspective
     Robert M. Price   257

Part 4 Conclusion

12   Ideology and Public Policy in Afro-Marxist Regimes:
     The Effort to Cope with Domestic and
     International Constraints
     Donald Rothchild and Michael Foley   281

     The Contributors   323

     Index   327

Tables

1.1 Afro-Marxist Regimes 1987   4

1.2 Populism and Leninism as Contrasted by Jowitt   9

7.1 Composition of the Derg 1975–76   163

7.2 Balance of Trade 1978/79–1983/84   169

7.3 External Trade Structure 1978/79 and 1982/83   170

7.4 Changes in Agrarian Structure 1984/85–1993/94   172

7.5 Cereal Imports 1975/76–1981/82   173

7.6 Ownership Structure in Manufacturing 1981/82   175

10.1 Principal Trading Partners of Ethiopia: Imports   235

10.2 Principal Trading Partners of Ethiopia: Exports   236

10.3 Trade Balance by Groups of Countries   247

Preface

Africa is increasingly an area of Cold War conflict and competition. Prior to the 1970s, both superpowers, when formulating and executing their foreign policies, placed Africa low in their priorities. U.S. involvement in Africa was minimal from the time of independence in the early 1960s to the mid-1970s and focused largely on such issue areas as economic aid and technical assistance. Exceptions to this tendency were the U.S. role in the Congo crisis and the U.S. military presence in Ethiopia's Eritrea Province. During the period, there was little evidence of a significant Soviet role in continental affairs. This Soviet low profile was partly explained by the continuing links that Africa maintained with the former colonial powers and by the suspicions that many of Africa's new leaders harbored about Soviet intentions. From their standpoint, the Soviets saw little opportunity for their brand of socialism to gain acceptance in Africa until recently; as these Soviet analysts perceived it, the necessary objective conditions—a relatively large proletariat, extensive industrialization, developed party and state institutions, and so forth—were absent.

By the early 1970s, however, the political environment began to change and the Soviets appear to have concluded that they could give effective assistance to selected national liberation movements on the continent. This reappraisal represented a significant shift of priorities, as the USSR, perceived by some African leaders as an active opponent of "neocolonialism," began to accrue considerable credibility in their eyes. Responding to this shift in Soviet policy toward Africa, the Nixon and Ford administrations took measures to head off an expanding Soviet influence on the continent, including covert aid to anticommunist elements in areas of international contention.

During the 1975 Angolan confrontation, superpower competition moved to another stage. With the demise of the Portuguese colonial establishment, three rival liberation groups engaged in an intense struggle for control. The U.S. Central Intelligence Agency used its support base in Zaire to provide the National Front for the Liberation of Angola (FNLA) with material and mercenary backing; moreover, regular South African troops fought alongside the National Union for the Total Independence of Angola (UNITA) forces. Separately, the FNLA and UNITA launched attacks upon the Soviet-supported Popular Movement for the Liberation of Angola (MPLA), but the MPLA proved more than a match for these opponents. The Soviets, in an effort to counter the covert U.S. initiative in Angola, gave extensive military aid to the MPLA, enlisting the direct involvement of its proxy, Cuba, on the side of the Afro-Marxist liberation movement there. Some 15,000 Cuban combat troops were sent to Angola, where they provided indispensable aid to the MPLA forces in the field. Meanwhile the U.S. Congress, fearing a repetition of the Vietnam fiasco, refused to respond positively to Secretary of State Henry Kissinger's appeals for increased U.S. involvement in the Angolan civil war on the side of the FNLA and UNITA.

Some clear lessons have emerged from the Angolan crisis. It was in Angola that the Soviet Union proved to have both the capacity and the determination to play a major role in the African arena. Its ability to project power was further demonstrated two years later in the Horn of Africa when the USSR switched its allegiance from "scientific socialist" Somalia, an ally of nearly ten years, to the larger and more strategically significant Ethiopia. This dramatic turn of events followed the souring of relations between Ethiopia and the United States as the radical regime of Colonel Mengistu Haile Mariam began to consolidate its political power. Fearing the rampant spread of Soviet influence in the Horn, the Carter administration decided to "draw a line in the sand" at the Horn. It initiated an encirclement strategy intended to confine "Marxism-Leninism" in Africa to Ethiopia. This approach involved the development of far-reaching military and economic relations with Ethiopia's neighbors, in particular, Egypt, Sudan, Somalia, Kenya, and Oman.

Given the recency of these developments, it is not surprising that little scholarly attention has been directed toward making a systematic investigation of these shifting alignments and influences. The most developed Afro-Marxist regimes lie in areas of intense conflict and hold out the prospect of enormous strategic importance, most notably in Southern Africa and the Horn. Not surprisingly, U.S. policymakers are coming to recognize that they must gain a fuller understanding of Soviet policies and motivations in Africa and the Third World generally if potentially dangerous conflicts on the international border zone are to be averted. A realistic policy toward the Soviet Union in the 1980s requires a greater knowledge about the nature and complexity of the Afro-Marxist regimes and their militant counterparts across the Third World.

The present book is an outgrowth of an international conference on "Ideology and Policy in Afro-Marxist States" held in Santa Barbara, California, from 6 to 8 December 1985. The conference was organized around three main themes:

1. The structures and functions of the so-called Afro-Marxist states
2. The extent and character of the relationship between these states and the Soviet bloc and United States
3. The strategic regional and global issues involved in these relationships

The assumption underlying the conference was that a more comprehensive and comparative appreciation of the nature and challenge of Marxist-Leninist ideology and practice in Africa might contribute to the avoidance of regional and global conflict in the area. Sparks that start seemingly peripheral conflicts along international frontiers could possibly ignite major wars between the patron-superpowers. A more comprehensive appreciation of the Afro-Marxist phenomenon will help to nurture a balanced perspective in the West regarding the purposes and structures of the regimes grouped under this label. Such is the essence, we feel, of a practical and constructive realism in foreign policymaking.

The primary catalysts for this project were two grants received from the University of California Institute on Global Conflict and Cooperation for the study of Afro-Marxism as it relates to issues of peace and security. Not only are we deeply grateful to the IGCC for its monetary support, but also for its strong intellectual input into this project. As important as the IGCC grants were to this undertaking, it could not have taken place without support from other sources. In this respect, we benefited greatly from a variety of other persons and institutions: in particular, Professor Carl Rosberg and the Institute of International Studies at the University of California, Berkeley; the Department of Political Science at the University of California, Davis; the Office of the Chancellor and the Provost at the University of California, Santa Barbara; and the University of California, Los Angeles, African Studies Center. We wish to express our deep appreciation to all the persons and institutions that responded so generously to our appeals.

The facilities for the conference were provided by the Robert Maynard Hutchins Center for the Study of Democratic Institutions at the University of California, Santa Barbara. This proved an ideal setting for a conference of this sort, especially as the meeting room allowed for an intimate dialogue among the participants, as well as a ready means of contact with the various observers. The center deserves our warm appreciation for generously making its facilities available to us.

Special thanks are also due to the participants, some of whom are represented in this volume. Participants not represented here, but who served well as discussants and *agents provocateurs*, included: Ruth B. Collier, E. Gyimah-Boadi, Michael Clough, David Laitin, William Cyrus Reed, Michael Lofchie, and Richard Sklar. Susan Henriksen deserves our appreciation for the professional way she edited our manuscript in its entirety. Needless to say, without an excellent support staff, coordinated by Rosie Conaway and including Kelly Brown, Coleen O'Brien, and Joyce Thompson, the conference would never have materialized. Our profound thanks go out to all involved.

Edmond J. Keller
Donald Rothchild

Afro-Marxist Regimes

Edmond J. Keller

Socialist ideals have appealed to African political leaders since the earliest stages of the nationalist period. Socialist thought ranging from indigenous African notions of socialism to Owen, Saint-Simon, Fourier, Engels, Marx, Lenin and Mao, all informed (and in some cases shaped) the notions many African leaders had of the ills that afflicted their respective societies and provided them with the vision of a framework for their liberation and empowerment. As the drive to independence unfolded in francophone Africa, for example, it was common for nationalist leaders such as Ahmed Ben Bella (Algeria), Modibo Keita (formerly Soudan, now Mali), and Sékou Touré (Guinea-Conakry) to borrow liberally from Marxist thought to justify their movements against a common enemy, European colonialism. Moreover, several of the nationalist parties in French-speaking colonies, including the multicolony Rassemblement Démocratique Africaine, were influenced by French socialist and communist organizations which provided them with technical advice.[1]

In anglophone Africa, Kwame Nkrumah established himself as the most ardent African student of Marxist-Leninist thought. He integrated Marxist-Leninist ideas into his philosophical writings, and even had intentions of utilizing Marxian ideology as a guide for transforming Ghanaian society.[2] Julius K. Nyerere in Tanganyika, on the other hand, came to represent the most common position of African leaders who endorsed "African socialism" or "Populist socialism" as an ideology over the first decade of independence.[3] Nyerere had been attracted to the brand of socialism preached by the Fabian Colonial Bureau and elements of the British Labour party after World War II, perhaps because the Fabians' social and political views coincided with his own. The principles of

1

egualitarianism and social justice were central to the Fabian position as well as to Nyerere's populist ideology, *ujamaa* socialism.[4]

Populist socialism, wherever it was found in the early to mid-1960s, was seen as being rooted in African traditions and not in the universal and immutable scientific laws of nature as envisaged by Marxists. It was a soft, diffuse, even amorphous ideology that left a lot of room for interpretation as long as its "Africanness" and populism were stressed. By definition, this ideology was non-Marxist; at the same time, however, it was not always anticapitalist. In Kenya, for example, the government of Mzee Jomo Kenyatta in 1965 published a white paper entitled "African Socialism and its Application to Planning in Kenya," which was essentially a reaffirmation of the Kenyan commitment to a welfare state utilizing a liberal market economy approach.[5]

No matter what form socialism took in the late 1960s, and no matter where it was found in Africa, rarely did ideology serve as a hard-and-fast guide to policy. In Ghana, for instance, even though Nkrumah acknowledged that scientific socialism would not spontaneously take hold in society, and had to be made real through policies, he was never really able to put his Marxist-Leninist ideas into practice. Even Julius Nyerere, who came closest to being able to apply populist socialism through his policies, had difficulty translating thought into concrete reality.[6] In other places, African leaders did not even attempt to link ideology and policy.

The factors that seem to have inhibited African leaders from following their ideological maps more closely were common to all regimes at the time, no matter what their ideological orientation. They tended to be politically independent, but remained economically dependent. They were characterized by a facade of state power and a substance of fragile political institutions; limited financial and technical resource capacities; and bureaucracies that were incapable of ensuring citizen compliance and social discipline. This syndrome has been described as the "soft state" by Gunnar Myrdal, Goran Hyden, and others.[7] When ideological exhortation failed to elicit necessary support for regime policies, raw coercion was often invoked at the expense of legitimacy. This was as true of Nyerere's Tanzania as it was of Touré's Guinea and Nkrumah's Ghana. Even though ideology and the one-party state came to be viewed by many African regimes in the immediate postindependence era as almost essential ingredients in some magical political potion, their effect proved to be at best neutral.

African socialism as an ideology reached its apogee in the early 1960s, and by 1967, when the Arusha Declaration was proclaimed in Tanzania, it was already on the wane. Although African or populist socialism has not been completely stricken from the lexicon of African politics, there is little doubt that its moral power has been considerably lessened. It has even lost its value as symbolic currency in Tanzania, the font of populist socialism in Africa. The moral undertones and volunteerism associated with this brand of socialism have proven difficult to sustain without tangible rewards for the sacrifices of the populace.

Ironically, as the currency of populist socialism has declined, the stock of scientific socialism, based on the principles of Marx and Lenin, has risen. After virtually being extinguished with the overthrow of Kwame Nkrumah by a military coup d'état in 1966, the language of Marxism-Leninism in Africa gained new life after 1969, and blossomed in the mid-1970s. In late December 1969, Major Marien Ngouabi, a year after he seized power in a military coup, proclaimed the establishment of the People's Republic of the Congo, which was to be organized around the principles of scientific socialism. This was the first African regime to reject a variant of populist socialism for what came to be known as Afro-Marxism.[8] The military regime in Somalia took the same path less than a year later. By 1986, there were six African regimes that claimed to be committed to the principles of scientific socialism or Marxism-Leninism (see Table 1.1). Zimbabwe, based upon the stated intentions of the government of Prime Minister Robert Mugabe and his politically dominant party, the Zimbabwe African National Union (ZANU), could be classified as an "aspiring Afro-Marxist regime."[9]

Several interesting and important questions arise from this trend. What factors most influenced the movement away from populist socialism as a regime ideology and toward Afro-Marxism? Were external or internal factors most influential? How different is Afro-Marxism from African socialism? How do we define it? How significant is Afro-Marxism as an ideology? Why is it important to understand the essence of Afro-Marxist regimes? These and related questions form the basis for the essays contained in this volume. The remainder of this introduction will attempt to provide some preliminary, more general answers by way of background.

The Origins of Afro-Marxism

When Marien Ngouabi declared the Congo a People's Republic, Western scholars and foreign policy makers alike hardly paid notice. However, with the Soviet and Cuban entry into the civil war in Angola on the side of the Popular Movement for the Liberation of Angola (MPLA) in 1975, Western governments, particularly the administration of Gerald Ford in the United States, feared a serious Soviet attempt to displace the influence of the West in Africa. This fear was reinforced several months

Table 1.1   Afro-Marxist Regimes 1987

Regime	Inauguration Year
Angola, People's Republic	1977
Benin, People's Republic	1974
Congo, People's Republic	1969
Ethiopia, People's Democratic Republic	1987
Madagascar, Democratic Republic	1975
Mozambique, People's Republic	1977

later when the Soviet Union came to the aid of Ethiopia in its efforts to ward off military challenges from Somalia and several ethnically based opposition movements in the country. In the space of a few months in 1977, the Soviets, Cubans, and other Eastern Bloc countries airlifted massive amounts of military supplies and equipment and provided technical assistance, as well as combat personnel to replace U.S. military support. President Jimmy Carter responded by vowing to halt the spread of communism in Africa.[10]

Some scholarly observers have suggested that the growing Soviet and Eastern Bloc activity in Africa is related to a "grand design" on their part to "recolonize" Africa.[11] Others, such as Kenneth Jowitt, without commenting on the geopolitical or strategic implications of these developments, downplay the prospects for the development of genuine Marxist-Leninist states in Africa. Jowitt contends, for example, that where such regimes appear, they are at best "imposters" and at worst "heretics" in that they tend to reject some Leninist tenets. Moreover, he maintains they have identifiably non-Leninist characteristics, but for particular reasons have formally adopted Leninist facades.[12] I contend that the evidence does not support these assumptions. First, the Afro-Marxism that we witness today was not imported from abroad, but is instead a product of internal processes that are unique to certain African states.[13] Second, there is Marxist-Leninist substance to the most well-articulated Afro-Marxist regimes if not to the more ideologically heterodox ones. The object of this book is to provide a critical understanding of the true essence and relevance of the concept of Afro-Marxism and the phenomenon of the Afro-Marxist regime.

One should not confuse the growing presence of the Soviet Union and other Eastern Bloc countries in Africa with a "communist invasion" intended to recolonize Africa. African leaders have willingly chosen to tread the scientific socialist path because of their felt need for more central control and social discipline. Samuel Huntington has correctly noted, "The political function of communism [i.e., scientific socialism] is not to overthrow authority but to fill the vacuum of authority."[14] In those African states where the establishment of Afro-Marxist regimes has gone the furthest (i.e., Angola, Mozambique, Ethiopia), this has been most evident.

Soviet and other Eastern Bloc influence on the formulation of ideology and policy in self-proclaimed Afro-Marxist regimes has grown over the past decade, but this occurred only after the fact. Even where foreign communist advisors are closely involved in institution building, ideology formation, and policymaking, there is little evidence that such involvement results in absolute influence in all situations.[15] The hold of the USSR and the Communist party of the Soviet Union over African clients, in fact, appears to be relatively weak. In contrast to the ideological and political conformity that the Soviet Union was able to demand of its Eastern European and Asian satellites as late as the 1960s, the authoritative center in the communist world today has lost a good deal of its power. Regimes that endorse the Soviet model are not now forced to comply with the letter of Soviet-style Marxist-Leninist doctrine. In fact, the opportunity for eclecticism in ideology formation and policy action is what seems to appeal to the current group of African leaders who have endorsed scientific socialism.

For whatever reasons, Soviet ideologues have rethought their positions on the prospects for socialism in Africa and on questions of doctrine. In contrast to the skepticism they had about the socialist aspirations of African states such as Ghana, Guinea, and Mali in the 1950s and 1960s, they now rationalize the legitimacy of Afro-Marxist regimes.[16] Today, they speak of Third World regimes of a "socialist orientation."[17]

David Albright notes, however, that Soviet analysts hold out no great hope for a "real" revolutionary breakthrough, although there is the possibility that there might be some "genuine Marxist-Leninist breakthroughs." In other words, socialism might come about even without a thoroughgoing social revolution in Africa.[18] Little hint is given as to what level of purity is necessary before such a breakthrough is achieved.

The Third World regimes which are said to have the highest potential for real progress in this direction are those that pursue a noncapitalist development strategy and pass through a phase of "national democratic revolution."[19] Soviet ideologues now suggest that the capitalist phase on the road to socialism can be skipped *if* "revolutionary democrats" engage in a genuine national democratic revolution. This phase is said to be made necessary by the fact that in Third World states, capitalism, according to Marxist-Leninist theorists, is at best immature; most economies are still characterized by "medieval survivals." Therefore, the objective conditions found in Africa are different from those that characterized Russia in

1917. The general theory and practice of socialist transformation in the eyes of Soviet ideologues, then, has to be adapted to the specific conditions of specific Third World countries. They emphasize that Lenin himself came out categorically against assuming the absolute necessity of technical-economic prerequisites, as well as against rigid, deterministic political preconditions for socialist revolution.[20]

What is clear is that the Soviets were able to benefit from the receptivity of some African regimes to the idea of scientific socialism, and opportunistically made adjustments in their positions on doctrine and process. Their entry onto the African scene in the 1970s was facilitated as much, however, by their willingness to provide military support to African clients. This fit right into the strategic game plan of the USSR, which had been unfolding since the conclusion of World War II.[21] At that time, the Soviets began to build a capacity to project their military might almost anywhere in the world. In part, the intention was also to be able to provide military supplies to clients in distant parts of the world as a counterweight to their Cold War adversary, the United States. This strategy was perfected during the Viet Nam War.

By the 1970s, the USSR had built up large stocks of surplus weapons that it could use to supply a growing number of client states throughout the world. It had also developed a long-range, blue water navy, an airlift capacity to further extend its reach, and foreign-based support facilities that allowed it to support what it termed progressive movements in the Third World.[22]

Through its efforts in aid of the MPLA in Angola in 1975, the Soviet Union showed that it not only had the capacity, but also the will to project itself militarily into the African arena. This ability to project its military power was further demonstrated two years later in the Horn of Africa when the Soviet Union abandoned Somalia, an ally of almost ten years, in favor of the larger and strategically more important Ethiopia. The net result was an escalation of superpower competition in Africa; a proliferation of modern weapons among the clients of the respective powers; and an intensified effort on the part of Western governments to prevent communism from gaining a firm toehold on the continent. Where communism is perceived to exist in Africa, the goal of the Western Bloc is to root it out.[23]

The object of this volume is threefold: (1) to gain a better understanding of the character of Afro-Marxist regimes through the comparative method; (2) to analyze the relationship between ideology and policy in these states; and (3) to explain the nature, extent, and relevance of the Soviet Bloc presence in Africa. Such understanding would serve the interest of scholars and policymakers alike.

Identifying Afro-Marxist Regimes

How would we know an Afro-Marxist regime if we saw one? How does it differ from other types of African regimes? How similar or different is it from other Marxist regimes?

B. D. G. Folson, in his article "Afro-Marxism: A Preliminary View," identified two types of Marxists in Africa: (1) African Marxists, and (2) Afro-Marxists.[24] African Marxists were described as individuals (i.e., African intellectuals and political leaders) who rigorously applied the principles of scientific socialism to Africa. In 1976, when he wrote his article, Folson could find not even *one* African Marxist regime! Afro-Marxists were described as those leaders who attempted to adapt the principles of scientific socialism to African conditions. According to Folson's criteria, Afro-Marxists use the terminology and the analytic categories of Marxism-Leninist doctrine. This tendency away from ideological purity, Folson suggested, was not uncommon in the annals of Marxist-Leninist praxis. Indeed, neither Lenin, Stalin, Mao, nor Che Guevara shied away from Marxist revisionism. Because African leftists tended to adapt Marxism-Leninism to fit African circumstances, Folson contended, there was a possibility that Afro-Marxists could make an original contribution to political thought, if not to politics.[25]

In an effort to distinguish Afro-Marxist regimes from other types of African regimes, Crawford Young relies primarily upon the ideological self-ascription of a regime's leadership.[26] At the same time, he attempts to evaluate the policy performance of such regimes in the context of their stated goals.

However, as noted above, Kenneth Jowitt is doubtful about the prospects for genuine Marxist-Leninist regimes in Africa. The reason for such a contention, he suggests, is that African regimes who dub themselves Marxist-Leninist in orientation are attracted by the ease with which they can avoid the hard choice of surrendering to doctrinaire scientific socialism as defined by the Soviets. Instead, they may freely construct their own eclectic model of scientific socialism to suit their own purposes. The reason this is possible, Jowitt maintains, is because the "Soviet Union is either unwilling and/or unable to enforce [or even loudly assert] its 'papal' convictions, while the United States finds it more difficult to intervene wherever an elite designates itself scientific socialist or Leninist."[27]

The main thrust of Jowitt's argument is that no matter what self-styled Afro-Marxist regimes call themselves, they do not come close to approximating the requirements of the designation of "Leninist" or "Marxist" or "Marxist-Leninist."[28] None oppose religion as a social institution; none have a sizable, politicized working class that serves as the basis for a vanguard party; and all tend to have more nationalistic and populist features than internationalist and Leninist ones.

Jowitt goes on to sketch out the populist features he finds in self-proclaimed scientific socialist regimes in Africa, and juxtaposes these characteristics against parallel features in Leninist doctrine. The populist elements include (1) a heavy reliance on a charismatic national leader; (2) a primary stress on moralism in defining social roles and in addressing issues of development; (3) an attempt to achieve national homogeneity through *political* mobilization; (4) an orientation toward social leveling and equalitarianism; (5) a perception that the colonial experience had a defining impact on the current African condition; and (6) an emphasis on the particular rather than general features of developmental relationships.[29]

On the other hand, Jowitt argues that Leninism (1) relies more on the "correct line" as a guide to action than on the charisma of a given leader; (2) emphasizes sociological rather than moral imperatives; (3) stresses the need for social mobilization (i.e., class war) rather than political mobilization; (4) identifies particular classes as constituents rather than the vaguely defined "people"; (5) downplays the relevance of the colonial experience in defining the current social situation; and (6) emphasizes general rather than particular features of social change (see Table 1.2).[30]

While Jowitt's argument is provocative, it is not entirely convincing. In light of what we know ten years after his article first appeared, his argument is grossly overdrawn. Jowitt himself admits that the differences between Leninism and populism are not absolute. Leninist regimes, for example, have been known to rely heavily upon charismatic leaders who sometimes interpreted the "correct line" to suit their own ends (i.e., Mao in China, Tito in Yugoslavia, Castro in Cuba). A second exaggerated dichotomy in Jowitt's analysis is the moral/sociological one. Leninism, in spite of its presumed scientific base, is rich in moral undertones (i.e., emphasis on the goal of social justice and equality). The distinction between populism and Leninism is certainly not absolute; and it is also not definitive as Jowitt contends.

Afro-Marxist regimes tend to be hybrids with both Leninist and populist traits. The most well-articulated among them grew out of national liberation movements in the name of the "African people" of their respective countries (i.e., Angola and Mozambique) or from a social revolution in the name of the "toiling masses" who were liberated from their "feudal chains" (i.e., Ethiopia). The significance of their respective national histories remains important even as leaders stress the roles of their people in the proletarian international movement. Some have possessed charismatic leaders (i.e., Agostinho Neto in Angola and Samora Machel in Mozambique), while being guided simultaneously by a "correct

Table 1.2   Populism and Leninism as Contrasted by Jowitt

	Populism	Leninism
Focus of the Movement	charismatic leader	"correct line"
Rationale for the Movement	moral base	sociological base
Type of Mobilization Advocated	political	social
Constituency	"the People"	working class
Evaluation of Colonialism	mostly negative; racially and culturally chauvanistic; all-important in defining present situation	somewhat positive; economic determinism; not all-important in defining present situation
Features of Social Change	particular	general

line." Class war is acknowledged as a prime requisite for social change, while the rubric of "revolutionary democrats" is flexible and broad enough to include even some elements of the bourgeoisie.

There is no denying that some features of the Soviet-style Leninist model are generally ignored or rejected as inappropriate in the African context. This does not necessarily make Afro-Marxist regimes "imposters." In fact, it should alert us to the possibility that what we might be witnessing in Africa is the evolution of yet another hybrid form of Marxist-Leninist regime. What is borrowed from orthodox Marxism-Leninism is the model and only selected parts of the doctrine. The tenets of particular Afro-Marxist regimes are fleshed out according to local conditions. The most well-articulated Afro-Marxist regimes attempt to follow orthodox doctrine more closely than those which are less well-developed. However, pragmatism often forces even the most committed Afro-Marxist regime to strategically withdraw from a rigid application of ideologically determined policies. This is clearly shown in the articles on the political economy of Afro-Marxist states in this volume.

Angola, Mozambique, and Ethiopia have established themselves as the most well-articulated Afro-Marxist regimes. This judgment is based upon the sophistication of their respective ideologies, the degree of institutional transformation they each have achieved, the tendencies in their policy preferences, and the trends in their policy application. States that have publicly claimed their commitment to Marxism-Leninism and have made incomplete attempts at any or all of the above mentioned criteria may also be considered Afro-Marxist, but it must be acknowledged that there is a significant qualitative difference between those Afro-Marxist regimes that demonstrate efforts and results in the direction of approximating the model more closely.[31] Benin, Congo, and Madagascar, for example, clearly do not belong in the same category as Angola, Mozambique, and Ethiopia. The former regimes are simply too ideologically and politically heterdox.[32]

Self-designation, while important, is not sufficient to ensure that a regime can be transformed into a viable, credible Afro-Marxist regime. Nor does it guarantee that, once declared, an African scientific socialist regime will forever "stay the course." The regime of Robert Mugabe in Zimbabwe has pledged to reorganize his society along scientific socialist lines. However, because objective conditions inhibit Mugabe, he has not been able to translate ideology into praxis. Indeed, he has yet to even clearly articulate his ideological orientation.

Peter Wiles and Alan Smith have suggested that once states of what they call "the New Communist Third World" completely adopt the Soviet model, it is unlikely that they will retreat from it. They contend that unless a state is "marginal," it does not "unbecome a communist state."[33] There are two reasons given for this assertion: (1) the Soviets will not allow it; and (2) if the instruments used for taking and keeping power are efficient, tightly knit, and complemented by a workable ideology and self-perpetuating elite, there is no need to abandon the system.[34] Wiles and Smith do not, however, indicate a threshold beyond which retreat is unlikely or impossible. The first point clearly is irrelevant to Afro-Marxist states at this moment in history. I would contend that no matter how well-articulated the objectives of the extant Afro-Marxist regimes might be, there is none that is solidly in the "communist camp." This is not to say, however, that they are not firmly committed to scientific socialism.

The second point made by Wiles and Smith seems to have more potential for validity among Afro-Marxist regimes than the first. The leaders of Afro-Marxist regimes seem to value the ideology and the institutions and policies that complement it, as much for what it allows them to do as for what it is. What they find convenient about the Soviet model of scientific socialism is that it allows the ruling elite to define the normative order, and it approves of the domination of a ruling oligarchy.[35] The same needs that gave rise to one-party states and military rule—unity, social discipline, and order—explain the appeal of Afro-Marxism for some leaders. One-party rule often created only the illusion of national unity and failed to ensure social discipline and order. Military regimes tend to be less concerned with achieving unity voluntarily than with social discipline and order. Neither proved to be able to achieve each of these ends along with legitimacy over the first two decades of African independence. The leaders of Afro-Marxist states are attracted to the promise of governmental efficiency, authority, and social discipline in the Soviet model. Huntington notes that:

> History shows conclusively that communist governments are no better than free governments at alleviating famine, improving health, expanding national product, creating industry, and maximizing welfare. But one thing communist governments can do is govern; they provide effective authority. Their ideology furnishes a basis of legitimacy, and their party provides the institutional mechanism for mobilizing support.[36]

Ideology, however, is not magic. Development is not guaranteed by the model. Effective leadership and adequate resource bases are inarguably more important. I shall return to this point below.

As mentioned above, Afro-Marxist regimes are not homogeneous in the ways in which they interpret the correct line or organize society or in the policies they follow. However, they do possess several common, defining characteristics. This is particularly true for the most advanced Afro-Marxist regimes: Angola, Mozambique, and Ethiopia.

Among Afro-Marxist regimes, five common threads stand out: (1) ideology is accorded the first order of priority; (2) the vanguard party is given a key role in the harmonization of ideology and policy and in providing political direction in society at large; (3) heavy emphasis is placed on developing a broad, deep, effective, and authoritative state apparatus; (4) serious efforts are made to place the state in firm control of the economy by involving it directly in economic production, distribution, and exchange; and (5) there is a commitment to a centrally planned economy.

Party, State, and the Theory and Practice of Scientific Socialism

Just prior to his ouster as prime minister of Ghana in 1966, Kwame Nkrumah asserted:

> Socialism is not spontaneous. It does not arise itself.... There is only one way of achieving socialism: by the devising of policies aimed at the general socialist goals. These policies must be based on the universal laws of scientific socialism adapted to the particular circumstances of a particular state at a definite historical period.[37]

Although Nkrumah was prevented by circumstances from following through on his dictum, it is central to the development strategies being followed by the most sophisticated of the current Afro-Marxist regimes.

Ideology is considered to be paramount along with the organizational weapon of the vanguard party. Angola, Ethiopia, and Mozambique, in the articulation of their ideologies, place their revolution at the stage of the "national democratic revolution." The ultimate aim is the creation of a socialist state, but the leaders of Afro-Marxist regimes realize that the road to socialism will be long and difficult.

A national democratic revolution in the scientific socialist doctrine of Marxism-Leninism is claimed to be needed to prepare the way for a genuine socialist transformation of society.[38] There are no pretentions that the simple adoption of an explicitly Marxist-Leninist ideology is a guarantee of transforming a society into a socialist one. It simply distinguishes between those African states that have adopted a version of the Soviet model of political and bureaucratic organization and those that have not.[39]

The ideology clearly identifies the friends and enemies of the revolution. Friends and cadre are considered "revolutionary democrats." They belong to a broad front of revolutionary forces. In Angola and Mozambique they are simply termed "the people." In Ethiopia this front is more specifically spelled out to include peasants and workers along with progressive elements in the bourgeoisie, including some elements of the military. In fact, soldiers are viewed as integral members of the revolutionary vanguard. The enemies of the revolution are variously referred to as "narrow nationalist," "comprador bourgeoisie," "bureaucratic bourgeoisie," "imperialist," "feudal remnants," "counter-revolutionaries." Ironically, "class war" as a concept is not universally central in the stated ideologies of Afro-Marxist regimes. It is most common in the line of the leaders of Ethiopia and Congo; but least prominent in the statements of Frelimo (The Front for the Liberation of Mozambique) and the MPLA (The Popular Movement for the Liberation of Angola).[40]

Although Afro-Marxist regimes commonly condemn capitalism, neocolonialism, and economic dependence in the ideological pronouncements, they cannot avoid dealing with the forces of capitalism, nor can they completely rid themselves of the dependency syndrome. This will be discussed more fully below. The point here, though, is that objective circumstances create a gap between rhetoric and reality. This is rationalized by Afro-Marxist ideologues who note that in Marxist-Leninist theory such contradictions are part and parcel of this stage of the national democratic revolution.[41]

The immediate mission of the revolutionary democrats is to lay the groundwork for the building of a socialist society. The only way this objective can be achieved is through intense political education and agitation, the strengthening of the state apparatus, the reorganization of the productive forces of society, the development of a centrally planned economy, and the establishment of an all-embracing Marxist-Leninist vanguard party. By following the correct line, it is felt that it will be possible to create societies free of the exploitation of man by man.

In Marxist-Leninist theory, the vanguard party is more important than the state. In fact, the state does the bidding of the party. The party has the central role to play in social transformation. It has the responsibility of defining the normative order, defining the normative content of its particular Afro-Marxist ideology. Moreover, it is responsible for dismantling the institutions and culture of the old order. Consequently, it is assigned the critical role in raising the political consciousness of the masses and, when necessary, mobilizing them to "consolidate the gains of the revolution."

As early as 1974, Samora Machel acknowledged the revolutionary necessity of vanguardism and called for the development of a "revolutionary vanguard within the 'heart' of the front."[42] In Ethiopia, despite pressures from Soviet patrons, the vanguard party was slow to develop. It was not even assigned a priority role by the military-dominated regime until 1979. Even when the Workers' Party of Ethiopia was founded in 1984, a decade after revolutionary forces seized power, the "vanguard party" was not totally civilian-based; nor was it characterized by democratic centralism, a stated goal of all scientific socialist regimes. Rather than being characterized by broad representation (i.e., classes and ethnic groups), the military remained dominant at all levels of the party, especially in leadership roles. Peasants, workers, and other oppressed groups were poorly represented. They are said to have input into party policy through mass organizations (i.e., trade unions and youth, peasant, women's groups). The important point is that a commitment to a correct line and vanguardism appear to be critical in differentiating Afro-Marxist regimes.

Even the aspiring Afro-Marxist regime of Robert Mugabe recognizes this. In 1984, ZANU's First National Congress declared its intention to pursue a scientific socialist path. It established the Herbert Chitepo College of Marxism-Leninism, and pledged to organize ZANU according to the principles of democratic centralism.[43]

Particularly in Mozambique and Ethiopia, the vanguard party has become extremely active in taking its assigned leadership role. In Angola, the party organization has been less effective. In both Mozambique and Ethiopia, on the other hand, the parties are organized closely along the lines of the Soviet model; they are not all-inclusive, but consist of a core of carefully selected cadre. At the Second Plenary Meeting of the Commission to Organize the Party of the Working People of Ethiopia (COPWE) in February 1981, Head of State Colonel Mengistu Haile

Mariam declared: "Although its importance cannot be underestimated, membership is not very decisive for the strength of an organization. What is decisive is the ideological purity of members being governed by organizational discipline and reliable organizational work."[44] Party membership is carefully regulated in Frelimo as well, but less so in Angola where the MPLA has had difficulty filling the ranks of the party even though it opened membership to the masses. Although it has yet to establish a true Marxist-Leninist state, ZANU has begun to screen party membership in the manner of a vanguard party.[45]

Much of the effort of Afro-Marxist regimes has been devoted to the development of an authoritative state apparatus. In large measure, this requires a loyal, effective state bureaucracy. In Angola and Mozambique, the Portuguese themselves filled the key roles in the colonial state bureaucracy. When they withdrew, they left a severely crippled bureaucratic institution. It has taken years to arrive at a point where either the Frelimo or MPLA governments have fashioned a disciplined public administration. Contrary to their desires, they have had to rely heavily upon expatriate managers and technicians. In Ethiopia, it has taken time to begin to effectively displace the remnants of the imperial civil service and its culture and to replace them with a bureaucratic core steeped in the correct line and committed to its implementation.

Of the three most well-articulated Afro-Marxist regimes, Ethiopia's state bureaucracy seems to have grown faster and become most effective over the past several years. This is not to say that it functions like a mirror image of the Soviet or Yugoslav bureaucracies, only that it has become progressively more effective in large parts of the country over the past several years. This cannot be said of the Angolan and Mozambican state bureaucracies in part because of the active destabilization campaigns being waged by UNITA and Renamo, respectively, with the aid of South Africa. In either of the three cases, however, the most important factor constraining the state bureaucracy's effectiveness is its limited resource capacity.

Despite their commitment to state control of the means of production, distribution, and exchange, Afro-Marxist states have been able to achieve control of economic processes only to a limited extent. Private enterprise is still to be found everywhere except in such strategic industries as mining, communication, and oil refining. In the cases of Ethiopia, Angola, and Mozambique, the regime has been unable to gain complete control of the economy because of limitations in technical and managerial manpower. They have, in some cases, rescinded nationalization orders, and are all purposively inviting private capitalists with good terms of investment. The governor of the National Bank of Ethiopia remarked that "...we should be given credit for being wise enough to appreciate that capital is a very shy animal and that if you play the game wrongly you will lose. We have decided we need [foreign companies] to invest and can be expected to act accordingly."[46] This does not mean that the commitment to socializing the economies of Afro-Marxist states has been completely abandoned, only that a strategic retreat in the face of severe economic pressures seems to be afoot. These governments still attempt to regulate and direct their economies—through the participation in joint ventures with foreign investors while controlling a predominant share of the assets invested, and by being selective about which foreign firms may participate in their economies. In Zimbabwe, Mugabe would like to socialize his economy, but he is constrained by the extent to which the free enterprise system has matured and the potential opposition of powerful capitalist classes.

Central planning is a goal of all Afro-Marxist states, but it is an elusive goal. Attempts to do this in Angola and Mozambique have been outright failures. In Ethiopia, the form of central planning is elaborately developed in the National Planning Council, but even there central planning amounts to a broad definition of economic goals in general by the council and decentralization at the points of program development and execution.

In the short run, Afro-Marxist regimes, despite their best efforts to socialize their economies, must be content with mixed economies. This is something their Soviet Bloc patrons are more willing to accept than the Afro-Marxist regimes themselves.[47]

From this discussion, it is clear that ideology is indeed not magic. Afro-Marxist leaders must be able to rely on an ample reservoir of resources to enhance their rulership. Better organization compensates to a degree, but it is not a guarantee of managerial success on the part of political leaders. The problem is that all Afro-Marxist states are "soft states." This is why they turned to Afro-Marxism in the first place: in search of managerial effectiveness and social discipline with legitimacy.

The term "soft state" was first used by Gunnar Myrdal to describe governments of South Asia that seemed unable to promote rapid development; political and social conditions prevented them from enacting public policies that demanded the meeting of substantial obligations by the general populace.[48] Even where there were rules, he found the governments to be weak and lacking in the authoritative capacity necessary to ensure the compliance of the people. Kinship and patron-client ties commanded more respect and legitimacy in the countryside than did the state.

African states, regardless of their ideological orientation, tend to fit the "soft state" mold. Most are saddled with weak, inefficient, and/or corrupt state bureaucratic structures. This fact sometimes inspires the soft state to become authoritarian and coercive. The resort to force, however, is more a reflection of the state's weakness or "softness" than it is of its power.

The pattern of failures in policy implementation, despite good, rational plans, can be traced to the low levels of resource capacity found in most African states (including Afro-Marxist states) and to the misguided policies of their leaders. A reckless attempt to socialize African economies without the necessary resources to do so, for example, might at best be considered too ambitious and, at worst, foolhardy. A better strategy would be to pay more attention to developing the conditions that would allow for a gradual socialization of the economy. Even when "soft states" such as the ones we consider in this volume attempt to plan rationally, they are often disappointed. They do, in some instances, possess planning bodies that are extremely well organized, but even then their policymaking quality is still poor and, above all, their capacity for implementation is almost nonexistent. In part, this is because local political cultures do not permit feasible intermediate-range, highly rational planning and partly because the needed inputs are so scarce.[49] Qualified manpower is scarce; modern, appropriate technology is limited; and financial resources (particularly foreign exchange) are difficult to come by.

Naomi Caiden and Aaron Wildawsky have suggested that such conditions are a manifestation of a severe lack of resource redundancy. Resource redundancy is a prime requisite for coping with change.[50] Civil war and natural catastrophe are the types of uncertainties that confront not only Afro-Marxist regimes, but a large number of African regimes on a regular basis. Where either condition exists, the vulnerability and dependence of the regime is accentuated.

External dependence is perhaps the most important factor besides state "softness" in explaining why the policies of Afro-Marxist regimes seem so full of contradictions. In every case, these regimes are heavily dependent on foreign capital, mostly provided by bilateral and multilateral aid agencies. As the African economic crisis deepens, this dependency increases. Moreover, the power of donors to demand some ideological and programmatic "backsliding" on the part of Afro-Marxist regimes is enhanced. Mozambique's signing of the Nkomati Accord can be seen in this light; so can its decision in 1985 to lessen state control over the economy at the encouragement of the International Monetary Fund (IMF).[51]

Although Afro-Marxist regimes tend to be economically dependent on the Western Bloc for aid, trade, and technology, this vulnerability has not forced the most determined among them to move too far off their scientific socialist course. The rhetoric that Afro-Marxist regimes espouse and the policies they prefer to follow are in the tradition of Marxism-Leninism. They are mainly attracted by the potential for organizational power implicit in the approach.

An affinity for the Soviet model, however, has not meant a total embrace of the Eastern camp, nor has it meant the unrestrained acceptance of Afro-Marxist states into the Eastern fold. For instance, Afro-Marxist states rely on the Soviet Bloc more for military than economic aid. None has been able to secure massive amounts of economic assistance from Soviet Bloc countries even in the worst of times; nor has any been able to secure more than observer status in COMECON. The Eastern Bloc is simply unable to challenge the West in the economic development sphere. Moreover, the fact of economic dependence on the West is likely to ensure that Afro-Marxist states will not have to make the hard choice of whether to become a full-fledged member of the Eastern Bloc.

Conclusion

The past decade has witnessed the emergence of new type of state, the Afro-Marxist regime. Currently, there are six regimes that fall into this category: Angola, Mozambique, Ethiopia, Benin, Madagascar, and Congo. Afro-Marxist regimes are partly self-defined and partly defined by the kinds of institutions they use for governing and the policies they pursue. Within this group of states, we can identify two subcategories, the most well-articulated Afro-Marxist regimes (i.e., Angola, Mozambique, Ethiopia) and the "marginals" (i.e., Benin, Congo, Madagascar). The former are characterized by clear attempts to approximate an orthodox scientific socialist model and the latter by extreme heterodoxy. The regime of Robert Mugabe has aspirations of becoming Afro-Marxist, but objective conditions are not favorable.

This introduction has attempted to trace the origins of the Afro-Marxist regime phenomenon and to identify its defining characteristics. The substance of these types of regimes are fleshed out in the subsequent chapters of the book.

The Plan of the Book

The purpose of this volume is to assess in a critical fashion the nature and policy performance of three Afro-Marxist regimes—Angola, Ethiopia, and Mozambique—and one aspiring Afro-Marxist regime, Zimbabwe. The essays in the collection attempt to evaluate the relationship between ideology and social organization, and ideology and policy.

The first section attempts to gain an understanding of how these Afro-Marxist regimes were formed and the social forces that facilitated or constrained their efforts to consolidate power in the hands of the vanguard party and the state. It is generally agreed that, in order to realize the goal of transforming society along socialist lines, the state must be guided by a clearly defined ideology and a vanguard party. These are the "weapons" that are expected to facilitate the socializing process. The questions we ask are: (1) To what extent are Afro-Marxist states able to follow this model? and (2) To what extent are objective conditions in Zimbabwe conducive to the development of an Afro-Marxist regime there? Prior to Zimbabwe's independence, some observers wondered if there would be a power vacuum when the white minority regime fell, as had been the case of Mozambique and Angola.[52] But this did not happen, and the opportunity to move quickly to the announcement of an Afro-Marxist regime may have been lost as a consequence.

In the second section, the contributors concentrate on the policy performance of Angola, Ethiopia, and Mozambique in the context of state "softness," dependence, and low resource capacities. The question here is: What factors facilitate/inhibit the implementation of an Afro-Marxist development strategy along strict scientific socialist lines? As far as Zimbabwe is concerned, the question is: What are the prospects for socializing the economy in the face of a well-established market economy with strong domestic, as well as international, links?

The final section deals with the arena of international and regional politics from the perspective of Afro-Marxist states. Particular attention is given to the relations of these states with the Soviet Union. The assumption is that a better understanding of the character of Afro-Marxist regimes and their domestic, as well as foreign, policy perceptions could contribute to a lessening of tensions between them and countries like the United States, who see them as Soviet pawns. An attempt is made to show that these states have their own national self-interest, which they act upon. Such interests have more to do with the need for regimes and state survival than with Cold War alignments.

Finally, the conclusion examines the ideologies and policies of Afro-Marxist regimes in relationship to the domestic and international constraints in which they operate. Such constraints combine the limitations in policy implementation encountered by "soft states" throughout Africa with those constraints that are unique to the Afro-Marxist experience. The cumulative result, as is apparent from the chapters in this volume, is to restrict the options open to Afro-Marxist regimes in the severest of manners. Their ideologies, organization of state institutions, public policies, and external alliances all represent efforts to cope with a difficult domestic and external environment; nevertheless, such coping mechanisms create new complications of their own. The final effect is a threatening gap between commitment and performance.

Notes

1. See Aristide R. Zolberg, *Creating Political Order: The Party-States of West Africa*. (Chicago: Rand McNally and Co., 1966), 60.

2. See Kwame Nkrumah, *Neo-Colonialism: The Last Stage of Imperialism* (London: Heinemann, 1965).

3. See Julius K. Nyerere, *Ujamaa: Essays on Socialism* (London: Oxford, 1968); and Crawford Young, *Ideology and Development in Africa* (New Haven: Yale, 1982), 97-182.

4. See Daniel R. Smith, *The Influence of the Fabian Colonial Bureau on the Independence Movement in Tangenyika* (Athens: Ohio University, Center for International Studies, 1985).

5. Republic of Kenya, "African Socialism and Its Application to Planning in Kenya" (Nairobi: Government Printer, 1965).

6. See John R. Nellis, *A Theory of Ideology: The Tanzanian Example* (Nairobi: Oxford, 1972).

7. See Gunnar Myrdal, *Asian Drama: An Inquiry into the Poverty of Nations* (New York: Twentieth Century Fund and Parthenon Books, 1968); and Goren Hyden, *Beyond Ujamaa in Tanzania: Underdevelopment and the Uncaptured Peasantry* (Berkeley: University of California Press, 1980).

8. There is some debate over the appropriateness of this term, which I will address below.

9. See "Zimbabwe," *Africa Contemporary Record*, 1984-1985 (New York: Africana, 1985), B877.

10. See Edmond J. Keller, "United States Foreign Policy on the Horn of Africa: Policymaking with Blinders On," in Gerald J. Bender, James S. Coleman, and Richard L. Sklar, eds., *African Crisis Areas and U.S. Foreign Policy* (Berkeley: University of California Press, 1985), 178-193.

11. See Michael Radu, "Ideology, Parties and Foreign Policy in Sub-Saharan Africa," *Orbis*, (Winter 1982); and Morris Rothenberg, *The USSR and Africa* (Miami: Advanced International Studies Institute, 1980).

12. Kenneth Jowitt, "Scientific Socialist Regimes in Africa: Political Differentiation, Avoidance, and Unawareness," in Carl G. Rosberg and Thomas M. Callaghy, eds., *Socialism in Sub-Saharan Africa: A New Assessment* (Berkeley, Calif.: Institute of International Studies, 1979), 135, 140.

13. See Crawford Young, *Ideology and Development*, 8; and David and Marina Ottaway, *Afrocommunism* (New York: Africana, 1981), 11.

14. Samuel P. Huntington, *Political Order in Changing Societies* (New Haven: Yale, 1968), 335.

15. See D. and M. Ottaway, *Afrocommunism*, 11; and Edmond J. Keller, "Revolutionary Ethiopia: Ideology, Capacity and the Limits of State Autonomy," *The Journal of Commonwealth and Comparative Politics*, XIII, 2 (July 1985), 112-139.

16. See John O'Connor, "Russian Revisionism in Africa," *America* (28 May 1966), 774.

17. See Jerry F. Hough, *The Struggle for the Third World: Soviet Debates and American Options* (Washington, D.C.: Brookings Institutions, 1986); and I.

Andreyev, *The Noncapitalist Way: Socialism and the Developing Countries* (Moscow: Progress Publishers, 1977), 101-103.

18. See ibid; and David Albright, "Soviet Policy," *Problems of Communism* XXVII (January-February 1978), 27.

19. See V. Solodovinikov and N. Garilov, "Africa: Tendencies of Non-Capitalist Development." *International Affairs* (Moscow, March 1976); and R.A. Ulyanovsky "Lenin's Concept of Non-Capitalist Development," *Political Affairs,* (Moscow, 1970).

20. See Ulyanovsky, "Lenin's Concept," 44.

21. Bruce D. Porter, "The USSR in Local Conflicts: A Historical Overview," in Bruce D. Porter, ed., *The USSR in Third World Conflicts: Soviet Arms and Diplomacy in Local Wars, 1945-1980* (Cambridge: Cambridge University Press, 1984), 13.

22. See Porter, "The USSR in Local Conflicts," 21-35.

23. See Edmond J. Keller, "U.S. Foreign Policy on the Horn of Africa," 186-191.

24. B. D. G. Folson, "Afro-Marxism: A Preliminary View," *African Review,* 6, 4 (1976), 92-117.

25. Ibid., 115.

26. Young, *Ideology and Development,* 8.

27. Jowitt, "Scientific Socialist Regimes," 166.

28. Ibid., 171-172.

29. Ibid., 151-152.

30. Ibid., 154-155.

31. Peter Wiles and Alan Smith, "The General View, Especially from Moscow," in Peter Wiles, ed., *The New Communist Third World: An Essay in Political Economy* (New York: St. Martin's Press, 1982), 13-52. The authors divide Third World countries of a socialist orientation into two categories: (1) those that have proclaimed themselves to be pursuing a scientific socialist path, which have close military ties to the USSR, but have not been officially recognized by Soviet ideologues as genuinely socialist regimes (i.e., Angola, Mozambique, and Ethiopia); and (2) doubtful or "marginal" self-proclaimed scientific socialist countries in the Third World, which are characterized by extreme heterodoxy and limited institutional transformation (i.e., Congo, Benin, Madagascar).

32. See Young, *Ideology and Development,* 96.

33. Wiles and Smith, "The General View," 20.

34. Ibid.

35. See Edmond J. Keller, "State, Party and Revolution in Ethiopia," *African Studies Review,* 28, 1 (March 1985), 2.

36. Huntington, *Political Order,* 8.

37. Kwame Nkrumah, "African Socialism' Revisited" in Kwame Nkrumah, *Revolutionary Path,* (New York: International Publishers, 1973), 440.

38. See A. S. Shin, *National Democratic Revolutions: Some Questions of Theory and Practice.* (Moscow: Wanka, 1982). Shin describes the national democratic revolution as a new type of revolution and a way of gradual transition to socialism where the working class, rather than leading the revolution, enters

into strategic coalitions with progressive members of the intelligentsia for the administration of the state in the interim. Among these might be progressive elements within the military. This revolution disdains imperialism, "tribalism" or narrow nationalism, and "feudalism." The revolution forms the material and spiritual prerequisite for bypassing or cutting short the capitalist phase of development on the road to socialism.

39. See V. Solodovinikov and N. Gavrilov, "Africa: Tendencies of Non-Capitalist Development," 33.

40. Wiles and Smith, "The General View," 21.

41. See Berhanu Bayie, "People's Gains in the Ethiopian Revolution." *African Communist* 74 (1978), 55-56; and "The Ethiopian Revolution: Its Present Stage of Development," *Meskerem*, 2, 7 (1981), 10-44.

42. Samora Machel, "O Processo da revolução democratica popular em Moçambique," in *A Nossa Luta*, (Maputo: Imprensa Nacional, 1975), 209-210; and Sonia Kruks, "From Nationalism to Marxism: The Ideological History of Frelimo, 1962-1977," in J.L. Markovitz, ed., *Studies in Power and Class in Africa* (New York: Oxford University Press, 1987), 251.

43. "Zimbabwe, "*Africa Contemporary Record, 1984-1985* (New York: Africana, 1985), B877.

44. "Development Strategy Outlined," *Yakatit Quarterly*, 4 (3), (1981), 4.

45. "Zimbabwe," *Africa Contemporary Record, 1984-1985*, B876.

46. "Ethiopia," Africa Research Bulletin (1983), 6836.

47. See Andreyev, *The Noncapitalist Way*, 30.

48. Gunnar Myrdal, *An Asian Drama*.

49. Y. Dror, *Public Policymaking Reexamined*, (San Francisco: Chandler, 1968), 111.

50. Naomi Caiden and Aaron Wildavsky, *Planning and Budgeting in Poor Countries*, (New York: John Wiley and Sons, 1974), 57.

51. "Mozambique," *Keesing's Contemporary Archives*, (May 1985), 34084A.

52. D. and M. Ottaway, *Afrocommunism*, 11.

part one

Ideology and State
Power Consolidation

State Power Consolidation in Ethiopia

Marina Ottaway

The problem of state power consolidation—by which we mean consolidation of central authority in any form—has been crucial in Ethiopia ever since the 1974 revolution. The collapse of the old regime left a vacuum of power and institutions, and although the military could quickly fill up the former, it took close to ten years for new institutions to be developed. The process was neither easy nor painless, but involved much violence and even civil war. Nor is the process totally completed, for some major problems still remain. Nevertheless, at the time of this writing, Ethiopia provided one of the most successful examples of state power consolidation among the Marxist-Leninist African countries.

State Power Consolidation Before the Revolution

Although this study deals with present issues and not with past history, it is worthwhile pointing out that the issue of state power was not opened by the revolution; this long-standing problem in Ethiopia was faced by Emperor Haile Selassie anew after he was reinstated on the throne in 1941. It was in the attempt to increase his hold over the country at this time that Haile Selassie first created many of the institutions of the modern state in Ethiopia. The confusion between state power and the power of the emperor, however, kept these institutions weak.

The process of political modernization was triggered above all by the emperor's desire to strengthen his own position. This had been undermined by his exile during the Italian colonization and by the heightened ambitions of many of the country's regional leaders, a result of their participation in the resistance against Italy. The most important threat

25

came from Tigre whose rulers had historically been among the major contenders for the imperial throne.

The attempt to build the Ethiopian state under Haile Selassie was distorted by his preoccupation with his own power. Haile Selassie selectively built up the state when this strengthened his position, but weakened it when the state became a potential obstacle. In other words, the emperor consolidated the state in the sense of the power of the central authority over the entire country, but did not seek to create a government of institutions. In this period, Ethiopia ceased to be an empire in which semiautonomous regions controlled by local rulers coexisted within the larger framework provided by the imperial authority. Instead, it became a state with a single center of power and a single sovereign government. To be sure, it was not a nation-state, characterized by a high degree of ethnic, linguistic and cultural homogeneity. Rather, it remained a diverse "empire-state," held together by a common authority at the top, but not by a commitment to unity on the part of the population.[1]

The elimination of the regional rulers, accomplished through a mixture of military repression and political maneuvering, was a task to which Haile Selassie devoted his wholehearted efforts. The process of building government and administrative institutions, also undertaken in this period, was carried out with a lot less enthusiasm. The problem in this respect was that Haile Selassie wanted administrative institutions to limit his authority. At the same time, he wanted the trappings of a modern state. The result was a system in which an elected parliament existed, but had little power; the cabinet served strictly at the pleasure of the emperor. The regional and local administration was in the hands of governors appointed by the emperor and supported by a small staff of what could more properly be called civil servants.[2] It was hardly a modern state: cabinet and administrators in Ethiopia were the personal staff of Haile Selassie, just as the public finances were also the finances of the emperor.

State building was a central concern of Haile Selassie's, because it directly involved his own power; nation building, on the other hand, was not. In other words, Haile Selassie only looked at the problem of authority from the top down, as one of organizing the channels through which his decisions would be implemented. The problem of creating a nation as well, as a body politic of individuals with a sense of belonging and a commitment to the state, was ignored. That the issue of nation building was not important to, and probably not understood by, Haile Selassie was seen in his handling of the Eritrean problem.

Eritrea, an Italian colony from 1890 to 1941, became part of Ethiopia in 1952, as the result of a United Nations decision. The solution chosen by the United Nations at the time, after much controversy, was to create a federation, within which Eritrea enjoyed a considerable degree of internal autonomy and even a measure of democracy. The federal solution was not welcome by Haile Selassie, who saw it only as a limitation of his own power, rather than as a means of defusing the potentially serious problem of Eritrean separatism. In 1962, he managed to engineer a vote by the Eritrean assembly that disbanded the federation and made Eritrea an integral part of Ethiopia; and he followed up this victory by appointing his own son-in-law as governor of Eritrea.[3] What Haile Selassie totally disregarded when he carried out this maneuver was the depth of nationalist feeling in Eritrea, a feeling which was manifested immediately in the creation of the Eritrean Liberation Front. In retrospect, it is easy to see that the dissolution of the federation strengthened the authority of the state, making it more extensive, but that it weakened the possibility that the citizens of Ethiopia would come to see themselves as willing members of a nation, rather than unwilling subjects of an empire.

By the time of Haile Selassie's demise in 1974, there was a modern state in Ethiopia, but only in certain aspects. In order to explain this point, we need to look briefly at the characteristics of the modern state. First of all, there are those characteristics that make a modern state such in its foreign relations, namely a fixed territory enclosed by internationally recognized borders and over which the government enjoys sovereignty. In this sense, the Ethiopian state existed, and had existed since the beginning of the twentieth century. Another characteristic of the modern state is the existence of a government distinct from any particular individual and bound by a set of laws nobody can modify at will. In this respect, there was no state in Ethiopia. The authority was Haile Selassie's, not the Ethiopian state's. The citizens owed allegiance to him personally, and his power was bolstered by a network of personal ties. Haile Selassie, like Louis XIV, tried to be the state—which amounts to saying that no state existed at all.

The modern state is also supposed to have a government capable of commanding the obedience of its citizens, by consensus when it can and by coercion when it must. In theory, Haile Selassie's authority was absolute. In practice, it was very limited, because of outright resistance in different parts of the country—in Tigre in the 1940s, in Eritrea since 1962, in Gojjam and Bale in the late 1960s, because of the weakness of the administrative structure, and because of the physical problems of implementing the dictum of any central authority in a country where roads were few and turned into rivers during the long rainy season.[4]

In short, under Haile Selassie the state existed as an international entity, enjoying sovereignty within recognized boundaries. Domestically, the situation was not so clear. The best answer is probably provided by Nettl's suggestion that the concept of the state should be regarded as a relative rather than absolute one. The issue is not whether the state exists or does not exist. Rather, it is what degree of "stateness" exists in a certain country, or to what extent a particular state corresponds to the model of what a state should be.[5] Ethiopia under Haile Selassie had a low degree of stateness. From a purely historical point of view, this low degree was probably more than Ethiopia had enjoyed in the past. History, however, did not make the problems the military regime inherited from Haile Selassie, or the new ones created by the revolution, any easier to solve.

The Disintegration of State Power After the Revolution

When Haile Selassie was deposed in September 1974, the weakness of the state became immediately manifest, because what disappeared was not only a person, but a network of relations cementing the country together. Haile Selassie was truly irreplaceable: his was not a bureaucratic position someone else could fill. To make matters worse, in a country used to personal authority, the new ruler was not a person, but the shadowy Derg, a military committee composed of individuals whose names (in fact even whose number) were not made public. It is not accidental that a joke popular in Addis Ababa in late 1974 transformed the Derg into a person. In that story, the military committee became Leul Derg, or "Prince Derg," an illegitimate son of the emperor whose existence had been concealed until that time.

This nameless, faceless military committee had no legitimacy— neither based on tradition nor on charisma. It did not even have a reliable administrative apparatus—there was no well-organized and apolitical bureaucracy the new rulers could simply appropriate. To make matters worse, the military had to contend with a mobilized country. It is true that there was no organized political movement, but since the previous February many groups had taken to the streets to present their demands. All of them, from students to labor unions or even charitable organizations, considered themselves the real authors of the revolution, denying that the military had a legitimate political role.[6] The Derg succeeded in staying in power in this period because of the disorganization and weakness of its opponents, not because of the strength of the state institutions it controlled. Even the military was divided initially, with some sectors, particularly the air force and the army corps of engineers, in a mutinous mood even after the military government had come to power.

The issue of state power, already serious at the outset, became much more acute after January 1975, when the Derg emerged from the ideological vagueness of the early months and proclaimed its intention to transform Ethiopia into a socialist country. While it was not clear what kind of socialism the Ethiopian leadership had in mind at this point—it was not until a year later that socialism became identified unequivocally with Marxism-Leninism—there was no doubt that socialism implied an enhanced role for the state.

The first socialist reforms did not cause significant problems because their scope was limited. In January, the government announced the nationalization of banks and insurance companies, as well as that of all major industrial enterprises. The measure sounded more far-reaching than it was in practice—given the country's underdevelopment there were only about seventy companies to be nationalized, and this did not overtax the resources of even a weak state. The real problem arose a few weeks later with the launching of the land reform; this was a measure with a nationwide impact, which needed to be enforced everywhere, not just in a few towns. The discrepancy between state power and state ambitions gave rise to one of the great paradoxes of the Ethiopian revolution: a government that had already manifested its authoritarian orientation and a great deal of ruthlessness and brutality created a network of decentralized and democratic peasant associations, endowed with a very high degree of autonomy and policymaking power, in order to implement the land reform.

The creation of the peasant associations stemmed from two major considerations. One was ideological, the other pragmatic. The ideological issue was raised by some of the younger officials in the Ministry of Land Reform, whose concept of a socialist organization of agriculture was based on the Chinese model of peasant communes—or, more precisely, on a romantic vision of that model. This group saw the creation of the peasant associations as the first step toward collectivization. The pragmatic consideration was simply that there was nobody to implement the land reform, unless the peasants could do it themselves.

From the point of view of the Derg, pragmatism was probably the major consideration at this time: in early 1975, the military committee had not decided yet to push for collectivization in rural areas. This is suggested by the fact that each peasant association was given the power to choose whether it wanted to promote collective cultivation, to redistribute land among its members in an egalitarian fashion, or simply to enforce the limit of ten hectares per family established by the land reform proclamation.

The peasant associations were the very first institutions created by the new regime. Within a few months, over 18,000 were formed.[7] This was an unheard-of success, particularly when we consider the difficulty most African countries have encountered in organizing the rural population. The success was due in part to the efforts of university and high school students who were deployed in rural areas by the government to spearhead the *zemacha*, a development and literacy campaign that had turned into a land reform project. Another reason the peasant associations could be formed so quickly was the vacuum of power in the rural areas, where the landlords had been the representatives of state power before the land reform. This both created the need for new institutions to fill that vacuum and removed obstacles to their formation.

There is little systematic information on the peasant associations and their leadership. The little that is available suggests they have some characteristics that are typical of grass roots organizations in many countries. Leadership of the associations was often taken over by the better-off peasants, or even school teachers and priests, but not by the large landlords, who either disappeared from rural areas or attempted to organize armed resistance.[8] A similar pattern was noticed in the *ujamaa* villages in Tanzania, in the Chinese villages at the time of the land reform, and even the community action programs formed in the United States during the 1960s "war on poverty"; all of them tended to be controlled by the better-off members of the poor communities. Later, there was a fair amount of internal strife in many associations, particularly when the various opposition movements tried to infiltrate them and turn them against the government. Beyond these rather vague and poorly documented trends, it is difficult to generalize. What is certain, however, is that what happened within each association was originally determined by the local balance of power, rather than by a national policy. Above all, the peasant associations were not controlled either by civil servants or by party representatives because there was no local administration below the district level and because the party did not come into existence until much later, as we shall see.

The rural land reform was followed in the summer of 1975 by an urban land reform, in which all urban land was nationalized and all houses except those occupied by the owners were confiscated. In the cities, too, the government created new institutions, the urban dwellers associations or *kebeles*. They were supposed to help provide services and promote small development projects if possible. Theoretically the equivalent of the peasant associations, the urban *kebeles* never acquired the same degree of autonomy. There was no vacuum of power in the towns, since the formal administrative structures functioned to some extent, and the associations became essentially tools used by the government to maintain control over the urban population—except in those cases in which they turned into tools of the opposition parties. In any case, the urban *kebeles* did not have the power to make policy on fundamental economic issues.

The Attempt to Restore State Power

The salient characteristic of the institutions created during 1975 was their decentralization. For a military regime that had been rejecting the idea of "people's government" since coming to power, the Derg brought into being a curiously participatory, democratic system, while state power was severely eroded. Such decentralization was not deliberate, but resulted from a temporary weakness of the military committee. In fact, as soon as the associations were created the government tried to limit their autonomy, weaving them into a centralized, hierarchical system controlled from the top down. Basically, the Derg followed two approaches. On the one hand, it organized the associations into a vertical hierarchy by building up district and provincial level associations, and finally forming the All-Ethiopian Peasant Association at the national level. On the other, it integrated these associations laterally into development committees, which included not only the representatives of the peasants, but also those of the ministries and other government agencies.[9] The purpose of both efforts was the same: to give the government the power of making and implementing policy choices for the entire country. There is no evidence that the Derg ever intended to renounce that prerogative, despite the broad powers initially given to the peasant associations. Rather, the government initially did not have the capacity to enforce its policies, and had to build up the institutions first. The Derg always interpreted socialism to mean centralized control over economy and society, rather than decentralized, participatory democracy. However, the reality of Ethiopia's low degree of stateness prevented this interpretation of socialism from being acted upon until the centralized institutions could be developed.

The military administration was not able to create the centralized system for several years, and in the interim period the peasant associations maintained a high degree of autonomy, with both political and economic consequences. The economic consequences of decentralization were felt, above all, in rural areas because the peasant associations were in a position to make major decisions concerning land allocation and cultivation. The land reform decree gave the associations the right to redistribute land among their members or to encourage collectivization, as we have seen. A few, very few, opted for collectivization. The information available on these early collectives is scanty, but it suggests that they were formed either at the instigation of the students, often collapsing as soon as they left, or by peasants who had been expelled from the land by the formation of mechanized farms before the revolution and came back to repossess their fields when the reform was announced.[10] Collectivization in these cases was facilitated both by the fact that the individual possession of land had already been interrupted, and by the physical transformation of the farms, plowed in large fields, obliterating old borders and markers.

What most peasants demanded—and most associations carried out—was not collectivization, but land redistribution. Land scarcity was a serious problem in most parts of Ethiopia; as a result, although the land reform in theory allowed family holdings as large as ten hectares, there was a great deal of pressure from the poorest peasants to redistribute land in an egalitarian fashion, taking into account family size and land quality. Again, we do not have any systematic, nationwide evidence concerning land redistribution. It is known, however, that whenever land redistribution was carried out, it became a continual, repeated process, as the associations tried to maintain equity while peasant families changed in size and composition. It is also known that redistribution created a serious problem of land fragmentation because individual holdings, already quite small, were made up of parcels of different quality land located in different areas.[11]

The urban associations did not make economic policy, and in fact their economic functions were very limited. They were given the task of collecting rent on the cheapest houses in their neighborhood and could use the money for improvement projects; however, these funds were extremely modest, and the projects carried out at the local level amounted to little more than cleaning up streets and market sites. The associations also participated in the rationing and distribution of scarce staple foods, such as sugar and oil, but in this capacity they were acting as agents of the government, implementing a policy decided upon at higher levels.

Neither the urban nor the rural associations were designed to play a role in the national political process. The Derg saw them as strictly local institutions and, as we have argued, even tried to limit their policy-making power at the local level. In reality, rural and, above all, urban *kebeles* became involved in politics. When they were first created, there were no channels for political participation in the country, because the party was not formed until 1984. Initially, there were only the urban and rural *kebeles*, democratic but with limited jurisdiction, on one side, and the military government, authoritarian and shadowy, on the other. Inevitably, the associations became involved in national political activity, particularly the urban *kebeles*, as contending groups tried to infiltrate their leadership.[12] The politicization of the *kebeles* was especially evident during the "red terror" period we will discuss below.

The building of the party was part of the process of state power consolidation. The choice of socialism made it ideologically necessary for the Derg to create such an organization; so did the practical requirements of governing the country. As we have already pointed out, the administrative structure was very weak, and the formation of the peasant associations, while crucial to the implementation of the land reform, made the situation worse by increasing local autonomy. The party thus was an essential tool. Its absence tarnished the image of Ethiopia as a socialist country and, more seriously, left the Derg without a linkage to the population, giving a free hand to the radical civilian groups that started organizing after the revolution.

Building a party in Ethiopia did not prove an easy task. The project was first undertaken in the fall of 1975, but the party was only launched in September 1984. The intervening nine years were filled with attempts and setbacks. Party formation was undertaken "from the top down," inevitably leading most radical civilians to conclude that the revolution, which they claimed started as a popular movement, was being betrayed by the Derg. There was, in reality, no other way the military council could have formed a party, regardless of ideological beliefs or personality traits of its members. An established regime has, by definition, a source of power, and if it organizes a party it will at best devolve some of this power to it, in a process "from the top down." It is only the opposition that needs to derive all its power from the party, thus building it "from the bottom up."

At any rate, while the Derg was trying to organize the government party, the two groups of radical intellectuals were trying to put together their own opposition movements. During 1976, in the most confusing episode of the Ethiopian revolution, the Derg's own attempt to build the official party from the top down and the attempt by one of the civilian groups to build an opposition party from the bottom up were superimposed. One of the two clandestine organizations, known as MEISON, pretended to cooperate with the Derg in organizing the official party, but in reality used the opportunity to build up its own strength as an opposition movement. The inevitable breakup led to the bloodiest period of the revolution.

The origins of this confusing episode go back to the years 1975-1976, when the Derg, having decided it needed a party, turned for help to the radical intellectuals. The radicals were reluctant. There was a great deal of hostility to the military on ideological grounds, and also because the military was perceived as having preempted the revolution, depriving the radical left of what it considered its legitimate role. On the other hand, the civilian left did not have its own party or organization. Rooted in the student movement, it had failed to move beyond the confines of the university. The Derg's request for help provided an opportunity to overcome that weakness. By mid-1976, after much debate within the ranks of the left, punctuated by a battle of semiclandestine leaflets, the radicals split. One faction chose an unambiguous opposition role, and formed the clandestine Ethiopian People's Revolutionary Party (EPRP). The other faction, MEISON, chose cooperation, in the hope that the party it was ostensibly organizing for the Derg could, in reality, be the instrument allowing the civilians to overcome the power of the military.

In 1976 and early 1977, MEISON members were busy organizing an aboveground, official institution, clumsily named the Political Office for Mass Organizational Affairs (POMOA). The Derg expected this organization to become a full-fledged political party once the groundwork had been laid. But behind POMOA was MEISON, an opposition party. All groups, EPRP, POMOA in its official capacity, and POMOA as MEISON, tried to establish control over the urban associations and, to a lesser extent, the peasant ones, thus dragging them into the national level political process.

The conflict between the EPRP, POMOA, MEISON, and the Derg came to a head in 1977. In the words of Derg Chairman Mengistu Haile Mariam, the red terror of the revolution destroyed the white terror of the counterrevolution. In less flowery language, hundreds of people were killed, particularly in the urban areas, as the military tried to reassert its control. The EPRP, MEISON, and POMOA practically disappeared.[13] The Derg triumphed over the civilian opponents, not surprisingly, since it controlled the military. But destroying the opposition did not mean acquiring the capacity for controlling the country and implementing policy in a systematic, orderly manner. For that purpose, the Derg needed institutions, but in this area it suffered a major setback. POMOA was totally destroyed and the other institutions, above all the urban and rural *kebeles*, were far too decentralized and autonomous to satisfy the Derg's need for control. In fact, the period of the "terror" showed very clearly the dangers of local power in the absence of an overall organization: many associations turned into centers of opposition.

The need for state power consolidation dictated that the Derg immediately undertake the task of building another party. Having learned its lessons about the pitfalls of the process, the military committee was extremely cautious. This caution, in fact, led to a considerable amount of friction between the Ethiopian government and the Soviet Union, which had started playing an important military role in the country in late 1977, when it had transferred its support from Somalia to Ethiopia in the midst of the Ogaden war. In fact, the strife has been interpreted by some observers as a sign that the Derg really did not want a political party, and that it only formed one because its Soviet allies forced it to do so. This interpretation is unfounded. The Derg had been working on the party ever since 1975 because it was an important instrument of control and its absence weakened the military's hold over the country. The party was formed because of need, not ideological conviction or subservience to the Soviet Union. There is no doubt, however, that the military was extremely cautious in its second attempt to form the party, and that this caution displeased the Soviets, who were anxious to see Ethiopia root its socialism in a strong organization. The Soviets probably also expected to have more influence over a party they helped form than over a military committee that had come to power and stayed there for three years, without their help or encouragement.[14]

The Derg's caution was reflected in much initial wavering in its second attempt at party formation. It first considered relying again on preexisting civilian groups, and for that purpose it promoted in 1979 the formation of a Union of Marxist-Leninist Organizations, including one that was almost exclusively rooted in the military. But the small parties squabbled, their leaders vied for power, and the Derg had little control over the membership of the organization, since each group screened its own adherents. The project was thus abandoned in favor of the idea of building up the party within the military—a self-defeating approach, since what the Derg needed was a better link to the civilian population, not to the military it already controlled.[15]

Eventually, the decision was reached to create a new organization from scratch. In December 1979, the Committee for Organizing the Party of the Workers of Ethiopia (COPWE) was set up. At this point, a long and painstaking effort to recruit and train party cadres was started with the help of the Soviet Union and East Germany. Cadres and party members were carefully screened on the basis of individual merit, not because of membership in some other organization. Cadres were trained at a special school in Ethiopia or in Eastern Bloc countries. In September 1984, during the celebration of the revolution's tenth anniversary, COPWE became the Workers' Party of Ethiopia (WPE). At this time, it had about 15,000 cadres, showing the dimensions of the effort undertaken in the previous five years.

The formation of the party was undoubtedly the most important and, above all, the most symbolic achievement in the process of state consolidation that followed the "red terror," but it was not the only one. Even before the party was officially launched, the Derg started forming and consolidating other centralizing institutions, whose collective importance is probably not lesser than that of the party. Mass organizations for women and youth were formed even before the party was set up. The ease with which these organizations were launched is explained by the fact that the regime could create them *ex novo*, without facing the problem of dismantling preexisting ones. The only exception was the labor union, which predated the revolution and had become an active center of opposition to the military government in 1974 and 1975.

However, the initial resistance was quickly suppressed, and in late 1977 a new organization, the All-Ethiopian Labor Union, was created under government control. Paradoxically, because of the small size of the industrial sector, the labor union lost its importance once it ceased to be an opposition force.

By 1984, the major mass organizations were well established. The Revolutionary Ethiopia Women's Association (REWA) claimed a membership of 5.2 million and the Revolutionary Ethiopia Youth Association (REYA) claimed 3.8 million adherents.[16] It is difficult to check the accuracy of the figures, and even more difficult to check the extent to which the members of these organizations participated actively in their activities. However, there is no doubt that REWA and REYA existed everywhere, and that their presence was felt strongly even in rural areas, together with that of the party.[17] All were very visible to the casual visitor, and a force to be dealt with by organizations working in the country, be they missions or famine relief agencies.

Among the centralizing institutions set up by the Derg was the All-Ethiopian Peasant Association (AEPA), as we have already mentioned. The Derg started forming district and provincial level peasant associations in late 1975, and the All-Ethiopian Peasant Association was set up in 1977. With the formation of the party, the leadership of the AEPA was absorbed in it, creating the lateral linkage between this specialized organization and the overall party.[18]

Centralization was also increased as the government started formulating a rural development policy of its own, rather than leaving the choice up to the peasant associations. The most important issue was that of collectivization. In 1979, the government issued guidelines concerning the formation of "producers' cooperatives," as the peasant collectives were officially called. Basically, the guidelines specified the stages a producers' cooperative would go through before reaching total collectivization. They also spelled out the relation between cooperatives and peasant associations; the most important rules were that only one cooperative could be formed in each association, that membership in the cooperatives was voluntary, but that the members of the cooperative would also control the peasant association they belonged to.[19] The next step, announced with the publication of the Ten-Year Plan in 1984, was the decision that 50 percent of all peasants would have to be members of producers' cooperatives by the end of the plan period.[20] The establishment of such an overall target meant that the choice between collectivization and land redistribution was taken away from the peasant associations.

The Unresolved Problems

By 1984, the Ethiopian leadership had been extremely successful in creating the apparatus considered necessary for the consolidation of central authority in a socialist state. The Derg started out in 1974 with no political institutions and a very weak administrative structure. In ten years, it built a party and mass organizations, formed the peasant associations, succeeded in limiting their autonomy, and finally began to formulate and implement nationwide economic policies. While the regime was undoubtedly an authoritarian one, and it never refrained from using violence and coercion to attain its goals, its accomplishments in terms of state power consolidation were remarkable. In fact, Ethiopia was probably the most successful of the African Marxist states in creating such a complex set of institutions. However, there were still two major unresolved problems of state power consolidation. One was the fierce opposition to the authority of the central government by the liberation movements of Eritrea and Tigre. The other was the fact that the political apparatus built since the revolution was not supported by a corresponding economic apparatus. Socialism in Ethiopia remained almost exclusively a political endeavor, rather than an economic one as well.

The basic facts concerning Eritrea and Tigre are well known, and we will review them only very briefly. Both regions were reluctant to accept the power of the central state already in the days of Haile Selassie, Eritrea because it claimed the right to be an independent country based on more or less accurate historical grounds, Tigre because of the long-standing competition between Amharas and Tigreans for the control of the throne. In Eritrea, the resistance to central control led to the formation of two competing liberation movements during the 1960s, the Eritrean Liberation Front (ELF) and the Eritrean People's Liberation Forces (EPLF). The latter group emerged during the 1970s as the most important and effective one. Tigre had no organized movements, and in fact it was rather quiet in the last period of the emperor's rule. With the revolution, the resistance to central control increased in both regions. In Tigre this was due in part to the EPLF's decision to support the Tigre People's Liberation Front.

The worst clash between the Eritrean nationalists and government forces took place in 1977, when a major Eritrean offensive was launched. Initially very successful, it was eventually stopped by the government. Since then stalemate, maintained at the cost of heavy fighting, has prevailed in the region, with the government controlling the main towns and movements in much of the rural areas, but with neither side able to win a decisive victory. By the late 1970s, the level of conflict also escalated in Tigre, eventually leading to a situation similar to that in Eritrea.

The existence of these resistance movements in Eritrea and Tigre poses a large number of questions, but only one is directly relevant to this study: to what extent is this resistance an obstacle to state power consolidation? Part of the answer is obvious; there is no doubt that the existence of these movements is a major obstacle to the consolidation of state power in Eritrea and Tigre. In these two regions, state power is tenuous at best, and it is maintained more by military than by political means. But does this failure in two regions point to a broader, more significant failure of state power in Ethiopia? In other words, does it make sense to conclude that state power has been consolidated everywhere except in these two regions? The answer is far from clear. The fact that Eritrea and Tigre have some unique characteristics suggests that their resistance to central authority is a regional problem of consolidation, rather than one affecting the very essence of the Ethiopian state. Eritrea was an Italian colony for half a century. Tigre has a unique history of competition for the throne in the recent past, and also a geographical position that has made it possible for the EPLF to provide help. Furthermore, liberation movements created in other parts of the country, especially the Oromo Liberation Front, have remained very marginal organizations, indicating that state power has penetrated most of the country.

Nevertheless, the fundamental problem remains that the state apparatus built since the onset of the revolution does not include mechanisms to cope with the great ethnic, linguistic, and cultural diversity that characterizes the country. Ethiopia was an empire, not a nation-state, and while it would be unwarranted to assume that it is the historical destiny of all empires to break up, diversity poses a special challenge in the process of state consolidation. The institutions created in Ethiopia so far simply ignore that challenge, rather than rise to meet it. Thus the major obstacle to state power consolidation in Ethiopia is not so much the fact that resistance continues in Eritrea and Tigre but that there is no apparatus for dealing with the great heterogeneity of the population, "the problem of the nationalities" in the Leninist jargon currently used in Ethiopia. The government is aware of this failure and the new constitution, to be announced in September 1986, is expected to provide a framework for solving the problem of the nationalities. Unfortunately, no concrete information is available at this time.

The other main problem in the process of state power consolidation is the absence of an economic structure underpinning the political one. This is a critical issue from many points of view. First, it is an untenable position for a government calling itself Marxist-Leninist to have a political superstructure that does not rest on an economic structure. The reality at the present time is that the complex political apparatus created by the Derg presides over what is still overwhelmingly a subsistence peasant economy. For all the efforts made by the government, state farms and producers' cooperatives together account for less than 5 percent of the cultivated land in the country.[21] The rest is occupied by small family farms, producing mostly for their own consumption and selling only marginal amounts on the market. Furthermore, what is being sold is handled mostly by private merchants because the government's own Agricultural Marketing Corporation has not succeeded in becoming the major purchaser of the surplus produced by the peasant sector.[22]

The weakness of the economic system underpinning the political one is not only an ideological problem, but a material one as well. Lack of control over the peasant sector makes it very difficult for the government to formulate a coherent economic policy and to prepare and execute a development plan. A Ten-Year Plan was published in 1984, but it is doubtful that it can be implemented, considering that the economy of the rural areas is still in the hands of the peasants, and that the industrial sector that the government does control is minute. It would appear at the present time that the government has to win the battle for economic control before we can conclude with confidence that the process of state power consolidation has succeeded.

There is a final issue concerning state power consolidation that needs to be touched upon here because it has been raised often with reference to Ethiopia, and that is the issue of the popularity of the regime. To what extent is the lack of popularity of the regime a major factor affecting the consolidation of state power? There is no doubt that the Derg has not been popular, although some of its policies, such as the land reform, have been well received. This has slowed state power consolidation. Thus the Derg was forced to organize a party twice before it succeeded, but the end result is that it succeeded. Similarly, by favoring redistribution the peasants have shown that they want a piece of land of their own and that collectivization will undoubtedly be an unpopular measure. But there are already some producers' cooperatives in Ethiopia, and they were not formed at gun-point. In other words, organization and apparatus can make up for the lack of popularity of a regime or the absence of charisma in a leader.

One of the attractions of Marxism-Leninism in Africa has been its claim to being an ideology that is universally applicable. Certainly, the Marxist message concerning the lack of justice in most societies and the need for a redistribution of both wealth and power has had very widespread appeal ever since it was formulated. The Leninist message, that the conditions existing in a country before the revolution are not as important to its success as the organizations that are created and the tactics that are followed, has also had considerable appeal because it seems to offer many Third World governments a blueprint for solving their problems. In Ethiopia, the Derg has undoubtedly seen Marxism-Leninism primarily as a blueprint for state power organization and consolidation. One example is not sufficient to draw conclusions concerning the universal applicability of this blueprint, and the process of state power consolidation is by no means completed in Ethiopia. Nevertheless, the Ethiopian case suggests that Marxism-Leninism—for better or for worse—does provide a model for the consolidation of state power that can work under very difficult conditions.

Notes

1. The term "empire-state" has been used by professor Richard Greenfield in a number of lectures and papers. It is borrowed here as a useful descriptive term, although not as a term having a derogatory connotation.

2. On this issue, see Christopher Clapham, *Haile Selassie's Government* (New York: Praeger, 1969); and Peter Schwab, *Decision-making in Ethiopia* (Cranbury, N.J.: Associated University Presses, 1972).

3. For more information, see Haggai Ehrlich, *The Struggle Over Eritrea, 1962-1978* (Stanford, California: Hoover Institution Press, 1983); and Haggai Ehrlich, *Ethiopia and the Challenge of Independence* (Boulder: Lynne Rienner Publishers, 1986).

4. On Eritrea, see Ehrlich; on the Tigre revolt, Patrick Gilkes, *The Dying Lion* (London: Julian Friedmann Publishers, 1975); and on the Gojjam and Bale revolts, see John Markakis, *Ethiopia: Anatomy of a Traditional Polity* (London: Oxford University Press, 1974).

5. J. P. Nettl, "The State as a Conceptual Variable," *World Politics*, XX, 4, July 1968, 559-592.

6. A call for "people's government" issued by the Confederation of Ethiopian Labor Unions right after the deposition of the emperor listed the following groups as entitled to participation: the labor unions, the teachers' association, two organizations representing university teachers, the student union, the civil servants' association, the businessmen's association, and the Ethiopian Women's Welfare Association; this particular document also included the armed forces among the legitimate participants in people's government, but not all such documents did.

7. In late 1984, there were 19,267 peasant associations in Ethiopia, suggesting that most of the organizing took place immediately, in the first few months after the launching of the land reform.

8. One study on this issue was carried out in 1979 by the World Employment Research Program; a series of case studies was also carried out by university students, as part of an overall project, in the same period. None of these studies has been published. A more recent, published study, on the other hand, finds that the leadership of the associations was representative of their membership, without

a particular bias toward the better-off peasants. See Dessalegn Rahmato, *Agrarian Reform in Ethiopia* (Uppsala: Scandinavian Institute for African Studies, 1984), 85. It is possible that later elections corrected the early bias in the leadership of the associations.

9. See Proclamation No. 71 of 1975, "A Proclamation to Provide for the Organization and Consolidation of Peasant Associations," *Negarit Gazeta,* December 14, 1975.

10. The issue of tenant expulsion from the land was becoming acute in some areas of Ethiopia, particularly around Addis Ababa and in the Arssi and Sidamo regions, during the last years of Haile Selassie's reign. Government policies encouraged mechanization, making the sharecroppers redundant. Most of the large commercial farms created in this period, though, became state farms after the revolution, rather than going back to the former tenants.

11. See Fassil Gebre Kiros, "Agricultural Land Fragmentation: A Problem of Land Distribution Observed in Some Ethiopian Peasant Associations," *Ethiopian Journal of Development Research,* 4, 2, October 1980, 1-12; and Dessalegn Rahmato, 40 ff.

12. See David and Marina Ottaway, *Afrocommunism* (New York: Africana Publishers, 1981), 152-154.

13. MEISON and POMOA disappeared completely, although some of the leaders remained active politically, resurfacing either within the new Marxist-Leninist parties formed in 1978, or in the ethnic opposition movements, particularly the Oromo Liberation Front (OLF). The EPRP survived as an organization, but it became much smaller and weaker, a marginal movement no longer active in the cities.

14. Soviet pressure to get the party formed was particularly evident in 1979, a time when the Derg was still debating how the problem of forming the party should be approached in order to avoid a new debacle. Mengistu went so far as to rebuke the Soviets in public for their insistence on speed in the speech in which he announced the formation of the Committee for Organizing the Workers' Party of Ethiopia, which in 1984 turned into the full-fledged Worker's Party of Ethiopia. See *The Ethiopian Herald,* December 18, 1979. For a discussion of Soviet-Ethiopian dissensions concerning the party, see also Edmond Keller, "State, Party and Revolution in Ethiopia," *African Studies Review,* 28, 1, March 1985, 11 ff.

15. See Keller, "State, Party and Revolution in Ethiopia," 9 ff.

16. These are the official figures released in Addis Ababa during the celebration of the revolution's tenth anniversary.

17. The plan followed by the regime was apparently to have at least a party cell and a cell of each mass organization within each peasant association. This served two purposes: it made it easier to reach the rural population by using the already existing peasant associations as a framework for all other organizations; and it helped the government bring the peasant associations under control through the party and the other political organizations.

18. The members of the AEPA Central Committee all became members of the WPE Central Committee in September 1984.

19. See Proclamation of June 26, 1979, "Establishment of Producers'

Cooperatives," *Addis Zemen,* June 26, 1979.

20. See Workers' Party of Ethiopia, "Guidelines on Economic and Social Development of Ethiopia, 1984/85-1993/94 (Draft)" (Addis Ababa: September 1984).

21. These are the figures provided by the Ten-Year Plan. they correspond to other informal estimates.

22. This conclusion is supported by a World Bank report, "Ethiopia: Recent Economic Developments and Future Prospects," I, March 31, 1984 and by a study of the Marketing corporation: Alemayehu Lirenso, "Grain Marketing in Post-1984 Ethiopia: Problems and Prospects," unpublished paper presented at the Eighth International Conference of Ethiopian Studies, Addis Ababa, November 26-30, 1984.

chapter three

State Power Consolidation in Mozambique

Herbert Howe
Marina Ottaway

In early 1987, the process of state power consolidation in Mozambique could only be considered a failure. With insecurity prevailing over much of the country, including the outskirts of Maputo, a weak and undisciplined military, and an economy in total disarray, Mozambique was moving further away from Frelimo's stated goal of building a coherent Marxist-Leninist state rather than closer to it. Yet, Frelimo itself remained a united party, reasonably popular, and with a proven capacity for self-criticism and self-renewal. In October 1986, it weathered successfully the potentially divisive crisis of the death of President Samora Machel in a plane crash, electing as successor Joaquim Alberto Chissano, a long-term Frelimo militant, member of the Political Bureau and, since independence, foreign minister. The party maintained its unity, although the choice of a successor was hotly contested, and it showed its strength as a collegial body.

In other words, a fairly successful process of consolidation of the party and thus of the regime itself had taken place. Frelimo's own house appeared to be in order, and after the death of Machel and the election of Chissano as president it was even clearer than before that the top leadership derived its power from the party and not the party from the leadership. In that sense, the regime was strong and well consolidated. The state, however, was another matter. The institutions linking the regime to the society were weak and in disarray. As the movement that led the country to independence, Frelimo maintained a degree of popularity, but popularity is not sufficient in a country in state of war. The state administration was in disarray, more unable than ever to cope with the economic and social problems of a country devastated by war and economic collapse. The army, forced to play a crucial role because of the war, was unable to defeat the Renamo guerrillas and contributed to political dissatisfaction in the country because of lack of discipline in its ranks.

How the regime could be strong while the state remained weak or even became weaker can be explained by several factors: the nature of Frelimo and its effort at organizing during the eleven years since independence; the rise of Renamo, the Mozambican National Resistance supported first by Rhodesia and, after 1980, by South Africa; and the difficulty the military encountered in building an effective conventional and counterinsurgency force out of a mass of largely illiterate recruits, relying on often inadequate Soviet weapons and training techniques.

The initial growth of Renamo was almost unrelated to the domestic policies of Frelimo. Renamo was not an indigenous movement but the creation of the Rhodesian Central Intelligence Organization. Yet the presence of Renamo, the destruction it caused, and the increasing hardship suffered by the population because of the rapid decline of the economy inevitably contributed to the growth of discontent inside Mozambique. However, the huge crowds at Machel's funeral suggested that Frelimo still commanded a large amount of respect and even emotional attachment in Mozambique.

The sudden attainment of independence after a protracted period of guerrilla warfare represented a double crisis for Frelimo.[1] It was not yet ready for independence, and it had to transform itself from a liberation movement in which military and political roles were fused into a party organized for and capable of ruling the country. At the same time, it had to create a new military organization to defend the new state—a difficult transformation few liberation movements accomplish smoothly and quickly. The problem was compounded by the fact that Frelimo had not yet won a military victory; rather, the Portugese Armed Forces Movement that overthrew the Caetano regime decided to dismantle the empire in order to concentrate on domestic problems.[2] As a result, Frelimo found itself in power—there were no other movements that could claim the leadership of Mozambique—but with a small number of cadres, a narrow geographic base in the northern provinces, and only a weak presence in the capital city.[3]

Having been thrust in power, Frelimo had to define its policies and thus its ideology. *De facto*, socialism had been the ideology of most of the leadership of the movement since Frelimo's beginning, but as long as the war lasted it was not necessary to define precisely what it meant. The first task was to win the war. Furthermore, the 1960s were a period in which even moderate or conservative leaders talked about socialism in Africa. But once the country was independent, socialism had to be translated into policies. The leaders' personal inclinations, and probably also the dissatisfaction with the failure of earlier socialist experiments that had become rather common by the mid-1970s, led Frelimo to opt for Marxism-Leninism. Officially, Frelimo proclaimed itself a Marxist-Leninist party at its first postindependence congress—the party's third—in February 1977, although the choice was by that time a foregone conclusion.

The ideology proved important because it was given a concrete policy content rather than remaining mere rhetoric. Reshaping the political organization of Frelimo to suit the Leninist concept of a party proved to be a difficult and dangerous task for Frelimo. Its strength as a liberation movement had resided not in being a rigidly structured organization of cadres, but in remaining open and flexible. As the name proclaimed, Frelimo was a front and a liberation movement. The latter meant that independence was the primary goal, and that everything else was subordinated to it; the former meant that membership was open to people of different ideological inclinations, as long as they shared the goal of independence from Portugal. It is true that following the death of Eduardo Mondlane in February 1969 the leadership of Frelimo experienced a split, resulting in the expulsion of the more moderate, "bourgeois" faction.[4] However, this purge affected the top levels of the organization only, and it is doubtful that it had much impact on the general membership, particularly in the remote rural areas where Frelimo operated.

The lack of ideological rigidity in the war years was accompanied by a lack of organizational rigidity. Frelimo had a limited number of cadres, some 10,000 at maximum. It had to wage a guerrilla war, provide political education to win more supporters for the cause, and, once the two northern provinces of Niassa and Cabo Delgado became liberated zones, it had to provide a minimum of political and administrative organization there. Although the reports of how well Frelimo had organized administration, educational services, and economic activity in the liberated zones were probably exaggerated, there is no doubt that it was engaged in a large number of very diverse and complex tasks for which it did not have sufficient cadres.[5] In these conditions, Frelimo's early style of rule developed. It was highly participatory, relying heavily on the population of the liberated zones. At the time of independence, this system of participatory democracy was extended to the rest of the country.[6] Frelimo had its major problems in Maputo where the Portuguese population had been concentrated and where the collapse of economic activity and public services was felt most acutely. Making things worse, Frelimo's organization in the cities was weak and the potential for opposition much stronger. The feared last-ditch resistance by Portuguese settlers unwilling to accept Lisbon's decision did not materialize. Instead, the Portuguese left in a mass exodus. Nevertheless, in Maputo Frelimo had to handle a diverse population with conflicting interests and concepts of what benefits they expected after independence. Frelimo responded by turning to the participatory democracy that had served it well in the war years. "Dynamizing groups" were organized in urban neighborhoods and workplaces under Frelimo's loose supervision. These groups undertook a large variety of tasks, from restoring order and a minimum of services to urban neighborhoods, to keeping enterprises functioning and workers on the job. Above all, they provided a political infrastructure, however loose, linking Frelimo to the population.

In rural areas, the participatory organizations envisaged in this early period were the communal villages. The concept was somewhat vague, but strongly reminiscent of the Tanzanian *ujamaa* villages: the rural population was expected to reorganize spatially into villages and politically into self-governing communities that would form cooperatives and move toward collective cultivation. Again, the emphasis was on spontaneity and participation.[7]

Frelimo's participatory solution did link the party with the population and also created a sense of trust. The first round of elections for local officials in Mozambique after independence showed participatory democracy at work through the endless questioning of the candidates' fitness for office and the dismissal of those considered corrupt or inefficient.[8] But participatory democracy also created problems for Frelimo, in that not all dynamizing groups were willing to accept the authority of the party without discussion or to follow policy decisions blindly.[9]

The Third Party Congress of February 1977 established an unmistakably Leninist line, suggesting that the initial choice of participatory democracy had been a matter of expediency more than of ideological commitment.[10] The party was put in control of all policy decisions, with the state administration as executor. The dynamizing groups were to be eventually disbanded and replaced by well-organized party cells, composed of screened party members accepting the party's discipline and working for the implementation of its decisions. And, while the communal villages continued to be extolled as the cornerstone of rural organization, the party also embraced what would later be known as the "large project approach" in agriculture, meaning that huge state farms, rather than the communal villages, became the focus of government attention and, more important, budgetary provisions.[11]

The decisions reached by the party congress had both positive and negative political repercussions for Frelimo. On the positive side, the party became a much stronger organization internally. A large effort was undertaken to train cadres, and above all to screen members, to make sure that only those accepting the ideology and discipline of the party would be accepted. Available reports suggest that the process was a rather traumatic one for many Frelimo adherents, because nobody was spared the scrutiny of the organization before membership was reconfirmed or denied.[12] The process thus engendered some discontent, while at the same time yielding a stronger party apparatus. But the participatory character of Frelimo was altered.

At the same time, while the party was undergoing the transformation described above, the economy was also becoming much more rigid, at least in the nonsubsistence sector where the government had some control. Centralization and rigidity became the hallmark of the economy because of a fatal flaw that appears to afflict socialist economies in all Third World countries: a desire for control, coupled with scarcity of personnel, leading to the formation of giant farms nobody can manage.[13]

The strictly economic implications of this trend toward centralization and giantism do not concern us here. The political implications were serious: by concentrating on the small state sector, Frelimo neglected everything else. Peasant agriculture received virtually no attention, as the government admitted. A typical Marxist notion that peasants are petty bourgeois, paradoxically coupled with a vaguely populist notion that small peasants have an infinite capacity to pull themselves up by their own bootstraps, provided an ideological justification for the neglect of peasant agriculture. Furthermore, the state farms absorbed the little money the government could devote to agriculture, making it materially impossible to aid the small producers. For example, nine years after independence the government had not yet lessened the acute shortage of hoes and other hand tools.[14] The neglect of the peasant sector meant that the government had very little influence in most rural communities and a purely political linkage to the mass of the population living in these areas. With the party changing from a mass, participatory organization to a Leninist one, the connection between party and population became weak.

This was all the more serious in that not all Frelimo's policies were welcomed by the population. The formation of communal villages was received without much enthusiasm, that of cooperatives with outright resistance. The permanent work force on the state farms was happy to receive a fixed salary, but the peasants who lost some of the country's best land were understandably resentful. The policies might have been made more acceptable to the population through more political participation. In reality, Frelimo's approach to the formation of communal villages and state farms was heavy-handed, triggering significant discontent and few economic benefits.[15]

In urban areas as well, Frelimo angered the population at times. The chronic food shortages were a constant irritant to the urban residents. A campaign to reeducate those who had collaborated with the Portuguese, including posting their pictures in the work place for a whole year so their coworkers would keep them under surveillance, obviously caused resentment. The attempt to stem and even reverse the growth of Maputo, which had doubled to 800,000 people between 1975 and 1983, also caused much damage to Frelimo. "Operation Production," launched in 1983, was an attempt to relocate over 50,000 unemployed people from Maputo to rural areas, where they would supposedly be more productive.[16] The unspoken goal of the operation was also to remove from the cities at least a part of a *lumpenproletariat* deemed potentially criminal and susceptible to recruitment by Renamo. But the people removed from Maputo were relocated in remote areas, mostly in the northern provinces of Niassa and Cabo Delgado, with very little assistance from the government. In short, they were put back into exactly the same conditions they had tried to escape by coming to Maputo. There is some evidence that Renamo did take advantage of the resentment to recruit among these resettled persons.

By the early 1980s, the leadership of Frelimo became aware that the party was becoming isolated and less popular than it had been at the beginning. The Fourth Party Congress had been scheduled for 1982, but as the date approached, doubts arose within the leadership of the organization about the situation that had been developing. There was real concern that Frelimo was losing its grip and its roots. The result was a postponement of the congress and a campaign to revive the spirit of the old Frelimo and the enthusiasm of the population, which was suffering because of the uninterrupted decline of the economy and the escalation of the war waged by Renamo. Few details exist about the discussion that must have taken place within the top leadership of Frelimo at this point because, as usual, the party succeeded in keeping dissension contained and unpublicized. It is clear, however, that two currents had emerged: a hard-line, strongly ideological one, insisting on a very orthodox interpretation of how the party and economy should be organized; and a more moderate, pragmatic one willing to take advantage of what had been Frelimo's strength in the past, its openness and flexibility.[17]

The moderate faction prevailed. As a result, a campaign was undertaken to discuss with the population the problems the country was facing and the options the congress would consider, as well as to air grievances. Some results were obtained, because the party gained new adherents.[18] The congress was finally held in April 1983 in a spirit of renewal. It confirmed the ascendancy of the more moderate faction, in part because economic conditions by this time had become so disastrous that a continuation of the "large project approach" was no longer feasible—although it still had its supporters.

The Fourth Party Congress was another turning point, signalling the change toward a less ideological and somewhat more flexible stance. The changes were seen above all in the economic policies pursued by Frelimo and in the country's foreign relations, but were not as clear concerning the functioning of the party itself.

By the time the congress was held, the economy of Mozambique had begun a process of disintegration, which replaced the slow improvement marking the first years after independence. The GNP was 111.9 billion meticais before independence in 1973, dropped suddenly to 71.1 billion in 1975, and rose to 83.7 billion by 1981. In 1984, it plummeted to 55.6 billion meticais, and it is estimated to have lost another 20 percent in 1985. Estimates for 1986 are not available, but there is no reason to believe the decline has been arrested.[19] Under the circumstances, it was not possible for the government to continue its past economic policies because funds were simply not available. An ambitious development plan calling for the creation of more state farms was thus shelved indefinitely and replaced by an emergency attempt to increase production in existing farms and state enterprises.[20] It is worth noting here that many within the Frelimo leadership never recanted on the desirability of large state-controlled projects and centralized control, although they reluctantly agreed that the policy could not be pursued immediately. The Fourth Party Congress was less a rejection of socialism than an admission that the country was bankrupt.

Following the congress, there was also some change in the country's foreign relations. Faced with increased aggression—Frelimo alleged that, between 1976 and 1984, South Africa and Renamo had caused one-third of a billion dollars of destruction—the Mozambican government signed a nonaggression pact with South Africa.[21] The Nkomati Accord, negotiated at the urging of the United States and with its mediation, committed the two countries not to allow the other's enemies to operate from their territory.[22] In other words, Mozambique agreed to close down the offices of the African National Congress (ANC) in Maputo and South Africa pledged to stop supporting Renamo. It is open to debate whether the signing of the accord represented a long-term trend toward moderation in the foreign policy of Mozambique or simply reflected the immediate difficulty the government was having in confronting Renamo. The latter certainly played a major role, and Mozambique had, in any case, always maintained close contacts with South Africa because of the large number of Mozambican workers in the South African mines and that republic's use of the port of Maputo.[23] In any case, the decision was interpreted by the United States as a sign that Mozambique was becoming less ideological and more pragmatic, a conclusion that appeared confirmed by the decision to join the World Bank taken later in the same year.[24] On that basis, the United States became more forthcoming in its policy toward Maputo. In May 1985, Mozambique introduced some economic reforms favored by the United States, including the liberalization of the marketing for some agricultural produce and the breakup of some state farms, and this opened the way for increased U.S. assistance. Aid reached $60 million in 1985 before being reduced to $40 million because of U.S. budget restrictions the following year. A very large part of this was humanitarian aid to those suffering famine because of drought and war. Economic development aid amounted to about $15 million in 1985, and it was channelled toward the private farm sector, meaning the larger commercial farms, not the peasant holdings.[25]

Political change, on the other hand, was more obvious before the party congress than after it. The campaign to revitalize Frelimo did not lead to the revival of the dynamizing groups or of participatory democracy. The top leadership of the party also remained stable, with the old guard firmly in control of the political bureau. The fortunes of the hard-liners declined for a period, but nobody was ousted from the party. A few prominent members of the political bureau were assigned as governors to the provinces, but it is not clear that this meant a demotion.[26] In fact, at the time of Machel's death, it became quite clear that they were still full-fledged and influential members of the central committee. In other words, while it is true that in 1977 the balance of power within Frelimo shifted in favor of the hard-liners and in 1983 it swung back toward the moderates, the composition of the top leadership of Frelimo had remained constant through all these shifts. Frelimo was controlled by an old guard of preindependence leaders, who did not always agree on all issues, but who remained firmly in control of the organization and were able to contain their disagreements within the party itself, presenting a united front to the rest of the world. Frelimo remained strong at the center, and this was confirmed by the fact that after the death of Machel the succession problem was solved within the party without any public show of disagreement. The choice of Chissano as the new president seemed to confirm the continued ascendancy of the more moderate group, but the hard-liners remained very much part of the organization.

The leadership of Frelimo had been consolidated quite successfully in Mozambique by the time Samora Machel was killed in October 1986. The party was reasonably well-organized and cohesive, the leadership capable of containing dissension, and the organization had demonstrated a capacity for self-criticism and self-renewal, although perhaps more fitfully than on a continuous basis. In comparison to most political parties in Africa, Frelimo was a remarkable success. The regime was strong, a collegial rather than a one-man regime, also something rarely found in Africa. Despite the success of the party, however, the state remained weak. In

1986, the major process in Mozambique was one of state disintegration, rather than consolidation.

The Renamo insurgency reduced Frelimo, despite its internal cohesion, to a battered fighter who surprised many onlookers by surviving all his fights but who increasingly was hanging on the ropes. For the past twenty-two years, Frelimo had fought continuously against a series of opponents displaying a confusing variety of styles. Having survived bouts with Portugal and Rhodesia, a still unified Frelimo could not effectively counterpunch against incessant jabbing from Renamo.

The Mozambican National Resistance (Renamo) had been created in 1976 by Rhodesia's Central Intelligence Organization (CIO).[27] Its earliest supporters included former Portuguese settlers in Mozambique and ex-Frelimo guerrillas disenchanted with the discipline imposed by the new government or purged from the reorganized ranks of the military and the party. Until the accession of Robert Mugabe as Zimbabwe's first prime minister in 1980, Renamo continued to operate from Rhodesian territory. Its goal was to obtain intelligence about ZANU (Zimbabwe African National Union) and only secondarily to fight either ZANU or the Mozambican army. Combat was the task of the Rhodesian forces, intelligence gathering that of Renamo. In the early period, as a consequence, the organization was only a minor factor of destabilization.

Renamo's power grew markedly after 1980. Forced to leave Zimbabwe, the movement was airlifted into South Africa by that country's military intelligence and started receiving much more support. Its forces grew from a few hundred at the time to perhaps 20,000 combatants in 1986. Furthermore, its activities changed from gathering intelligence to sabotaging the transportation infrastructure and disrupting an already fragile rural economy. In early 1987, only the major towns were reasonably safe from Renamo's attacks, and it appeared the insurgents might be changing their tactics from "shoot and scoot" to holding captured territory. The growth of Renamo compounded the country's economic problems by forcing it to devote about 40 percent of its budget to defense, while at the same time making it more difficult to carry out development projects and precluding large-scale foreign economic assistance. The disruption created by Renamo was greatly increased by the fact that it was able to operate from Malawi as well as from South Africa, thus stretching the Mozambican Armed Forces' (FAM) limited logistical and manpower resources.

By early 1984, according to Joseph Hanlon, Frelimo controlled a smaller portion of the country than Portugal had controlled in 1974, when the decision was reached to grant Mozambique independence.[28] The increasing threat from Renamo was important in convincing the Mozambican leadership in early 1984 to sign the Nkomati Accord in an attempt to stop the flow of aid from the republic. But South African aid to Renamo continued, as shown by documents found at the movement's Gorongosa Mountains headquarters in 1985.[29] At the same time, however, the movement started diversifying its sources of support. At present, reports indicate that Renamo continues to receive aid from embittered former Portuguese residents and that it has also attracted the support of private U.S., Brazilian and West German citizens. Several countries, including Saudi Arabia, Somalia, Malawi, and the Comoro Islands also are believed to be providing support for Renamo.[30]

The threat from Renamo and South Africa, and until 1980 from Rhodesia, made Mozambique very dependent on its armed forces, causing it to undertake a military buildup program while it was still trying to reorganize the party and to relaunch the economy. But the FAM has encountered many constraints and dilemmas that have prevented it from becoming an effective force. Major constraints include low education, poor morale, and lack of loyalty. The dilemmas involve the choice between training the FAM for conventional warfare or counterinsurgency, when both are needed and Mozambique lacks the resources to do even one adequately; and the fact that Soviet military equipment, which is readily available, is often unsuitable, while the probability of receiving more adequate Western equipment is decreased by the present reliance on Soviet arms. It should also be added here that the job the FAM was called upon to do—stopping infiltration by South Africa or Renamo—was almost impossible under any circumstances, given the reality of Pretoria's massive military machine and of Mozambique's geography: the country is twice the size of California, has a 1,500-mile coastline, a 300-mile border with South Africa, a 625-mile border with Malawi, and an inadequate transportation infrastructure.

The shortage of skilled manpower has badly affected the FAM, as it has all other sectors of Mozambican life. The departing Portuguese left Mozambique saddled with a 90 percent illiteracy rate. Not surprisingly, this resulted in "the low scientific and educational level of the majority of the [military] candidates," as Machel put it.[31] Poor administrative-logistical skills perhaps were the single most damaging factor to the FAM. Without the staff capable of implementing regular salary payments, as well as food, clothing, and ammunition shipments, and without the personnel able to read manuals or maps, the FAM suffers both low morale and inefficiency. The high number—relative to the FAM's size—of Soviet and Eastern European advisers attached to Mozambican units is at least in part the result of the incapacity of FAM personnel to handle technologically sophisticated material. In 1985, there were 1,600 advisers in the FAM, or one for every seventeen soldiers. In addition, Frelimo is caught in a dilemma between loyalty and meritocracy. Traditionally it has chosen loyalty, shifting rather than demoting, incompetents. While this policy has consolidated the party by lessening factional splits or outright disloyalty, it has probably lowered military efficiency.

There is a weak esprit de corps among FAM members. In part, this is explained by Mozambique's lack of a military tradition; the war for independence was waged by semiautonomous guerrillas, and there was some resentment when Frelimo imposed tighter discipline after 1975. Additionally, 75 percent of FAM personnel are conscripts, many of them unwilling. Some observers describe the Mozambican recruiting as sometimes akin to impressment. President Machel acknowledged many times that the draft system was arbitrary and that this had created "damaging" and "incapacitating" consequences, notably a "lack of political conscience."[32] Indiscipline by FAM and the secret police angered the citizenry and prompted President Machel to institute a continuing "legality offensive" to curb the excesses of the security forces, but apparently with little success.[33] Reports have continued of abuses by security forces, including stealing by hungry troops who do not receive adequate food supplies.

Even more damaging to Mozambique's security has been the disloyalty of the military. A number of high-ranking officers have either defected from Mozambique or been accused of being South African agents.[34] Following a raid by South Africa in 1981, Machel admitted that Pretoria possessed substantial information about the FAM's combat readiness, its deployment, and its defense systems. Defectors to South Africa have included high-ranking officials in the Ministry of Security. At lower levels, desertion from the FAM is also common. According to U.S. intelligence sources, the "extensive" problem at this level is caused by insufficient food, inadequate weapons, irregular pay, inadequate clothing, and low morale because of continuing Renamo attacks. By late 1986, defections were increasing throughout the FAM's ranks.

A final constraint on the effectiveness of the FAM is insufficient manpower to counter the 20,000-strong Renamo force, as well as possible South African incursions. Mozambique's armed forces include some 30,000 regulars and an additional 30,000 border guards and people's militia, but this only represents less than 30 percent of the number needed to maintain the one-to-ten ratio considered necessary for successful counterinsurgency. The fact that FAM is organized and equipped as a cost-intensive conventional force, coupled with the country's declining economy, makes it financially impossible for Mozambique to increase the number sufficiently.

The military's problems are compounded by the necessity of preparing for two possible types of warfare—conventional against a South African threat and counterinsurgency against Renamo—while lacking the resources to master even one. South Africa's main role in Mozambique has been that of supplying, training and transporting Renamo forces. Direct intervention has been limited to small reconnaissance commando operations, as well as attacks against purported African National Congress areas. Yet the possibility of a direct South African attack threatens Mozambique sufficiently for it to retain and even increase its conventional fighting capabilities.

Frelimo's decision following independence was to transform its guerrilla force into a conventional army. This was a natural decision for an independent state, particularly one threatened by Rhodesia and South Africa, but it also entailed significant costs, creating a sharper division between military and civilians and leaving Mozambique unprepared to fight the counterinsurgency war against Renamo.

The initial decision to build a conventional fighting force was strengthened by Rhodesian incursions. Between 1975 and 1979, Rhodesia's Special Air Service, Selous Scouts, light infantry, and air force staged over 360 attacks within Mozambique, mostly against ZANU camps. The Soviet Union supplied Mozambique with weaponry that was fairly modern by African standards, and at the Nampula training camp Soviet trainers taught conventional techniques, such as large force movements and the use of tanks, heavy artillery, and missiles. At the same time, Frelimo demobilized most of its guerrilla veterans. FAM also reorganized its command structure along conventional lines: in 1980, it introduced a formal system of ranks to replace the informal breakdown into commanders, trained men, and recruits that it had maintained until that point.

It is worth pointing out here that this change took place at the same time that Frelimo was reshaping itself into a Leninist party, also becoming more rigid and hierarchical. The change in the nature of the military cannot be attributed exclusively to the influence of the Soviet military advisers or the incursions by Rhodesia. Clearly, the ideological choices of the Frelimo leadership affected the military, as well as the party structure. The result was that the military, like the party, became more isolated from the population and more prone to indiscipline. The creation of a more formal organization in the military thus decreased rather than increased the military's efficiency.

Building the FAM into a conventional force did bear some fruit immediately. The Mozambican military succeeded in blunting several Rhodesian strikes in 1979, something that helped boost the Lancaster House negotiations.[35] But after 1980, the FAM had to face Renamo, not the Rhodesian army, and being a conventional army became a liability. The process of building up the badly needed counterinsurgency capability proved very difficult. The FAM had equipped itself with conventional weaponry at high initial costs. The weaponry received little use, but maintenance costs remained high nevertheless. For example, the air force received its first MiG fighter in March 1977, and had the equivalent of six squadrons by 1984, including some forty-four MiG-21s.[36] But the Mozambican pilots never ventured into South African air space to hit Renamo bases, and apparently they never scrambled to intercept South African planes that regularly resupplied Renamo, at least until the signing of the Nkomati Accords. But equipment more suitable for the task of fighting Renamo, such as helicopters, four-wheel-drive vehicles, field radios, and above all fuel, small arms, and combat rations, was in short supply.

Once again, there is a striking parallel here to what was happening in the civilian sector. The decision to provide the military with heavy and costly equipment is similar to that of endowing the state farms with tractors and combine-harvesters. The heavy machinery was poorly used because of constant breakdowns, but its high initial price and continuing maintenance costs depleted the agriculture budget, preventing the country from buying hoes and other hand tools the peasant population needed to produce food.

As in the civilian sector, the decision to move toward hierarchy and mechanization had political as well as efficiency costs. By separating the soldier from the rural support base developed during the war for independence, the transformation of the FAM into a conventional force helped increase the tension between military and civilians. Frelimo had been both a party and an army, and its members had identified themselves with the peasants—Frelimo even maintained farms in the liberated zones to raise its own food supplies. But with the transformation of FAM into a conventional army, the public started complaining of military indiscipline and belligerence toward civilians. Machel did his best to remind his countrymen that the military and the civilians were engaged in the same battle. In his 1981 May Day speech, for example, he stressed that "defense and economy are two muzzles of the same gun," and that "the gun [the soldiers] are bearing has the same value as the peasant's hoe or plow...."[37] He further stated that each soldier should work in a communal village, cooperative, or state farm. But the idea was apparently put into practice in only a few cases, and the gap between military and civilians continued to grow.

Just as the decision to form a conventional army had some immediate benefits but caused longer term problems, so did the decision to rely on Eastern Bloc equipment solve an immediate problem but create new ones at a later date. Eastern Bloc equipment could be obtained quickly, and Frelimo had every reason to believe that it would continue to be provided reliably. Obtaining Western equipment would have been a lengthy process, even assuming Frelimo could have gotten any, and in any case Western military aid is often subject to yearly reviews that make it undependable.

But the training and equipment Frelimo received from the Soviet Bloc was often unsuitable. FAM officers acknowledge the costly and outdated nature of Soviet equipment. Details of the agreements are unclear, but observers believe that Mozambique obtains its arms either through concessionary cash sales or through barter deals. It would probably be very difficult for Mozambique to break these agreements not only because such action would greatly upset the Soviet Union, but also because Mozambique is unlikely to find an alternate and reliable source of weapons in the West. In early 1985, the U.S. Congress rejected a Reagan administration plan to supply Mozambique with slightly over $1 million worth of training and "nonlethal" military equipment.[38] Britain is providing increasing military support: British officers are training FAM officers inside Zimbabwe and at Sandhurst; former Special Air Service (SAS) personnel are doing the same in Mozambique; specialized communications equipment has been provided and advanced Lee-Enfield assault rifles have been pledged. But such aid serves a largely symbolic purpose and falls far short of Mozambique's needs. So far, the opening toward the West has not proven to be the solution to Mozambique's security problems any more than it has to its economic problems.

The FAM is thus caught between a rock and a hard place: Soviet assistance is reliable—unless Mozambique turns openly to the West—but inadequate in quality. British assistance, while more suitable to Mozambique's counterinsurgency needs, is totally inadequate in quantity. U.S. assistance would depend on Mozambique's moving away from the Soviet Union to begin with, and even then it would remain dependent on domestic political events.

Mozambique increasingly is turning to another alternative—African and nonaligned countries—which can provide military support without antagonizing the Soviet Union or the West. Foremost among these countries is Zimbabwe, which has provided 14,000 soldiers out of its total force complement of 40,000. Most have been deployed along the Beira corridor, but with the increased Renamo activity in northern Mozambique some Zimbabwean soldiers were reassigned to active combat there. The Zimbabwean defense force also has an air base in Chimoio. Increased Zimbabwean manpower depends upon a rapprochement between ZANU and ZAPU or upon the presence of a garrisoning force from another country, probably India.[39] Both possibilities would free more Zimbabwean troops for Mozambique without lessening Zimbabwe's security. Tanzania has provided several hundred advisors and, by late 1986 had begun supplying combat troops. Surprisingly, the final source of African assistance is Malawi, which until late 1986 was giving sanctuary to Renamo. Under pressure from the frontline states, Malawi agreed in December 1986 to permit Zimbabwean and Mozambican military units to cut across southern Malawi while moving from Tete to Niassa and Zambezia provinces in pursuit of Renamo. Given the domestic financial and economic situation of African countries, African assistance is bound to remain limited—an addition to, rather than a substitute for, Soviet aid.

The fight against Renamo and South Africa has greatly weakened Mozambique and prevented the consolidation of state power. Not only has the lack of security brought economic activity to a standstill and made it impossible for Frelimo to govern many parts of the country, but it has also undermined the military, threatening to turn it into an organization at odds with the civilian population and potentially with the party. The problems that must be surmounted at present to consolidate state power in Mozambique are enormous. Frelimo, despite its internal strength, is in a poor position to do so. The question that arises is whether Renamo itself might become a future catalyst for the consolidation of state power. Is Mozambique, in other words, likely to move from the ineffective government by Frelimo to a much more effective government by Renamo? This is highly doubtful, given Renamo's uncertain goals and limited popularity, as well as the fact that South Africa does not appear enthusiastic about the prospect of a Renamo takeover.

The organization started as a military rather than political one during its Rhodesian days, and was heavily dependent on white external leadership. To date, it remains a predominantly military organization with some ethnic-traditional support, notably in Manica province and especially among the Ndau. It has spelled out some of its goals—in rural Mozambique it has received some support by pledging to allow polygamy and to reinstall the *regulos* or chiefs deposed by Frelimo. But its national political goals remain unclear and, while the leadership contains more Africans, it remains divided and diffuse.[40] No leader of charismatic appeal, with whom the population can easily identify and who can represent Renamo abroad, has emerged. There is, in other words, no Jonas Savimbi in Mozambique.

South Africa, for its part, has helped Renamo survive and increase its fighting capability, but it has not provided the massive support that might have helped it to overthrow Frelimo. Between 1980 and March 1984, the South African government provided Renamo with bases, sanctuary, training, equipment, and transportation into and out of Mozambique. But apparently the South African government was using Renamo as a spoiler not to topple the Machel government, but to cripple a Marxist-Leninist state, force it to sign a nonaggression pact with South Africa, and disrupt the transportation system of those front-line states trying to lessen their economic dependence on South Africa.

To this end, the south African government deliberately supplied Renamo with military equipment of limited capability. For example, at one time, Renamo's field radios reportedly could link with a central point—either in South Africa or at Renamo's main base in Mozambique's Gorongosa Mountains—but not with each other. This effectively prevented the carrying out of large scale operations independently of a central, South African-controlled source. Additionally, even after most observers were quite aware of Pretoria's involvement, and secrecy was thus pointless, South Africa never launched any joint strikes with Renamo, for example by providing air cover for a guerrilla ground attack. The largest weapons supplied by South Africa have apparently been some 12.7-mm antiaircraft guns. South Africa's manpower involvement appears to have been limited to individual or small-unit reconnaissance commandos operations against purported ANC installations, above all in the period preceding the signing of the Nkomati Accord.

South Africa certainly has the means to topple Frelimo militarily, but it does not appear to have the will. The extent of South Africa's intervention in Mozambique has been much smaller than in Angola—and it is not even clear whether South Africa is trying to install UNITA in power there. A possible explanation is that South Africa believes that direct intervention against Mozambique would lead to a stronger reaction by other African countries than its invasion of Angola in 1975. At that time, there was no legitimate government in power in Luanda, and UNITA had some support among Black African nations—at least before the South African invasion. Renamo has not received any official support in Africa in its opposition to an internationally recognized government.[41] Furthermore, a direct South African move against Frelimo would almost inevitably prompt a reaction by Zimbabwe and possibly other front-line states, given the importance of the transportation routes through Mozambique as the only alternative to dependence on South Africa. The Botha government also realizes that the invasion of a sovereign state could further inflame unrest within South Africa and step up pressure for sanctions in the West.

Finally, the long-range cost of keeping Renamo in power would prove daunting. The initial operation would only be the beginning. A South African-installed regime would remain dependent on Pretoria for support, encountering great difficulty in finding other sources of aid. Given the present economic crisis of Mozambique, and the fact that Frelimo would undoubtedly continue fighting, South Africa would face a long-term financial and security drain. South Africa would thus be confronted by a conflict that could conceivably spill across its borders.

Some observers have argued that, although South Africa has not sought to install a Renamo government in power, Frelimo might collapse on its own. The combination of Rhodesia's, Renamo's, and South Africa's attacks, on one side, and Frelimo's inability to defend the state and revive the economy on the other, have created a vicious circle. Renamo's strength makes it difficult for Frelimo officials to reach the villages, which in turn further strengthens Renamo or at least creates a power vacuum in rural areas.[42] The besieged Frelimo could also become increasingly authoritarian, alienating the population. Conceivably, Frelimo could topple without any additional force being exerted against it, with a government of national unity emerging that incorporated Frelimo and Renamo members. This seems a remote prospect, however, because Frelimo is still reasonably popular.

A second possibility discussed by some analysts is that the war's continuing toll might prompt a military *putsch* against the new Chissano government. The regime has instituted policies that lessened the state's security, and younger officers complain that Frelimo has allowed the older *"historicos"* of the liberation struggle to retain their positions and thus block promotion possibilities. Yet Frelimo's long-standing cohesiveness and collegiality, its ability for self-criticism and renewal, and the personal popularity of Minister of Defense Alberto Chipande suggest that such military action is unlikely. Finally, while morale in the armed forces has been low and the behavior of the officer corps has been less than professional at times, the military's sense of corporatism and professionalism undoubtedly has been bolstered by recent British assistance, as well as the deployment of 14,000 Zimbabwean troops to protect the Beira corridor. While one can never rule out the possibility of a military coup d'état, there is no indication that one is likely to take place.

After more than ten years of independence, the process of state power consolidation in Mozambique has not been accomplished. In fact, despite some initial progress, the process has stalled and is not likely to resume unless the security situation improves drastically. And yet Mozambique has a strong regime, which has proven capable of maintaining its cohesion and collegiality under the difficult conditions created by the war and, more recently, by Samora Machel's sudden death.

How the regime could be strong despite the weakness of the state is a paradox that can be explained specifically in terms of the history of the independence movement in Mozambique, some characteristics of the country, and the political situation in the region. In more general terms, however, the paradox is explained by the fact that in all countries the strength of the regime and that of the state require very different assets.[43]

We have already discussed the reasons for the strength of Frelimo and the regime it has formed. It may be worth reiterating here that Frelimo's role as the country's sole independence movement cannot be underestimated because it provides the party with a legitimacy that has survived the most controversial policies and the most obvious mistakes. It is also worthwhile stressing that the legitimacy of Frelimo was aided by the lack of major ethnic cleavages in the country, which made it easier for the movement to be national in scope, rather than identified with one ethnic group.

The weakness of the state, on the other hand, is explained by the administrative and military deficiencies of the newly independent country, coupled with South Africa's policy of destabilization. The Mozambican state at independence was probably no weaker than many others in Africa. The intervention of South Africa through Renamo transformed that weakness into an active process of state disintegration, rather than leading to a condition of stagnation, as has frequently been the case elsewhere.

In more general terms, the discrepancy between regime strength and state strength can be explained by the fact that the former is mostly a question of internal organization and legitimacy, while the latter is a question of power and mobilization of material assets. The policy choices made by Frelimo, its internal organization, the affective linkages it has established with the population during the war of independence, and the mechanisms created for discussing problems and managing internal disagreements are the major factors that influence the legitimacy of the regime and its internal strength.

The consolidation of the state is something very different. The key here is power, or the capacity to make things happen, through coercion if necessary. Power requires material assets. Some of these assets are economic—a bankrupt state has a very limited capacity to make anything happen. Some are organizational—the existence of a linkage between the regime and the population that ensures that policies are applied even when the population is not enthusiastic about them. This kind of organization is very different from the internal one of the regime. Thus the collegiality of Frelimo's Political Bureau enhances its legitimacy by presenting the population with an image of united and cohesive leadership; what would enhance state power is the restoration of Frelimo's rural network, as well as of the administrative and security apparatus.

The critical problem for Mozambique is that it would need particularly large material resources to consolidate the state, because of South Africa's backing of Renamo. Not only are South Africa's assets immeasurably greater than those of Mozambique, but the task of destabilization undertaken by Pretoria requires fewer resources than that of state consolidation.

The consolidation of the state in the long run depends on the regime's capacity to generate material assets. Mozambique cannot do this on its own since it is fighting not only an internal opposition, but also South Africa. However, at the present time, it is caught in a vicious circle because its incapacity to generate enough assets to maintain security means that it cannot generate the foreign support it needs to reestablish security. Soviet aid has been and still is necessary to the survival of the Mozambican state, but insufficient to promote its consolidation. Western aid and investment that might generate greater material assets are hampered by the lack of security and the ties to the Soviet Union. In late 1986, Mozambique was caught in a chicken and egg dilemma: it needed security to attract aid and investment, but it needed aid and investment before it could improve security.

When the Frelimo leadership adopted the Marxist-Leninist blueprint for organization at the 1977 congress, it viewed it as a means for consolidating the state, not only the regime. Marxism-Leninism was seen as a form of political organization, to be sure, but also as a form of economic organization that would generate material assets, further helping the consolidation of the state. Poor economic policy and the Renamo insurgency prevented the generation of material assets, yet the model helped the consolidation of Frelimo as a political organization, leading to the present paradox of a strong regime presiding over a very weak state.

Notes

1. Frelimo was founded in 1962 as a front uniting three smaller movements that had been in existence for a few years. The initial process of unification was fairly difficult, but by 1964 the war started in Mozambique's northern provinces. The political orientation of Frelimo was not totally clarified until a meeting of Frelimo's Central Committee in January 1969, during which the more conservative, purely nationalistic leaders of the movement were expelled and the socialist-oriented group prevailed. The victory of the radicals was confirmed by Samora Machel's election to the presidency of Frelimo in May 1970. Since then, Frelimo has not suffered any major internal splits.

2. The Caetano regime was deposed by the Armed Forces Movement on 24 April 1974. On 7 September of the same year, the Armed Forces Movement agreed to transfer power to Frelimo within a year. A transitional government led by Joaquim Chissano was set up on 20 September 1974 and Mozambique became independent on 25 June 1975. Frelimo therefore had very little time to plan the transition to independence.

3. Frelimo forces were estimated at about 10,000 by 1974. Most of them

62   Herbert Howe & Marina Ottaway

were concentrated in the liberated zones, that is the provinces of Niassa and Cabo Delgado in the extreme north of the country. Frelimo was also operating in Tete province since the late 1960s, but it was not active in the southern part of the country until 1973. Even then, its presence in the south was weak, because the distance from its rear bases in Tanzania and the concentration of the Portuguese population in the southern part of the country made operations more difficult. For more detail, see Allen and Barbara Isaacman, *Mozambique from Colonialism to Revolution, 1900-1982* (Boulder: Westview Press, 1983), 105-107.

4. The split within Frelimo had been in the making for some time. In fact, when Eduardo Mondlane was killed by a letter bomb in Dar es Salaam, there were allegations that the rival faction of Frelimo, led by Lazaro Nkavandame, was responsible.

5. An interesting account of Frelimo's accomplishments in the liberated zones is contained in Anders Johansson, *Struggle in Mozambique* (New Delhi: Indian Council for Africa, n.d.). The pamphlet is based on a visit to the liberated zones in 1968. At this time, Frelimo had about 8,000 cadres.

6. For an account of the organization of Frelimo in the early postindependence period, see Allen Isaacman, "A Luta Continua: Creating a New Society in Mozambique," Fernand Braudel Center for the Study of Economies, Historical Systems and Civilizations, State University of New York at Binghampton, 1978.

7. The communal villages were first organized in the liberated zones. After independence, the process apparently slowed down. Communal villages fell into four categories: those formed before independence; former Portuguese regroupment villages organized to isolate Frelimo from the population; villages created to relocate the victims of floods and natural disasters; and finally those organized for political purposes after independence.

8. See Isaacman, "A Luta Continua," 36 ff.

9. As a consequence of the problems encountered with some dynamizing groups, party officials tried to limit their political role and to reduce them to local grievance committees. While this trend was decried by high party officials, it started making the party more aloof from the population. For a criticism of the trend, see Oscar Monteiro, "L'Action du parti dans l'appareil de l'état," Ministry of Information mimeo, n.d.

10. For more detail on the 1977 congress, see Marina Ottaway, "The Theory and Practice of Marxism-Leninism in Mozambique and Ethiopia," in David Albright, ed., *Communism in Africa* (Bloomington, Ind.: Indiana University Press, 1980).

11. The issue of how much help the communal villages should receive remained controversial within the government. Frelimo's commitment to the villages was reaffirmed at the 1977 congress, but by 1980 there were no laws governing their formation. Minister of Agriculture Joaquim de Carvalho was dismissed in August 1978, in part for having neglected the communal villages and favored the state farms. But after his dismissal, the policy did not really change and state farms continued to absorb most of the agriculture budget. See also Joseph Hanlon, *Mozambique: The Revolution Under Fire* (London: Zed Books Ltd., 1984), 121 ff.

12. See Isaacman and Isaacman, *Mozambique from Colonialism*, 122-123.

13. Some examples will help illustrate the dimension of the problem of centralization in the economy, above all in agriculture. The Limpopo Agro-Industrial Complex, which had been created by the Portuguese as a small holder scheme grouping 1,500 Portuguese families was run as a single unit in 1979. At that time, it had 15,000 hectares of land under cultivation, producing rice and vegetables. According to the director, the ultimate goal was to enlarge the scheme to 90,000 hectares, still under central management. Around the same time, the Ministry of Agriculture was trying to set up an office to organize the repair and allocation of tractors and farm machinery on a nationwide scale. See David and Marina Ottaway, *Afrocommunism* (New York: Africana Publishers, 1986), 88. The Ten-Year Plan, approved by the People's Assembly in 1981 but never implemented because the country was bankrupt, called for the organization of ten giant "integrated agro-industrial complexes," which by 1990 would produce 75 percent of agricultural products, 78 percent of the meat, 83 percent of the milk, and 53 percent of the eggs in the state sector. See Isaacman and Isaacman, *Mozambique from Colonialism*, 152.

14. See Hanlon, *Mozambique: The Revolution*, 110.

15. By May 1982, there were only 1,352 so-called communal villages, containing about 19 percent of the rural population. Most of these villages were not "communal" at all, because the peasants cultivated all of their land individually. Only 229 villages had organized a cooperative and were at least in part communal. See Isaacman and Isaacman, *Mozambique from Colonialism*, 155.

16. See *Africa Confidential*, 25, 15, 1 August 1984; and Harold D. Nelson, ed., *Mozambique: A Country Study* (Washington, D.C.: Government Printing Office, 1984), 277.

17. See "Frelimo Fourth Congress," *Communist Affairs*, 3, 1, January 1984, 31-39.

18. At the time of the Fourth Party Congress, Frelimo had 110,000 members and candidates. This represented a more than tenfold growth since independence.

19. *Quarterly Economic Review of Tanzania and Mozambique*, 1, 1986, based on statistics released by the National Planning Commission of Mozambique.

20. The 1982-1985 plan called for only one-third the investment envisaged by the shelved Ten-Year Plan. Even this plan proved to be overly ambitious. In 1982, high Frelimo officials were warning that no growth could be expected before 1985, in retrospect an optimistic appraisal. See Hanlon, *Mozambique: The Revolution*, 86-90.

21. *The Guardian*, 5 March 1984. The government estimated that 900 rural shops, 495 primary schools, and 140 communal villages were destroyed.

22. See Hanlon, *Mozambique: The Revolution*, 290, for excerpts from the accord.

23. During the colonial period, up to 100,000 Mozambicans had worked in South African mines, under a contract highly lucrative for Portugal, which received the workers' wages in gold and paid them in the local currency. A new agreement negotiated in 1978 reduced the number of miners to 35,000 and abrogated the gold payment clause. The number later increased again, reaching

about 61,000 by late 1986. In October 1986, after a landmine exploded in South Africa near the Mozambican border, Pretoria accused Mozambique of having violated the Nkomati Accord by allowing the ANC to operate from its territory. In retaliation for the alleged violations, South Africa banned the recruitment of additional Mozambican miners and announced that it would not renew the contracts of those already in the country. This could be a serious blow to Mozambique, for the remittances from South Africa account for close to one-half of Mozambique's foreign exchange earnings. See *Africa News*, XXVII, 8, 27 October 1986; and William Claiborne, "Poverty Above the Ground, Wealth Below," *The Washington Post*, 31 October 1986.

24. Mozambique formally joined the World Bank in September 1984. A short time later, it also joined the Lome Convention. This represented a major change for a country which a few years earlier had unsuccessfully tried to join the Eastern Bloc Council for Mutual Economic Assistance (CMEA).

25. See Claiborne, *Mozambican News Review*, 15, 8, 13 September 1985; and *Quarterly Economic Review of Tanzania and Mozambique*, 1, 1986.

26. Among those transferred to the provinces at this time was Marcelino dos Santos,one of the founders of Frelimo and a known supporter of the large project approach. Dos Santos, who had occupied a number of major positions in the government and party, was named governor of Sofala Province. Nevertheless, he remained part of Frelimo's inner circle and a member of the political bureau. For more detail, see *Mozambique: A Country Study*, 220; and *Africa Confidential*, 25, 15, 1 August 1984.

27. On the early history of Renamo, see David Martin and Phyllis Johnson, "To Nkomati and Beyond," in David Martin and Phyllis Johnson, eds., *Destructive Engagement* (Harare: Zimbabwe Publishing House, 1986).

28. Hanlon, *Mozambique: The Revolution*, 219.

29. "Counting on Colonel Charlie," *Africa News*, XXV, 9.

30. See *Africa Confidential*, 25, 28 November 1984 and 26, 7, 3 April 1985; and *The Observer*, 2 December 1984.

31. *Mozambique, A Country Study*, 266.

32. Ibid., 267.

33. See *Quarterly Economic Review of Tanzania and Mozambique*, 3, 1984, 16-17.

34. Following a successful South African reconnaissance commando raid on Maputo in January 1981, the Mozambican government arrested eight high-ranking FAM officers, two of whom later escaped.

35. Hanlon, *Mozambique: The Revolution*, 232.

36. By 1985, Mozambique had four attack squadrons that included MiG-17s, MiG-21s, MiG-23s, and SU-22s. It also had three interceptor squadrons that included MiG-19s and MiG-21s. The approximate number of planes in the seven squadrons was 140.

37. *Mozambique: A Country Study*, 265.

38. Herbert Howe, "US Plans Military Aid for Marxist Mozambique," *Christian Science Monitor*, 14, January 1985.

39. At the 1986 meeting of the Nonaligned Movement in Harare, suggestions

were made for the creation of a Third World peace-keeping force to help Mozambique. Among the possible participants, India, Ethiopia, Kenya, and Tanzania were mentioned.

40. See Mozambican National Resistance, "Manifest and Program" Cascais, Portugal, September 1985.

41. Malawi, Somalia, and the Comoro Islands have reportedly provided some aid to Renamo. Malawi has turned a blind eye to Renamo guerrillas operating from its territory, Somalia and the Comoro Islands have apparently served as transshipment points for military ordnance. None of these countries has officially expressed support for Renamo.

42. According to the Machester *Guardian*, 27 February 1984, refugees from Tete province reported that they had not seen a Frelimo official in two years.

43. The idea of the difference between the strength of the regime and that of the state originally stemmed from a conversation with Naomi Chazan. Whether she would accept what we have done with it, we do not know. We are indebted for the inspiration, but she bears no responsibility for the consequences.

chapter four

The People's Republic of Angola: A Radical Vision Frustrated

John A. Marcum

When he departed the besieged city of Luanda on 10 November 1975, a day before scheduled independence, Portugal's last high commissioner for Angola left three nationalist movements locked in violent competition for political succession. The following day, the Movimento popular de libertação de Angola (MPLA), whose traditional political base was Luanda and its ethnically Mbundu hinterland, declared itself political successor and proclaimed the creation of an independent People's Republic of Angola (PRA).[1] The MPLA's principal external backers, the Soviet Union, Cuba, North Vietnam, other communist states, and the governments of other former Portuguese colonies, promptly made good on prior commitments to extend diplomatic recognition to the MPLA polity.[2] The MPLA also successfully opposed and prevented any last-minute initiatives by the Organization of African Unity (OAU) designed to press it into a negotiated settlement with its civil war adversaries.[3]

In the face of this winner-take-all strategy, most African states initially withheld recognition of the MPLA/PRA and continued to call for a ceasefire, a transitional government, and free elections to determine the political future of Angola. As Western journalists uncovered and publicized evidence of South African intervention on the side of the MPLA's rivals, however, continental attitudes quickly shifted. The specter of armored columns striking north from South African-administered Namibia aroused a greater fear and animosity than did large-scale, and ultimately decisive, Soviet and Cuban intervention on behalf of the MPLA. It was apartheid, not communism, that constituted a locally recognizable threat. Beginning with the preeminent regional power, Nigeria, a country that had previously criticized Soviet assistance to the MPLA, African states responded to South African intervention by recognizing the MPLA state and government.[4] To the consternation of the United States, reeling at the time from its defeat at the hands of communist forces in Vietnam, radical nationalists beholden to Soviet and Cuban benefactors moved to secure political hegemony over a large, resource-rich area of southwest Africa: Angola.

During the ensuing decade (1976-1986), the MPLA attempted to realize the vision of a radically new socialist society that had inspired its senior leadership over the previous two decades (1955-1975) of anticolonial struggle. Despite a persistent MPLA commitment to this goal, however, Angola today does not seem much closer to becoming the modern, disciplined, and prosperous society these leaders envisioned. To the contrary, ravaged by insurgency within and battered by military incursions from without, the MPLA government depends upon the costly presence of a foreign army merely to survive. The Angolan experience illustrates how determined would-be architects of radical Third World polities may find themselves overwhelmed by limiting social realities and victimized by their own impetuous or inflexible strategies.

Colonial Conditioning and the Roots of Radicalism

Throughout the formative decades of contemporary African nationalism just before and after World War II, Portugal was governed under the personalized autocracy of António Salazar. Repressive policies limited civil liberties and perpetuated an inequitable, largely preindustrial class structure. The weakness of the Portuguese state was reflected in a dependence on secret police, press censorship, and colonial mercantilism. This weakness helps to explain why it did not emulate British, French, and Belgian policies of reform and, finally, political retreat that led most of Africa to independence by the mid-1960s. Portugal's African colonies were obliged to fight (1961-1974) for their independence. The cruelties of guerrilla war and counterinsurgency ultimately combined with colonial conditioning under political dictatorship to deprive lusophone Africa of even that brief, flawed, but heuristic exposure to democratic values and processes that was experienced by most other African territories.

Portuguese authorities anxiously attempted to contain nationalism as it spread over Africa in the wake of a global conflict that had fatefully weakened European colonial power. Despite expanded border and political police networks and tightened travel restrictions, and despite the social constrictions of illiteracy (90 percent) and economic marginality, collective awareness of political developments elsewhere in Africa and of socioeconomic injustices inside Angola spurred indigenous political organizing. The government penetrated and smashed formative dissident movements, be they student, religious, cultural, labor, or ethnic. Political consciousness and activism nonetheless spread and persisted in those urban, coastal, and agricultural highland areas heavily influenced by centuries of colonial economic, educational, and cultural presence. Of these impact areas, the most salient was Luanda with its tens of thousands of Portuguese residents. Luanda constituted the core of a modernized and bureaucratized "central society" incorporated into a colonial political economy.[5] It was in Luanda that the MPLA's founders and subsequent leaders, mostly disaffected professionals and intellectuals that included Portuguese and *mestiço* Marxists, first organized, determinedly survived, and ultimately emerged to form the government of a new state.

During the course of Angolan nationalist insurgency against Portuguese rule, the MPLA, in the segmented, tridimensional form of a political underground, guerrilla force, and exile movement functioned as an eclectic front. Its leadership rejected proposals from within that it declare itself a "revolutionary party," preferring to wait until such time as a solid nucleus of ideologically trained cadres could be prepared.[6] Its Marxist roots were, however, arguably stronger than those of any other nationalist movement that led a sub-Saharan colony to political independence. Its ideological stance as presented in public statements and documents consistently stressed egalitarian, multiracial, and anti-imperialist themes compatible with a Marxist perspective.[7] In considerable measure, the MPLA's Marxist tendencies were a logical consequence of rigid Portuguese policies that over time had frustrated, alienated, and radicalized politically conscious Africans in all of Portugal's African territories.

According to contemporary MPLA and Soviet accounts, young Luandans and other urban dwellers exposed secretly to Marxist thought by Portuguese and Brazilian teachers, civil servants, and commercial employees responded to mounting government coercion in the 1950s by forming political groups of a "revolutionary character."[8] Writing expansively, one distant Soviet enthusiast alleged that during the period 1955-1956 a Marxist underground created "hundreds of mobile libraries" and clandestine schools in the African quarters of Luanda.[9] Within this context, the MPLA took form in 1956 as a broad umbrella movement. It reportedly incorporated a clandestine Partido comunista de Angola (PCA), cited prominently in Soviet publications during the 1960s, but since dismissed by Soviet researchers as having constituted little more than a group of a dozen or so persons.[10]

MPLA founders included persons whose writings and interviews displayed a sophisticated grasp of Marxist-Leninist thought.[11] And Dr. Agostinho Neto, President of the MPLA from 1962 until his death in 1979, received his formative political experience in Portuguese leftwing politics while a medical student (and sometime political prisoner) in

Portugal.[12] After escaping to Africa in 1962, Neto lobbied for support in
Western capitals. But he had little success in generating material support
or in altering perceptions of the MPLA as pro-Soviet, a failure that he
attributed to the biases of Western "imperialism." The MPLA was left to
rely externally on small-scale, fluctuating but sustained assistance from
communist states (some $60 million in Soviet assistance according to
U.S. government estimates) up to the time of the April 1974 military
coup that overthrew the post-Salazar government of Marcello Caetano.
This assistance was funneled in part through the Portuguese Communist
Party (PCP) with which the MPLA maintained close ties.[13]

In 1966, Cuba joined the Soviet Union and Eastern Europe as a major
provider of military and technical training for MPLA militants. As
noted in the columns of *Pravda*, a principal aim of such assistance was to
spread "the ideas of socialism and revolutionary anticolonial ideology."[14]
When the MPLA underwent periods of military adversity and political
stress, the analytical and organizational skills of Soviet- and Cuban-
trained leaders helped to sustain and revivify the movement. One
celebrated example of such leadership was provided by the military
instructor and ideologue, Commander Gilberto Teixeira da Silva ("Jika"),
whose posthumously published *Reflections on the Struggle for National
Liberation* offers insight into the theoretical and functional sophistication
with which the MPLA approached its bid for power.[15] When, in
September 1974, Neto loyalists assembled in a remote zone of eastern
Mexico province to salvage a faction-torn movement and to lead it into a
new era of legalized political activity, socialist-trained cadres assumed a
crucial role. Confronted with the breakaway of two sizeable internal
factions, hastily reorganized and locally augmented MPLA ranks fell far
short of providing the human resources necessary to win military and
political control over a new Angolan state.[16] Other potential cadres were
at least temporarily lost to two competing movements.

In the north, a predominantly Bakongo movement, the Frente
nacional de libertação de Angola (FNLA), led by a professed anti-
communist, Holden Roberto, received substantial support from the
United States and Zaire. On the eve of independence, the FNLA made its
move to become Portugal's political succesor. Its numerically superior,
partly Chinese-trained army moved south from bases in Zaire to storm
Luanda. To the south, a third nationalist contender, the *União para a
independência total de Angola* (UNITA), led by a young political
pragmatist, Jonas Savimbi, first attempted to parley its evident
following among some three million Ovimbundu of the central highlands
into political ascendancy. As Portuguese authority crumbled in the period
1974-1975, however, UNITA lost its principal hope for such
ascendancy—free elections promised by Lisbon. In desperation, Savimbi

turned to South Africa for political survival. South Africa obliged in September-October 1975 with a crash program of military training for UNITA and a motorized expeditionary force that swept northward toward Luanda.

In the end, it was a dramatic, global outreach and inpouring of Cuban troops and Soviet armor that won the day. Assistance from only a few hundred, first-arrived Cuban soldiers equipped with Soviet artillery and rockets was required for the MPLA to route the poorly led forces of the FNLA from the outskirts of Luanda to the Zaire border.[17] It took a more massive delivery of men (10,000-15,000) and material to prompt South Africa's withdrawal and, with it, the retreat of UNITA forces and followers into the vast emptiness of Angola's southeastern forests and savannah. After a harrowing "long march," Jonas Savimbi and remnants of UNITA did manage to escape annihilation at the hands of MPLA pursuers and dispersed into the protective wilderness of the southeast.[18] But the MPLA victory appeared essentially complete.

Independence and the Radical Agenda

The MPLA moved quickly to consolidate power and to convert itself into a "party guided by Marxism-Leninism, the ideology of the proletariat."[19] It strove to eliminate residual or potential opposition, rejecting any "reactionary" notions of political pluralism. Illustrative of this approach, it squashed the beginnings of an independent labor movement through which Luanda dockworkers had wrung economic concessions from Portuguese authorities in 1974 and imposed its own affiliate, the *União nacional dos trabalhadores angolanos* (UNTA) as the country's sole labor organization.[20]

In late 1976 and early 1977, an ambitious organizer of political action groups in Luanda and a veteran of guerrilla bands active in the Mbundu country of the interior, Nito Alves, mounted an early internal challenge to senior MPLA leadership. Exploiting popular resentment over the salience of *mestiços* and whites within the government and movement, Alves and his followers alleged that "ideological laxity" and administrative mismanagement were responsible for crippling food shortages. In May 1977, these *nitistas* attempted a coup d'état and, in the process, slew several prominent MPLA officials. The fact that Alves had been a vocal advocate of tightening ties to the Soviet Union and had enjoyed close contact with the Soviet embassy compounded the damage. It raised doubts about the reliability of the MPLA's principal external backers.[21]

Though severely shaken, Agostinho Neto and the movement's resiliant loyalists pressed ahead with their plans to transform the MPLA into a Marxist-Leninist party. According to MPLA Administrative Secretary Lucio Lara, militants embittered by the "anticommunist" intervention of South Africa, Zaire, and the United States pushed the leadership to move toward this goal more quickly than it believed prudent.[22] At the time, few MPLA members were familiar with even the most basic concepts of Marxism-Leninism. They knew little or nothing of dialectical materialism, democratic centralism, or dictatorship of the proletariat. Faced with this reality, in February 1977 the MPLA opened a National Party School in Luanda to train political cadres and raise their level of ideological comprehension. Unprepared to delay realization of the desired new political order, MPLA leadership decided simply to declare the adherence of thousands of MPLA followers to the pursuit of "scientific socialism" as a given. This adherence was said to be grounded in popular "trust" in the movement and its guide "Comrade President Agostinho Neto."[23]

A lack of conversance with Marxist-Leninist doctrine as opposed to good intentions was not to be a bar to party membership (an elite of some 35,000 members in a population of roughly eight million as of early 1986). Moreover, the standard panoply of affiliated labor, youth, women, student, and other "mass organizations" that flesh out a Marxist-Leninist single-party system did not require even a nominal adherence to Marxist-Leninist ideology as a prerequisite to membership, at least not at an early stage.

The formal conversion into vanguard party took place at the MPLA's First Congress on December 10, 1977, the movement's twenty-first birthday. A new MPLA-Partido do trabalho (MPLA-PT) "guided by the scientific ideology of the proletariat, Marxism-Leninism," emerged in predictable form. It assumed a pyramidal shape, from a base of local cells of three to thirty members on up (via indirect elections) through area, district, and provincial committees to the party congress, its central committee, and finally to the latter's political bureau. The congress confirmed the personal authority of Agostinho Neto as leader of the party and thus of the entire political system in which the government was to implement, not formulate, policy. The MPLA-PT assumed "political, economic and social leadership over the State" and its "efforts to build a socialist society."[24]

The fervor and intensity with which the MPLA-PT set out to build that new society were characteristic of the early phases of a revolutionary regime. The party attached an urgent importance to two tasks: political education and economic reconstruction.

It took monopoly control over all news media, the country's press agency, daily newspaper *(Jornal de Angola)*, radio (the Catholic church's Radio Ecclesia was shut down) and television stations. It assigned these institutions a major role in mobilizing and educating Angolans about the "objectives of socialist revolution." Perceiving a need to reeducate "backward" social groups, the party undertook to reduce the "counterrevolutionary" influence of religion. Religion represented a "distorted reflection of social reality."[25] "The struggle for a free, scientific and materialistic consciousness" was "an integral part of the struggle to build a new society." The MPLA-PT barred religious "believers" from party membership and eliminated church schools.

In its approach to economic reconstruction, the MPLA-PT turned initially to a by-the-book prescription of socialist formulas— nationalization, centralization, collectivization. Relying on political exhortation rather than economic incentive, it undertook to build a planned economy in the disabling absence of managerial personnel, commercial trade networks, functional transport, and private capital that had disappeared with the exodus of over 300,000 resident Portuguese in 1975. An influx of thousands of technicians, health practitioners, and teachers from Cuba and Eastern Europe helped avert total economic collapse. But this assistance could not have been financed without an early concession to economic pragmatism under which Sonangol, Angola's state-owned oil company, acquired a controlling partnership in a U.S. oil subsidiary, Cabinda Gulf. This arrangement, followed by similar agreements with other Western oil firms, insured an uninterrupted inflow of civil revenue. As of 1984, this income had grown to some $2 billion annually and enabled the government to survive.

It was in a noneconomic political sector of external relations, however, that the revolutionary zeal of the MPLA was most evident and most fateful. Mindful of how newly independent and self-consciously revolutionary Algeria had provided a formative MPLA guerrilla army with military training and arms in the years 1962-1964, the MPLA accepted a similar revolutionary mission with regard to nationalists (South West Africa People's Organization [SWAPO]) seeking to overthrow South African rule in neighboring Namibia.[26] In the flush of its own 1975-1976 victory, the MPLA made two related and fundamental assumptions. It assumed that South Africa, chastened by the Angolan misadventure of 1975, would not risk the international opprobrium or military costs of a head-on clash with MPLA and Cuban forces that anti-SWAPO incursions into Angola might provoke. It further assumed that UNITA no longer posed a serious threat and lacked either the internal political appeal or the external backing necessary to rebuild and reemerge as an effective adversary. Ideological blinders or casual, wishful thinking, or both surely contributed to these flawed calculations.

What Happened: the Inevitable and the Avoidable

Any political movement(s) coming to power in 1975 would have faced horrendous problems. The legacy of Portuguese rule—political inexperience, general illiteracy, rural poverty, and regional particularism, combined with the disjunctive departure of those (the Portuguese) who ran things, and the bloodletting of an externally armed civil war could not but render Angola extremely difficult to govern. What Keith Somerville aptly describes as the inheritance of a "crippling shortage of educated and politically conscious cadres" was to bedevil the efforts of any successors to Portuguese rule.[27] Those who would judge harshly what ensued must keep this inevitability in mind.

On the other hand, the calamity that was to befall Angola was not altogether unavoidable. It was evident from the outset of its rule that the MPLA would "need more than the weapons and the men of the Soviet Union and Cuba" to construct a new, unified society. It needed "to surmount the limits of its own social origins and reach out to those who [saw] it as an instrument of alien [Portuguese/Cuban] rule. The alternative [was] rule by force with continued rural violence."[28]

Given its mostly urban origins, Portuguese schooling, and high proportion of *mestiço* leadership, the MPLA always had difficulty relating effectively to rural areas and people. Its first secretary general, Viriato da Cruz, underscored this when he broke with the movement in 1963, charging that failure to develop an effective rural insurgency was attributable to a failure to understand that, in circumstances of white settler domination, African peasants logically viewed the independence struggle in racial, not class, terms.[29] Ten years later, a gulf of incomprehension between the still predominantly urban, multiracial MPLA leadership, on the one hand, and the ill-educated, rural black militants on the other was at least partially responsible for the collapse of a promising MPLA insurgency in rural eastern Angola.

As early as 1962, the MPLA formally recognized the peasantry to be Angola's largest and "most exploited" class and declared rural recruitment to be be a high priority.[30] Yet twenty-five years later, its leadership remains overwhelmingly urban. At the MPLA-PT Second Party Congress in December 1985, only twelve out of six hundred delegates were reported to be peasants—although some 30 percent of party members were said to be agricultural workers and peasants.[31]

It appears that continuing ideological rigidity prevented the MPLA from reaching out to preempt the growth of internal dissidence and organized opposition. Its strident campaigns against organized religion alienated Protestants and Catholics and converted churches into focal points of resistance to government policy. The Catholic church, led by a new, postcolonial hierarchy of local seminary-trained blacks not only survived, but has become what one former Protestant missionary has termed the "only truly national institution" in contemporary Angola. [32] Regionally divided Protestant denominations have also persisted, even flourished. The Methodist church, whose schools in the Luanda-Mbundu region educated many MPLA leaders, reportedly grew from 42,000 in 1975 to 100,000 in 1986. [33] As further evidence of just how counterproductive the antireligious policy proved to be, in the Ovimbundu highlands and to the southeast, a resistant Church of Christ in the Bush developed in tandem with UNITA.

Rejecting ethnicity ("tribalism" in MPLA parlance) as a valid variable, the MPLA refused to take affirmative action to bring underrepresented Ovimbundu into the ranks of top party leadership. Consequently, ten years after independence, Ovimbundu and other rural central-southern communities (Chokwe, Ganguela, Ovambo) remain unrepresented in the MPLA-PT political bureau and underrepresented in its central committee. A policy of "national reconciliation" inaugurated by Agostinho Neto in 1976 persuaded substantial numbers of former FNLA leaders and followers to make their peace in return for amnesty and civil service jobs or the right to resettle in rural areas. But this policy did not succeed in attracting significant defections from UNITA. [34]

Arguably, UNITA might not have reappeared in the late 1970s as a potent political/military challenge if its defeated and demoralized army had not been retrained and reequipped in Namibia by the South African Defense Force (SADF). But MPLA ideological hostility to popular racial, religious, and ethnic sentiment was also central to this reappearance. It presented UNITA with a cluster of popular grievances. On one count, the MPLA did change. President Eduardo dos Santos gradually built up his own power base and team of supporters after assuming office in 1979. One apparent consequence was that the number of mestiços in top party posts declined markedly in the years 1985-1986. But UNITA could still appeal to racial grievances by citing the presence of some 35,000 Cubans as a form of continuing alien white rule. (In the absence of free opinion polls, it is not possible to establish the extent to which Cubans are so viewed by the populace at large.)

Despite a relaxation of antireligious policies beginning in 1982, at the MPLA-PT's Second Party Congress President dos Santos reaffirmed the MPLA's fundamental hostility to religion. He warned against the "proliferation of sects" prone to pursue "counterrevolutionary goals," called for legislation to facilitate "effective control over religious activity," and urged "more attention to propagating the atheist concepts expressed in Marxist-Leninist theory." He thus affirmed the continuing exclusion of Angolan Christians from participation in the political process.[35] (The full significance of this exclusion can be appreciated by recalling that in the colonial years those fortunate few who did benefit from education attended church schools.) Although the MPLA endorsed cultural freedom, including ethnic expression in the arts and literature, the Angolan Writers' Union, the only available vehicle for literary publication, is governed by Luanda-Mbundu-*mestiço* intellectuals, publishes almost exclusively in Portuguese, and excludes dissident political views.[36]

Possibly the most decisive factor in fostering the "maintenance and growth" of organized UNITA opposition was the government's economic incapacity.[37] Its inability to revive agricultural production and to deliver essential goods and services to the outer reaches of central and southern Angola combined with an underestimation of both Jonas Savimbi's skill and appeal and South Africa's willingness to intervene to fuel a dramatic resurgence of UNITA.[38] This inability was due as much to ideological rigidity as to the violent and disjunctive transition to independence. It was soon compounded by the brutal, destructive impact of UNITA's hit-and-run insurgency.

Policies of centralization, mechanization, and collectivization in agriculture and policies modeled on Soviet experience paralleled and reflected the MPLA's general neglect of peasant needs and opinions. Illustrative of the consequences of these policies (and of continuing war), coffee production, previously a major source of foreign exchange, fell from 5.2 million sacks in 1974 to 283,000 sacks in 1983. By the time of the Second Party Congress, the MPLA was ready to acknowledge errors of haste and insensitivity and to accept a revisionist need to permit "all types of enterprise in rural areas, notably family types of enterprise and private initiatives in farming and livestock."[39]

Confronting economic imperatives, the MPLA came to accept the need for policies that were more "realistic." Indicative of its new willingness to compromise in the economic sphere, the party determined that it was better to raise official prices and legalize private trading and traders than to endure blackmarket trading that persisted, corrosive of authority, "outside the law." It concluded that small private enterprise "beginning to appear in agriculture" might be to the country's advantage and that such enterprise might even appropriately "develop in other low technology sectors where the lack of initiative from the state as well as the private sector has often led [Angolans to resort] to foreign companies."[40] The government dismantled a number of state farms and turned them over to smallholders and to local associations of farmers.

Meanwhile, UNITA insurgency developed into a formidable obstacle to economic revival. James Brooke, one of the few Western journalists permitted access to the area, reported in late 1985 that the International

Red Cross was flying four hundred tons of food weekly to tens of thousands of persons starving in Angola's fertile central highlands. UNITA rebels had effectively shut down road transport, blocked rail traffic (the Benguela railroad was utilizable only on short stretches), and progressively fostered such insecurity so that it became unsafe for peasants to cultivate or transport crops.[41]

Obliged to divert human and financial resources to combat an insurgency that reportedly had received over $1 billion in South African assistance by mid-1986, the MPLA found its efforts to move ahead with national reconstruction stymied.[42] Its school system remained underfunded and understaffed. Many students sent abroad to study failed to return or adjusted poorly when they did. The government made little progress toward reducing the disabling scarcity of skilled human manpower.

MPLA officials openly acknowledge their plight. They state that "the principal cause" of continuing insurgency is their inability "to provide Angolans with the goods and services that they need."[43] In turn, the persistence of UNITA insurgency renders the government unable to devote those resources that it is able to muster to the development of human and material resources with which to meet pressing societal needs. It is forced, instead, to divert it energies and capital into fighting an insurgency that further exacerbates rural misery, social discontent, and the magnitude of unmet needs.

Repeated "rectification" campaigns to forge party discipline, eliminate administrative corruption, and raise governmental effectiveness have borne minimal results. MPLA rule is geographically and demographically circumscribed. A French military analyst, Bernard Expédit, likens the MPLA's circumstances to those of ancient Rome in the civil war of 91-88 B.C.—a beleagured, "coastal-based" power center (Luanda and other air-linked cities) confronted by a hostile hinterland.[44]

Although it refuses to negotiate a power-sharing settlement with UNITA (the frequently stated goal of Jonas Savimbi), the MPLA attempts doggedly to break out of the UNITA/South Africa checkmate by following two related policies. On the one hand, it seeks, receives, pays, and increasingly borrows for ever more sophisticated Soviet weaponry with which to pursue its internal war.[45] On the other had, it embraces pragmatic economic policies that yield crucial oil revenues and that some external observers view as sparking a significant retreat from Marxist-Leninist ideology. In its struggle for survival, is the MPLA abandoning its radical social vision?

Angolan Socialism: Challenged Vision

Some Western bankers and businessmen, impressed by the forthright, pragmatic, and responsible manner in which Angolan officials interact with them, tend to conclude that the MPLA's commitment to "scientific socialism" is less than total. They speculate that only its dependence on Soviet weaponry and Cuban soldiers in coping with security and counterinsurgency needs prevents the MPLA from abandoning a nominal commitment to Marxism-Leninism in favor of a more rewarding, market-oriented economic and social system. In support of this thesis, they can point to growing Western investment in and trade with Angola and to a measure of "liberalization" in Angolan government policies.

Not only are Western oil firms (including Chevron, Texaco, and Conoco) investing in and pumping from petroleum reserves estimated at 1.7 billion barrels, but Western influence has grown in other economic sectors such as banking, food processing, and transportation as well. Inevitably, these relations tend to spill over into cultural areas. When an official of Sonangol takes crash courses in English and business administration at a U.S. university, his exposure to U.S. thought and practice helps to compensate for the absence of U.S.-Angolan cultural relations, an absence perpetuated by a diplomatic boycott imposed since 1975 by the United States.

Within the MPLA party and government there are individuals and groups reportedly inclined toward a generous interpretation and implementation of the official policy of "national reconciliation."[46] Measures have been taken to decentralize and devolve considerable economic authority to the provincial government level and to broaden the representative base and the latitude for legislative discretion in provincial and national assemblies. These constitute politically significant moves that take greater account of local and group interests.[47] MPLA leadership has all along maintained that, although guided by Marxist-Leninist principles, it would devise and construct a socialist system responsive to and reflective of the country-specific characteristics and needs of its own people.

The MPLA has consistently declared that Angola is no one's satellite despite the presence of 35,000 Cuban troops and a mutual security pact (1976) with, and continuing arms deliveries from, the Soviet Union. It has also steadfastly proclaimed the constancy of its commitment to Marxism-Leninism. The commitment appears serious and likely to continue.[48] Economic pragmatism and political adjustments notwithstanding, President dos Santos sounds a more fundamental note when he continues to declaim against "liberalism" and "individualism" and to extoll the importance of centralized leadership and party control.[49]

Reinforcing this commitment, Cuba has maintained roughly 400 teachers in Angola since 1978 and has provided over 1,000 places at a time for Angolan students in Cuba. Another 1,000 are studying in the Soviet Union at any given time. The only foreign publications available in Angola are Cuban and Soviet. The East Germans provide security training and personnel. The Cubans and Soviets provide military training in their military academies and in the field.

On the face of it, there would seem to be little reason to expect, as the U.S. Defense Intelligence Agency (DIA) apparently does, that U.S. assistance to UNITA (notably Stinger surface-to-air missiles) will so reduce the effectiveness of MPLA airpower and batter hopes for a decisive victory over the insurgents that it will create the political-psychological conditions for a coup and, finally, a negotiated settlement with Jonas Savimbi.[50] A more widely held view is that open U.S. assistance to UNITA effectively "close[d] the door to all hope for a negotiated settlement" that might include withdrawal of the Cubans.[51] The failure of U.S. diplomacy to broker a timely agreement incorporating such a withdrawal by getting South Africa to carry out an internationally sanctioned plan (UN Security Council Resolution 435) for Namibian independence opened the way to pressure from conservative political forces in the United States, pressure that culminated in a policy of active assistance to "anticommunist" UNITA.

The MPLA's conviction that it has a "political, moral and ideological" obligation to support SWAPO insurgents "whatever the consequences," further locks its political orientation in place. In the words of Assistant Foreign Minister Venancio de Moura, Angola cannot be free as long as neighboring Namibia is not. South African retaliation (periodic armed incursions beginning in 1978) "will not deter" Angola from continuing its support for SWAPO and for the African National Congress (ANC) of South Africa as well.[52]

Thousands of war amputees (from land mines), unschooled and underfed children, and foreign troops and technicians together present a human specter that contrasts utterly with the MPLA's vision of a new, independent society. Preferring to spend much of its oil revenue on arms and soldiers to negotiating with UNITA, the MPLA seems captive to a political immobilism that can only leave the internal war to continue its sanguinary course until one side or the other is exhausted.

MPLA leadership, like that of South Africa, appears bereft of the political imagination, initiative, and cohesion necessary for breakout from debilitating stalemate. The longer the devastation of civil war and external incursions persists, the more insecure, intolerant, and arbitrary MPLA rule may become. In the process, realization of the MPLA's radical, utopian vision will be at best delayed or at worst fatally frustrated.

Notes

1. For a documented account of the transfer of authority, see *A descolonização portuguesa. Aproximação a um estudo,* vol. 2 (Lisbon: Instituto Amaro da Costa, 1982), 248-251.

2. In a hastily convened meeting in Lourenço Marques (Maputo) on 9 November 1975, Mozambique's President Samora Machel, along with allied nationalist leaders from Guinea-Bissau, Cape Verde Islands, and São Tomé e Principe, called on all "democratic forces of the world" to recognize the state and government that the MPLA was readying. *Facts and Reports* (Amsterdam), 29 November 1975.

3. See the interview with MPLA President Agostinho Neto in *Afriscope* (Lagos), August 1975, 6-14.

4. For an analysis of Nigeria's critical policy reversal see Fola Soremekun, *Angola: The Road to Independence* (Ile-Ife, Nigeria: University of Ife Press, 1983), 198-204.

5. F. W. Heimer usefully distinguishes between the "central society" integrated into the dominant economic system of the colony and the outlying "tributary societies" of African peasants and herders that constituted the bulk of the population. See Heimer, *The Decolonization Conflict in Angola, 1974-1976. An Essay in Political Sociology* (Geneva: Institut universitaire des hautes études internationales, 1979).

6. Paulo Jorge, *Interviews in Depth: MPLA Angola* (Richmond, B.C.: Liberation Support Movement, 1973), 29.

7. See *História de Angola: Apontamentos,* vol. 2 (Algiers: Centro de estudos angolanos, 1965); and Agostinho Neto interviewed in *Révolution africaine* (Algiers), February 7/13, 1970.

8. Mário de Andrade, "Et les colonies de Salazar?" *Démocratie nouvelle* (Paris), 14, 9, September 1960.

9. V. Sidenko, *Angola v ogne* (Moscow: Polizdat, 1961).

10. See the Soviet handbook, *Africa Today* (translated in *Mizan Newsletter,* London, 4, 5, April 1962) for the contemporary assessment later challenged by Soviet researchers, such as Vladimir Kokorev interviewed at the Africa Institute, Moscow, 1984.

11. See the writings of acting MPLA President (1960-1962) Mário de Andrade, "Le mouvement de libération dans les colonies portugaises," *Partisans* (Paris), 29-30, May-June 1966; and (with Marc Ollivier) *La Guerre en Angola. Etude socio-économique.* (Paris: Maspero, 1971); and those of the first MPLA secretary general (1956-1963), Viriato da Cruz, "O futuro dos brancos em Angola," in *Angola através dos textos* (São Paulo: Editora Felman-Rego, 1962); and "What Kind of Independence for Angola?" *Revolution* (Paris), 1, 9, January 1964. See also the address by MPLA Administrative Secretary (1963-1985) Lucio Lara to MPLA cadre school, *Vitória ou morte* (Léopoldville), April 27, 1963.

12. Dr. Neto was arrested in Lisbon in 1952 because of his participation on the central committee of an anti-Salazarist youth group, the Movimento de unidade democrática juvenil (MUDJ).

13. The PCP was generally regarded as the prime mover in an exile coalition of Portuguese oppositionists, the Frente patriótica de libertação nacional (FPLN), with which the MPLA and nationalists from other Portuguese territories formed a formal alliance in 1966. See John A. Marcum, *The Angolan Revolution*, vol. 2. *Exile Politics and Guerrilla Warfare, 1962-1976* (Cambridge, Mass.: MIT Press, 1978), 226.

14. *Pravda*, 22 April 1965.

15. Jika, Reflexões sobre a luta de libertação nacional (Luanda: União dos escritores angolanos, 1979).

16. The *revolta activa* faction led by dissident intellectuals including the MPLA's former acting president, Mário de Andrade, and the *revolta do leste* faction, eastern-based followers of Daniel Chipenda, the MPLA's ranking leader from the populous Ovimbundu community.

17. For a first hand chronicle of the FNLA's military collapse, see Fernando Luis da Camara Casudo, *Angola: A Guerra dos traidos* (Rio de Janeiro: Block Editores, SA, 1979).

18. For a vivid description of the long march and survival of Jonas Savimbi and his UNITA followers, see Fred Bridgland, *Jonas Savimbi: A Key to Africa* (London: Mainstream Publishers, 1986), 194-218.

19. MPLA, *Documentos. 3ª Reunião do comité central do MPLA* (Luanda, 1976).

20. The *Confederação nacional dos trabalhadores angolanos* (CNTA). See Marcum, *The Angolan Revolution*, 245.

21. According to informed accounts, neither the Soviet or the Cuban embassy gave warning of Alves's intention to overthrow the government. For an official MPLA version of the incident, which acknowledges that Alves enjoyed influence among diplomats from "friendly countries," see MPLA, "Informação do bureâu politíco sobre a tentativa de golpe de 27 maio," *Boletim do militante* (Luanda, July 12, 1977).

22. Interview, Luanda, October 1984.

23. MPLA, *Documentos e teses ão l congresso* (Luanda: *Jornal de Angola*, 1977).

24. For a description and analysis of MPLA-PT structures and authority, see Keith Somerville, *Angola: Politics, Economics and Society* (Boulder: Lynne Rienner Publications, 1986), 83-115.

25. MPLA, *First Congress: Central Committee Report and Theses on Education* (London: Mozambique, Angola and Guinea Information Center, 1977).

26. Marcum, *The Angolan Revolution*, 62-66.

27. Somerville, *Angola*, 183.

28. Marcum, *The Angolan Revolution*, 279.

29. da Cruz, "What Kind of Independence?" 16-17.

30. MPLA, *First National Conference of the People's Movement for the Liberation of Angola* (Léopoldville, December 1962), 14.

31. Somerville, *Angola*, 105.

32. Former United Church of Christ missionary Lawrence Henderson in testimony at U.S. Senate Forum, 9 September 1986. Catholic clergy are active in UNITA-held as well as government-held territory.

33. According to Angolan Methodist Bishop Emilio Carvalho, *West Africa* (London), May 1986, 1054.

34. Daniel Chipenda, a sometime rival of Savimbi for leadership among the Ovimbundu and a 1974 defector from the MPLA who formed a regional (central-south) faction within Holden Roberto's FNLA (1974-1975), did respond to MPLA "national reconciliation" overtures. In late 1986, he announced support for the MPLA from exile in Lisbon. Chipenda said that some 70,000 professionally trained Angolans living in exile should return and replace Cuban and Eastern Bloc technicians in Angola. Arguing that a policy of reliance on its own human resources could move the country toward a political solution, his public stance was seen by some observers as reflecting "a growing Angolan determination to break dependence on Soviet aid and to find an alternative method for dealing with UNITA. Angola's debt to the Soviets is about $1.5 billion." Jill Jolliffe reporting in the *Christian Science Monitor*, 31 December 1986.

35. Central Committee Report presented by President dos Santos in MPLA, *Documents: Second Congress of the MPLA-Workers' Party, Luanda*, 2-9 December 1985. (London: Angop, 1986), 17.

36. Agostinho Neto set a relatively tolerant tone by seeming to endorse cultural, as distinct from political, pluralism. He rejected the imposition of a literary dogma such as Soviet "socialist realism," urged Angolan writers to be sensitive to their own cultural heritage, and encouraged open-mindness and debate in the quest for a new national culture. Agostinho Neto, *On Literature and Culture* (Luanda: União dos escritores angolanos, 1979).

37. This thesis is cogently set forth in Gerald Bender, "The Continuing Crisis in Angola," *Current History*, March 1983, 128.

38. See Bridgland, *Jonas Savimbi: A Key to Africa;* and John A. Marcum, "The Politics of Survival: UNITA in Angola," *CSIS Africa Notes*, 8, 18 February 1983.

39. MPLA-PT Secretary for Ideology, Roberto de Almeida, in *AfricAsia* (Paris) 25, January 1986, xvi; also MPLA, *Documents: Second Party Congress*.

40. Ibid.

41. *New York Times*, 28 December 1985.

42. *Los Angeles Times*, 18 September 1986.

43. See "L'échec économique 'met en cause' la survie de la révolution," *Le Monde*, 3 September 1985.

44. Bernard Expédit, "Jonas Savimbi: Mao's Military Disciple?" part 2, *African Defence* (Paris), June 1986, 79.

45. This weaponry includes Mig-23s, tanks, mobile radar, and other sophisticated equipment that often requires the presence of Soviet and Cuban technicians for use and/or maintenance.

46. Some war-weary MPLA leaders reportedly went so far as to propose creation of a supragovernmental council including former adversaries. It was

argued that giving such a dramatic thrust to "national reconciliation" would attract dissidents away from bush insurgency and exile, incorporate new talent within the thin ranks of public service, and hasten an end to internal conflict. *Jeune Afrique* (Paris), 13 February 1985, 55.

47. Candidates for the second People's Assembly elected in 1987, although all sanctioned by the MPLA-PT, were subjected to public discussion of their qualifications. A few were eliminated before the final, single list was presented for pro forma voting in a direct, as contrasted with previous indirect, election to the Assembly. *Afrique-Asie* (Paris), 389, 15-28 December 1986, 23.

48. See Somerville, *Angola,* 186-188.

49. See, for example, dos Santos's speech to the national party conference, Radio Luanda, 0930 GMT, 14 January 1985 in Foreign Broadcast Information Service, *Southern Africa,* 15 January 1985, U2.

50. See *Africa Confidencial* (Lisbon), 7, April 1986, 10.

51. See Alain Louyot, "Le casse-téte angolais," *L'Express* (Paris), 1805, February 1986, 12.

52. *Jeune Afrique,* 17 September 1986, 25.

chapter five

State Power Consolidation in Zimbabwe: Party and Ideological Development

Masipula Sithole

Zimbabwe achieved its independence on 18 April 1980, ending ninety years of British colonial sovereignty and white Rhodesian settler rule. Independence came as a result of long years of African nationalist agitation and armed struggle from which many political parties and factions of varied ideological persuasions emerged. In February 1980, the Zimbabwe African national Union (ZANU) under the leadership of Robert Mugabe won a general election and came to power espousing a socialist ideology. In 1985, ZANU won another brilliant victory with an increased majority committed to the same policies and advocating the establishment of a one-party state organized on the principles of Marxism-Leninism. Since 1980, ZANU has been involved in the struggle to consolidate state power, and has committed itself to the establishment of a socialist one-party state.

This chapter discusses state power consolidation in Zimbabwe. It is organized in five sections. The first section outlines ZANU's road to power. This is a brief historical account of the origins and development of ZANU in the context of factionalism in the nationalist movement. The second section focuses on the organizational transformation of ZANU. Here the emphasis is on party organization and methods of work during the liberation struggle and since independence. Section three focuses on ZANU in power; it discusses steps taken by the ZANU government in consolidating state power during the initial years of independence. Here the discussion focuses on the reorganization and reorientation of the organs of the state: the civil bureaucracy, the courts, and the military and police. Section four deals with party ideological transformation and orientation during and after the liberation struggle. The final section deals with problems and prospects in Zimbabwe. Here some of the major issues such as the conflict in Matebeleland, and other factors that militate against or facilitate state power consolidation, socialist transformation, and the drive for a one-party state in Zimbabwe are examined.

ZANU's Road to Power

Zimbabwe's ruling party, the Zimbabwe African National Union (ZANU), was formed on 8 August 1963 as a splinter party from the Zimbabwe African People's Union (ZAPU), the country's main opposition party, which was founded in 1962. While several factions sprung up in the 1970s, particularly toward the end of the decade, they suffered speedy decline immediately after independence in 1980, leaving ZANU and ZAPU dominating the political landscape, with the former enjoying decisive preponderance, though not total hegemony. Zimbabwe's two main political parties, ZANU and ZAPU, are also the oldest in the country; they have been around for nearly a quarter of a century. This section sketches the political history of ZANU from 1963 to its present position of preeminence.[1] Here, and in the next section, an attempt is made to show how ZANU achieved political hegemony that led up to independence.

Countrywide agitation for African majority rule in colonial Rhodesia began in earnest with the formation of the African National Congress (ANC) of Southern Rhodesia in 1957, which united the formerly Bulawayo-based ANC with the then Salisbury-based Youth League.[2] The enlarged ANC was founded under the leadership of the present opposition ZAPU leader Joshua Nkomo who also led the National Democratic Party (NDP), founded in 1960 after the ban on the ANC. When ZAPU was formed in 1962 following the ban on the NDP, Nkomo again led this successor organization. It is not until 1963 (eleven months after the ban on ZAPU), that a different organization (ZANU) was founded by high-ranking personalities within Nkomo's national executive, led by Ndabaningi Sithole, to challenge his leadership and give the nationalist movement a different tone and direction.

The formation of ZANU was the result of two main factors, namely: Nkomo's vacillating leadership and the incipient intransigence of white settler attitudes, manifest in the arrival into Rhodesian politics of the right-wing—if not reactionary—Rhodesia Front in 1962. Hitherto, Nkomo had exhibited what his former colleagues believed to be "cowardice" and "indecision" by failing to take bold steps when the situation in the country called for it. Moreover, Nkomo seemed to focus much attention on creating international pressure against white Rhodesia as the main strategy for achieving majority rule. And, curiously for a "cowardly" and "indecisive" leader, his colleagues also accused him of "dictatorial" tendencies.[3]

In the circumstances of the ascendancy of right-wing attitudes within the white community, the need for a more radical (if not militant) nationalist movement was all the more apparent. Hence the formation of ZANU in 1963 to "usher in the new politics of confrontation," under the slogans, "We are our own liberators," and "Leaders will come and go, but Zimbabwe remains," was a direct response to challenges of the time.[4] Thus, right from its inception, ZANU was confrontational, representing the more radical streak in the nationalist movement.

ZANU was banned in 1964—only a year after its formation—but immediately resurfaced in exile to compete with ZAPU. While in exile, as we shall see in the next section, the Zimbabwe nationalist movement in general, and ZANU in particular, transformed methods of struggle from mere confrontational rhetoric to confrontational practice in armed conflict. At this point, the movement also began to pay some attention to Marxist-Leninist discourse and practice.

Inside the country, the political vacuum created by the ban on the parties and the incarceration of the leadership in 1964 was not filled until the end of 1971, when Bishop Abel Muzorewa's African National Council (later UANC) was formed primarily to unite the African people in order to reject Anglo-Rhodesian settlement proposals. ZANU and ZAPU sympathizers in the country worked under Muzorewa's leadership to reject the proposals in 1972. However, when the main nationalist leaders were released toward the end of 1974, disunity resurfaced as ZANU and ZAPU, while working within the UANC, sought either individual identity or to capture the leadership of the broadened council from Muzorewa.[5] The latter fought to retain his leadership of the council, emerging with a faction or party of his own which lasted for fourteen years until the election of 1985—five years after independence.

In exile, the nationalist movement was further factionalized when dissident members of ZAPU and ZANU came together to form the short-lived Front for the Liberation of Zimbabwe (Frolizi). However, the formation of Frolizi disadvantaged ZAPU more than it did ZANU.[6] In fact, the Frolizi incident may have been decisive in the rise of ZANU to the position of dominance over ZAPU and, subsequently, over the liberation struggle and its eventual outcome.

At its inception in 1963, ZANU was strongest in the Manicaland and Masvingo provinces, with a somewhat modest following in the Midlands Province. ZAPU. on the other hand, retained its strongest support in Matebeleland, as well as in Mashonaland (i.e., Harare and its surrounding areas). It was not until the formation of Frolizi in exile in 1971, following another major split in ZAPU, that that party lost the support of a very significant portion of its top Shona leadership led by James Chikerema and George Nyandoro. These men were household names in Zimbabwe nationalist circles in the 1950s and early 1960s. They, in fact, were the founding leaders of the Youth League of the 1950s. ZAPU's appeal in Harare and surrounding areas was largely because these leaders remained loyal to Nkomo in the ZANU split of 1963. In 1971, Frolizi left ZAPU a largely Ndebele party. But when Frolizi could not take off on its own, it leaned toward Muzorewa's council.[7] However, as Mugabe triumphed in the ZANU leadership, reestablishing control and stability in that party following a period of internecine infighting (1974-1976), Harare significantly accelerated the drift toward ZANU, leading to the political eclipse of Muzorewa in 1980.

Most important, however, the Frolizi development led to organizational "paralysis" in ZAPU at a crucial juncture in the course of the liberation struggle in Mozambique and Zimbabwe. ZANU had approached Frelimo (now in control of the Tete Province in Mozambique) with a view to allowing ZANU "safe passage" in opening operational zones in northeastern Zimbabwe. Frelimo, then in a closer international alliance with ZAPU, gave that party first preference in the use of Tete. ZAPU could not take advantage of the offer because of the "paralysis." T. G. Silundika, then ZAPU secretary for publicity and information explains:

> Our friends approached us when we had real difficulties. Any decision had to be taken by a full executive committee, including Chikerema, and at the time he was not cooperating....The war council was no longer working. So paralysis was starting within ZAPU at the time when our friends were making these proposals and therefore the question of our responding to them immediately was just not practical.[8]

It was only then that Frelimo agreed to the ZANU request, though begrudgingly.[9] The Frelimo preference had been ZAPU.

Further, unlike the 1963 ZANU split, the Frolizi split brought to the surface latent Ndebele-Shona and intra-Shona subethnic tensions for the first time.[10] Having lost its Shona component in the formation of Frolizi, ZAPU was now a largely Ndebele party, and for this reason could not operate from the northeast or the whole of the eastern border with Mozambique, which is Shona-speaking. This was the actual significance of the "paralysis"—otherwise those who remained in control of ZAPU could have used Tete Province to overcome the "paralysis" by appearing to be the more performance-oriented faction. This is what, in fact, won the day for ZANU. However, it would be stretching the imagination too far to suggest that ZANU would have succeeded in Mashonaland even had it been led by Ndebele leaders. It is therefore significant that had Frolizi not been formed, ZAPU would have retained Shona loyalty and the Tete offer would have been accepted, leaving ZANU in the lurch. Frolizi was therefore an *accident* that altered the whole course of the Zimbabwe struggle and its outcome. Moreover, once the Zezuru in the exiled ZANU leadership defected to Frolizi, ZANU developed factional competition and tensions that culminated in the assassination of its chairman and leader in exile, Herbert Chitepo, in March 1975.[11]

Toward the end of 1974 and early in 1985, ZANU experienced serious internal problems, including the Nhari rebellion that culminated in the assassination of Chitepo.[12] These events almost destroyed the party. In fact, the ZANU political machinery was completely decimated. The party was saved by its military wing and the ascent of Robert Mugabe to the ZANU leadership. By the end of 1974, as we shall see in the next section, the Zimbabwe African National Liberation Army (ZANLA), the ZANU military wing, had entrenched itself within the country so that it could act independently of either the front-line states or any "deviating" leader in the nationalist ranks.

Upon his release from detention, Mugabe escaped with the help of the ZANLA machine from Rhodesia into Mozambique. As secretary general of the party, Mugabe was the third most senior ZANU leader. Sithole, the president, also released in 1975 and exiled to Tanzania, became a victim of front-line state politics, which he either paid too much attention to or handled without tact.[13] Leopold Takawira, the vice-president, died in detention in 1970. This left Mugabe the most senior living nationalist leader among the guerrilla forces in Mozambique. It is from this base that he rose to the ZANU leadership by first gaining the confidence and control of ZANLA, then regrouping the party's disarrayed political wing, and finally striking an alliance (Patriotic Front) with Joshua Nkomo, by then also in exile. This alliance lasted until immediately after the Lancaster House Constitutional Conference at the end of 1979, when ZANU pulled out so that it could run the impending election campaign separate from ZAPU. This would decide the question of leadership that had remained a problem for the Patriotic Front: that is, was the future leader going to be Nkomo or Mugabe? In the election of February 1980, Mugabe led his party to a brilliant victory, defeating ZAPU and seven other parties. ZANU's brilliant victory in this election, and in the subsequent election of 1985, as well as its hold on the electorate, can be attributed in part to the organizational and ideological transformation that the party underwent during and after the liberation struggle.

The Organizational Transformation of ZANU

In this section we discuss the organizational transformation of ZANU from 1964 to 1984. At its First National Congress in 1964, ZANU decided to prepare for armed struggle. The party was banned and its leaders incarcerated later in the year. In 1965, senior members of the central committee smuggled a document from detention empowering the late Herbert Chitepo, as senior member of the central committee in exile, to rally party members and supporters abroad in order to implement the congress's resolution to wage war. Chitepo organized a group of other exiled central committee members and began the training and infiltration of armed guerrillas. At a consultative meeting in 1969, the group called itself "Dare re Chimurenga" (War Council), otherwise known simply as "Dare." This became the institutionalized political wing of ZANU in exile. A decision was taken in 1969 to institutionalize biannual consultative conferences.

At the next consultative biannual conference in 1971, a major decision was taken to reject feelers for unity with the Chikerema faction following the infighting in ZAPU. Those in ZANU who had advocated such unity lost their positions in Dare and subsequently defected to Frolizi, denounced by the party as a grouping of "cousins and relatives."[14] Another important decision related to this matter was made at the 1973 biannual conference requiring persons, such as those who had defected to join Frolizi but now wished to rejoin ZANU, to serve long probationary periods before full membership could be conferred. By the end of 1973, many wanted to join or rejoin ZANU because it had sustained a spectacular guerrilla offensive since the end of 1972. However, the long and selective probationary period became an effective instrument to keep an important Zezuru element (who now wished to rejoin the party) out of Dare. This resulted in a sharp bipolar competition between the Manyika and Karanga groups within the Dare, leading to serious internecine infighting in ZANU at the end of 1974, which left protracted ethnic tensions in the party. Prior to the Frolizi split, the ethnic composition of the Dare included the three main Shona subgroups: Manyika, Karanga, and Zezuru. With the Zezuru now pulling out, the factionalism became bipolarized and the infighting more intense—such that, by the end of March 1975, the Dare had completely collapsed as a result of the infighting. There was no consultative meeting in 1975.[15] When Mugabe finally regrouped the party at the end of 1976 and early 1977, Dare was reconstituted and enlarged. Individuals and groups who were formerly alienated from the party, as well as new personalities, regrouped in ZANU or at its doorsteps. In this way, ZANU regained its former equilibrium, which it retains to this day, although somewhat tenuously as evidenced by recent (1986) vitriolic exchanges in the Zimbabwe parliament and the party central committee, suggesting that cleavages now exist between Karanga and Zezuru groups in the new grand coalition of ethnic forces in ZANU.[16]

In 1969, the ZANU armed wing was named ZANLA. While it was the responsibility of the Dare to expand and map out the political objectives, orientation, and strategy of the liberation struggle, the onus for implementation lay on ZANLA. Thus ZANLA guerrillas had a political orientation right form the outset. Its detachments had members of the political commissariat responsible for the political program of the party and orientation of the masses during mobilization. The commissariat was responsible for the content of messages transmitted at *pungwes* (marathon night meetings) held right through the period of the liberation war. Further, ZANLA instituted an elaborate network of "feet-eyes-and-ears of the revolution," the *mujibas,* persons who served as intelligence gatherers and transmission belts between the guerrillas and the people engaged in enemy activities.

Thus, when ZANU experienced instability at the political top (1974-1976), its politicized war machinery at the bottom remained intact on the war front and saved the party from both disarray in political leadership and from either the misjudgement or mischievous machinations of some front-line states and international actors during the détente exercise.[17] At the consultative conference of 1977 at Chimoio, a decision was taken to include leaders of the ZANLA high command in the central committee in order to facilitate better coordination and communication between the political and military wings of the party.[18] When the general election of 1980 came as a result of the Lancaster house conference, the party earned its victory of the ZANLA machine, as described above. The party, outlawed in Rhodesia for some fifteen years, had no organizational political infrastructure within the country, and so relied heavily on its guerrilla military and paramilitary structures established during the war. In the general election of 1985, however, ZANU owed its victory to superior political organization as a party and to its control of the state as the incumbent party.

The consultative conferences that ZANU institutionalized during the liberation war kept the party revitalized both in personnel and ideas. Moreover, it enabled the party to maintain its self-critical outlook and a democratic tradition that attracted people from every strata of African society. On the other hand, it is in the nature of democracy and protestantism to encourage inter- and intra-group competition which, if improperly managed, can be destructive to organizations and the body politic. ZANU experienced this. At any rate, ZANU's emphasis on politicization and mobilization in the war front gave it a mass appeal whose momentum was to assure its electoral victory and enable it to consolidate power at independence. After the war, this investment began to be depleted and there was talk of a vanguard Leninist party to guide society as it maintained the gains of the past.

Theoretically, ZANU is organized on the Leninist principle of "democratic centralism," whereby free discussion and self-criticism take place within party structures, and lower organs of the party report and answer to organs immediately above them as policy directives flow from top to bottom. In practice, however, this has not always been the case. This is not surprising since "democratic centralism," like any principle, is an "ideal type"; organizations in real life can only approximate it.

The supreme organ of ZANU is the national congress, which (since the party's Second National Congress in 1984) is scheduled to be held every five years—or a year before national general elections, which are held every five years.[19] The national congress consists of members of the party central committee, as well as representatives of the provincial organs of the party who themselves are selected at provincial congresses before the national congress. Representatives to provincial congresses are selected at interbranch meetings at the district level (provincial congresses are themselves interdistrict). The lowest party organ is the cell. Party branches are selected at meetings of party cells convened for that purpose. It is important to note that when ZANU returned from exile in 1980 it had a makeshift central committee without these other elaborate structures. By 1984, however, these structures were all in place as the party moved aggressively to consolidate its power in the country for postwar politics. The congress discusses and makes broad and far-reaching policy decisions for the party. The central committee of ninety members (1984) implements these decisions between congresses. From 1984, the work of the central committee and other policy issues are overseen by a fifteen-member politburo selected from members of the central committee by the party first secretary, who is assisted by the second secretary (Mugabe and Simon Muzenda, respectively, 1984). In ZANU's twenty-one-year history, this is the first time it has had a politburo. The politburo meets more often than the central committee and schedules meetings and decides on agenda for the central committee. For this reason, the politburo is the most powerful party organ and membership in it is coveted and prestigious. The method of selection to the politburo makes the position of first secretary most powerful. This marks the final triumph of the consolidation of Mugabe's position within ZANU, despite possible future dangers of such concentration of power.[20]

Since its formation in 1963, ZANU has undergone discernible organizational transformation and innovations necessitated by the demands of exile conditions, the circumstances of prosecuting the liberation struggle, and the conditions of peace. In the course of its initial twenty-three-year history, ZANU has shown marked organizational flexibility, dexterity, and adaptability—if not also instability. We will now discuss the steps ZANU took to consolidate power once in government.

ZANU in Power

Apart from party hegemony, ZANU's consolidation of power in Zimbabwe has, of necessity, been approached through other organs of the state: the civil bureaucracy, the military and police, and the judicial system.

The public (civil) service is a major element of state power in any society because it is the instrument with which policy, as made by politicians and political parties, is translated into actual programs affecting the masses on the ground level.[21] Moreover, permanent secretaries, as top civil servants, play a key role in both policy formulation and in overseeing the execution of policy. As such, any strategy for consolidating power in the postcolonial era must necessarily involve changes in orientation, if not structure, of the public service to achieve orientational compatibility with the new political bosses. In Zimbabwe, the initial years after independence witnessed marked change in the area of the public service.

To begin with, the public service in Zimbabwe is a constitutional matter.[22] The Zimbabwe public service consists of all personnel who serve under the different ministries and departments of government. These numbered 83,904 employees as of July 1985, and 92,129 employees are envisaged for the 1985-1986 authorized establishment.[23]

The general organization of the Zimbabwe public service is regulated and controlled by the Public Service Commission. This central mechanism is directed by the constitution. The commissioners themselves are not public servants as such; they remain outside it in order to protect their independent and impartial role. Further, they are not to hold office in political parties, although they may belong to parties and espouse political views like everyone else in society as long as this does not impair their impartiality.

At the preindependence constitutional talks in London in 1979, the nationalists successfully negotiated for the inclusion of "Chapter VII section 75, subsection 2" into the constitution. It reads:

> The President may give general directions of policy to the Public Service
> Commission with the object of achieving a suitable representation of the

various elements of the population in the Public Service and the Prison Service.[24]

Subsequently this clause facilitated transformation of the Zimbabwe public service. The president, acting on the advice of the prime minister, was quick to effect this clause. On 2 May 1980 (hardly a month after the 18 April independence celebration), he issued general directives of policy to the Public Service Commission as follows:

1. Recruit staff to all grades of the public service in such a manner as will bring about the balanced representation of the various elements that make up the population of Zimbabwe.
2. Give more rapid advancement to suitably qualified Africans in appointments and promotions to senior posts in the public service.
3. In carrying out these directions, have due regard to the maintenance of a high state of efficiency within the public service and the need to satisfy the career aspirations of existing public servants.
4. Make annual reports on progress.[25]

The objective of these directives was to create, as early as possible, a "balanced service fully representative of all elements of the population, and with the skills appropriate to the country's needs."[26] This policy is largely responsible for the change and direction of the public service since independence. At independence in 1980, established officers in the public service totaled 10,570. Only about 32 percent of these were both black and of junior rank. There was no black secretary, deputy secretary, or under secretary in any ministry; the highest rank held by an African being that of senior administrative officer. By July 1981, the number of black officers had increased to 63 percent, and by 1983 to 86 percent. Significantly, while all thirty permanent secretaries at independence in 1980 were white, by July 1981 there were thirteen black permanent secretaries. Today virtually all ministries have black permanent secretaries.[27]

In addition to the consolidation of power through the civil bureaucracy, Prime Minister Mugabe created a system of provincial governors appointed by the president upon recommendation by the prime minister. These are responsible for all facets of development at the provincial level, and are supervised by the minister of state in the prime minister's office who is responsible for political affairs and provincial coordination. Further, at the local level, all city and district councils and mayorships have been democratized and are now controlled by Africans. ZANU controls most of these councils except those in Matebeleland, which are largely ZAPU. The critically important area in ZANU's path toward consolidating power has been in the armed forces. With the help of the British Training Unit, the program to retrain and integrate the formerly separate and warring armies, ZANLA, ZIPRA, and the Rhodesian army, into one army has been quite successful. One Zimbabwe National Army (ZNA) has been created and has largely remained intact.[28] Further, a team of North Korean military experts was also involved in the training of some aspects of the army, mainly the Fifth Brigade and the paramilitary force.[29] This would suggest that the army has two orientations or biases: the one British, and the other North Korean, making another reintegration of the national army imperative.

Related to the military is the police force. The former Rhodesian police force was renamed the Zimbabwe Republic Police (ZRP). Hundreds of new recruits from former ZANLA and ZIPRA forces were incorporated into the ZRP, which maintained a largely nonpartisan, professional outlook and commitment to the maintenance of law and order, as well as loyalty to the state. However, during the violence that broke out a few days after the 1985 polling, the police in some areas demonstrated negligence of duty when many stood by watching members of the opposition parties being beaten up and unlawfully evicted from their residences. Many observers thought that either the police had become inept (which was unlikely) or they had taken sides according to party affiliation (which was more likely). Moreover, Enos Nkala, the new minister of home affairs after a cabinet reshuffle following the elections, warned and threatened to dismiss elements in the police force disloyal to the government.[30] This was in apparent reference to some members of the former Rhodesian police force, as well as those with sympathies towards ZAPU and dissidents in Matebeleland. Important in terms of consolidating power in the military and police force is the fact that the ZANU leadership acted swiftly and decisively in changing personnel at the top rank. Former Rhodesian Commander of Combined Operations Peter Walls was sacked and exiled and replaced by the former ZANLA Commander Rex Nhongo, while Josiah Tungamirayi, another former ZANLA commander, took over command of the Zimbabwe air force. Moreover, at the 1984 ZANU Second national Congress, both Nhongo and Tungamirayi were appointed to the politburo, the highest policy body of the party. Changes in high-ranking personnel in the police force were mainly internal promotions involving Africans who had served in the Rhodesian police force for a long time. Unlike in the army and air force, the Zimbabwe chief commissioner of police is not from the former freedom fighters of ZANLA or ZIPRA, but is an African of long-standing in the Rhodesian police force.

The courts are another important component of state power. Although there are a number of white judges and magistrates in the Zimbabwe judicial system, many have been replaced by blacks. For instance, Chief Justice Enoc Dumbutchena, and Attorney-General Godfrey Chidyausiku occupy the highest offices in the country's judicial system. At the local level (closer to the people), Africanization of the legal system has been implemented even more comprehensively with the creation of primary courts run by trained presiding officers who do not have executive functions.

The Zimbabwe judiciary has a good reputation for its independence, professionalism, and impartiality. In his article, "Reds, and Rights: Zimbabwe's Experiment," Richard Sklar shows how the judiciary in Zimbabwe has, on a number of occasions passed decisions that have not only contradicted the expectations of the state, but have been controversial and embarrassing.[31] Moreover, the judiciary has not been under any undue political pressure from either the party or individual politicians.[32] The selection of judges, magistrates, and presiding officers has been mainly on professional rather than political grounds. Although both Dumbutchena and Chidyausiku were closely identified with the liberation movement, they remained in the legal profession throughout the liberation period.

We have, up to this point, discussed the history and organization of ZANU, as well as the steps it took to consolidate its hold on state institutions once it assumed office. What is the ideological foundation of ZANU's rule?

ZANU's Ideological Development

A simple definition of ideology is that it is a set of ideas, beliefs, and values that guide the actions of organizations. What then is the set of ideas that guide ZANU? What is its ideology? A mild partisan answer is that ZANU's ideology is "socialism," while a militant partisan response is that ZANU's ideology is "scientific socialism" based on the principles of "Marxism-Leninism." While such responses and interpretations may be partisan-correct, they are however analytical distortions that are misleading. To the extent that ideologies guide actions, ZANU and the Zimbabwean society are guided by an eclectic ideology that embraces nationalism, pan-Africanism, internationalism, socialism (both in its "utopian/Fabian" and "scientific Marxist-Leninist" sense) and, as we shall argue, capitalism.

At its inception in 1963, ZANU declared itself as embracing nationalism, pan-Africanism, and socialism (in its Fabian sense). "Scientific" socialism or Marxism-Leninism was absent from the policy statement made in both the initial party constitution and the earlier *mwenje* party publications.[33] The articulation of Marxism-Leninism and Maoist thought progressively became conspicuous in the Zimbabwe nationalist movement generally, and in the party in particular in the 1970s. In fact, at its formation in 1971, Frolizi claimed that both ZANU and ZAPU were ideologically "bankrupt" and lacked a Marxist-Leninist "scientific" outlook, claiming that it (Frolizi) had emerged to fill this ideological vacuum.[34] In ZANU, notwithstanding sporadic pronouncements of "scientific" socialism (Marxism-Leninism) by individuals in the party and in some of its literature, the official adoption of Marxism-Leninism as an element of party ideology took place in 1977. As Mugabe explained at the party's Second National Congress of 1984:

> After the abortive Geneva Conference, and having regard to some weaknesses and contradictions in the structure of the Party, we convened a Conference of the party Central Committee at Chimoio, Mozambique, in March 1977. At the Chimoio Conference, significant organizational, structural and political modifications were made to the Party, but especially: (a) the Central Committee was enlarged—(b) *the adoption of scientific socialism based on Marxism-Leninism and to include elements of Maoist thought* (my emphasis).[35]

The adoption of Marxism-Leninism, however, did not mean that other earlier "isms" were excluded or became secondary. Marxism-Leninism was simply additional. Moreover, Marxism and the other "isms" are not necessarily mutually exclusive—except when nationalism and pan-Africanism became "narrow" and inimical to internationalism in its positive global sense. At any rate, three years after adopting "scientific socialism" as part of its guiding ideological tools, ZANU was swept to power by a largely peasant electorate and a proletariat largely illiterate as to what Marx may have meant by "dialectical materialism." Moreover, many in the central committee itself were only getting some initial impressions. *Das Kapital* demands a fair amount of literacy in political economy, and some amount of intellectual discipline is required for one to begin to appreciate Karl Marx's epochal contribution.[36] Moreover, usage of the concepts "scientific socialism" and "Marxism-Leninism" in the Zimbabwe political discourse has yet to be clearly articulated. To date, there is no body of literature attempting to do this. At any rate, the party's Second National Congress in 1984 endorsed "scientific socialism" based on "Marxist-Leninist" principles. As such, this has now been an element of official party doctrine for nine years since 1977.

But to what extent is Marxism-Leninism dominant in the eclectic ideological spectrum of "isms" suggested above? If by "dominant" one means, in this case, values actually (in action) shared by a preponderant number of people either in an organization or in the larger society, then *nationalism* and not any of the other "guides to action" has consistently been dominant in Zimbabwe politics during and after liberation. It is the contention here that, throughout the liberation war, ZANLA was inspired much more by the sentiment of nationalism and opposition to white settler political domination than by a Marxist analysis of the capitalist colonial economy. Moreover, ZANU was swept to power twice (1980 and 1985) not because of its Marxist-Leninist pronouncements, but in spite of them. ZANU, as an organization, and Prime Minister Mugabe, as its leader, were both times perceived as vigilant and appropriate for the consolidation of the gains of independence and for checking possible reactionary tendencies among whites and among other blacks, regardless of their class background.[37] Further, the choice of personnel in the state institutions, discussed earlier, had more of a nationalist basis than class. These appointments amounted to Africanization, more than proletarianization—let alone peasantization—of state institutions of power.

At the time of the second general election in 1985, the propensity for private accumulation by the rank and file in the ZANU leadership was commonplace. Yet the masses swept the party back to power by even larger majorities. Was it because they were more persuaded by "scientific" socialist pronouncements than by the actual evidence of private accumulation within officialdom? The contention is that the propensity for accumulation was seen in individuals of all parties. However, ZANU distinguished itself as more vigilant, patriotic, and less puppet-like on the immediate question of "genuine" independence and majority rule. Class consciousness is still not very salient in the Zimbabwe political milieu. Moreover, when Matebeleland voted overwhelmingly for ZAPU and the Shona regions voted for ZANU in both the 1980 and 1985 elections, it did not mean that the bourgeoisie was in one region while peasants and the proletariat were in another, but that ethnicity (subnationalism) in Zimbabwe society was currently more salient than class.[38] Serious quarrels in the Zimbabwe nationalist movement throughout the liberation struggle, as we have seen, hinged either on effective methods to fight the white minority's settlerist domination or on ethnic and personal ambitions, but not on whether one belonged to a bourgeois or proletarian faction. Similarly, after independence, the conflict in Matebeleland, as well as quarrels in the Zimbabwe parliament and in ZANU earlier in 1986 had no class basis. It would be stretching the Marxist tool of analysis a bit too thin to see a quarrel between Byron Hove (lawyer) and Herbert Ushewokunze (physician) as a surface manifestation of underlying class struggle. There need not be a class reason for two people shouting at each other across the floor of parliament. Of note is the fact that the censure of both men (who are themselves practicing businessmen and politicians) was on the basis of the emotive, personal, and ethnic tone of their debate, and not its ideological "class" content.

Finally, on this question of ideological eclecticism and the dominant thrust of nationalism, a comment by Herbert Ushewokunze (then secretary for the commissariat and culture, and also number four in the politburo), is instructive in its wide-ranging perceptions of the ideological milieu in Zimbabwe:

> In Zimbabwe, the fundamental thrust of politics is along [sic] nationalism. Of course, the spectrum goes from a radical form seeking to transform society along socialist lines to the conservative seeking to establish South African hegemony over Zimbabwe. Mainstream politics in Zimbabwe does not concretely utilize class as a basis to re-organize society, but deals much more with the struggle between national and international capital, or the struggle between the mainly white large Zimbabwe capital and the emergent African capital. In ideological terms, all the political parties in Zimbabwe can comfortably exist in one organization that calls for a self-reliant nation, struggling for social justice. This is not to deny the existence of tendencies inside some of the political parties for a radical restructuring of society, using a Marxian model. But these have existed within the nationalist movement quite comfortably.[39]

The "nationalist thrust" has, thus far, been the dominant guide to political action in Zimbabwe society, and ZANU has been perceived by the mass public to encapsulate the nationalist sentiment more genuinely than any other political group.

Problems and Prospects in Zimbabwe

In conclusion, we consider problems and prospects in Zimbabwe insofar as power consolidation may still be incomplete given the continuing conflict in Matebeleland and the ZANU leadership's advocacy of the one-party state. Further, what is the likely ideological completion of such a one-party state?

The performance of ZANU in consolidating power since 1980 has been impressive by any informed and objective criteria. Notwithstanding the conflict in Matebeleland, Zimbabwe has largely been a stable country over this period. Moreover, those who cite the conflict in Matebeleland have often overlooked the fact that the conflict did not start when ZANU came to power; it is a conflict with a much longer history running back not only to the ZAPU-ZANU split of 1963, but even predates colonialism in the nineteenth century.[40] It is a historical conflict, as well as cultural, psychosocial, and political. It is a problem that had to be worked out sooner or later. An offshoot of the Zulu of South Africa, the Ndebele, invaded Shona territory and dominated them from the 1830s until British colonial conquest in 1890, when both groups fell under colonial rule. There were unsettled disputes between the Ndebele and Shona on the eve of colonialism. The uneasy feelings between the two groups largely remained latent under colonial rule but began to resurface as the nationalist movement gained momentum.

The conflict in Matebeleland, brutal and costly as it is, in many ways is the process of working out the earlier problem. Eventually, ZAPU had *to test ZANU's will to rule,* and the latter had to pass this challenge before a realistic accommodation could be reached. The tragedy is the human and material cost involved, but maybe *the will to rule* cannot be demonstrated any other way when the authority of a constitutional government is faced with physical resistance.

An important question arises, however, whether the consolidation of state power necessarily means consolidation of "Afro-Marxism" in Zimbabwe. The answer must be no, certainly not, from the evidence in this chapter. If anything, the evidence demonstrates the fact that Africans have taken and consolidated state power in Zimbabwe, that those Africans mainly belong to ZANU, and that this party has the support of the overwhelming majority of the people of Zimbabwe. Marxist socialist commitment has not been a dominant guide to action.

The ideological content of power consolidation in Zimbabwe would require that we go beyond the stated preferences of ZANU, or any party for that matter, and examine the class identity and/or orientation of the "critical," or "pivotal," or "opinion-forming" personnel in the party, the public service, the army or police, the courts, and indeed in society as a whole. Certainly, a "proficiency test" in Marxism-Leninism has not quite been the criterion for advancement or promotion in any of the state organs of power discussed or in those not discussed. Such criteria have neither been obligatory nor necessary at this necessarily national democratic stage of the Zimbabwe revolution, a stage that need not be hurried through as if there were a definite prize ahead.

Some final observations and comments on the ZANU drive for a Marxist-Leninist, one-party state are necessary at this point. Having won the 1980 elections constitutionally, ZANU proceeded both cautiously and constitutionally on the two questions of a socialist economy and on the one-party state. The ZANU government proceeded to buy (and not seize) land on a "willing buyer, willing seller" basis. Where government sought involvement in certain industries, such involvement followed amicable discussions and mutual agreement with the industries concerned. Moreover, government has tended to take active interest in previous parastatal organizations as well as in establishing new ones. But the Zimbabwe economy still remains basically a market economy. The private sector controls roughly 65 percent of the economy although it is regulated by government labor laws. The focus has been on economic performance rather than on ownership. Moreover, this performance is rated quite highly by Zimbabwe peasants and workers, the two classes that should celebrate socialism.[41]

ZANU has particularly been constitutional in its approach to the one-party state issue. In a resolution adopted at the party's Second Congress in 1984, a year before the general elections, ZANU was unequivocal in its commitment to constitutional procedure in pursuing the goal of the one-party state:

> That is the settled and determined will of the people and their Party to bring about a one-party state in the fullness of time and in *accordance with the law and the constitution* [my emphasis][42]

To this end, the approach to the one-party state has focused on a strategy of party building with a view to establishing ZANU hegemony throughout the whole country. This would then be followed by a legislative establishment of the one-party state as a natural consequence of party hegemony, much in the manner TANU (now Chama Cha Mapinduzi, CCM) established itself and the one-party state in Tanzania.

The ZANU leadership, consistent with its constitutional commitment as mentioned above, has largely favored organizational hegemony. The emphasis has been to make ZANU so entrenched and popular that other parties become irrelevant and simply wither away. For instance in 1983, a group of some 500 women assembled outside Prime Minister Mugabe's office agitating for the ban on minority opposition parties and declaring Zimbabwe a one-party state. They demanded to see the prime minister on the issue. The message of his brief talk to them was that he agreed with them that Zimbabwe should become a one-party state. To that end they were instructed to go back to their various communities and organize the party so that opposition parties would be rendered irrelevant.

This approach is often repeated by many in the ZANU leadership. A central committee member and chairman of the party in the Manicaland Province, Edgar Tekere, did not believe in a "piece of paper" declaring a one-party state. He believed in what he called "organizational efficiency," in outperforming other parties.[43] Another central committee member and chairman of the Masvingo Province, who is also minister of justice, legal and parliamentary affairs, Eddison Zvobgo, had a similar approach. Asked what sort of majority would be considered a sufficient mandate for declaring the one-party state, he replied:

> This is not a mathematical sort of thing. Naturally, like every other proposal, any majority is good enough. And there is no question that we are going to come back from the hustings with an increased majority. But the one-party state is not an issue that this government wants to

foist on anyone. The Prime Minister has been very clear on this. We will not outlaw any other parties; they will just vanish by loss of support from the people. Ultimately what you will have is a *de facto* one-party state—if not at this general election, then at the next one.[44]

Actually ZANU did increase its 1980 victory from 57 to 64 percent of the vote in the 1985 elections. Opposition parties have been practically wiped out in most parts of the country except in Matebeleland, where ZAPU remains entrenched and resilient; demanding, perhaps a totally different approach than either Tekere's "organizational efficiency" or Zvobgo's assertion that ZAPU "will just vanish by loss of support from the people" in Matebeleland.

There were numerous attempts to unite ZANU and ZAPU during the liberation struggle but all failed, including the Patriotic Front that lasted for three years, 1976-1979. After independence, there was another unsuccessful unity attempt in 1983. The latest unity initiatives began in August 1985 and are still tenuously in progress. The resilience of ZAPU in Matebeleland is likely to determine whether the populist approach policy on the one-party state question continues to be pursued and what form that one party takes. However, the latest unity talks were apparently the result of government's "get tough" policy, on the one hand, and the realization of the extent of the ZAPU impact in Matebeleland on the other.[45]

A "get tough" policy often causes deep wounds among contending groups in society. This is usually the case if such a policy is implemented over a long period. Protracted hostilities alienate society, or part of it, from its authority. It is therefore incumbent on the ZANU leadership to solve the problem with some finality within a reasonable time. If, on the other hand, the ZAPU leadership begins to be perceived as refusing what are considered "reasonable offers" by the ZANU leadership, it risks alienating itself from its constituency in the long run. The question, however, is whether an accommodation can be reached outside the one-party state formula. If, for instance, dissident activities stop in Matebeleland and ZAPU commits itself to constitutional approaches to power, it should be possible to bring Nkomo back into government without requiring the dissolution of his party. National unity is often brought about by a willingness to work together with or without the one-party framework.

But, if ZAPU were agreeable to a one-party state, would it also agree that such a party be Marxist-Leninist? Not necessarily. Although ZAPU has had a long history of association with the Soviet Union, its leader has had an even longer and more intimate history with Tiny Rowland, executive director of Lonrho.[46] It is unlikely that the ZAPU leadership would be particularly enthusiastic about the inclusion of Marxist-Leninist phraseology, even though opposing this might cause some embarrassment. At any rate, the commitment to Marxism-Leninism seems only an illustration in a society of men and women (in both parties) who are busy accumulating capital. The import of this contradiction cannot be minimized.

Nationalism, more than Marxism, is likely to guide Zimbabwe patriots of both ZANU and ZAPU for quite some time to come in the essentially national democratic phase of the African revolution. To date, both subjective and objective conditions for "scientific socialism" do not sufficiently exist in Zimbabwe or in most African countries. But such conditions have begun to exist for democratizing African polities. To push the Marxist-Leninist matter too hard and prematurely, as some critical leftist analysts are prone to instigate, would fail and lead to official frustration with its attendant dangers of authoritarianism.[47] The Zimbabwe leadership seems to recognize these subjective and objective limitations. It is for this reason that it has charted a cautious and pragmatic course on both questions of the economy and the one-party state.

Notes

1. For a detailed account of the political history of ZANU, see David Martin and Phyllis Johnson, *The Struggle for Zimbabwe* (Harare: Zimbabwe Publishing House, 1981).

2. The ANC is the subject of a Ph.D dissertation by Tapera O. Chirau, *The African National Congress of Zimbabwe* (Ann Arbor: University Microfilms International, 1986.

3. For an analysis of the ZANU-ZAPU split, see Nathan Shamuyarira, "The ZAPU-ZANU Split" in his *Crisis in Rhodesia* (London: Andre Deutsch, 1966). See also Masipula Sithole's, *Zimbabwe Struggles Within the Struggle* (Salisbury: Rujeko Publishers, 1979), the chapter on "Contradictions in ZAPU," 27-46, especially the document by Ndabaningi Sithole quoted on pp. 31-34.

4. These slogans are attributed to Ndabaningi Sithole, founder president of ZANU.

5. For a discussion of the politics of Muzorewa's United African National Council, see M. Sithole, *Zimbabwe Struggles*, the chapter titled "Contradictions within the ANC," 98-115.

6. See "Contradictions in Frolizi," in ibid., 88-97. The formation of Frolizi disadvantaged ZAPU because, while only marginal ZANU leaders defected to the new party, defections from ZAPU included its acting president and the secretary-general—very senior posts in any party.

7. In fact, Chikerema became Muzorewa's vice-president when he returned from exile in 1977. Nyandoro became secretary-general. Subsequently they split from Muzorewa, and by 1980 they were largely sympathetic to ZANU.

8. David Martin and Phyllis Johnson, *The Struggle for Zimbabwe*, 18; also a fuller discussion of the foundations of ZANU's relations with Frelimo, 14-20.

9. Ibid. 17-18.

10. I discuss the role of ethnicity in the Zimbabwe liberation movement in "Ethnicity and Factionalism in Zimbabwe Nationalist Politics 1957-1979" in *Ethnic and Racial Studies*, 3, 1 (January 1980).

11. For discussion of polarization within ZANU and the events leading to the assassination of Chitepo, see "Who Killed Chitepo?" in M. Sithole, *Zimbabwe Struggles*, 67-87; also David Martin and Phyllis Johnson, *The Chitepo Assassination* (Harare: Zimbabwe Publishing House, 1985) for a different interpretation.

12. See "What of the Frontline States?" in M. Sithole, *Zimbabwe Struggles*, 129-146.

13. Sithole first concentrated his energies on observing the behavior of the front-line states, acquiescing to their advice and machinations. He perceived a unity of purpose and approach by the front-line states and often used a Shona proverb to describe their relationship: *Zvikomo zuinopana mhute* ("Hills share fog"). When he finally fell out of grace with them, he spent enormous energy attacking their "interference." However, he did this from a position of weakness—front-line capital cities—rather than from the guerrilla bases from which Mugabe made vitriolic attacks on the activities of at least one of the front-line states, Zambia.

14. See a statement issued by Richard Hove, then ZANU publicity Secretary in exile, Lusake, 9 October 1971; also quoted in M. Sithole, *Zimbabwe Struggles*, 91.

15. All members of Dare still alive and not on the run as the result of infighting were detained by the Zambian government following the assassination of Chitepo.

16. See "Pointers: Zimbabwe Party Games" in *Africa Confidential*, April 1986.

17. The detente exercise was an attempt by U.S. Secretary of State Henry Kissinger, South African Prime Minister John Vorster, and the African front-line states, Zambia, Tanzania, Mozambique, Botswana, and Angola, to reach a peaceful solution in Rhodesia. Many in ZANU believed Zambia looked for an outcome that favored ZAPU.

18. See *Central Committee Report*, by the ZANU President R. G. Mugabe to the Second Party Congress (Harare), 8 August 1984, 5.

19. This is required by the constitution. However, ZANU's holding of its congress a few months before the general elections is tactical: it gains momentum for the election campaign.

20. While many people believe that Mugabe will occupy this position and execute his duties with probity, there is doubt that such a quality is present in most men. At any rate, concentration of power and public trust is a risky affair in any organization and society.

21. In fact, the public service is the government. Hence its control was a contentious issue at the Lancaster House constitutional talks in 1979.

22. *The 1979 Zimbabwe Constitution*, Chapter VII, (73) (1).

23. This number does not include employees of local authorities and parastatal organizations because they are not civil servants as such. But local authorities are under the ministry of local government, while each parastatal falls under the jurisdiction of a particular ministry, depending on area of activity. However, according to Ibbo Mandaza, one of the commissioners of the Public Service Commission, an exercise is currently under way designed to rationalize the terms and conditions of service of such personnel with those of the public service. See Madaza's paper: "The Zimbabwe Public Service" presented at the United Nations Inter-Regional Seminar on Reforming Civil Service Systems for Development (Beijing, China, 14-24 August 1985). This section relies heavily on this paper.

24. From *The 1979 Zimbabwe Constitution*. See also Ibbo Mandaza, "The Zimbabwe Public Service," 8.

25. Quoted in Madaza, Ibid., 8.

26. Ibid.

27. Ibid.

28. Notwithstanding some defections from the ZNA of some former ZIPRA cadres sympathetic to dissidents in Matebeleland, most former ZIPRA fighters remain loyal to the army and the state. (Also in July 1982, saboteurs [allegedly former Rhodesian officers collaborating with South African agents] destroyed thirteen Zimbabwe military aircraft).

29. The Fifth Brigade is presumed to be an all-ZANU "crack" unit. It gained both fame and notoriety in the campaign against dissidents in Matebeleland. The paramilitary are locally trained people's militia for local defences.

30. Minister Nkala, a long-standing senior member of ZANU, is popularly known for his uncompromising "get tougher" policy towards the ZAPU leadership before and after independence.

31. In *Issue: A Journal of African Opinion*, XIV (1985), 29-31.

32. In a conversation with Chief Justice Dumbutchena on 14 November 1985, I asked him pointedly whether the party or the politicians as such have tried to do his work. He replied very unequivocally: "No, never, not once," and said that he found this feature in our government "admirable." When I asked for his permission to quote him on this, he said: "Oh yes, by all means do."

33. See the 1964 ZANU constitution as adopted at the First National Congress, 21-23 May 1984.

34. See the entire Frolizi statement in Gideon Nyandero and Christopher Nyangoni, *The Zimbabwe Nationalist Movement: Select Documents* (London: Rex, 1978), 171-184. Also quoted in M. Sithole, *Zimbabwe Struggles*, op. cit., 134.

35. From *Central Committee Report*, op. cit., 5.

36. South African colleague Victor Khabo, studying for a Ph.D in economics at the University of Cincinnati in 1974, once commented in a discussion, rather poignantly, that many in the Ph.D program would not want to even pretend to understand *Das Kapital* let alone have confidence to explain it.

37. This sentiment was expressed by a lot of people during a study of voter attitudes conducted by the author during the 1985 election.

38. The issue of the inappropriate use and misuse of class analysis is the subject of my article on "Use of Class Analysis in Explaining Factionalism in the Zimbabwe Nationalist Movement," in *African Studies Review*, (March 1984).

39. From the speech, "Political Systems in Zimbabwe," he delivered at the Zimbabwe/Federal Republic of Germany Symposium (Harare: Parliament of Zimbabwe, 6 November 1985), 4.

40. The Ndebele came into present-day Zimbabwe in early nineteenth century and dominated the indigenous Shona population until the advent of colonialism. The Shona emerged the dominant group after colonialism. I deal with this in greater detail in a chapter "Zimbabwe in Search of a Stable Democracy" in a forthcoming volume, *Experiences with Democracy in the Developing Nations*, edited by S. M. Lipset, J. Linz, and L. Diamond.

41. In a survey this author conducted during the 1985 election, a question was asked: "Are you better off today than you were five years ago?" There was overwhelming satisfaction, particularly among peasants.

42. Resolutions of the Second ZANU National Congress, Harare, 1984.

43. See a special interview in *Moto*, July 1984. Tekere repeated this theme in another "exclusive interview" with *Prize Africa*, May 1985. When asked what he would do with those who don't want a one-party state, he replied: "They will be overwhelmed and I'm going to make sure we eclipse everybody."

44. See the interview in *South Magazine*, June 1985, 24-25.

45. This observation is shared by many enlightened local analysts, the belief being that both ZAPU and ZANU now fully realize the need for and prudence of an accommodation.

46. David Martin and Phyllis Johnson quote a journalist as having observed that, "Nkomo could have breakfast at the Kremlin, lunch in the Lonrho boardroom, and dinner at the White House in the same day." op. cit., 287.

47. More radical commentators on Zimbabwe since independence tend to be critical of the fact that the revolutionary zeal in ZANU seems to be finished, or has "lost its way," or some such superficiality. See A. Astrow, *Zimbabwe: A Revolution That Lost Its Way?* (London: Zed Press, 1983); or Ronald Weitzer, "Continuities in the Politics of State Security in Zimbabwe," in *The Political Economy of Zimbabwe*, edited by Michael Schatzberg (New York: Praeger, 1984); or Christine Sylvester's "Zimbabwe's 1985 Election and the Search for Ideology," a paper presented at the ASA Conference in New Orleans, 23-25 November 1985. What is glaringly missing in these critiques are coherently realistic options or alternatives, given the circumstances Zimbabwe finds itself in in the international political economy and because of its own domestic and regional realities. Suicide has never been an option open to rational men.

part two

Public Policy and Policymaking in Afro-Marxist Regimes

Development and Counterdevelopment Strategies in Mozambique

John S. Saul

Mozambique's socialist experiment, thrust forward by the long years of guerrilla struggle and increasingly based on a Marxist approach to social transformation, began with high hopes at independence in 1975. It now lies in tatters. Why has this occurred? This is a big question, but not an unprecedented one. Why, Marxists and others have asked, are there the many negative features that had also scarred Russia's postrevolutionary society? These features have substantially blurred the image of the numerous achievements that also sprang from Russia's October Revolution. It is not surprising, therefore, that historians and activists struggle, to the present day, to provide convincing explanations: the drag of inherited backwardness, the weaknesses in the Bolsheviks' own project, and the pressure of imperialist encirclement. Self-evidently, the relative weight to be attached to such factors cannot be established with the precision of a chemical experiment. Most usefully, the debate continues and it also has resonance elsewhere. Indeed, certain parallel considerations spring to the fore when one confronts an event like Mozambique's signing of the "Nkomati Accord" with South Africa in March 1984, or its expelling (at South Africa's insistence) the last remnants of the African National Congress's official delegation from Maputo in January 1987.

Perhaps the canvas upon which the Front for the Liberation of Mozambique (Frelimo) has sought to depict its revolution will appear to be more modest than that which was available to the Bolsheviks. But for the people of Southern Africa, Frelimo's victory over Portuguese colonialism and its coming to power (in June 1975), with a socialist program of increasingly self-conscious Marxist provenance, was a major step forward. It gave substantial inspiration—and, equally important, crucial logistical backup—to those Zimbabweans who were soon to overthrow the Smith regime. It helped, tangibly, to stoke the fires of resistance in South Africa in the period leading up to the Soweto uprising. And for Mozambicans, it provided the promise of a process of liberation that would continue, moving on from political triumph to a socialist future.

How different the situation was to appear a decade later! By then the Nkomati "Agreement on Non-Aggression and Good Neighborliness" with South Africa had found Mozambique forced to compromise dramatically on its support for the African National Congress (ANC) of South Africa. Now, too, Mozambique sought further integration into the very grid of South African regional economic hegemony, which had been identified as one of the major barriers to Mozambican development in the first heady days of independence. More generally, the country's economy lay in chaos, and the government was forced to go cap in hand to the World Bank and the IMF, among others, for succor. With counterrevolutionary guerrilla activity rife in virtually every one of the country's ten provinces and with its own armed forces in considerable disarray, the Frelimo government was unable even to guarantee the physical safety of a large proportion of its citizens.

Inherited backwardness? Weaknesses in Frelimo's own project? Imperialist encirclement? All these factors (and others, including an extraordinary string of natural disasters) have had a role to play in producing the present grim denouement to Mozambique's revolution. In this chapter we will examine each in turn, focusing special attention upon problems that seem defined by tensions and contradictions within the Mozambican government's own development strategy. Certainly it would be a misguided form of solidarity with a revolution—even one as beleaguered as is Mozambique's—to fully accept the crucial importance of external aggression as any kind of apologia. To its credit, the Frelimo leadership itself has avoided, by and large, the temptation to hide its own failures of omission and commission behind such an emphasis.

That being said, however, we will find ourselves forced to return, again and again, to the hard fact of South African aggression. We are forced to accede to the truth of the late President Samora Machel's 1984 conclusion that the single most important cause of Mozambique's current problems "lies in the situation in Southern Africa and in the wars that have been forced upon us."[1] More, we will have to acknowledge features of these wars that, it can be argued, make them qualitatively different from the "imperialist encirclement" experienced by the USSR. They mark a new sophistication in the techniques of global counterrevolution, South Africa's destabilization strategy partaking of the same brutal universe of discourse that has spawned the parallel U.S. strategy of "low-intensity conflict" and its principal concrete manifestation, the Nicaraguan *contras*. As directed against Mozambique, first by Rhodesia and later by South

Africa, "destabilization" has been crafted quite cynically and self-consciously to grant the revolutionary regime in Mozambique no margin for error and little room to learn from experience. It has been planned, in short, as the cutting edge of the effort to deny the possibility of significant development in Mozambique, planned, inhumanly but systematically, as *a counterdevelopment strategy.*

Development Strategy in Mozambique

For a more detailed elaboration of a number of the points made in this section, see John S. Saul, ed., A Difficult Road: The Transition to Socialism in Mozambique *(New York: Monthly Review Press, 1985), esp. Chapters 1 and 2.*

Mozambique was colonized by the most backward of European powers operating in Africa and so paid doubly for its servitude. Portugal operated, in large measure, as a *rentier* colonialist. In the late nineteenth and early twentieth centuries, this meant farming out much of its colonial exploitation on a regional basis to various, largely parasitic, companies. In this century, its role as middleman vis-à-vis a more economically assertive South Africa had much the same character; the Portuguese colonial state lived, to a considerable extent, off profits reaped from subordination of the Mozambican economy to South Africa (labor to the mines of Transvaal, charges on transit to Mozambican ports, and the like). Indeed, such subordination to South Africa was one crucially important legacy that a postcolonial Mozambique would have to shoulder.

In addition, various bursts of economic nationalism in Portugal led to the instrumentalization of certain sectors of the Mozambican economy in order to service more directly Portugal's own development requirements (forced cotton cultivation, for example). However, by the 1960s, multinational corporations were also being invited in. As much as anything else, this was done to make firm international support for Portugal's colonial project, but it also did begin to impart some economic momentum to the economy. Nonetheless, the socioeconomic picture remained bleak to the very end of the colonial period, various brands of forced labor and a particularly ugly form of cultural and political subordination (product of the malevolent interplay of fascist state and Catholic church) locking backwardness into place. The end of centuries of Portuguese domination saw Mozambique come to independence with a formidably dependent and underdeveloped economy, even by African standards—a situation marked, for example, by an overall literacy rate of well under 5 percent and a staggering paucity of trained personnel.

The reverse side of the coin of "ultracolonialism" was revolutionary nationalism. Portugal had far too weak an economy to sustain economic control of a territory like Mozambique without continuing use of the colonial state, its guarantor of privileged "middleman" status. Therefore, the neocolonial solution to emerging nationalist demands was not nearly so available to Portugal as it was to other, more economically self-confident colonial powers. Portuguese intransigence meant, in turn, that fledgling nationalist politicians in Mozambique were forced to deepen their revolutionary practice beyond the conventions of most prior African experience—in order to mount a guerrilla war. This involved establishing a much more democratic link to the peasantry, the latter's support being so important an ingredient of guerrilla war success; it also meant, in order to hold that support, having to begin to exemplify the egalitarian promise of anticolonial struggle in the newly liberated areas themselves, in advance of victory. There was strife within Frelimo regarding this apparent radicalizing logic of guerrilla warfare, and the more opportunistic of the nationalists were to fall by the wayside. What began to emerge, however, were progressive and collective practices—in the spheres of democratic participation, health, education, gender relations, and economic activity—which foreshadowed a socialist future for an independent Mozambique. Also occurring was the crystallization of Frelimo's fluid and developing ideology into an ever more self-consciously Marxist mold. As Eduardo Monlane, Frelimo's first president, put the point shortly before his death in 1969:

> I am now convinced that Frelimo has a clearer political line than ever before....The common basis which we all had when we formed Frelimo was hatred of colonialism and the belief in the necessity to destroy the colonial structure and to establish a new social structure. But what type of social structure, what type of organization we would have, no one knew. No, some did know, some did have ideas, but even they had rather theoretical notions which were themselves transformed by struggle. Now, however, there is a qualitative transformation in thinking which has emerged during the past six years which permits me to conclude that at present Frelimo is much more socialist, revolutionary and progressive than ever and that the line, the tendency, is now more and more in the direction of socialism of the Marxist-Leninist variety. Why? Because the conditions of life in Mozambique, the type of enemy which we have, does not give us any other alternative. I do think that, without compromising Frelimo, which still has not made an official pronouncement declaring itself Marxist-Leninist, I can say that Frelimo is inclining itself more and more in this direction because the conditions in which we struggle and work demand it.[2]

Yet the grim inheritance remained. Moreover, the immediate terrain for Mozambique's launching of a transition to socialism was rendered even more treacherous than it might otherwise have been by the manner of the departure of the Portuguese from the scene. Such had been the character of the latter's brand of settler colonialism that they had monopolized positions very deep down into the Mozambican social structure. When the vast majority of these settlers chose, with Frelimo's coming to power, to cut and run (while also indulging in a staggering amount of willful and gratuitous sabotage as they departed) they brought acute crisis to an already backward and dependent economy. Industries and agricultural enterprises were abandoned or milked dry, and Frelimo found itself forced into a pace of nationalization and state control that would quickly outrun its immediate strengths in terms of trained cadres and its capacity to provide firm economic leadership. Especially disastrous (although its full implications were not immediately grasped) was the collapse of the formerly Portuguese-dominated network of commercialization, particularly in the countryside. From the very start, Mozambique was forced into an emergency mode of activity from which it never fully recovered—especially when its enemies began to move, quite consciously, too exacerbate the crisis that the Frelimo leadership had thus inherited.

But let us stay with the difficult terrain for the moment—a terrain that would become even more difficult as wars waged first by Rhodesia and, subsequently, South Africa and a cruel run of natural disasters (drought, then flood, then drought again) closed around Mozambique. Here we must ask what the instinct, carried forward from the liberated areas, for popularly based and collective solutions to development problems would be made to mean, in and of itself. Frelimo sought to make concrete its commitment, in the first postindependence decade, on two broad developmental fronts, the sociopolitical and the economic. As regards the first of these, the chief challenge was seen to be the consolidation, in power and policy, of the interests of the popular classes, the workers and peasants. In policy terms, the immediate effort to shift such sectors as education, health, the role of women, urban planning, and the like in a direction that would service these interests has been well documented.[3] Needless to say, the centrality of the interests of the popular classes was also to be the basis for articulating economic policy.

To this latter point we will return. Particularly prominent in political terms, however, was the felt need to consolidate "people's power" in Mozambique as a guarantor of the further progress of the revolution. This imperative had been well sounded by one of the key Frelimo leaders in the days of the armed struggle itself. Asked how it might be ensured that the "collectivist effort" of the liberation period be carried over into the new phase, Marcelino dos Santos argued that "if our organization maintains its true revolutionary leadership, the special circumstances of our liberation open up real possibilities for an advance from liberation to revolution". But, he quickly added, "the main defense must be to popularize the revolutionary aims and to create such a situation that if for one reason or another at some future time some people start trying to change these aims, they will meet with resistance from the masses".[4]

There is a tension here, of course, between the competing claims to centrality, within an attempted transition to socialism, of "true revolutionary leadership," on the one hand, and of the action to be taken by the popular classes on the other. The hard fact is that both claims have merit, although the tendency in relatively underdeveloped settings is for the bearers of "true revolutionary leadership" to expand their prerogatives in ways that threaten to become disproportionate. In Mozambique, as elsewhere, there are various "good reasons" why this should happen. Perhaps inevitably, the new leadership becomes charged with virtually constituting the new society in extremely important ways, with, in effect, constituting the context within which viable socialist democracy might come to function. This involved, for example, continuing the effort begun in the liberated areas to focus a transethnic sense of nationhood. Even more important for a socialist-inclined leadership it has involved, to some degree, the necessity to *create* the very class base for continuing revolution—"create" in this context, implying the giving of a sense of "classness" and of progressive class potency to both a large but widely dispersed peasantry and to a small, historically repressed working class. And this was in a setting where any nascent sense of democratic empowerment had been systematically quashed by centuries of colonial brutality.

To these pulls toward a magnified definition of the leadership's role as "legislator" must be added the apparently centralizing imperatives of economic planning in a context of scarce resources and (in particular) the apparently centralizing imperatives of military defense in a situation that, in Mozambique as in so many other fledging socialist environments, quickly becomes one of external siege and the most malevolent kind of internal subversion. Itemized here, in fact, is a list of tasks that the Mozambican leadership shouldered with vigor; equally important, they shouldered them in a manner that manifested a real, not metaphorical, commitment to the interests of ordinary Mozambicans.

Indeed, the great strength of the Mozambican leadership team—a team forged in the armed struggle but, in essence, still in place through the first independence decade—is that it has remained "true" to its revolutionary calling. the implicit bond it forged with the Mozambican people in struggle against colonialism and at independence remains as a constitutive "myth" (in the best sense of that term) central to the very definition of the new Mozambique and still its strongest guarantor of continuing socialist accomplishment. To be sure, hardship has frayed that bond but the evident commitment and the lack of venality of the leadership has meant that it has not been broken. Where Frelimo has been less successful is precisely on the development side of this equation in its efforts to ensure a continuing renewal of its revolution by advancing, over time and in line with its theoretical commitments, a positive and effective *empowering* of the people.

This is not for want of some conceptualization of the issue, as the earlier citation from dos Santos will already have suggested. Moreover, in practice, the very first order of business established by Frelimo—as it moved to extend its political presence beyond the liberated areas and throughout the country during the period of the "transitional government" (from the signing of the Lusaka Agreement in September 1974, to independence in June 1975)—is highly suggestive in this respect. For it encompassed the effort to establish political institutions that would give the populace in the rest of the country a politicizing experience equivalent to that which had been felt to characterize life in the liberated areas. Thus emerged the *grupos dinamizadores* (dynamizing groups), organs of popular involvement in the work place and the locality, ones fraught with contradictions and difficulties but genuine schools of democracy and nascent class consciousness nonetheless.

In retrospect, Frelimo's decision to move beyond the *grupos* experiment to an ever firmer institutionalization of the "vanguard party" format in 1977 seems to have been almost inevitable, and as a strengthening of the role of "true revolutionary leadership" it had its merits. Nor did Frelimo neglect an attempt to match that initiative with the construction of fresh organs of popular participation. Not only were there distinctively democratic aspects to the process of selection of recruits to the new party, but a network of popular assemblies began to be constructed, as well as "production councils" to help to ventilate from below the country's economic enterprises. Nonetheless, future historians may well question the wisdom of the move toward the vanguard party model. Did it tend more to stifle than to expand the democratic promise of the liberated areas and of the *grupos dinamizadores?* If so, part of the problem may have lain in the uncritical adoption of what is merely one strand within the Marxist tradition, that less liberatory strand incarcerated historically within the grim political practices of the Soviet Bloc.[5] As I have written elsewhere, "too often...the comforting nostrums of a certain brand of Leninism have served to paper over challenges that require even more creative responses" in the political sphere in

Mozambique, with even "the very best of the leadership...sometimes [seeming] a little too reluctant to risk 'too much democracy.'"[6] Some would go further with this line of criticism. Thus Dan O'Meara, in a review of an earlier book of mine on Mozambique, notes that I "correctly [dwell] on the democratic work methods, political imagination and courage which made Frelimo such a unique movement in the 1960s and 1970s" but that I still tend to underestimate such things as "the long-term consequences of the profound formalism of Frelimo's political style":Some would argue that the overweening emphasis given *forma correcta* [the correct form] at every level of public life has been an important factor in the profound depolitization of present-day Mozambique—a depolitization which I think is underestimated by Saul. Likewise an emerging cult of the personality around President Machel, strong centralization of decision-making in the President's office as state power weakened under destabilization, and an information policy which deprives Mozambicans of real information about their own society and encourages the most outrageous forms of rumor-mongering, are all significant aspects of the Mozambican "reality"....[7]

This almost certainly overstates the case, although other observers might want to carry this kind of criticism even further, seeing in any such deviations not so much evidence of self-righteousness (however well-intentioned) and failure of political imagination on Frelimo's part as the self-interested closure of the polity by a nascent bureaucratic class.[8] To be fair, however, it is Frelimo leaders themselves who have been most clearsighted about any such possibility. No doubt this reflects, in considerable measure, the strength they derive from commitment to a Marxist perspective, for those lodged more firmly within a merely "African socialist" view of the transition process have found it virtually impossible elsewhere to comprehend the class dynamics of that process. The following striking passage from the key document presented by the party's Central Committee to Frelimo's Fourth Congress in 1983 illustrates this point:

> Our country has a social stratum that enjoys levels of consumption unavailable to the overwhelming majority of the people. From the social point of view, it consists chiefly of citizens originating from the social strata that were already privileged in the colonial period. Politically, this social stratum is opportunist, elitist, unscientific and hopeful of transforming itself into an authentic bourgeoisie. All it admires in the bourgeoisie is its corrupt consumerist nature.From the cultural standpoint, aspirants to the bourgeoisie are alienated and estranged. They are unaware, or pretend to be unaware, of the value of Mozambican culture and they spurn the people's wisdom and knowledge. These individuals are slaves to everything that comes from Europe, and

particularly from the West. For this reason, they try to distort the class character of our revolution by transforming it into a technocratic process through which they can control power.This social stratum actively opposes any measures that aim at simplifying organization and methods, democratizing leadership or increasing the workers' share in planning and controlling production. Because of their book learning, aspirants to the bourgeoisie despise solutions from the people. They are unable to learn from the people. So they reject the experience of the liberated areas. They reject the small-scale projects that require the intelligence, sensitivity and understanding of the people and prefer the projects that come ready made from abroad.The characteristics of aspirants to the bourgeoisie make this social stratum vulnerable to the insidious action of the enemy. Strict class vigilance must be exercised over these individuals.[9]

Nor have such perceptions remained merely on the printed page. Since 1980, Frelimo has struggled to find innovative means to move against abuse of bureaucratic and political position. In this regard, the dramatic pairing of the "Political and Organizational Offensive" and the "Legality Offensive" merit careful consideration, even if, all too characteristically, they remained more "top-down" than "bottom-up" means of shaking up and cleaning the state system in the popular interest.

At the same time, it must be admitted that, in independent Mozambique, there has been considerable pull upon even the most committed leadership cadres toward precisely the kind of technocratic, large-scale solutions to the economic development challenges that are being condemned in the paragraphs quoted above. Is this because the failure to keep the link to the popular classes, as open and vibrant as it was in the days of the armed struggle, has allowed the leadership instead to find its most active reference group in the aforementioned "social stratum" ("opportunist, elitist...") that staffs the middle levels of party and state? Perhaps in part, but one must be wary of any too glibly class reductionist explanation here. In the case of the leadership (and not merely at the very top), many of the problems seem to have arisen primarily from distortions in the very *definition* of their development project (although it is also true that such distancing from an effective interaction with the populace as has occurred make such distortions all the more likely).

"Distortions in the very definition of their development project"? Alongside the cruel fact of continuing destabilization, there are numerous factors that help explain Mozambique's failure in the economic sphere. There have been natural disasters, certainly, of trade, rising oil prices, and the like); but also, as noted earlier, there has been the sheer weight of historical backwardness; I have written elsewhere that

After independence [not in comparison with the challenges of the liberation struggle period] the scale became infinitely vaster, the stratum of middle-level cadres too thin on the ground and too ill-trained, the challenges...literally overwhelming in their scope and variety....Not surprisingly, even the most solid of senior leaders have been reduced under such circumstances to fire-fighting a seemingly endless series of emergencies rather than finding time to concentrate on the slow, patient, on-going...work which would serve to consolidate a firmer...base for the revolution.[10]

Nonetheless, one major factor in economic decline seems to have reflected a much more self-conscious choice (and a rather surprising one, in light of the nature of the actual war of liberation): the choice to downplay the importance of the peasant sector within the country's economic development strategy!

True, Frelimo first found itself pulled away from the peasantry by the threatened collapse of the former settler farm sector in the Limpopo Valley and elsewhere, this being a crucial source of food supply for the cities. The takeover of these farms created the state farm sector—large-scale, high technology—which became, in turn, a virtual magnet for the bulk of scarce resources and organizational energies that were to be devoted to the agricultural sphere. What tended to happen, however, was that too much of a virtue was soon being made of this necessity, dovetailing (as the concentration upon the state farms did) with other emphases forming within Frelimo's postindependence strategy on economic development. More generally, "big projects" were becoming the core of that strategy, a familiar enough temptation in all Third World countries; it was difficult not to interpret it as bearing, in the Mozambican case, the stamp of a certain kind of Marxism (of Eastern European provenance) that places such exclusive emphasis on "development of the productive forces" as a prerequisite for the emergence of genuinely socialist relations of production. As I have documented elsewhere, Frelimo was to seek, with time, to inch its way toward a less rigid brand of Marxism, one truer to its own history, just as it was to inch its way toward a more promising economic strategy.[11] But in the short run, the new government did find its attention diverted from the seriousness of the negative impact on agricultural production and peasant life of the simultaneous collapse of the network of commercialization and of the goods-supplying industries.

Thus a quite one-sided notion of "sacrifice" for economic development (albeit development conceived as being in the "long-run interest" of the mass of the populace) carried the day—rather than a sense of the manner in which the interacting expansion of agricultural and industrial spheres might both drive each other forward *and* begin at once to meet more immediate popular needs (a model that I have termed, elsewhere, "the socialism of expanded reproduction").[12] And, as implied, the cumulative impact of the disastrous combination of goods shortage and marketing problems deepened the crisis of reproduction for peasant households throughout the country. In consequence, rural production tended to fall and with it the availability of marketed surpluses both for internal consumption and overseas sale (read: foreign exchange). Moreover, when at first the government did seek to overcome such problems it did so by increasing the money supply (the new money, in the absence of readily available goods, quickly being swallowed up by inflation or by the black market) rather than addressing the structural parameters of the crisis of the peasantry.[13]

The Fourth Congress of Frelimo must be seen, in this context, as a very real harbinger of potential renewal of the Mozambican revolution, both politically and economically. As Frelimo turned back toward the peasantry at that congress, its innovative resolutions reflected the impact of the markedly open period of debate at the grass roots level that had been part and parcel of the preparation of the congress. For, in the forums provided, peasants had raised their voices loudly and clearly about the negative impact upon them of misguided development policies. Now, however, the emphasis, economically, was to be on downplaying big projects (both within the agricultural sector and beyond), overcoming the goods crisis and servicing the peasants' needs. Positive adjustments can be interpreted, to a considerable degree, as a creative renovation of Mozambique's Marxist discourse on the imperatives of economic development. These adjustments exemplify many of the terms of an innovative structural analysis of the economy's problems while casting proposed solutions for those problems along lines which parallel aspects of Lenin's New Economic Policy (NEP).[14]

Some analysts have been critical of the economic content of such proposals, however. As the allusion to the NEP suggests, the linking mechanism for delivering fresh incentives to the "family sector" was to be, to a significant degree, a market one. And such critics wonder aloud whether Frelimo has not underestimated the extent to which this is likely to prove a substantial retreat from, rather than merely some kind of step forward toward, a more "feasible socialism." Where, they ask, is the socialist thrust that had originally foreseen a strong move toward production cooperatives as an essential ingredient of any transformation of the peasant sector? True, after the enthusiasms of the first few postindependence years, this intention had tended to become buried under the one-sided emphasis on the state farms. But was it now to be lost again in a groundswell of enthusiasm for the capitalist farmer? Certainly Mark Wuyts has suggested this to be a real threat, arguing that Frelimo has in any case long underestimated the danger of class formation within the peasantry and the threat that that could pose to a long-term sustaining of the socialist impulse in Mozambique.[15] From this perspective, one reads with interest the recent findings of Otto Roesch in Gaza Province where, apparently, the NEP has led to some rejuvenation of rural economic life, but where also "one could see that capitalist farmers, and entrepreneurs generally, were exhibiting much greater public assertiveness and an increasing tendency to play a more active role in local political affairs."[16]

When some of these risks are viewed alongside the much more solicitous approach by the Frelimo government toward Western investors to help meet the pressing need for foreign exchange, capital investment, and know-how, leftist critics do begin to query the future of socialism in Mozambique. Not that the Mozambican leadership is indifferent to such worries and concerns (a point to which we must return in the final section of this chapter). Yet, as we will then emphasize, by the time such policy adjustments had begun to be made, this could no longer be done with reference merely to the presumed imperatives of the struggle for socialism. Instead, the contest that increasingly framed them was the struggle for sheer survival—survival in a setting of unrelieved siege. What can be affirmed, however, is that, despite this setting, a significant learning process, a refinement of Marxist practice in Africa full of risk but also full of promise, had been underway in Mozambique, and the fecund debate that swirled around the Fourth Congress was a significant moment in point.[17] We can note, too, the fact that even in advance of this congress and during the only brief period of peace experienced by Mozambique since independence (the period between Rhodesia's defeated sponsorship of a war of aggression against Mozambique and South Africa's reactivation of that war) the economy did experience a momentary up-turn. Yet, even as Frelimo moved further at the 1983 congress to firm up the internal logic of its revolution, the hard fact remained that it was already too late to expect such "internal" preoccupations to be quite the heart of the matter. The clouds of South Africa's ever more aggressive destabilization were already closing around Mozambique and an ever greater number of counterrevolutionary guerillas stalked the land.

Counterdevelopment Planning: The South African Factor

The following two sections incorporate some materials from my article, "Mozambique: Destabilization and the Counterrevolutionary Guerilla," which appears in the Canadian journal, Studies in Political Economy *(Spring 1987).*

Marxist regimes can create some of their own difficulties. Yet, as the case of Mozambique also demonstrates, a regime that retains many of its links to a process of popular based revolution has a good chance of recouping lost ground and moving creatively toward fresh solutions. How important, therefore, to reaffirm the fact, noted in the introduction to this chapter, that it is precisely these latter efforts to regenerate the Mozambican revolution that South Africa has sought, quite consciously, to short circuit through of its war of destabilization. For North American readers, it may be helpful to compare this latter war with the remarkably parallel counterdevelopment strategy mounted by the United States vis-à-vis Nicaragua; although we will see that there are also important reasons for distinguishing the two cases and, in particular, for defining South Africa's counterrevolutionary role with clear reference to the realities of its own region.

The most important link between the two cases is the *global* context within which they both fit—a point of critical importance to any student of the challenges that confront "Third World" Marxist regimes, not least in Africa. Wielders of power in both South Africa and the United States like to paint their "enemy," in Southern Africa and the Caribbean basin respectively, as being primarily the manifestations of some presumed "Soviet menace." While certain died-in-the-wool Cold Warriors may be able to convince even themselves of their own rhetoric and of such a reading of the situation, their basic instincts have, nonetheless, been much sounder. For what both South Africa and the United States seek to place in question is rather the precedent and practice of popularly based movements, whether they be in power or in gestation, which mount a radical-democratic and/or socialist-cum-Marxist challenge to the global status quo.

From this perspective, the imperial project becomes one not of "confronting the Soviet Union" but, instead, of attempting to undermine the popular bases of these regimes and discredit the promise of their socialism in the eyes of their own people. When, in 1984, I visited a Nicaragua already under sharp attack by *contras*, it had some of the feel of the Mozambican situation that I knew so well: an inspiring struggle and a humane and vital revolution being slowing bled to death. A Jesuit priest, working in Nicaragua's agrarian reform sector, but also active in Chile before the coup there, put the point to me with scalding simplicity. "In Chile," he said, "the Americans made a mistake. They cut off the revolution too abruptly. The killed the revolution but, as we can see from recent developments there, they didn't kill the dream. In Nicaragua they're trying to kill the dream."

Not that counterinsurgency strategy—which, in confronting a guerrilla challenge, adds economic, social, and psychological dimensions to military operations in an aggressive tactical mix—is entirely new to imperial planners: witness Britain in Malaya or the United States in Vietnam, to go no further afield. No more unprecedented is the attempt, mounted on various fronts and at different levels, to undermine and destabilize established regimes that challenge global capitalist hegemony: Chile, Cuba, and the like. What is more innovative, however, is a new sophistication of the diverse means of such destabilization and, in particular, the manner of deploying a newly prominent centerpiece in that approach, *the counterrevolutionary guerrilla.*

For comparative purposes, let us look at the Reagan administration's model of "low-intensity conflict" or "low-intensity warfare" (LIC/LIW), about which enough has recently been written to identify its main components. "LIC," Michael Klare observes, "is counter-insurgency and a whole lot more" and he identifies three variants of it: "classic counter-insurgency," "'active' defense against terrorism," and, most important for our discussion of the role of the counterrevolutionary guerrilla, "pro-insurgency."[18] In the words of one of the key strategists of LIC/LIW (Colonel John D. Waghelstein), "LIW is revolutionary and counterrevolutionary warfare. It is total war at the grass-roots level—one that uses all the weapons of total war, including political, economic and psychological warfare with the military aspect being a distant fourth in many cases," Nonetheless, as two recent critics of this policy's implementation have written, it is "permanent but low-key military aggression" that ties the strategy together and which, when it becomes a forward strategy against revolutionaries in power (as in the case of the contra assault on Nicaragua), gives it definition as a "war of attrition."[19]

Such a war, they write, is designed to "pound away at the social and economic fabric" of the target society, seeking to limit a revolution's "ability to meet the material needs of the population and [whittle] away at its base of support." LIC/LIW "seeks first to crack the logic of the revolution, deciphering its internal cohesion and understanding the tactics it employs to advance its interests, and then to devise a strategy that will warp its logic, undoing its internal cohesion and rendering its tactics ineffective—in short turning the revolution against itself." These critics then cap their point by quoting yet another establishment theorist of LIW, Edward Luttwak, to the effect that "in low intensity wars victory is normally obtained by altering the political variables to the point where the enemy becomes ineffectual, and not by actually defeating enemies in battle!"

More positively, apologists for low-intensity conflict make much of the mobilizational aspects of their kind of warfare vis-à-vis the local population; in the words of the key CIA manual on LIC, "Psyops [psychological operations] are conducted to exploit grievances and raise expectations, to influence the population and to promote the loyalty of insurgent members." It is apparently intended, at least in theory, that the destructive aspect of LIC aggression against a targeted revolution be complemented by the development of an "internal front," a counterhegemonic project and the generation of a popular base for counterrevolution. However, the transition to "people's war" has proven to be virtually impossible for counterrevolutionary guerrillas to make, a result that may not appear particularly surprising given the venality of the overall project and given the "antipeople" elements from which these forces are generally stitched together. Thus "the contras are still beset by power struggles, abusive leaders, lack of discipline in the field and internal conflicts, despite the [CIA] manual's plea for 'self-criticism and group discussion' to build 'a spirit of democratic cooperation.'"[20]

Such rebels seem much more comfortable with the same manual's more horrific and Machiavellian suggestions about the wisdom of provoking "riots or shootings which lead to the killing of one or more persons who will be seen as martyrs" or of hiring professional criminals "to carry out specific selective jobs," including the "neutralization" of Nicaraguan judges and other key Sandinista cadres. As Sara Miles elaborates,

> Overall, there is a conscious effort to reduce the presence of the civilian government, to remove successful social programs and the ideological influence that comes with them. The strategy aims to create the impression among the local population of government weakness and *contra* strength. In practice, this means the targeted torture and assassination of teachers, health workers, agricultural technicians and their collaborators in the community. This is not, as many critics charge, 'indiscriminate violence against civilians.' Nor are the killings random acts of terror by incorrigibly brutal ex-National Guardsmen. Rather the violence is part of a logical and systematic policy, and reflects the changing pattern of the war.[21]

And yet, given the character of the counterrevolutionary guerrilla, "indiscriminate violence against civilians" is scarcely absent from the picture. Indeed, as will be documented in greater detail below, South Africa has made even less attempt than the United States to give destabilization or "low-intensity conflict" a positive political coloration vis-à-vis target populations. In fact, there is no place where the practice of the counterrevolutionary guerrilla can be understood as having taken a leaf from the book on classic guerrilla warfare. To a surprising degree—as exemplified by both the *contras* in Nicaragua and the Mozambique National Resistance (MNR or Renamo), South Africa's surrogate force in Mozambique—this type of guerrilla actively disdains to seek the support of the peasantry; intimidation and naked terror directed against the civilian population quickly becomes the dominant approach. A review of South African practice will also confirm the point that the planners of this kind of warfare have indeed developed a quite sophisticated sense of the kind of economic linkages whose establishment is necessary to move an underdeveloped country forward. And they have crafted their intelligence and operational capacities quite consciously to identify such linkages in the making and to destroy them in the countries that have been targeted. Their main purpose reduced itself to wearing down the population, through induced economic hardship and the undermining of the people's sense of security. By these means, too, they seek to render the target government vulnerable, if not necessarily to total collapse, at least to extortionate demands from the outside and to a possible compromising of first principles. Note, for example, Sara Miles's conclusion:

> The war in Central America cannot be reversed by theory alone, and already it may have progressed so far that it is too late for the United States to roll back the challenge of revolutionary nationalism. If that point has been reached, Washington may be capable of no more than inflicting pain—which given the available options, may in itself become a goal of low-intensity strategy. Along with its redefinition of battlefields, the innovation of low-intensity doctrine has been its redefinition of victory. Even if the United States is unable to win outright, it can cause enough physical destruction and political damage over a long period to guarantee that the revolutionaries will not truly "win" either. It can settle for weakening its opponents to such a point that their political goals become unattainable. If their experiments can be aborted, the United States will be able to claim at least a partial victory.[22]

As we shall see, this was precisely the manner in which Mozambique was bludgeoned into accepting the Nkomati Accord with South Africa in 1984, at which time the Frelimo government sought to offer sufficient concessions to South Africa and its Western allies to lift the cruel weight of aggression from its back (albeit with no very great success). Indeed, it is far from clear that South African war aims have ever included an "outright" victory for the MNR in Mozambique—a victory that would, after all, involve South Africa in the embarrassing and costly business of shoring up an unpopular post-Frelimo government and a desperately broken-backed economy. Whatever the case in this respect, the more immediate aims of Pretoria's destabilization strategy throughout the region (including for Mozambique) can be specified. Broadly speaking, the goal is to reinforce its domination of the regional environment in defense of its narrow economic and political interests. More specifically, Pretoria seeks to undermine support by neighboring states for the African National Congress, to sabotage attempts by the Southern African Development Coordination Conference (SADCC) to establish a regional economic grid outside the orbit of South African hegemony, and, where appropriate, to facilitate such a measure of economic and social decay in specific countries as to tarnish the image of the alternatives of "socialism" and "black majority rule" in the region.

But we have mentioned the U.S. parallel. What, in fact, is the likely degree of overlap between South African-sponsored destabilization and the rather similar U.S. approach toward its own radical neighbors? By the very nature of the case, evidence of active collusion is difficult to pin down—except during certain periods of the continuing Angolan operation when the United States's coordination of counterrevolutionary action with South Africa (and through their joint cat's-paw, UNITA) has been much more overt. In fact, there has been greater ambiguity about the extent of coincidence of war aims between South Africa and the United States in the case of Mozambique. Yet Mozambicans themselves have certainly felt, at least, that some of the authors and agencies of U.S. overseas policy are operating in concert with South Africa in stoking the flames of counterrevolutionary guerrilla activities in their country. Consider a mid-1985 report from Mozambique by Michael Valpy in Toronto's *Globe and Mail:* "And the U.S. connection? A senior Mozambican official was asked who could be clever enough to guide the MNR's campaign of terror and sabotage. 'I'll never say this into your tape recorder,' he said. 'The Americans.'"[23] Consider, too, the comment by Deputy U.S. Ambassador to the United Nations, Charles Lichtenstein, in late 1983 when he stated that "destabilization will remain in force until Angola and Mozambique do not permit their territory to be used by terrorists to attack South Africa."[24]

There are good reasons, of course, why U.S. and South African political-military planners should talk the same language and have a shared strategic interest—whatever the tactical differences that might also exist—in the global counterrevolution alluded to above. Moreover, as Philip Frankel points out in his book, *Pretoria's Praetorians,* some of them have, quite literally, gone to school together:

> While American literature on counter-insurgency abjures the totalist flavor of its French counterpart, the intellectual pedigree of [South Africa's] total strategy also contains technical and programmatic elements drawn directly from United States experiences in combatting communism in Latin America and Vietnam. It is perhaps not insignificant for the political role of the South African Defense Force that many of the Latin American coups of the sixties and seventies were

initiated by officers trained at Fort Leavenworth or Inter-American Defence College—both of which placed considerable emphasis on civic and political action by the military as a vital ingredient in the management of "communist-inspired" internal warfare. It is also perhaps not insignificant that the current Minister of Defence and previous Chief of the South African Defence Force, General Magnus Malan, is a Fort Leavenworth graduate—one of the few South African officers to have received American training.[25]

Yet Frankel insists even more strongly on the importance to South Africa's thinking of precisely that "French counterpart" with its "totalist flavour." Thus,

> if the ideological and strategic spirit of the South African military is particularly and peculiarly Francophile in character and if there is any single figure whose writings have had a formative influence on how the current generation of Defense Force leaders interpret the world in relation to counter-insurgency, it is above all the French general, André Beaufre, whose various works are at the basis of virtually every lecture at the Joint Defense College—the primary institution for socializing South Africa's military elite,one of the main contact points for communication between government, the private sector and the state security apparatus, and, since the early seventies, the think-tank for the formation and development of South Africa's total strategy. The term "total strategy" is taken directly from Beaufre's An Introduction to Strategy....[26]

"Total strategy" as a key to understanding the recent activities of the South African state, both domestically and in the Southern African region, has been well analyzed by a number of observers. In Beaufre, however, lies a systematization of the sense that "warfare has become a total form of social interaction," especially important in this respect being Beaufre's notion of "total strategy in the indirect mode," where (in Frankel's summary) "contestants maneuver for advantage on a broad social plane and where the brute actualities of military combat are only one dimension of the competitive process." Or, to return to Beaufre's own words, "action is total and...must prepare...and exploit the results expected from military operations by suitable operations in the psychological, political and diplomatic fields." "Old style warfare with its battles was a sort of bloody surgical operation. The new style war with its nuances is more analogous to the creeping infection of an illness." In the end, it is the "moral disintegration of the enemy [which] causes him to accept the conditions it is desired to impose upon him!"

In short, says Frankel, "there can be no doubt that the intellectual element of the SADF as well as their civilian counterparts working within the logic of the total strategy have absorbed the totalist and embracing spirit of counterrevolutionary action at the center of Beaufre's programme." At the same time, Frankel also cautions against giving the South African defence establishment too much credit for deep thinking, suggesting that its version of total strategy remains "still basically viscerotonic, more of a mood composed of imperfectly linked semi-developed ideas than a sophisticated and carefully articulated formula for the direction of society." Elsewhere, I have discussed with Stephen Gelb some of the implications of this "total strategy" concept for the internal defensive actions taken by the increasingly integrated civil-military leadership in South Africa, noting, not least, the distinct tendency (given the intractable conditions that exist in that country) for it to collapse, all its reformist pretentions to the contrary notwithstanding, into mere repression. As a forward political-military approach to be wielded against its neighbors, thinking cast in terms of "total strategy" has undoubtedly had an important role to play as well, helping identify the broad front across which South Africa and its counterrevolutionary guerrillas have attacked the Mozambican development effort. Yet, just because total strategy is, in Frankel's phrase, more "mood" than "formula" in the South African case, it also behooves us to look at more specific and immediate determinants of South African practice. It is in this connection that I would give particular emphasis to the considerable creativity shown by the Rhodesians in first beginning to craft for the region the practices of aggressive destabilization, which have found their cruelest expression in Mozambique. Indeed, it was precisely the Rhodesian initiative against Mozambique that the South Africans would ultimately inherit and into which they would breathe new life.

Interestingly, the target initially proposed by the Rhodesians (in 1971) was not Mozambique, but already independent Zambia. This is revealed in a "very secret" document of the period entitled, in its Portuguese language version, *Operações especiais* (Special Operations).[27] In trilateral discussions with the Portuguese and the South Africans, Ken Flower of the Rhodesian Central Intelligence Office (CIO) identified Zambia as a crucial rear base for both Frelimo and ZANU guerillas entering Tete Province, and proposed a multifaceted offensive against that country, one designed quite explicitly to force it to "expel all terrorists [sic] from its territory and to forbid their through transit." The operation would have "economic aspects": delaying the transit of crucial goods into Zambia and of exports out of the country, raising rail charges and port fees discriminatively, refusing to accept payment in Zambian *kwachas*. But, as Alves Gomes points out in an important article on the document under discussion, it is in this document's emphasis on "immediate direct action" and "long-term action" that the seeds of the armed banditry, which has become all too familiar in Mozambique, lie.

Thus not only was it suggested that equipment and machinery bound for Zambia might be selectively sabotaged in transit, but also that there be "the creation of a climate of uncertainty" by means of the "indiscriminate killing of Zambian government and party functionaries." Even more important, despite the absence of any large numbers of Zambian refugees in neighboring countries, there was to be established in Mozambique a special center for "Africans, Asians and others" to act (primarily in Zambia, but Tanzania was also mentioned) as secret agents and "troublemakers," with one specific task to be "recruiting and organizing dissidents in the target territories." There are indications that South Africa's then Minister of Defense P.W. Botha and his lieutenants were more enthusiastic about such plans than Prime Minister John Vorster. In any event, the Portuguese (and the South Africans) rejected the option offered by such *Special Operations,* choosing instead to concentrate primarily on their high-powered *Relâmpago* and Gordian Knot offensives against Frelimo-controlled areas *within* Mozambique. Moreover, linked to these latter offensives, was the creation—with South African assistance and with the shifting of such officers as Alvaro Cardoso from Angola to Mozambique—of various hard-boiled commando units and special forces (e.g., the *Flechas,* the *Grupos especiais* (GEs), the Special Paratroop Groups (GEPs), the *Commandos africanos,* the *Serviços especiais de informação e intervenção* (SEIs), all organizations "of sad memory in Mozambique," as Alves Gomes phrases it in his above mentioned article.

Yet, ironically, even as Flower's initial blueprint for destabilization and counterrevolutionary guerrilla warfare was thus being shelved, the Portuguese's own alternative was creating the concrete basis for its long-term reactivation—although this time to be directed against Mozambique itself. For it was precisely the military and paramilitary organizations just cited that provided the first recruits whom the Rhodesians were to mold into the MNR. The network thus made available to the Rhodesians fanned back into the broader structures of the Portuguese security apparatus (the notorious PIDE), but also reached beyond the Portuguese colonial state per se. For a number of the "special forces," initiatives of the waning days of Portuguese colonialism had borne the stamp of private enterprise. The key site for the latter was Sefala Province, in the very center of the country, and the key actor was Jorge Jardim, an extremely wealthy (and formidably reactionary) Beira-based businessman.[28]

For Jardim and other die-hard Portuguese, the war against African nationalism had not stopped with the coming of Mozambican independence—an attitude that many of those who have survived Jardim (he died in 1982) still retain. In the event, Jardim's former private secretary, Orlando Cristina, became the crucial link-man with the

Rhodesians, helping establish the anti-Frelimo radio station, *Voz da Africa livre* (Voice of Free Africa) in Rhodesia in 1976 and apparently providing much of the inside knowledge of names and organizations, state and private, that facilitated recruitment. As Alves Gomes notes, other familiar faces resurfaced in the early days of stitching together what was to become the MNR. Thus Jack Barry, who had been coauthor, with Flower, of the 1971 *Special Operations* proposal, became the first instructor at a camp established in early 1977 at Odzi as an important rear base for destabilization activities in Mozambique. And Alvaro Cardoso, the military commander mentioned earlier as being linked to the genesis of Portuguese commando operations, now found himself leader of one of the first such destabilization actions, directed against the Musuzi hydroelectric operations in Manica Province; later he was also to become an instructor at Odzi.

It was at Bindura, however, that the first real training camp was established, in 1975 or early 1976. Joseph Hanlon writes, "When Mozambique imposed sanctions on Rhodesia on 3 March 1976, it gave Flower the excuse he needed. The first MNR bands moved into Manica and Tete Provinces and attacked shops and health posts near the border."[29] As time went on, the Rhodesians made some effort to give the MNR more of an African coloration, welcoming such black Mozambicans as André Matzangaissa and Alfonso Dhlakama into leadership roles within their organization; these two, who have been particularly prominent within the MNR (Matzangaissa until his death in action in 1979, Dhlakama to the present), had both been cashiered from Frelimo for corruption. Attacks on villages and commercial linkages inside the Mozambican border with Rhodesia was the MNR's main activity, the aim, certainly at that state, being to bleed the Frelimo regime rather than attempt to overthrow it. Indeed, the launching of the counterrevolutionary guerrilla was still defined fairly modestly as merely one specific ploy—alongside airstrikes, dramatic acts of sabotage (e.g., the attack on the Beira oil storage dumps, with South African assistance, in 1979), and the like—designed to make Mozambique pay for its continuing support of ZANU guerillas.

It is true that by 1979 the Rhodesians were pushing the MNR further into Mozambique, helping establish a major operational base in Gorongosa and supplying it by air. But the handwriting was already on the wall. The Mozambican arm struck effectively at Gorongosa; with Matzangaissa's death, various factions within the MNR fought destructively amongst themselves; Rhodesia itself made ready to face the music at Lancaster House. After more than fifteen years of war, Mozambicans looked eagerly to some breathing room in which to advance, single-mindedly and without distraction, the reconstruction of their country. Indeed, as seen, the pace of economic development momentarily began to quicken. Unfortunately, however, Mozambique's trial by destabilization had only just begun, as South Africa now prepared to pump fresh life into the MNR.

It bears emphasizing that South Africa had not been entirely absent from the MNR initiative during the early period. Contacts were maintained and, as one example, Bureau of State Security (BOSS) agent Gordon Winter claims (in his book, *Inside BOSS*) that a major part of his work at that time was to act as chief propagandist for the MNR, both within South Africa and abroad.[30] Nonetheless, it was still primarily Rhodesia that was making the running with the MNR. By the period, 1979-1980, however, the scene had begun to shift, setting the stage, for South Africa to revitalize the fading MNR even as Rhodesia exited from the historical stage. Long-time Defence Minister P. W. Botha's 1978 ascension to the prime ministership had now placed the tough-minded and assertive notion of "total strategy"—a concept increasingly dear to the hearts of South Africa's military, as we have seen—firmly on South Africa's political agenda. It was no longer the old-fashioned *realpolitik* of Vorster's *détente* approach to newly liberated neighbors, but instead the notion of a far more active reshaping of the key parameters of choice for those governments—Mozambique's not least among them—with whom any future dealings would have to be carried out. And, as hinted earlier, the importance to South African decision makers of Ronald Reagan's rise to power in the United States, with his own parallel set of aggressive premises about dealing with recalcitrant denizens of the Third World, also bears noting here.

Beyond this, we need only remind ourselves that it had been Botha, as minister of defence, and his cronies, rather than Prime Minister Vorster, who had shown the most active interest in Flower's destabilization scenario back in 1971. It is not too surprising then that in the late 1970s, according to Flower's own account, the Botha team, now ensconced in power, showed much greater interest than its predecessors in Rhodesia's Mozambique operation. The evidence also suggests that the new Botha government began to give that operation much more concrete support. Certainly, as Rhodesia slipped away, South Africa was to prove itself quite willing to adopt the Mozambican counterrevolutionary guerrilla as its own: "a C-130 airplane from the South African air force flew to the base of Grand Reef, near Mutare, only one week before Zimbabwean independence, to take back to Voortrekeroptke in Pretoria the men whom we had used against Mozambique," says Flower.[31] Cristina was once again the link-man, Hanlon notes, selling the Dhlakama faction of MNR (the faction that had, in any case, won the recent shoot-out within that movement) to the South Africans as the cutting edge of further destabilization. The MNR—which had been " on the road to total destruction," as Dhlakama himself was subsequently to state—was back in business.

The fact that South African sponsorship was now crucial to the fortunes of the MNR quickly became an open secret. As the (London) *Economist* summarized the new situation in a 1983 special issue on "Destabilizing Southern Africa":

> the MNR directorate was flown south to Pretoria, lock, stock and barrel. It was established first at the Phalaborwa military base in northern Transvaal and its commander, Alfonso Dhlakama, was openly welcomed by General Malan. Since then, it has emerged as a major guerilla force some 10,000 strong. It is financed and armed by the SADF and given logistical support in the form of training, command and control equipment, helicopter transport and special operations. Its radio, the Voice of Free Africa, broadcasts regularly into Mozambique from South African soil.[32]

Even the U.S. State Department was prepared, in early 1983, to issue a statement acknowledging that the MNR "receives the bulk of its support from South Africa."[33] Of course, the South Africans continued to deny such obvious realities, although the truth did poke its way through in various of its hypotheses. Thus, in 1982, a Pretoria spokesman warned that "if the neighboring states continue to harbour anti-South African forces, they should not be surprised if South Africa considers doing the same for them."[34] The minister of defence, General Malan, spoke even more directly in early 1983, suggesting that South Africa would fight against its enemies "even if it means we will have to support anti-communist movements...and allow them to act from our territory."[35] However, it was not until mid-1985 that Foreign Minister Pik Botha would admit in parliament that there was "naturally" a time when South Africa had aided the MNR and that it would do so again "in similar circumstances"—this statement in turn prompting Colin Eglin to accuse Botha and his government of "making a 'farce' of parliament by making the admission after years of denying opposition charges that South Africa was destabilizing its neighbors."[36] The Nkomati Accord had brought an end to all this in any case, Botha responded. In the event, only a few months later Botha had to make even more damaging admissions concerning the extent of South Africa's continuing support for the MNR *long after* the signing of the accord.

It is important to underscore the extent to which South Africa began effectively—and far more aggressively than the Rhodesians—to link MNR incursions to its overall strategy of undermining the Mozambican economy. The latter goal has long been evident in South African policies.

(Although the MNR remains South Africa's preferred means of exerting direct physical force on Mozambique, it should be remembered that Pretoria has also been prepared, on numerous dramatic occasions, to intervene more directly: the January 1981 raid on Maputo that left twelve dead, for example, the May 1983 raid, nineteen dead, and the parcel bomb that killed Ruth First.) Thus an important report prepared by the Mozambique government in January 1984, in order to specify to creditors the reasons for its parlous economic state, documented the manner in which "the apartheid state since the independence of Mozambique implemented a global strategy of reduction of its economic and commercial relations."[37] The report cited, among other things, the reduction of traffic of goods through Maputo's port, the reduction in the number of Mozambicans working in South Africa's mines, and the unilateral change in the terms of payment of these workers (to the detriment of Mozambique's balance of payments). Now, in addition, military targets were to be chosen, with considerable sophistication, in terms of the extent of the damage that could be inflicted on Mozambican (and SADCC) development.

The pattern of MNR activities would itself provide sufficient evidence of this, but MNR documents captured at their Garagua base in December 1981 reinforced the point that careful planning was involved. Thus notes from meetings held in October and November revealed not only Dhlakama's fawning attitude toward his South African contact (variously referred to as "Colonel Charlie" and "Colonel Van Niekerk"), but also the nature of the chain of command, with Colonel Charlie presenting Dhlakama with the "list of targets for the MNR's 1981 campaign. These included the Beira-Umtali pipeline, the railways linking Zimbabwe to Mozambique's ports, and the roads in the center of the country. The border areas of Zimbabwe had lost their previous importance, and the stress was now on disrupting the economies of both Mozambique and Zimbabwe by hitting at their most vulnerable point, their communications."[38] Constantino Reis has testified that this continued to be the pattern of South African-MNR relations during his period with the MNR in 1983:

> Asked about other work he did besides broadcasting, Reis said he "worked on files that Cristina had in his office at the camp and I also did some translations for him. It was from documents in these files that I understood better that nothing was done without orders from the South Africans." And they often overruled Cristina and Dhlakama. "For example, the South Africans decided that the armed bandits had to attack the Beira-Zimbabwe pipeline and the railway from Beira to Malawi. Cristina and Dhlakama didn't want to do this because they were afraid of

losing a lot of men and because it would only benefit the South African economy. But they had to attack, they had to sign the orders."[39]

Of course, in the case of the more complex sabotage actions the South Africans were even more directly involved: the blowing up of the road and rail bridges over the Pungwe, the railway operation that cost South African Defence Force lieutenant Alan Gingles his life (by his own bomb) deep inside Mozambique, the destruction of the marker buoys in Beira harbour (carried out, almost certainly, by South African frogmen). But, as hinted earlier, the South Africans were also slowly but surely pointing the MNR toward more modest but, cumulatively, even more devastating targets—in effect, the entire infrastructure of Mozambique's development effort in terms of physical plant, social and economic institutions and linkages, and human resources. The precise extent of the damage done in this way is impossible to quantify, although anecdotal evidence does begin to suggest both the low cunning and absolute ruthlessness, in terms of realizing the long-term goal of destabilization, of South African-cum-MNR actions. There were the firing, on the very eve of one province's marketing season, of a garage containing a fleet of trucks (relatively few in number but painstakingly readied for the purpose), the lightening attack on a sugar factory that permitted the destruction of precisely those machine parts that would prove the most difficult to replace, the identification and calculated murder, in innumerable villages, of the few people—generally speaking, all those with modern skills—linked to the central structures of party and state, the cruel harassment of activities to relieve drought-stricken areas of the country, which undoubtedly multiplied the number who perished. But perhaps Samora Machel's words, presented as part of the explanation for Mozambique's signing of the Nkomati Accord, best capture something of the overall impact of South Africa's war of destabilization (this despite the fact that the figures he cited are by now, unfortunately, understatements of the damage done):

Our people had their property looted, their houses destroyed, their granaries looted, their crops pillaged and flattened, their cattle stolen and killed, their tools burnt and destroyed. The communal villages and cooperatives, the schools and clinics, the wells and dams built by the people with so much effort and sacrifice became targets for the enemy's criminal fury. The systematic destruction of economic infrastructure, bridges and roads, shops and warehouses, sawmills, plantations, agricultural and industrial machinery, electricity supply lines, fuel tanks, lorries and buses, locomotives and carriages has prevented the implementation of economic development projects of the utmost importance for the well being of the Mozambican people.

840 schools have been destroyed or closed, affecting more than 150,000 schoolchildren. Twelve health posts, 24 maternity clinics, 174 health posts and two centers for the physically handicapped have been sacked and destroyed. 900 shops have been destroyed, hampering marketing and supplies for about four and a half million citizens.

The bandits have murdered and kidnapped peasants and members of cooperatives, parliamentary deputies and Party militants, teachers and students, nurses, lorry drivers, engine drivers, agricultural, construction and commercial workers, technicians in various sectors, nuns, priests, private shopkeepers, journalists and civil servants. This is the enemy's cruel nature—kill everything, steal everything, burn everything.[40]

Yet even the above quotation does not quite capture the extent to which South Africa's war of aggression has been waged not merely against the Mozambican populace itself (the peasantry in particular). Here, too, the shift from Rhodesian to South African sponsorship appears to have been of some importance. Thus, in the early days, the MNR had made some small attempt to legitimate its activities in the eyes of local populations—albeit by appealing, first and foremost, to tribal and subtribal resentments and to quasi-traditional superstitions and fetishisms. Under South African tutelage, these latter methods did not disappear altogether. Nor did the occasional effort to airbrush MNR activities with a patina of anticommunist and—laying an altogether illegitimate claim to the mantle of Eduardo Mondlane—anti-Machel rhetoric. Yet, as noted above, what has been most marked about MNR activities has been its terrorist methods, involving, as virtually all observers of the war agree, an almost unimaginably savage brutalization of local populations. The cost of this kind of activity to Mozambique's future is incalculable; elsewhere in the speech quoted from above Samora Machel speaks of the "severe wounds" thus inflicted:Only future generations will show the precise extent of the social trauma caused by the horrors and barbarity of the armed gangs. The children who witnessed atrocities and repugnant acts of violence and destruction will grow up with the nightmare of their tragic memories. Men and women have been permanently mutilated and maimed, both physically and psychologically. They will be living evidence of the cruelty of the war waged against us.[41]

We have suggested reasons why a movement like the MNR might be reluctant to tackle Frelimo head-on in political terms. But even then it may seem a bit surprising that it has not, especially given the difficult times through which Mozambique has been passing. After all, as we have seen in the previous section, Frelimo's own policy failures have made some contribution to the situation in which the regime finds itself. In the economic realm, it seems clear that, by concentrating on big projects, state farms and the like, the Frelimo did far too little to service and activate the peasant economy. Moreover, without being notably repressive, Frelimo's political structures, particularly at the base, became less liberating and less stimulative of the release of popular energies than might have been anticipated in light of the movement's formative experience of "people's war" against the Portuguese. No doubt these realities, in and of themselves, helped to eclipse some of the popular enthusiasm that had accompanied the movement into power.

Yet, as we have argued, Frelimo's revolutionary leadership has, by and large, remained "true" and therefore cannot easily be made to seem illegitimate. In consequence, the MNR and its sponsors have accepted that, under the circumstances, the most they can hope for would be further to demobilize the population—economically, but also in terms of that population's confidence in the ability of the Frelimo government to act effectively in its defense. Thus, even if no alternative project to that offered by Frelimo were to be established, this particularly gross and cynical form of destabilization could become a check to Frelimo's recovering its equilibrium. What is the result of South Africa's success in this regard? It is a downward spiral of economic decay and social distemper in Mozambique that has profoundly shaken the Frelimo government's fragile structures and unleashed anarchic forces of truly disturbing proportions. As one academic observer close to the South African defense establishment could write coolly in the immediate aftermath of the signing of the Nkomati Accord, "SA's hawkish strategy towards its neighbors has had the intended effect of producing or aggravating domestic instability in the target states!"[42]

This is probably one reason why the war remained so relatively invisible for an extended period: the key to success for the South Africans was less a question of dramatic military gains of their own than the slow attrition—and the gradually compounded vulnerability—of the Mozambican state itself. It is, of course, true that many young Mozambicans have been recruited to sell the initial core group of the MNR described above. Interviews with captured MNR members and defectors from the organization indicate that this recruitment is often carried out by kidnapping villagers and involving them in terrorist acts, thus giving them little possibility of a retreat from bandit life. Others were recruited in Swaziland or South Africa where they sought work (and often after their initial arrest, at which point the choice offered them was jail or the MNR). With the downward spiral of the Mozambican economy, the counterrevolutionary-cum-bandit life may also have begun to seem a "job option" for some young Mozambicans, the MNR thus feeding on the results of its own destructiveness. Occasionally, too, specific actions taken by Frelimo may have helped produce some recruits. This has been said, for example, of the 1983 "Operation Production," which deported "surplus populations" from Maputo's urban areas to remote Niassa Province, and also of the policy of "villagization" in some parts of Nampula Province around the same period. Nonetheless, it seems clear that the MNR could not have grown or sustained itself without South Africa's continuing stewardship. And, to repeat, the absence of a project of popular mobilization remains a marked feature of the MNR noted by virtually all observers.

The signing of the Nkomati Accord bound South Africa, in principle, to wind down support for the MNR. It is now clear that this was not done. For one thing, South Africa had actually set itself the task of beefing up the MNR in the period immediately prior to the signing, sending fresh men across into Mozambique as well as some six months' supply of ammunition and material. Far from MNR activity slowing down, therefore, it actually began to intensify, most notably in Maputo Province, the most southerly and most proximate to South Africa of the country's ten provinces. True, with the coming into effect of the accord, the South Africans did take some actions, such as shutting down the MNR transmitter in the Transvaal. But from very early on, Mozambique complained that, on the bilateral Joint Security Commission formed to monitor implementation of the accord, South Africa was tight-lipped about what was being done regarding the "armed bandits" still garrisoned in their territory; soon, too, it was evident that fresh men and material were entering Mozambique from South Africa. Small wonder that before the year was out, Samora Machel could accuse the South Africans in no uncertain terms of ignoring the accord: "We are not fooled. The key to the problem of terrorism lies with South Africa. That is why we signed the Nkomati Accord with them." The South African government, he said, continued to "sustain, develop, equip, infiltrate and supply" the rebels.[43]

Needless to say, South Africa rejected such charges and attempted to cover its tracks. But up to the present, "armed banditry" has continued to spread to virtually every province, retaining most of its by now familiar shape and substance of economic disruption and rural terror. It seems probable, too, that in some areas the wasting effects of the war have begun to have greater impact on popular loyalties, not so much in earning the MNR a popular base as in helping to neutralize, in a kind of political limbo, at least some of the members of a tried and drained citizenry. It will be readily apparent that, to the extent this is the case, one important goal of the enemies of the Mozambican revolution will have begun to be realized. As I noted, after a visit to Nicaragua, of a roughly comparable process there,

>...the result...does begin to approximate that achieved by the South
>Africans in Mozambique, even if the process has not gone nearly so far:

an economy in tatters, with lack of foreign exchange, a severe constraint, a goods shortage, rising prices. Needless to say, these and other developments hit the proverbial "man [and woman] in the street" pretty hard....Even when they could see the American-cum-contra role in all of this, some people grumbled—not going over to the other side, it seemed, but a little less wholeheartedly enthusiastic about the revolution than before. Some of the blame for economic crisis must stick to socialism, so the Americans apparently calculate. Who'll dare to raise their heads for another fifty years after we get through, who'll dare to dream: this too seems part of the calculation.[44]

Soon fresh evidence was to document graphically the continuing centrality of South Africa to the MNR's activities—in spite of the signing of the Nkomati Accord. This fact was documented more clearly than ever after the fall of "Casa Banana." Of course, as stated, South Africa's continuing entanglements with the MNR had all along been an open secret, given the men and arms that continued to flow into Mozambique, the extensive violations of Mozambican air space that were monitored, and the exposés of such practices as police empressment (inside South Africa) of Mozambicans into the MNR.[45] But documents captured at Casa Banana showed an even more broad-gauged pattern of post-Nkomati support than perhaps had been suspected. They provided substantial further evidence of those actions taken by South Africa to strengthen the MNR inside Mozambique just prior to the signing and evidence, as well, that South African arms supplies saved the MNR from almost certain defeat in the *second half* of 1984.[46]

Confronted with this evidence, Pik Botha, South Africa's foreign minister, had no alternative but to admit, before a press conference, to most of the charges arising from the documents: that South Africa had been supplying the MNR (though most often, he claimed, with "humanitarian" materials), had built an airstrip for the movement inside Mozambique, had transported MNR chiefs in and out of Mozambique by submarine, had maintained regular radio contact between the MNR and the South African army, and even arranged a series of visits to Gorongosa by senior South African military officers *and* by Louis Nel, South Africa's deputy foreign minister. Grotesquely enough, after these admissions, he claimed such violations of Nkomati to be merely "technical." Many observers of the Mozambican situation had warned at the time of Nkomati that, even were South Africa to lift its support of the MNR, disruption might have continued for some time because of the conditions of social anarchy South Africa had seen fit to create in many parts of the country and because of the widespread distribution of arms that had occurred. Many of the "armed bandits" (in the Mozambican government's characterization of the counterrevolutionary guerrillas) might have been expected to carry on, free-lance fashion, with their banditry even if no longer very much coordinated as a counterrevolutionary force.

But it was now more apparent than ever that the South Africans had, in any case, little intention of withdrawing their support. If anything, they have merely increased the pressure, as witness continuing evidence of airspace violations and the stepping up of MNR incursions via South Africa's client state Malawi; consider, for example, "the events of September/October [1986] when the spectre of a Mozambique cut into tow and apartheid on Tanzania's doorstep seemed a real possibility. September brought a massive influx of people from Malawi, with some 8,000 MNR forces flooded into Zambezia and Tete, arriving in trucks and cars. They included Mozambicans taken into Malawi and others flown from South Africa for infiltration into Malawi and others. There were very big military operations, some including white commanders, and a series of district capitals fell. Quelimane, the capital of Zambezia was the target, and the invading forces came very close to reaching their goal."[47]

Although this invasion has slowly been beaten back in recent months (with Zimbabwean and Tanzanian assistance), it is small wonder that Frelimo leaders have come to speak of a "new phase of regional aggression" and noted the return in South Africa to the "total onslaught" rhetoric of the pre-Nkomati period. A threat to send back the full complement of Mozambican miners from South Africa, with the range of devastating implications this would have for the Mozambican economy, meshed neatly with these other, latest destabilizing moves and indeed has prompted observers to raise fresh questions as to just what South African war aims do indeed lie behind its approach to Mozambique. But if not the overthrow of Frelimo, certainly the sustaining of a counterdevelopment strategy designed to do as much as possible to neutralize Mozambique as a progressive actor in the region remained very high on Pretoria's agenda—and with effects that, for Mozambique, have continued to be devastating.

Survival Strategy

For Mozambique, then, the situation has continued to get worse rather than better. When, in early 1987, a Canadian fact-finding team (including a prominent Conservative member of parliament) visited Mozambique, it confirmed the grisly balance sheet on Mozambique's first independence decade sketched above.

> We found a situation in which almost four of the fourteen million children and women and men populating Mozambique are in imminent

danger of starvation—a tragedy of Ethiopian proportions. We found more than 42 percent of the population on the move, forced to abandon fields and homes by the massive bandit activities throughout the rural areas. In every province, the provincial and district capitals are swollen with refugees. More than 250,000 have fled to neighboring countries. The under-five mortality rate which had decreased by 20 percent between 1975 and 1980, thanks to the solid health programs of the new Frelimo government, has actually increased from 270 per thousand in 1980 to 375 per thousand in 1987. One in every three children now dies before the age of five. Forty-two percent (484) of the total health posts have been destroyed since 1982.

The team also echoed the explanation that this chapter has sought to document, "apartheid as the principal factor in Mozambique's present state of emergency."

Whether through direct military involvement, through its surrogate, the MNR, through economic destabilization, or through disinformation campaigns, South Africa is systematically engaged in a wrecking operation in Mozambique. Whatever the impact of historic underdevelopment, drought, the international economic crisis or policy errors in causing this situation, all these pale into insignificance against the systematic destruction and terror being perpetrated by the apartheid regime.[48]

Viewed in more general terms, Mozambique's case suggests just how well the tactic of the counterrevolutionary guerrilla can be made to work and just how likely it is that we will see similar scenarios being played out by imperialist planners against other Third World attempts at Marxist-cum-socialist creativity in the future. For Mozambicans one grim lesson is clear: their own fate depends upon the efforts of the South African people to drag down the apartheid monster from within. Only when that happens will Mozambique really be freed from what we have now seen to be the most serious obstacle to realization of its development aspirations. In advance of the fall of apartheid and racial capitalism in South Africa, however, the Mozambican people must struggle primarily to survive, while also hoping to safeguard whatever they can of the socialist goals they have established for themselves. The planning of this struggle for survival has manifested itself in three spheres that we can look at briefly, in turn, in concluding this chapter: the diplomatic, the economic, and the political-military.

Mozambique's diplomatic strategy—involving measured adjustments to the realities of global and regional power—was most clearly exemplified in the Nkomati Accord itself. This "nonaggression pact" was signed, with much fanfare, by South Africa and Mozambique in March

1984. It is indicative of how easily South Africa has been able, internationally, to get away with its policy of naked aggression against its neighbors that the first time many North Americans knew there was a war going on was when "peace" was declared! On the positive side, South Africa was now, for the first time, to acknowledge its responsibility for the MNR's activities. Frelimo leaders even claimed the accord as a victory because South Africa had failed to overthrow their regime.

> [South Africa's] objective was to overthrow the socialist and progressive systems of the region. In relation to our country, the objective was also to destroy our people's revolutionary state. The objective was to destroy the alternative civilization Mozambique represents....[But] the policy of regional destabilization did not have the desired effect. South Africa did not achieve the political objectives for which it launched the war....[I]t has failed to achieve armed victory....With the signing of the Accord of Nkomati, the main project, the destruction of our state, failed. In signing the Accord of Nkomati we guaranteed the objective of our fight—peace.[49]

Victory? It is true that when "peace talks" began in late 1982, South Africa wanted far more substantial concessions from Mozambique then were eventually included in the treaty. Yet, as we have seen, there is room for debate as to whether South Africa really desired outright destruction of the Mozambican state. Add to this the fact that South Africa was to do little enough, even in the short run, to call off its "dogs of war." Meanwhile, for its part, Mozambique was left with little alternative but to constrain severely the activities of the ANC on its soil (activities which, however, had never included the presence of military bases). Mozambique also appeared ready to open itself up to further economic integration with South Africa. Given these latter facts it was difficult even for many sympathizers not to feel that Frelimo would have been far better advised to refrain from claiming victory at Nkomati and to adopt instead the tone of Julius Nyerere:

> We think [the Nkomati Accord] is a humiliation. We don't want any more Nkomatis. It is the success of the South African policy of destabilizing the front-line states and it is assisted in this by the USA. And it is proper that we view it completely frankly. It is a defeat on our part. We understand *why* Mozambique had to look for some accommodation at Nkomati—but they haven't even got the minimum they thought they would get out of it. But we *understand* why they did it, because there was a promise that South Africa might stop supporting the MNR and Mozambique decided they needed peace to start new development in their country.[50]

Certainly such a tone might have been more comprehensible to Mozambique's supporters abroad—and less likely to raise false hopes at home. Moreover, some senior Frelimo leaders do admit that there was a certain amount of pride involved in the way they chose to present things. But they also argue that the pomp, ceremony, and publicity that made so many outsiders uneasy about Nkomati at the time served another purpose: by making the war visible and by so attaching South Africa to the "peace," the accord could serve as some established point of reference against which further to expose South African aggression. Indeed, the Mozambicans go further, stating, with some apparent justification, that there was reason to fear South Africa's actually intensifying its aggression by modifying its form, possibly to the point of intervening directly by air and on the ground in Mozambique, as in Angola. Nkomati, they suggest, made it far more difficult for the South Africans to be seen to do so.

These latter points do make sense, although many will feel that we are not talking about "victory" here but, as suggested, survival strategy.[51] Moreover, the underlying logic of this survival strategy lay even deeper, suggesting that, in fact, central to the the calculations of the Mozambican leadership was the premise—the gamble—that South Africa (and the Western capitalist camp more generally) might not necessarily be bent on the total overthrow of the Frelimo government after all. Perhaps, it was argued, South Africa sought merely to weaken Mozambique sufficiently, economically and politically, as to place it in a weaker bargaining position vis-à-vis international capital and the South African state. With scant room to maneuver, the Mozambicans felt they had little alternative but to structure their strategy on the very knife's edge of the ambiguities they thought might exist within South Africa's destabilization project. The editors of *Southern Africa Report* summarized Frelimo's consequent approach thus:

> In the absence of alternative sources of support, whether in the Eastern bloc or elsewhere, Frelimo has felt compelled to play a complicated game on the international plane. Apparently Mozambique has wagered that in both South Africa and in the international capitalist world at large there is a division between one group of policy-makers who think they can now ensnare a severely weakened Frelimo in the toils of neo-colonialism and a second group who prefer to pursue the overthrow of the present government by means of brute force. Perhaps by making judicious concessions to the neo-colonizing group, reasons Frelimo, it can help strengthen the neo-colonizers' hand in policy-making vis-à-vis Mozambique. If so, such concessions as membership in the IMF and acceptance of U.S. food and South African investment could serve to ensure both economic and political survival and, with survival, the

necessary breathing space within which Mozambique can seek, in turn, to strengthen its long-term resistance to neo-colonialism.[52]

Critics have tended to caricature this strategic departure on Mozambique's part as being either hopelessly naive or a complete sellout. In contrast, my own discussions with senior Mozambicans have revealed a sophistication of analysis regarding their attempts to maneuver for breathing room on the international plane which might surprise many of these critics. Certainly the leaders I talked with (a group that included President Machel) presented a pretty full catalogue of the possible forces ranged against them, while also weighing quite coolly the odds for and against their complicated strategy of trying to play off neocolonizers against militarists in the South African (and broader imperial) camp. Opinions will differ as to the basis for South Africa's decision not to shift definitively from stick to carrot in its handling of Mozambique, of course. As one example, South Africa's Financial Mail speculates thatit has been suggested that SA's security agencies perceived far greater long-term gains in maintaining proxy pressure on Maputo to get rid of its pro-Soviet hardliners [sic] than the doubtful short-run economic advantages that would flow from Nkomati.[53]

It may be that South Africa's decision makers—as has also been the case on a number of domestic fronts—have had some difficulty in making up their minds as to just which strategy to follow, tending, in consequence, to oscillate between options. In truth, however—and, once again, as on the domestic front—there has remained a very strong pull toward use of the stick. Moreover, Pretoria has been reluctant (with reason) to trust that Frelimo has abandoned once and for all its socialist project and become ready for any easy cooptation, even if it is forced to acknowledge that Mozambique has scrupulously honored its side of the Nkomati bargain with respect to the ANC. In any event, Frelimo was soon to realize that South Africa would not rest content with its gains at Nkomati and would continue to press for more concessions; thus, at the time of the signing of the Pretoria Declaration of October 1984, when Frelimo accepted South Africa's request to offer an amnesty to the MNR, South Africa tried to transform this (in the words of one Frelimo leader) "into negotiations between the Mozambican government and the bandits." And, as seen in the previous section, there has remained the stark fact of continuing aggression.

Part of Mozambique's strategy has been, in turn, the attempt to go over the heads of the South Africans, directly to the United States and other Western countries. In fact, the U.S. establishment has itself seemed uncertain about how to deal with Mozambique. On the one hand, the MNR began to emerge in recent years, as one more darling of the international right wing, its representatives received with open arms at such conferences as the San Diego meeting of the World Anti-Communist League (September 1984) and the second meeting of the International Conference for Resistance in Occupied countries held in Paris (November 1984).[54] As one conservative think tank (the Heritage Foundation) argued the case:

> In 1984 the United States designed an economic assistance program for Mozambique that will supplement existing U.S. food assistance for this drought-stricken nation. In general, a coordinated approach is underway by Western nations and South Africa to wean the Mozambique government away from its Marxist heritage. It appears that President Samora Machel may be willing to abandon gradually much of his Marxist dogma and compromise with his political opponents. The U.S. should encourage this process.One of the principal reasons Machel may be willing to change is due to pressure against his regime by the Movement of National Resistance [MNR] in Mozambique....If, by early 1985, Machel is not decisively moving away from Marxism, then a clear alternative exists through support for MNR by the United States.[55]

Almost simultaneously, however, the voice of a more liberal capitalist approach could be heard from no less a figure than Melvin Laird, a former U.S. secretary of defense. Bucking the neoconservative offensive, he penned an op-ed piece on the subject in the *Washington Post* in which he called for an even more active "opening to Mozambique," a "balanced relationship that includes diplomatic contacts, private investment, trade, economic and humanitarian assistance and a modest military training and assistance program." As Laird elaborated the point: "I recognize there are those who argue the United States should have nothing to do with a self-styled Marxist state. I disagree. The only way we can advance U.S. strategic goals in the Third World is if we compete in relevant ways—on the ground, through our programs, our presence, our diplomacy. The United States should be ready to respond constructively to openings that advance our interests whenever they occur."[56]

Just where the Reagan administration has stood with respect to this policy divide over imperial strategy toward Mozambique is less clear. Some aid did come, albeit aid carefully crafted along lines that paralleled the suggestions of the Heritage Foundation.[57] Yet who was to say which other U.S. agencies might be involved in more shadowy undertakings? Certainly the Mozambicans, as cited earlier, have had their suspicions. In any case, when Samora Machel met with Ronald Reagan in Washington and with businessmen in Texas in September 1985, it was the delicate game of attempting to tilt the U.S. government in the direction of Laird's "liberal-imperialist" option that he came to play. Machel brought with him strong evidence (including the Casa Banana materials) of South Africa's continuing complicity with the MNR, despite Mozambique's compliance with the Nkomati Accord's main terms. Here was proof, he said, that South Africa has "continued to recruit, train, organize, finance, equip and give logistical support to the armed bandits in my country." There were polite noises heard from the Reagan team on these matters, and at least the president and his advisors have seemed prepared, to date, to grant Mozambique a much lower place on its international "hit list" than, say, Angola. But right-wing pressure also has continued to build; the Heritage Foundation, for example, had sufficiently made up its mind about Mozambique, by early 1987, to be actively lobbying (along with others of its ilk) both against all aid to Mozambique and for military assistance to the MNR. Indeed, a senior administration official could now describe Mozambique to David Ottaway as a "hot issue" within the Reagan camp. The level of U.S. aid to the Frelimo government has "steadily declined" under conservative pressure. And while David Ottaway would find that "most top State Department officials" continue to oppose support for the MNR, he also found that "some senior Pentagon officials and the Defense Intelligence Agency favor it"![58] In short, it remained less than clear just what type of response Mozambique could expect to get, in the longer run, from the United States government.

In light of our earlier analysis it bears underscoring just how the Mozambican question is posed for discussion, by all sides, in this U.S. policy debate. Virtually no mention is made of the means by which Mozambique has been bullied into its relative supine posture, of how it is that the country's will has been, if not broken, at least greatly sapped by the "low intensity warfare" of racist South Africa. In fact, it is the Mozambicans, not the South Africans, who must pass muster: are they non-Marxist enough, antiterrorist (read: anti-ANC) enough, distanced enough from contact with the Soviet Union? One of the few cards—other than brute force—that the South Africans have to play is precisely the card of anti-Marxism, antiterrorism, and anti-Sovietism, seeking thereby to shift, by sleight of hand, the onus of responsibility for conflict in Southern Africa away from the crisis of racial capitalism that actually spawns it. And the "Reagan doctrine"—by painting Third World revolutionary regimes as inherently conflictual, as representing (in Michael Klare's phrase) "terrorism, political turmoil and Soviet expansionism," and by seeking to make heroes of the most grisly of counterrevolutionaries—does grant South Africa space for maneuver in this respect.

What of economic survival? In an earlier section, Mozambique's bow toward the market place, both local and worldwide, was noted. Strong positive arguments have been made for such a Mozambican style of "New

Economic Policy," notably at Frelimo's Fourth Congress in 1983. In part a response to the severe limitations Frelimo had found inherent in Eastern Bloc economic assistance, this policy departure also sprang from a self-criticism of some of the party's own policies in the first postindependence years. In this context, it was felt to mark a step toward a more "feasible socialism." But, as was also hinted, one may wonder whether Mozambique would ever have felt compelled to move so strongly in this direction if its economy had not been so badly battered by South African-cum-imperialist assault. We can now see more clearly how much some of these "concessions" were also part of the diplomatic offensive designed to gain room for maneuver for Mozambique.

Moreover, as Mozambique's economy plunged further into disarray and bankruptcy, additional areas of choice threatened to be wrenched from the country's own hands. Particularly significant in this regard was the increasing subjection of Mozambique to IMF and World Bank formulas for the development priorities of those Third World countries that are driven, cap in hand, to these agencies. Insistence on a deepening of the free run of the market combined, in early 1987, with "a massive devaluation...with the exchange rate shifting from 40 meticais to the dollar to 200 meticais to the dollar. While urban wages increased 50 percent, prices have quadrupled or quintupled. Fees for medical services were being introduced and the progressive housing policies that had kept rents pegged to salaries were to shift to a policy establishing rents in relation to property values."[59] How much, many wondered aloud, of Mozambique's substantial advances in such fields as education and health would be left standing when the IMF got through? Yet, as the country's minister of cooperation told the above-mentioned Canadian fact-finding team, "Mozambique was left with little choice but to carry out these measures. Various Western governments had made clear that unless this package recommended by the IMF were accepted, they would freeze all flow of credits to Mozambique."[60]

Mozambican leaders are, of course, good enough Marxists to know that bearers of Western capitalism—insofar as they are prepared to accept the renewed post-Nkomati invitation to come into Mozambique—do so only because they are confident of their own long-term capacity to hollow out from within any continuing commitment to real socialist goals that the leaders may be seeking to retain. Perhaps Mark Wuyts, cited earlier, is correct in his hunch that Frelimo underestimates the difficulties of controlling the socioeconomic forces released by its compromises (the long-term impact of domestic class formation in the private sector, the possible suborning of a potential "state-class" in the making, and deepening international entanglements). Yet there is some solace in the fact that Frelimo leaders can speak quite frankly about such dangers to Mozambique's socialist project. Thus Foreign Minister Joaquim Chissano, in private conversation a year or so before his elevation to the presidency after the untimely death of Samora Machel, discussed the emphasis now being placed upon *privados* (private farmers) in state planning and also the implications of the fact that U.S. agricultural assistance was being tied to facilitating the private sector. In so doing, he stressed bluntly the eventual necessity of hastening the pace of forming peasant cooperatives in order to counter any consolidation of new and privileged classes in the rural areas. Most dramatic, perhaps, was the conscious manner in which another minister put the point to me when he admitted there does exist, inherent in Frelimo's present approach, the distinct danger of the movement waking up one day only to discover that *nos não somos nos* ("we are no longer ourselves")!

Needless to say, the most disturbing fact of all has been the absence of any real economic turnaround. However, recent visits to Mozambique have at least suggested other indications of a renewed rigor in the economic calculations of many of the country's economic planners. These calculations are now made within the framework of a new overall policy guideline, that of the *economia da guerra* (war economy). Not surprisingly, this guideline is very far removed from the high hopes for a renovated economic strategy that marked the Fourth Congress. But, even if the apparent imperatives of pragmatism and survival economics did seem sometimes to threaten a blurring of the socialist vision, it was clear that the current crisis has also served to bring Mozambican planning ever more firmly down to earth and to a confrontation with the *real* possibilities of production at the district and provincial levels under the very hard conditions, economic and logistical, that exist. While obviously focused on the immediate need to underwrite the war effort, such a trend may also be having the long-term effect of helping to make planning for economic development a less abstract and far more effective exercise in Mozambique than it has sometimes been in the past. Thus Maureen MacIntosh, after a careful analysis of recent Mozambican economic policies, shares the concern that Mozambique may now be placing excessive reliance on *deregulation* of the economy, a market strategy she is not convinced can "work" even in sheer production terms, especially under wartime conditions. But she also hails the government's simultaneous (and somewhat contradictory) attempt "to retain and strengthen its capacity to plan," especially insofar as this "involves a very substantial reorientation of the planning process" in terms of "decentralization and local control of economic policy"![61]

In short, Frelimo continues the struggle to find the key to economic survival. But this is not merely a matter of economic strategy. For, given the counterdevelopment thrust of South Africa's own strategy towards

Mozambique, there can be no real hope of economic advance without military advance—without, that is, the consolidation of an increasingly effective capacity to defend the integrity of the development process. Small wonder that even 1984, in the heyday of the Nkomati experiment, Mozambican Minister Jacinto Veloso could assert forcefully that "these negotiations with the South African government are not at all the principal factor in stopping violence and creating peace and stability." He continued, "I think there is no doubt that the main factor that will lead to the normalization of the life of our people is the military action on the ground by the Mozambican armed forces."[62] But there are also problems in this respect, for there does exist a vicious circle: if it is true that there can be little economic advance without military advance it is equally true that there can be little military advance without economic advance.

The hard reality is that every kind of military effort is constrained by the severe economic limits within which the Frelimo government is operating. Most visibly, the regular army is crippled by lack of the wherewithal to fight—not just arms and transport, but boots, uniforms canteens, and food. Eastern Bloc assistance has been of some importance, but unfortunately (and ironically, given the fetishization by conservatives in the United States of the "Soviet menace" in Mozambique) such assistance has been far from adequate. Indeed, it has proven to be no more of a key to breaking the foreign exchange and other roadblocks to military success than it has been in other spheres. Mozambique has found its best friends closer to home. It is the Zimbabwean army that has been of the most direct help—in the struggles that have surged around Casa Banana in recent years and in safeguarding, currently, the "Beira corridor," for example. And, in the present Zambezia counteroffensive, Tanzania has begun to emerge as an important military actor as well.[63]

Nonetheless, the bottom line of any attempt, by sheer force of military-political will, to break out of the vicious circle into which South Africa has sought to lock Mozambique must be the domestic war effort. In this area, after a slow start, some fresh advances also have begun to be made. There was a slow start because Frelimo had anticipated (not entirely unreasonably) a rather more conventional form of military attack from Rhodesia and South Africa, and not the rise of the counterrevolutionary guerrilla. In consequence, in the first postindependence years, Mozambique had moved rather far from the successful "people's army" format of the days of armed struggle against the Portuguese and toward a much more conventional military model. In contrast, current military advances have come when Frelimo has been able to discover some contemporary equivalent of that earlier rooting of the war effort in the exertions of the local populations themselves. Thus, in several provinces, the grouping of such populations into defensible villages and their organization into effective militias seems to be advancing. Even more innovative has been the development of military units intermediate between local militias and the army per se, units made up of local people but given a higher degree of military training than mere militia members; returned to their localities where they will have a particularly clear familial and economic stake in the war effort, these citizen soldiers continue to operate under army discipline, available for offensive action against the "armed bandits."

These and other steps toward a politicization of the war effort remain a key, then, locally. But this is also true nationally, and it is here that even some sympathetic critics have expressed most unease, in effect echoing misgivings about certain aspects of Frelimo's political practices noted earlier in this chapter. Thus Judith Marshall, drawing comparisons with the situation in Nicaragua, suggests that the degree of ventilation of the political arena remains a continuing problem. In terms of mobilization efforts, she found far too little "political work going on around economic questions. People confronting the food shortages in Maputo had little sense of an economic strategy at work. Neither the government's efforts to channel scarce resources in a rational and responsible way within the limits of a war economy nor Renamo's actions bent on systematic destruction are very visible in the media. Laudable policies existed, such as guaranteeing resources first to the army, setting higher prices for rural producers, channeling consumer goods to rural areas through the parastatal AGRICOM, and giving workers' canteens priority in the distribution of scarce items. They were presented piecemeal, however, with no implication of coherent strategy at work." Even more worrying was the fact that "the information policy on the war has been more often characterized by silence than by an attempt to create an informed, and to that extent, mobilized population....Mozambique showed a marked reticence to deal publicly and politically with the war. Attacks that had the entire country agog were often not mentioned by the national newspapers"![64]

It is not that a state of siege necessarily provides the context best suited to drawing out the alternative potential for further democratization, which is present in Frelimo's past practices and current ideology. Still, Marshall in her account also lays considerable emphasis on meetings—of the expanded Political Bureau and of the Organization of Mozambican Youth—in the months before Samora Machel's death, in which he was facilitating a very searching, open discussion of the very real weaknesses of the military and of what political and organizational steps might be necessary to set things right. Of course, the president's own death (in a plane crash under the most suspicious of circumstances) is itself a genuine setback for he was an extraordinary man by any standard.[65]

Perhaps we will never know the truth about those "circumstances" of his death. Accidents do happen, after all. Yet the fact that so many observers could immediately suspect the South Africans of having helped to engineer it is itself no accident. Such an act would be perfectly consistent with South Africa's brutal record of aggression, assassination, and destabilization. What is true, moreover, is that Machel would not have been in Zambia, from which country he was returning on the night of the fatal crash, if it were not once again to help rally the front-line states of Southern Africa against South Africa's latest threats. In any case, so much Mozambican blood is visible on South Africa's hands that the point is almost academic.

This, then, was a grievous setback. Yet what has been most remarkable about the postassassination period in Mozambique has been the manner in which the Frelimo leadership team has stood firm and the smoothness with which the transition to Joaquim Alberto Chissano's presidency has been realized. Ill-informed speculation about the existence of warring camps of "hard-liners" and "moderates" within Frelimo faded before the reality that at least the "true revolutionary leadership" term of the Mozambican equation remained in place and that *a luta continua.* "The struggle continues"—this is Frelimo's watchword, worn somewhat thin through repetition, but still true. Thus Chissano has embraced unequivocally the unwelcome necessity, in his words, to "continue with war in order to finish with war," to struggle for "the complete elimination of banditry," fully aware that the MNR's "banditry is an integral part of the regional destabilization carried out by the South African apartheid regime."

The challenge? Even as Frelimo works "to restore peace and tranquility to all citizens," it declared that it will "proceed with the recovery of our economy," linking the needs of the country's defense and the economy "so that the economy may support the war against the bandit gangs and so that the defense effort may create the necessary security for economic activity." And the goal? By this route, too, he emphasized, "we will reach socialism because all our people want socialism."[66] In short, some strength remains. The struggle does indeed continue to redeem the promise of Mozambique's revolution and its Marxist project.

Notes

1. Mozambique Information Agency (MIO), "President Machel Addresses the People's Assembly," *News Review* (27 April 1984).

2. I have transcribed and translated this statement from a tape in the possession of the late Aquino de Braganca, who conducted the interview and was kind enough to lend me the tape.

3. See, for example, the chapters on these various sectors in John S. Saul, ed., *A Difficult Road:* Judith Marshall on education, Carol Barker on health, Stephanie Urdang on women, and Barry Pinsky on "urban life."

4. Interview with Marcelino dos Santos (conducted by Joe Slovo), "Frelimo Faces the Future," *The African Communist*, 55 (1973).

5. For a general perspective on this issue, see my essay, "The Role of Ideology in the Transition to Socialism" in Richard R. Fagen, Carmen Diana Deere, and José Luis Coraggio, eds., *Transition and Development: Problems of Third World Socialism* (New York: Monthly Review Press, 1986); for a first-hand account of "ideological class struggle" in Mozambique, see John S. Saul, ed., *A Difficult Road*, Chapter 2, 136-147 (subsection entitled, "The Ideological Front").

6. John S. Saul, ed., ibid., 103.

7. Dan O'Meara, "Review" in *Labour, Capital and Society*, 18, 2 (November 1985): 452.

8. This hypothesis is advanced, to some extent, in Joseph Hanlon, *Mozambique: The Revolution Under Fire* (London: Zed Books, 1984).

9. Central Committee of Frelimo, *Out of Underdevelopment to Socialism* (Maputo: 1983), 71-72.

10. John S. Saul, ed., *A Difficult Road*, 101.

11. John S. Saul, ed., *A Difficult Road*, Chapter 2.

12. Ibid., where "the socialism of expanded reproduction" is contrasted with "primitive socialist accumulation" as an alternative model of economic development.

13. This is discussed in a particularly illuminating manner in Mark Wuyts, *Money and Planning for Socialist Transition: The Mozambican Experience* (unpublished thesis, the Open University, August 1986).

14. Compare, however, O'Meara, "Review," 452, who argues that "in my view, Saul has overestimated the rejuvenative impact of Frelimo's Fourth Congress on both economic policy and the political life of the country....I am more pessimistic about the prospects for Mozambican socialism than is Saul—though I hope desperately that he is right."

15. Wuyts, *Money and Planning*.

16. Otto Roesch, "Mozambique's Agricultural Crisis: A Second Look," *Southern Africa Report*, 2, 3 (December 1986). Roesch concludes, nonetheless, that "the Fourth Congress reforms represent a genuine attempt to correct past policy mistakes and to pursue a more balanced rural development strategy" and, interestingly, even suggests that "these reforms may well be viewed in Mozambique as a necessary tactical retreat, aimed at grounding future efforts to build a socialist rural economy on a firmer productive basis."

17. For a further specification of this point, see my essay, "Ideology in Africa: Decomposition and Recomposition" in Gwendolen M. Carter and Patrick O'Meara, eds., *African Independence: The First Twenty-Five Years* (Bloomington: Indiana University Press, 1985).

18. Michael Klare, "Low-Intensity Conflict: The New U.S. Strategic Doctrine," *The Nation* (28 December 1985/4 January 1986).

19. William I. Robinson and Kent Norsworthy, "Nicaragua: the Strategy of Counterrevolution," *Monthly Review*, 37, 7 (December 1985), where Waghelstein and Luttwak are also quoted.

20. Sara Miles, "The Real War: Low-Intensity Conflict in Central America," *NACLA Report on the Americas* 2 (April/May 1986): 34, where the CIA manual, *Psychological Operations in Guerilla Warfare* is also quoted; see, in addition, Tom Barry, *Low-Intensity Conflict: The New Battlefield in Central America* (Albuquerque: The Inter-Hemispheric Education Resource Center, 1986).

21. Ibid.

22. Ibid., 45.

23. Michael Valpy, "Strange War Saps Mozambique," *The Globe and Mail*, 3 June 1985, 11.

24. As quoted in Sean Gervasi, "Southern Africa: Dr. Crocker's Secret War" (paper delivered to the Socialist Scholars' Conference, New York, 20 April 1984).

25. Philip H. Frankel, *Pretoria's Praetorians: Civil-Military Relations in South Africa* (Cambridge: Cambridge University Press, 1984), 65.

26. Ibid., 46 ff.

27. This document is cited in detail in Alves Gomes, "'Operações especiais': As origens do banditismo na Africa austral" in *Tempo* (Maputo), 754 (24 March 1985).

28. Paul Fauvet and Alves Gomes, "The 'Mozambique National Resistance,'" in *Supplement to AIM Bulletin No. 69;* see also Fernando Semede and João Paulo Guerra, *Operação Africa: A conspiração antiafricana em Portugal* (Lisboa: Editorial Caminho, 1984). Fauvet and Gomes write that "Jardim had organized elite military units to fight against Frelimo, units consisting mainly of black troops, better paid than the regular army, and soon gaining an unenviable reputation for brutality and atrocities." Unfortunately, their "brutality and atrocities" were to continue under first Rhodesian, then South African, auspices.

29. Hanlon, *Mozambique: The Revolution*, 220.

30. See Gordon Winter, *Inside BOSS* (Harmondsworth: Penguin, 1981).

31. Quoted in Alves Gomes, "'Operações especiais,'" 33.

32. Simon Jenkins, "Destabilization in Southern Africa," *The Economist* (16 July 1983), 19.

33. Quoted in Hanlon, *Mozambique: The Revolution*, 224.

34. Quoted in Jenkins, "Destabilization," 19.

35. Ibid.

36. Cited in *Facts and Reports* (Amsterdam), 15, K (24 April 1985):9.

37. National Planning Commission, *Economic Report* (Maputo: National Planning Commission, January 1984), 30.

38. Fauvet and Gomes, "'Mozambique National Resistence,'" 8.

39. Mozambique Information Agency (AIM), "The MNR From Within," *Supplement to AIM Bulletin No. 102.*

40. Samora Machel, "Accord of Nkomati: A Victory for Peace," speech of April 1984, published as *Supplement to AIM Bulletin No. 94*, 8-9.

41. Ibid.

42. Quoted in Robert Davies and Dan O'Meara, "Total Strategy in Southern Africa: An Analysis of South African Regional Policy since 1978," *Journal of Southern African Studies,* 11, 2 (April 1985):203; this Davies-O'Meara essay is extremely valuable for providing a broader context within which to situate the Mozambican case.

43. Samora Machel in a speech in Dar es Salaam as quoted in *The Guardian,* 28 December 1984.

44. John S. Saul, "Nicaragua Under Fire," *Monthly Review,* 36, 10 (March 1985).

45. See Eric Marsden, "Mozambique Rebels 'Press-ganged' in South Africa," *Sunday Times,* 7 July 1985.

46. See MIO, *News Review,* 62 (27 April 1984), "Special Issue: Dossier: South African Violation of Nkomati Accord."

47. Judith Marshall, "Mozambique: Apartheid's Second Front," *Southern Africa Report,* 2, 5 (April 1987):18.

48. Ibid., 17; Marshall's article is an account of this "fact-finding" mission by one of the participants.

49. Samora Machel, "Accord of Nkomati...," 6, 7, 8.

50. Julius Nyerere, as quoted in *New African* (January 1985); note also the comment of Kenneth Kaunda of Zambia: "Yes, humble Swaziland agrees, humble Mozambique accepts, humble Zambia hosts meetings of unequal neighbors like South Africa and Angola. What else can we do? But we are not doing it with happy hearts. We do it out of fear, but that fear will end one day. It is bound to." (As quoted in Kenneth W. Grundy, "Pax Pretoriana: South Africa's Regional Policy," *Current History,* 84 [April 1985].)

51. MIO, "People's Assembly Ratifies Nkomati Accord," in *News Review,* 28 (27 April 1984). It is worth noting that some Mozambican leaders at the time of Nkomati did come close to viewing things in this light, even publicity. Witness then Foreign Minister Joaquim Chissano, who "criticized the 'ultra-left myopic revolutionaries' who objected to the agreement. 'They don't hesitate in asking us to die so they can applaud us as heroes,' he remarked caustically. Mozambique did not mind when the sacrifice was useful, as it had been during the independence war, 'but we ought to tell them that our people don't just die to win applause. They don't die so that statues can be built to them.' Mr. Chissano warned that, in itself, the agreement 'will not bring us happiness. It is not the Nkomati Accord that will eliminate hunger, or provide us with clothing.' What the Accord did was 'create conditions for our efforts in production to give better results.'"

52. In *Southern Africa Report,* 1, 1 (June 1985).

53. *The Financial Mail* (Johannesburg), 5 October 1984.

54. See, for example, the article "Southern Africa is Extreme Right's Target" in *Indian Ocean Newsletter* (Paris), 12 June 1985.

55. Heritage Foundation, *Mandate for Leadership II* (Washington, 1984), chapter on Africa by Jeffrey B. Gaynor, 357.

56. Melvin Laird, "Opening to Mozambique" in *The Washington Post* 17 June 1984.

57. See, for example, the useful article by Victoria Brittain entitled "Mozambique feels the pain of war", *The Guardian,* 1 August 1986, where she notes that "donors now frequently use their aid to try to enforce policy changes, say officials. The U.S., for instance, has put a large amount of high profile aid behind successful large private farmers—a symbolic contradiction of Frelimo's commitment to poor peasants."

58. David Ottaway, "Rightwingers Press Reagan to Back Mozambique Rebels," *Manchester Guardian Weekly,* 22 February 1987, originally printed in *The Washington Post.*

59. Marshall, "Mozambique: Apartheid's Second Front," 19-20.

60. Ibid., 20.

61. Maureen MacIntosh, "Economic Policy Context and Adjustment Options in Mozambique," *Development and Change,* 17, 3 (July 1986).

62. As quoted in MIO, News Review, 3B (5 October 1984).

63. News report from the Tanzanian *News Agency,* datelined Dar es Salaam, 7 May 1985. Note also in this regard the tone of the following statement: "Tanzanian President Julius Nyerere has said Tanzania would provide the rear base for a fresh war to liberate Mozambique and South Africa if the Pretoria maneuvers to overthrow the Frelimo government succeeded. The government-owned Daily News reported in a front page story that the [then] Tanzanian leader told party officials...that Tanzania would not sit back and watch South Africa topple the Mozambican government. 'Mozambique President Samora Machel will return to Nichingwea [in southern Tanzania] and the liberation war will start afresh,' the President declared. he said this time the onslaught would thoroughly involve Frelimo and the African National Congress [ANC] of South Africa and sweep right through to Capetown. 'We want our enemies, especially apartheid South Africa, to understand this: We won't allow the Frelimo government to be overthrown,' Nyerere said."

64. Judith Marshall, "Mozambique and Nicaragua: The Politics of Survival," *Southern Africa Report,* 2, 1 (June 1986):17, 19.

65. I have published an obituary in *Southern Africa Report,* 2, 3 (December 1986); an extremely moving account of Machel's funeral by Jennifer Davis ("The Funeral: 'A People Cannot Bid Farewell to Its Own History'") appears in the same issue.

66. As quoted in the editorial "A Luta Coninua" to *Southern Africa Report,* 2, 3 (December 1986).

chapter seven

The Political Economy of Development in Ethiopia

Dessalegn Rahmato

This chapter has a limited objective, namely to discuss the broad outlines of the developmental process in Ethiopia since the overthrow of Haile Selassie's absolute monarchy in 1974 and to briefly sketch the context within which this process has taken place. With the deposition of the monarchy, and the consolidation of military government in the mid-1970s, Ethiopia ceased to be a political anomaly in Africa. In the space of a few years, and largely as a result of a "revolution from above," its ancient form of state and its medieval class structure were swept away and replaced by the present provisional military government (the PMAC), a social structure excluding nobility and rural gentry, and a state-dominated economy. In this sense, Ethiopia's government and economy resemble those of Benin, Congo, and the lusophone countries that have been variously described as socialist, Afro-communist, or Afro-Marxist.

The Ethiopian experience regarding political and economic change raises a number of important issues that are difficult to reconcile with current theories of socialist transition. It is hoped that the analysis presented here, covering the decade 1974 to 1984, will serve to show that social change—socialist or otherwise—is far more complex than it is made out to be in the general debate on underdevelopment and socialist transition.

Abbreviations used in the text are explained at the end of this chapter.

The Process of Political Change in Ethiopia

The civil unrest that broke out in Addis Ababa in February 1974 (preceded in the previous month by mutinies in several military camps) was a manifestation of discontent among sections of urban Ethiopian society.[1] The unrest, which took the form of strikes, demonstrations, criticism of men in high office by the "underground press" and other acts of civil disobedience, involved a small portion of the country's population, and was mainly concentrated in the capital and a few major provincial towns. The main social elements that played an active part in the movement were civil servants (the bureaucratic petite bourgeoisie), workers in transport, municipal services and printing, religious groups (both Moslem and Coptic), teachers and students. The majority of workers in manufacturing were uninvolved, but these workers were not a significant force and their involvement would not have had a significant impact. On the other hand, the peasantry, potentially the most powerful class in the country, was also quiescent, except in a few areas in the south of the country where some peasants carried out acts of violence against selected landlords.

The protesters' demands were surprisingly mild and political: they called for administrative reform, the removal of higher officials alleged to be corrupt and unjust, for redress of individual grievances, and for improvements in wages and working conditions. If political issues were raised, they were raised by students and young, radical intellectuals. By the latter part of June, at the moment when the civil movement had virtually spent itself, a new political force appeared on the scene; this was the Coordinating Committee of the Armed Forces and the Police, later to be widely known as the Derg. From this point on, the center of opposition shifted from the civilian sector to the military, with the latter assuming uncontested responsibility for the struggle against the old regime.

The idea of overthrowing the monarchy, and instituting a military government was *not* part of the original plan of the Derg, which began to seriously consider such a step some eight weeks after it was formally established, toward the end of August 1974. All the evidence suggests that the coup of 12 September, which deposed the aging emperor and placed power in the hands of the Derg, was a precipitate act and not the outcome of a carefully thought-out plan or strategy.[2] It was the pressure of events set in motion, partly unwittingly by the Derg itself, and the momentum created by the ensuing political crisis that drove the military to remove Haile Selassie and take power for itself. Second, neither before the coup, nor for quite a while after, did the Derg articulate any social, economic, or political policies that indicated that its ideological orientation was anything other than nationalist.

The political history of the country during the last decade may be broken down into three major periods. Each period is significant because it reveals in one way or another the changes that took place in class relations, between the state and society, and in the political outlook of the Derg itself.[3]

The Populist Period: 1974-1975

This was a period of political euphoria, which at times was mixed with uneasiness and confusion and in which the men in power actively sought real popular support from all sectors of society. This was also the period of collective leadership: although the two vice-chairmen of the PMAC held effective power, the chairman (first General Aman, later General Tefferi Bante), not himself a member of the Derg, served as the ceremonial head of state, and a number of the officers shared power as heads of influential committees.

Soon after the coup, teams of Derg members began to travel around the country addressing crowds of peasants, laborers, and civil servants, explaining what was called the "philosophy of *Ethiopia Tikdem*," ("Ethiopia First") or the "philosophy of the revolution."

Although the official policy of the country was declared to be *hibrettesebawinet*, and although policy statements were couched in radical language, the Derg at this time was by no means socialist in the Marxist sense of the term. *Hibrettesebawinet* (which has erroneously been translated as "socialism," but really means "communalism") and *Ethiopia Tikdem* were said to be one and the same: both were described as involving equality, self-reliance, the dignity of labor, the supremacy of the common good, and the indivisibility of the nation. The bases of the new philosophy were:

1. The political philosophy should spring from the culture and soil of Ethiopia; and should, moreover, emanate from the aspirations of the broad masses; and not be imported from abroad like some decorative article of commerce.
2. It should be a philosophy that brings Ethiopia closer to those of her progressive neighbors committed to fairness and human justice, as well as to the broad masses of humanity.
3. It should finally be capable of providing effective solutions to our long-standing political and economic problems....The political philosophy which emanates from our great religions which teach the equality of man, and from our tradition of living and sharing together, as well as our history, so replete with national sacrifice, is *hibrettesebawinet*....[4]

This period is also interesting for the political experiments that were initiated and later abandoned. One such experiment was the establishment of the *memakirt shengo,* loosely meaning parliament, to which representatives continued to be elected in the provinces all through the first year of the revolution. There were no clear indications at this time that the military was contemplating sharing power with civilian bodies. On the other hand, the Derg continued to insist that it was not seeking to hold on to power and, that as soon as the people became capable of establishing a "genuinely popular" government, it would return to the barracks. General Tefferi Bante, in one of his early public speeches, underlined three essential tasks that the Derg hoped to fulfill before it returned to where it came from. These were: to organize the people into associated forms of life, and teach them the philosophy of communalism; to establish a political organization to lead and preserve the country's progressive movement; and to enable the people to establish a popular government (Addis Zemen, 28 Megabit 1967 E.C.).

Most, if not all, of the widely supported economic and social reforms of the military regime were adopted in the first year of the revolution. The nationalization of financial institutions, and of some seventy or so manufacturing and commercial enterprises took place in January and February of 1975. The legislation initiating land reform which was the most enthusiastically received reform measure of the PMC to date, was published in March 1975. This reform nationalized all rural land, abolished landlordism and tenancy, provided usufruct rights to all self-laboring peasants over land not exceeding ten hectares in size, and established peasant associations. Nearly half a million people in Addis Ababa alone turned out for a mammoth march and rally the day after the reform was announced; similar demonstrations of support, all spontaneous and heartfelt, took place in several cities in the provinces. Interestingly enough, the peasantry for whose benefit the reform was enacted remained passive and unmoved throughout this period. Land reform was followed, some four months later, by the nationalization of urban land and rental houses, which was also greeted with a good deal of popular approval. Earlier, the government had launched a national *zemacha,* a campaign in which more than 80 thousand students and teachers were deployed in the rural areas for the purpose of organizing and politicizing the peasantry.

All these reforms and new initiatives, which were strongly laced with populist flavor, were attempts by the military authorities to accomplish the following tasks: (1) eliminate all opposition to the new order of things; at this time the main threat to the regime was thought to come from the aristocracy and other landed elements; (2) gain legitimacy and consolidate power; (3) placate and win the support of the politically active elements in the urban areas, in particular students and the radical intelligentsia. The militant student movement of the 1960s and early 1970s, and the political ideas that it had popularized long before the military came to power served as the inspiration for the social reforms of the period.

The hope of the new authorities was that these far-reaching reforms would not only meet what was believed to be the general expectations of the majority of the people, but also usher in a period of stability and growth. However, the political climate soon turned sour, and civil unrest spread from the urban areas to the countryside.

The Period of Political Confrontations and the Struggle For Power: 1975-1977

This period marks the most decisive turning point in the history of military rule in Ethiopia. It was here that the very survival of the new regime, as well as the integrity of the country, was threatened by enemies from within and without, and the country was plunged into a series of acute social crises. While the Derg emerged from this bloody trial victorious, with its internal as well as external enemies either prostrate or in disarray, the experience, nevertheless, was to leave an indelible imprint on both state and society, and to determine the course of future events. In these two critical years, the Derg had to silence first the right, then the left opposition, to contend with a costly secessionist insurgency in the north, to defend the country (with Cuban and Soviet assistance) from a full-scale Somali invasion, and, through a series of bloody purges, to eliminate all dissenting elements from within its own ranks.

The right opposition seemed, at least in official thinking at the time, to pose the greatest threat to military government. It was believed that a serious counterrevolutionary offensive was imminent, and the contending forces, led by the landed classes, were thought to possess far more power and political influence than they actually did. The right opposition, however, was deeply fragmented, and consisted in the main of three elements: (1) Feeble resistance to the implementation of the land reform by small groups of rebels in the southern provinces. The men involved were frequently frightened into rebellion by the threatening propaganda carried on in the media at the time, which railed against unnamed "exploiters and saboteurs" and incited the people to take measures against them. This kind of instinctive reaction for self-defense occurred largely in southern Shoa and central Sidamo provinces. A few incidents of this type were also reported in Arssi and Wollega. This movement was quickly brought under control by local forces made up of peasants and law enforcement agents. (2) Armed action by rebels consisting of up to two hundred or more persons, and operating in traditional *shifta* (outlaw) fashion. These events took place in the highlands of northern Shoa, and in

Wollo province (in Lasta, Lalibella, and Borena *awrajas* or mid-level national administrative units). These opposition movements required the deployment of a sizeable unit of the armed forces and took longer to put down. In both this and the previous case, the rebel forces, made up for the most part of members of the local gentry, were poorly armed, poorly deployed, and were in no condition to withstand the countermeasures launched by their opponents. (3) A feeble attempt at modern-style insurgency by a group calling itself the Ethiopian Democratic Union (EDU), a group formed and based in the Sudan.

The high point of activity of the forces of the right occurred at the close of 1975. It was not until about the middle of 1976, however, that the resistance of the propertied classes—a resistance remarkable for its ineptitude and conventionality—came finally to an end. It is true that the EDU continued to be a nuisance, particularly in Tigre and Gonder provinces, nevertheless, the threat from the right, never serious in the first place, receded into history after the latter part of 1976.

The struggle against *the left opposition* was, unlike its counterpart, a more complicated and protracted affair, which on several occasions threatened to split apart the Derg itself. The left opposition was predominantly urban-based, while the right operated almost exclusively in the rural areas. We may include in this group all dissident activities ranging from those of students, teachers, trade unionists, individual publicists in the "underground press" (which continued to thrive up to the latter part of 1977), to those of the extremist organization known as the Ethiopian People's Revolutionary party (EPRP). One important factor that made the activities of these forces more complicated, and in the end brought on the self-destruction of the opposition, was that the struggle was not just against the military government, but also against other elements within the urban movement. The hostility of one sectarian group toward another was such that it soon led to bitter recrimination and bloodletting.

Although the fratricidal conflict within the urban opposition had ideological overtones, it will not be unfair to say that the real reasons behind it had to do with rivalry for power and influence among the groups, and fear, jealousy, and mistrust on the part of the individuals concerned. Toward the end of 1975, a group within the movement, which previously had been mildly critical of the military regime, decided to break ranks and come out in support of the government. It was rewarded for this action with several senior and middle-level posts in the bureaucracy, and given prominent representation in the body set up in early 1976 to provide ideological advice to the government. This group of political adventurers, known by its Amharic initials as MESN, bore the brunt of the terrorism launched by the extremist groups. In the end

MESN abruptly broke up, with many of its leaders going into hiding when it realized that the state no longer needed its support or services. The government announced this ignominious act of its erstwhile ally on 24 August 1977, a few days after the invading Somali forces had overrun most of the Ogaden.

The first major confrontation between the government and the forces of the urban opposition occurred at the beginning of October 1975, when the authorities, in a surprise overreaction, declared a state of emergency in response to a general strike called by the Confederation of Ethiopian Labor Unions (CELU), the country's trade union federation representing some 80,000 workers in industry and commerce. By 1976, the confrontation had reached a high level of intensity and precluded the possibility of a compromise or rapprochement. The escalating hostilities, which so far had mainly involved verbal ideological warfare, turned to violence, when in the latter part of 1976, some extremist elements began armed attacks against selected individuals. Interestingly enough, those picked out for assassination were not senior members of the military or of the government but rather individuals belonging to MESN, trade union leaders, officials of the newly established mass organizations, and petty functionaries known for their strong support of the Derg.

Violence bred more violence, and assassinations led to bloody countermeasures. The year 1977 should be called the Year of the Terror, for it was then that the dogs of war were let loose throughout the country. The feeble but irksome terror of EPRP was now answered by the massive terror of the state. It is beyond the scope of this chapter to provide an account of the terror and counterterror of this period; suffice to say that, by the beginning of 1978, the urban opposition had been thoroughly decimated, and the authority of the state was reasserted in the political-ideological field as well.

The importance of this period to the political evolution of the Derg cannot be overemphasized. It was in this period, in particular as a consequence of its confrontation with the urban opposition, that the state became more and more radical and began to adopt measures consciously chosen for their "socialist" content. The radicalization of the military state was in a sense a response, in the political-ideological realm, to the opposition of the subsequent struggle against the various elements of the left. It is, of course, impossible to point to a specific date, event, or policy decision as indicating the turning point in the government's political orientation, but it may be argued that the process of conversion, and the formal adoption of Marxism-Leninism as the state ideology was completed at about the end of 1976. The emergence of Colonel Mengistu as undisputed authority in the PMAC in March 1977 was to assure that socialist thinking would permeate all levels of government and all aspects of policy making.

Insurgency and war with Somalia. Secessionist insurgency in the north of the country was a legacy inherited from imperial rule. Of interest to us here is the response of the government to the sudden escalation of hostilities in Eritrea, and the increasing strength of the insurgents in 1976 and 1977.[5] This took the form of massive deployment of regular and paramilitary forces, the latter consisting of a poorly trained and armed peasant militia. Later, in the second half of 1977, the Somali invasion of the country, which was unexpected and for which the government was ill-prepared, elicited a similar response; something like 200,000 peasants were given short military training and sent to the battlefront in the Ogaden in the space of a few months. Both of these efforts stretched the country's economy, already shaken by several years of neglect and civil unrest, to its very limits.

The lasting legacy of insurgency and war in the period under discussion consisted of the following elements: (1) a vast increase in the country's military apparatus; (2) The new government's breaking the long-standing political ties between Ethiopia and the West, substituting them with ties with Soviet Bloc countries; (3) the Derg's gaining added confidence in its own ability to hold the country together in the face of acute political and military crises. From this point onward, the military authorities were to be encouraged in their view that they *were capable* of providing political leadership, and the old idea of the Derg's eventually returning to the barracks was given a quiet burial.

The struggle for power within the state. The fourth conjuncture shaping the political evolution of the state reached its peak of intensity toward the end of 1976, and the problem was finally resolved in February 1977.

The military men who formed the Derg came from diverse backgrounds and exhibited differences in training, experience, and exposure to the wider world. As a result, they held a wide variety of views on political and social issues. The exact number and composition of the Derg may be a matter of debate, but according to our own findings, summarized in the table below, the membership numbered about 106 men, and was numerically dominated by noncommissioned officers. On the other hand, middle-level officers, who constituted about one-third of the total, provide the leadership in all except a few instances.[6]

A body of this size and diversity could not be free from conflict and factional infighting. The disagreements that occurred *after* 1976 were quite critical for, with the greater politicization of the Derg at this time

Table 7.1   Composition of the Derg 1975–76

	High Officers	Middle-level	NCOs	Privates	Total
Number	5	38	58	5	106
Percent	5	36	55	5	100

Source: Tallied from *Addis Zemen* reports of roving Derg teams in the provinces.

Note: High officers: those who were lieutenant-colonels and above.
Middle-level officers: lieutenants up to majors.

and the greater infusion of radical thought within the membership, differences now became more ideological than previously. An attempt to diffuse the growing tension was made at the end of 1976 with the enactment of legislation defining the powers and responsibilities of PMAC members, and reorganizing working procedures in the ruling body (Proclamation No. 108, 29 December 1976). This, however, further exacerbated the conflict; indeed, it was this attempt that precipitated the final showdown in early 1977 in which Colonel Mengistu emerged victorious. In this dramatic confrontation (3 February 1977), General Tefferi Bante, along with seven senior members of the Derg were killed. The execution of the vice-chairman of the PMAC, Colonel Atnafu, later in November 1977, was the last act of a mopping-up operation that swept the forces of the "right" from the ruling body.

The victory of Colonel Mengistu, who now assumed chairmanship of the Derg, was hailed as a victory for the forces of the left within the state. The main task was now seen as strengthening the powers of the PMAC, and building a political following loyal to it within the framework of Marxist-Leninist ideology. The state now emerged unambiguously committed to socialism, and more closely tied to the Soviet Union and its allies. .

The Period of Consolidation of Power and
Institutionalization of Socialist Reforms: 1978 and After
The political unrest and civil conflict that were so much a part of the earlier period came now to an end, at least in the urban areas and the central parts of the country. This period is one of steady consolidation of power, accomplished largely through legislation and administrative reform, and greater institutionalization of the revolution. The major effort of the state was directed to creating or strengthening the institutional mechanisms for political reform and policy implementation. Existing, or newly created mass organizations, involving trade unions, peasants, youth, and women, as well as urban neighborhood associations (known as *kebeles*), were more elaborately structured and were closely

integrated into the machinery of the state.

The emerging polity revealed certain characteristics that are also to be found, as a kind of universal landmark, in all countries traveling along the socialist road. First, with the greater consolidation of power came also the greater expansion of the machinery of the state. This was not merely a result of the assumption by the state of social and economic functions previously carried out by private bodies, but was brought on by a process of accretion. New tasks and new structures continued to be created all through this period. Second, the period witnessed a greater centralization of the decision-making apparatus. By the beginning of the 1980s, "centralism" became a key slogan both in the media and in official statements.

But there was one major political anomaly that continued to plague the leadership: here was a socialist state without a socialist party. Allies overseas and supporters within the country would both remain uncertain of the prospects for the revolution until this problem was resolved. The government, however, had continually stressed that the socialist transition would not be completed without a Marxist-Leninist party, but it was not until 1984 that such a party was finally established.

The attempt by the authorities to form a political organization may be traced to February 1977, when official sanction was given to five disparate political groupings to form an alliance. This organization, known as the Union of Ethiopian Marxist-Leninist Organizations, chose to remain an underground organization for reasons that many found impossible to comprehend, and the state thus found itself in the bizarre position of nurturing a clandestine political body. The anomaly was finally resolved by disbanding the union, and creating a formal body charged with founding the party (named COPWE) in December 1979. COPWE, which virtually operated like a party, soon extended itself far and wide, and by the time it gave way to the Ethiopian *Senategnoch* party (ESP) in September 1984, a formal party structure was already in place down to the *woreda* (lowest national administrative unit) level.[7]

The Process of Economic Change

A recent study of the process of development in Ethiopia tried to argue, quite unconvincingly in our opinion, that the country's economy should not really be called a "command" economy.[8] A look at the structure of the economy is sufficient to dispel any notions that we are dealing with a mixed or free economy. Virtually all medium and large-scale manufacturing, all large-scale trade and service enterprises, and all financial institutions are under state control. The private sector consists of a large number of very small-scale manufacturing, cottage enterprises, and petty trade, most of which, however, depend on the state-run distribution network as well as state industry for their raw materials and inputs. The rural sector is, of course, dominated by independent peasant production; however, state agriculture continues to swallow up a vastly disproportionate part of government expenditure on agricultural development. Additionally, greater effort is being made to bring the peasant economy under state control through government procurement of grain, fixed grain prices, and state control of modern inputs needed by the peasantry. Although not fully effective, a central planning apparatus has been set up, and the state sector, as well as a considerable proportion of the private sector, is controlled through this apparatus.

Since 1974, the state's predominance in the economy has been enlarged in all sectors. By extending the frontiers of public ownership far and wide and dislodging private enterprise from all areas except small-scale production and petty trade, the military government has succeeded in establishing what may be termed a full-fledged *state economy*. The previous economic system, it should be noted, was also dominated by the state, (as we have tried to show elsewhere) but the critical difference now is that, while this is a state-centered economy, its predecessor was an open economy in which the state played a disproportionately large role.[9]

The New Economic System
It may be useful to start with a brief discussion of the policy framework for the new economic system, and the justification for the choice of this particular path of development. The basic theoretical argument stresses that prerevolution Ethiopia was a semifeudal and semicapitalist economy that predominantly served the interests of the feudal and bureaucratic-capitalist classes, and the goals of imperialism. The earlier version of the theory, contained in the 1976 program of the National Democratic Revolution (NDR), argued that the friends and beneficiaries of the revolution were to be workers, peasants, and the petite bourgeoisie. More recent thinking has introduced a change, and now identifies workers, peasants, the revolutionary armed forces, and revolutionary intellectuals as the forces of the revolution. The NDR program envisaged a centralized economy with a strong public sector, but proposed that private enterprise owned and operated by Ethiopian nationals should be allowed to participate in the development process within the framework set by the government (*Addis Zemen*, 13 Miazzia 1968 E.C.)

It is worth noting that this program, with its lukewarm but fairly explicit endorsement of a role for private domestic capital and a period of mixed economy, has not been taken into account in policy decisions, nor has it been expressly renounced. While policy statements and official documents occasionally make references to the need for completing the presocialist phase of the transition, all too often actual reforms and policy decisions have not been favorable to or tolerant of private enterprise. Indeed, over the last ten years, the government has conducted a bitter media campaign against the private sector, accompanied by waves of nationalization that have left the sector badly battered.

The strategy recently mapped out by the government regarding the transition to socialism aims broadly at accelerating capital accumulation, boosting the productive forces, and improving the living standard of the people. The centerpiece of this strategy, however, is surprisingly modest: its focus is the solution of immediate economic problems and the satisfaction of the needs of primary consumption. The major tasks are seen to be the improvement of food production and the achievement of self-sufficiency in food in the coming ten years, the amelioration of the housing shortage, the provision of clean water to the rural population, the expansion of health and transport facilities, and the expansion of educational opportunities.[10] The old Soviet strategy of rapid capital accumulation, based on the prior development of heavy industry, has been jettisoned in favor of a more humble approach. Although some Marxist writing of late has seen in this "basic needs" approach a more novel and worthwhile experiment in socialist transition, the approach itself has been adopted in a good number of countries following the nonsocialist road of development.[11]

Insofar as development priorities are concerned, agriculture is given pride of place, with industry playing a supporting role. The agricultural sector is to provide the surplus for development and the raw materials for industry, and is to be the main source of foreign exchange earnings. At the same time, agriculture is to undergo a radical transformation, in which the present predominance of private peasant production will be replaced, a decade from now, by that of rural producers' cooperatives and state farms. Initially, the industrial sector will consist of small- and medium-scale enterprises and cottage industries, the former already under state control, the latter to be rapidly organized into cooperatives.

The basic guidelines of the "socialist transition" have only recently been worked out, in the form of a Ten-Year Guiding Plan (TYGP), formally adopted by the government in September 1984. Up until that time, economic policy had restricted itself to short-term measures and to solving immediate and critical problems that cropped up successively all through the decade. The economy itself went through several phases of change and restructuring, of which the following three are particularly important.

The period of economic dislocation: 1975-1978. In this period, the economy suffered its most serious crisis. The nationalization of financial and industrial enterprises and, later, the land reform—the earliest major economic measures taken by the new government—failed to usher in a period of improved economic performance and general prosperity. On the contrary, battered from all sides and starved of new investment, the economy, particularly the fragile urban sector, lurched to the brink of collapse. The immediate causes for the general malaise are many and varied.

To begin with, the uncertainty created in many quarters—planners, managers, the international donor community, private sector businessmen, etc.—did not provide an atmosphere conducive to concerted and increased economic effort. This uncertainty was economic and political: economic because the process of nationalization was not thought to have come to an end, and the economic policy of the government was far from clear; political, because the process of power consolidation took a long time to complete, and the nature of the political system emerged in full only much later. Furthermore, the extension of state control over a large number of small and large enterprises was not adequately prepared for, so that great difficulties arose in connection with the management and restructuring of enterprises and in the coordination of productive activities. This period was also marked by considerable social unrest (as discussed above), and government officials and planners had a difficult time working out production plans or asserting sufficient control over the activities of enterprises or the sources of raw materials.

Further factors that fueled the economic crisis were the damage and dislocation caused by insurgency in the north and war with Somalia in the east. A number of industrial plants and agricultural projects were shut down or completely destroyed, economic activity in parts of the country—notably in the north (where about one-third of the country's industries are located) and the east—came virtually to a standstill, and transport was severely crippled. To all these must be added the breakdown of discipline among workers in industry and services, especially between 1976 and 1978. This was caused by the continuing unrest and political strategies in the urban areas. The "exposure campaigns" conducted to clean out opposition elements from enterprises and government offices in 1977 and early 1978, had a severely damaging effect on many sectors of the urban economy.

This period brought with it shortages in all basic consumer goods, rising prices, and rising unemployment. The severity of the economic crisis is shown by the fact that, in the period as a whole, GDP (at constant factor cost) grew by an average of 1.8 percent annually, far below the rate of population growth, which currently is said to be 2.9 percent per year.

The period of the annual plans: 1979-1983. In October 1978, the Supreme Planning Council (the state's central planning agency), which since June 1984 has been renamed the National Committee for Central Planning, was established, and a one-year "development campaign" together with a similar one-year plan was soon launched. Since then, five more campaigns and five yearly plans have been assigned and implemented. The plans were meant to bring the industrial sector in particular under stricter control and to revive the economy. Overall, the purpose of the first few campaigns was to solve pressing economic problems such as the deteriorating food problem and the shortage of consumer goods, and generally to rehabilitate the economy from the ravages of the past five years.[12] Some positive gains were made in these years, largely as a result of the reactivation of damaged or closed enterprises, the utilization of plants and equipment at their full capacity, and the improvement in transport in the wake of the cessation of hostilities in both the northern and eastern fronts.

Although temporary gains were made, the yearly plans revealed major structural and other fundamental weakness in the economy, of which the following were identified by the TYGP as being critical: low productivity of labor, shortage of skilled manpower, high dependency of local industry on external economies, technological backwardness, and shortage of capital equipment and spare parts. The documents also noted that investment was very low over the period of the yearly plans, and unemployment was rising sharply.[13] Another official document, an assessment of the six yearly plans period, also painted a gloomy picture; in addition to the problems just mentioned, it cited shortage of raw materials, obsolete machinery, market and financial constraints, and poor management as being the prime factors contributing to the critical defects in the economy. Industrial growth in this period showed a declining trend, with the high point having been reached at the beginning of the campaigns.[14]

According to a team of ILO experts, the period between 1975 and the end of 1980 was "characterized by stagnation in per-capita income and a large fall in real private consumption per head. This decline is accompanied by an increase in the incidence and intensity of urban poverty, and by...erosion of the gains of the redistribution land reform in the rural areas. In short, the story is one of impoverishment without growth."[15] In the period since 1980, the situation has not improved much; according to statements by senior government officials and documents from the central planning agency, the prospects for real improvements in income and output appear to be dim.

In line with the government's policy of socialist transition, the public sector absorbed the lion's share of total investments in the period

under discussion. State agriculture, in particular, became the darling of
the economic planners, who believed it would become the flag carrier of
the transition process in the countryside. In reality, state farms, whose
land area was expanded almost threefold at one point, and which ate up
56.2 percent and 60.5 percent of the total budget allocated to agriculture
in 1978/79 and 1982/83 respectively, turned out to be a costly
experiment. Despite this massive assistance, the subsector's contribution
to total agricultural production actually fell between 1979 and 1983.
Obviously, a review of policy on this question was needed, but policy
makers decided to settle for retrenchment and consolidation.[16] The state
industrial sector, which was enlarged at this time by a spate of
nationalizations that brought some twenty private enterprises under state
control, fared slightly better, but here too, there was not much to rejoice
about as the real rate of growth was a miserly one, and substantial new
investments were not in the pipeline. To make matters worse, peasant
agriculture, which had registered modest gains in the first few years of
the land reform, performed badly in the period under discussion, further
exacerbating the problem of food shortages.

In the area of foreign trade, the record was also quite discouraging, as
the figures in Table 7.2 indicate. The burgeoning trade deficit was largely
caused by the fact that Ethiopia's chief export, coffee, declined in value
between 1979 and 1983 in the international market; in 1983, a ton of
Ethiopian coffee fetched nearly half what it did in 1977/78.[17]

There has been some change in Ethiopia's external trade structure,
although overall the capitalist countries still remain the dominant
trading partners of the country. The shift has been in the direction and to
the benefit of the Soviet Bloc countries, which now export far more and
import far less than they did earlier as shown in Table 7.3.

The Ten-Year Guiding Plan: 1984 and after. The Ten-Year Guiding Plan
(TYGP), which was formally endorsed in 1984, but whose
implementation is now raising difficulties, has been seen by many as an
overambitious attempt to invigorate, and subsequently transform, an

Table 7.2   Balance of Trade 1978/79–1983/84 (million birr)[a]

	1978/79	79/80	80/81	81/82	82/83	83/84
Exports	712.2	1006.3	818	852.3	844.8	962.9
(of which coffee was	519.5	685.6	493	497.1	513.6	576.9)
Imports	1261.2	1436.7	1384.2	1641.0	1752.9	1766.3
Balance	−549.1	−430.4	−566.2	−788.7	−908.1	−803.5

Source: NRDC–CPSC, *Assessment*, 160–173.
[a]2.07 birr equals U.S. $1.00.

Table 7.3   External Trade Structure 1978/79 and 1982/83
(percentages)

	1978/79	1982/83
Ethiopia's Exports to:		
Developed countries	64.3	69.8
Third World	20.9	26.7
Socialist Bloc	14.8	3.4
Imports from:		
Developed countries	66.1	59.9
Third World	22.8	9.2
Socialist Bloc	11.2	30.9

Source: Assessment, 150–51.

ailing economy. There are two important elements in the plan that continue to disturb analysts and cast doubt on the viability of the entire project. The first is the external content of the plan: the development strategy envisaged is a foreign aid-dominated strategy. The second aspect has to do with the modesty of the objectives sought in comparison with the huge investment finance required. The plan has also been criticized for other failings, and the team of experts from the ILO suggested that it be "stood on its head," to reflect greater concern for poverty alleviation and employment creation.[18]

We have already dealt with the major goals of the plan in the discussion above, so in the following lines we shall present a brief review of the more concrete objectives of the development strategy contained within.[19]

The plan, originally to run from 1984/85 to 1993/94, sets 6.5 percent as a target for annual GNP growth, with agriculture expected to rise by 4.3 percent yearly, industry by 10.8 percent, and services by 6.9 percent; per capita income is to grow by 3.5 percent annually. The economy is to be significantly restructured, with the emphasis dramatically shifting from the rural to the urban-industrial sector. The share of agriculture in total output is to decline from about 48 percent at the beginning of the plan period to 39 percent by the end, and that of industry to rise from 16 percent to 24 percent. Total investment for the whole period was set at 32.0 billion birr at 1980 prices, or 41.8 billion at current prices (15.5 or 20.2 billion U.S. dollars); 55.5 percent of this was to come from local sources, and the rest (between seven and nine billion U.S. dollars) from foreign sources. Of the roughly twenty-six "strategic tasks" identified in the plan, the great majority are of the "basic needs" variety discussed above. Second in importance are tasks of a "restorative" nature, among which the following were given prominence: preserving the country's ecology, its soil, forest and water resources; improving labor productivity and the quality of goods. The third variety of strategic tasks involves exploration for mineral resources, better utilization of energy, and expansion of the role of science and technology in production.

More than 17 percent of the planned investment was to go to industrial development, three-fifths of which was for new projects and new plants. On the other hand, the restructuring of the sector (i.e., the change of emphasis from light to heavy industry) was to be a gradual process. At present, the manufacturing industry consists of small- to medium-scale (with a few large-scale) enterprises, which produce almost exclusively light goods for primary consumption and rely heavily on foreign sources for their raw materials and spare parts.

The Rural Sector

It is now exactly ten years since the land reform, the most significant and far-reaching measure of social transformation by the present government, was promulgated and implemented. Since 1975, rural production has been freed from the heavy hand of "external forces"—landlords and landlord obligations—which in the past inhibited developments in agriculture. The land reform finally brought the landlord system to an end, abolished tenancy, and brought about the distribution of land to individual peasants organized in peasant associations. Although the legislation put a ceiling of ten hectares for the maximum size of plots to be held by individuals, plot sizes in fact are at present extremely small, measuring from 0.25 to 0.50 hectares in some areas, to 1.50 to 3.0 hectares in others. Thus rural Ethiopia remains, even after land reform and partly because of it, a land of small holders and subsistence producers.

There is another aspect of the reform that has serious adverse consequences for peasant production, and this is that land reform has given rise to a process of continuous diminution of peasant plots. A peasant has access to land only in his *kebele*—i.e., the area over which a peasant association has jurisdiction. The land and other resources in the *kebele* are fixed, and new peasants who become eligible for land acquire it only when land is alienated from those considered to possess larger plots. The peasant does not own the land he works on, he has only usufruct rights over it, hence it can be alienated from him at any time. This progressive leveling down of land possessions, and the deep uncertainty it is creating among the peasantry—which we have discussed at length elsewhere—is the single most critical defect of the land reform.[20]

Some gains were made in peasant production in the first few years of the revolution, however these were not significant enough to have lasting effects on the rural economy. The positive effects of the reform have now been lost, and this loss, coupled with the ill-advised government policy that has increasingly become hostile to smallholder peasant agriculture, has dampened prospects for rapid improvements in the rural sector.

The agrarian structure, at present, consists of three subsectors: private peasant agriculture, rural cooperatives, and state agriculture. The government is now very keen on accelerating the pace of cooperativization in the countryside (its earlier emphasis was on state farms); rural cooperatives are believed to hold the solution to the problem of agricultural stagnation, and are expected to provide the bulk of the domestic surplus in years to come. According to the Ten Year Guiding Plan, cooperatives are expected to provide nearly half of all the main crops in demand, and to occupy more than half of the cultivated area for such crops (see Table 7.4).

This dramatic transformation, if successful, will certainly create many serious problems for planners, and will be very unsettling for the rural population. In addition to the great push toward cooperatives, there have been two rural policies that have been vigorously pursued by the government. First, fixed grain prices have been in effect for several years, and peasants have been forced to sell at these prices, which they find quite unattractive; however, prices of primary goods bought by the peasantry have gone up sharply. Second, peasants are required to deliver a state-determined quota of grain to the state purchasing agency, AMC, which pays at the official rates. The main objective of this measure is to gradually eliminate the private grain merchant, and private trade in general, from the countryside.

Both of these policies are bitterly resented by the peasantry. The net result of the measures has been to inhibit increased effort by rural producers, to drive up grain prices sharply, and to create serious food shortages in the urban areas. This last has been exacerbated by the restrictions imposed, especially by provincial authorities, on interregional grain movements and free circulation of goods.

It should be pointed out that the country, which is believed to have considerable agricultural potential, has been unable to feed its population in good times as well as bad. During the last two decades, Ethiopia has

Table 7.4   Changes in Agrarian Structure 1984/85–1993/94
(percentage changes in output and area for main crops)

Subsector	1984/85		1993/94	
	Area	Production	Area	Production
Peasant	94.9	93.1	40.3	38.1
Cooperatives	1.4	1.4	52.1	49.6
State Farms	3.1	5.0	6.0	11.0
Settlement	0.6	0.5	1.6	1.3

Source: TYGP, vol. 2, 51.

been becoming a net importer of food, and the volume of food imports has risen sharply in the last ten years. The deteriorating situation in agriculture, and the continuing decline in the marketed surplus of peasant production, are among the major factors that led the country to import about 1.7 million tons of food between 1975 and 1982, as shown in Table 7.5.

The burden on the economy would have been heavier had it not been for food aid, which made up nearly two-thirds of total imports in this period. Food aid dependency has been further aggravated as a result of the worsening drought, which since 1977 has seriously crippled agriculture, and the famine of 1984/85, which is still not under control.

We will leave the subject of famine in Ethiopia and the government's response to it out of the discussion with only a few words.[21] Two devastating famines have occurred in the space of a decade, in a country that is fairly well endowed, and whose farming people are hardworking. This appalling record will continue to shame many Ethiopians for a long time to come. The famine of 1973/74 is believed to have claimed some 200,000 human lives and an untold number of livestock. Comparable figures for the 1984/85 tragedy are at present not available, but by all accounts, including official sources, the latest famine is far more severe and far more extensive than the previous one. At the height of its intensity, nearly a quarter of the country's rural population was affected and in need of assistance. In short, the economic and human costs of this disaster will continue to weigh heavily on the country long after normal conditions have returned to the rural areas.

The Urban Sector

The state is most visible and most predominant in this sector of the economy. Successive acts of nationalization since 1975 brought under public ownership not only the major productive establishments of the country, but also such small-scale enterprises as grain mills, woodworks,

Table 7.5   Cereal Imports 1975/76–1981/82 (in thousand tons)

Year	Commercial	Food Aid	Total
1975/76	32.0	60.6	92.6
1976/77	119.8	65.0	184.8
1977/78	109.0	206.4	315.4
1978/79	116.2	244.7	360.9
1979/80	188.9	134.4	323.3
1980/81	51.0	152.2	203.2
1981/82	38.6	182.0	220.6

Source: World Bank, 1981, vol. 1, 24.

coffee-cleaning outfits, small hotels, and grocery stores. According to information from all nationalized industrial enterprises, about half of the establishments under its control have an annual gross value of production of less than five million birr. Of these, nearly a third probably fall under the category of small-scale industry.[22]

The structure of the urban economy reveals three major divisions, reflecting three forms of ownership: state, private, and cooperative. State-owned establishments include large, medium, and small industrial, commercial, and service enterprises, while the private sector is almost exclusively restricted to small-scale and handicraft production. Cooperative enterprises are to be found only in cottage and household industries.

Although much is still unknown about it, cottage and household production provides employment to nearly 400,000 persons (mainly self-employment), contributes about 4.5 percent to GDP, and is scattered throughout rural and urban Ethiopia. This subsector relies mostly on domestic raw materials and supplies a variety of products that are cheap and act as substitutes for manufactured goods. Of the tens of thousands of craft enterprises in the country, only a small number have, so far, been organized into cooperatives, of which the most widely favored are service cooperatives. The majority of such cooperatives are in the tailoring business, with weavers coming in second. Most cooperatives (service as well as producers') operate under great difficulties, and the success rate, so far, has not been encouraging. Indeed, the pace of cooperativization, which had been relatively high between 1975 and 1977, has dropped considerably of late, indicating that the novelty of the experiment has worn off, and that the stringent requirements placed on cooperators by the authorities are beginning to tell. Most cooperative enterprises are unstable in two senses: enterprises break up or close down a short while after they are established as cooperatives, and there is a high turnover in the membership of the enterprises.[23]

It will be seen from Table 7.6 that private enterprise is an insignificant force as far as manufacturing is concerned. The table does not include all private establishments, only those employing ten or more persons, nevertheless, even if establishments with less than ten employees, (of which there are a great number) were included, the picture would not change significantly.

Overall, the manufacturing industry has been, and still remains a relatively weak force in the economy. In 1974, this subsector (excluding building, power, etc.) contributed 4.3 percent to GDP. In 1983, this figure had risen to only 6 percent.

A recent study published by the ILO strongly argues that in the last twenty years, i.e., in the years between 1960 and 1980, the contribution

Table 7.6   Ownership Structure in Manufacturing 1981/82
(value in thousand birr)

Sector	Number of Establishments	Gross Value Production	Value Added[a]	Work Force (permanent)	Wages Paid	Fixed Assets
Public	189	2,421,045	572,048	74,650	176,245	404,985
Private	230	102,157	29,549	7,168	16,994	22,345
Total	419	2,523,202	601,598	81,818	193,239	427,330

Source: CSO, Industry Survey, 1981/82.
[a]At factor cost.

of manufacturing to the development process—measured by employment, economic surplus, and income generation—has been quite neglible. This same document goes on to argue that the rate of growth of industrial output has shown a declining trend in the period, the last half showing the worst performance record. Industrial output at constant prices grew at an average annual rate of 12 percent between 1960/61 and 1973/74 (the prerevolution period), with manufacturing rising by 22.3 percent, and handicraft and small-scale industry by 7.3 percent. In the period 1974/75 to 1979/80 the annual growth rate was 4.4 percent, with manufacturing showing a 7.9 percent, and handicraft and small-scale production a 1.2 percent rate of growth.[24]

The poor performance of the modern economy has brought great hardships to the urban population, which has sustained high unemployment, estimated by one authority as being 20 percent of the labor force (ILO, 1982, 146 ff), a rapidly rising cost of living, and severe shortages of basic consumer goods. The shortages were primarily caused by restrictions on imports, and by the state distribution system for local manufacturers, which has become overly bureaucratic. Although these hardships were borne by all social classes, it is those in the lower income brackets that have suffered the most. The incidence and intensity of urban poverty has increased steadily since the latter part of the 1970s, and real living standards of all sectors of society, including employees of state administration and public enterprises, have declined considerably.

Conclusion

One aspect of the "transition" in Ethiopia, which outside observers may quickly lose sight of, is the high ideological content of public policy. Far too often, the choice of long- or short-term measures or decisions is made on ideological grounds rather than grounds of practicality. Economic questions have been turned into political ones, and the planner must view even the most technical problems through ideological spectacles.

The developmental strategy chosen by the government, which, as expressed officially, aims at "completing the national democratic revolution and laying down the foundation for socialism" (*Program* of the party), will have to solve two interrelated problems if development is to be successful, namely the problem of capital accumulation and of dependency. These two problems, which also happen to be central in all Third World countries, socialist or otherwise, do not respond positively to ideological manipulation. Indeed, our analysis has tried to show, first, that the performance of the economy in the decade under consideration places severe constraints on the process of accumulation; in fact, the rate of accumulation in this period in general has been much lower than in the decade before the revolution. Second, the economy has become greatly dependent, both in terms of its long-term plans and its sources of capital earnings on foreign, especially Western, economies.

Here are a few more thoughts on this last point. As was noted above, the country's long-term strategy relies for its success on a hefty dose of external loans and grants, much of it from the capitalist countries. Almost 90 percent of the nearly one-billion-dollar development aid provided to the country between 1971 and 1981 came from Western sources and UN agencies. Three donors, the EEC, UN agencies, and Sweden provided 75 percent of the total aid in this period.[25]

The same sort of external dependency is to be observed in the sphere of foreign trade, which relies mainly on the export of coffee. The United States still remains the most important single market for the country's coffee, although its significance has declined considerably in recent years. In the early 1970s, the U.S. market absorbed more than 70 percent of Ethiopia's coffee; in the early 1980s, however, the figure has gone down to less than 50 percent. In contrast, three EEC countries, West Germany, Italy, and France, which together took about 10 percent of the commodity in the early 1970s, have increased their imports to nearly 40 percent in the early 1980s. The socialist countries are of negligible importance in this area.[26]

The Ethiopian experience is, in many respects, quite similar to that of a number of "Afro-Marxist" countries, old and new. Yet, a good deal of the literature on underdevelopment and socialist transition has failed to incorporate these experiences in its scheme of analysis, and to benefit from them. The essays in a recent work that has been commended in many circles, for instance, illustrate this failure quite well.[27] Socialist transition in conditions of extreme backwardness, which is characteristic of all "Afro-Marxist" countries, is a perilous course, often full of consequences that tend to reinforce backwardness rather than progress, scarcity rather then abundance. The debate on the subject will become a great deal clearer and more relevant if this fundamental fact is not lost sight of, or brushed aside by tendentious rhetoric.

Abbreviations

AMC	Agricultural Marketing Corporation
CSO	Central Statistical Office
COPWE	Commission for the Organization of the Party of Workers of Ethiopia
HASIDA	Handicraft and Small-scale Industries Development Agency
ILO	International Labour Organization
NRDC-CPSC Central	National Revolutionary Development Campaign-Planning Supreme Council
PMAC	Provisional Military Administrative Council
MESN	All-Ethiopian Socialist Movement
RRC	Relief and Rehabilitation Commission

ADMINISTRATIVE UNITS: The *woreda* is the lowest unit of the administrative division of the country. Above it is the *awraja,* and above this is the province.

CALENDAR: The Ethiopian calendar (E.C.) is roughly seven to eight years "behind" the Gregorian Calendar (G.C.).

Notes

1. For a history of the revolution, see the following: Glen Bailey, *An Analysis of the Ethiopian Revolution* (unpublished M.A. Thesis, Ottawa: Carleton University, 1979); Zoltan Gyenge, *Ethiopia on the Road of Non-Capitalist Development* (Budapest: Institute for World Economics, 1976); Fred Halliday and M. Molyneux, *The Ethiopian Revolution* (London: Verso, 1981). For a perceptive and critical evaluation of this work, see John Markakis's review in *Review of African Political Economy,* no. 25 (1982); V. Korvikov, *Ethiopia, Ye-Abyot Amettat* [Amharic] (Addis Ababa: Novosti Press, 1979); R. Lefort, *Ethiopia: An Heretical Revolution* (London: Zed Press, 1983); Colin Legum, *Ethiopia: The Fall of Haile Selassie's Empire* (London: Rex Collins, 1975); David and Marina Ottawa, *Ethiopia: Empire in Revolution* (New York: Africana Publishing, 1978); R. Valdes Vivo, *Ethiopia: The Unknown Revolution* (Havana: Editorial de Ciencias Sociales, 1977).

For an official history, see PMAC, *Ye-Tigle Mi'raf, Special Publication Prepared for the First Anniversary of the Popular Revolution* [Amharic] (Addis Ababa: PMAC, 1975). Hereafter cited as *Ye-Tigle.*

2. PMAC, *Ye-Tigle,* 25-32. The following documents published between 1974 and 1977 are also important: PMAC, *Declaration of Economic Policy of Socialist Ethiopia* (Addis Ababa, February 1975), hereafter cited as *Declaration*

1975; PMAC, Declaration of the Provisional Military Government (Addis Ababa, December 1974), hereafter cited as *Declaration 1974;* PMAC, *Ethiopia in Revolution* (Addis Ababa: ERIC, 1977); PMAC, *The Ethiopian Revolution* (Addis Ababa, 1975); also, Ethiopian Serategnoch party, *Program* (Addis Ababa, September 1984).

3. The discussion that follows is based on published official documents, the Amharic language daily newspaper *Addis Zemen,* and on my own personal experience.

4. PMAC, *Declaration 1974,* 7. See also PMAC, *Declaration 1975.*

5. The most perceptive and balanced account of the conflict in Eritrea is Zewde Gabre-Selassie, *Eritrea and Ethiopia in the Context of the Red Sea and Africa,* (unpublished ms., Washington: Woodrow Wilson International Center, March 1976). Another work is H. Erlich, *The Struggle Over Eritrea, 1962-1978* (Stanford: Hoover Institution Press, 1983).

6. Major Fisseha, a senior member of the Derg has stated there were 108 members at the formal establishment of the pre-Derg on 28 June 1974 (see *Addis Zemen,* 22 Sene 1976 E.C., 29 June 1984 G.C.) See also Pliny the Middle-Aged, "The PMAC: Origins and Structure," *Ethiopianist Notes,* 2, 3, (1978-1979).

7. For a discussion of party formation in thee post-1975 period and of the activities of COPWE, see COPWE, *Espaco be-Party Misretta* [Amharic] (Addis Ababa: COPWE, January 1983).

8. World Bank, *Economic Memorandum on Ethiopia,* Report No. 35526-ET (East African Regional Office, December 1981), 11. See also the same agency's *Ethiopia: Recent Economic Development and Future Prospects,* Report No. 4783a-ET (East African Regional Office, May 1984) for another sympathetic assessment.

9. Dessalegn Rahmato, *Political Power and Social Formation in Ethiopia under the Old Regime, Notes on Marxist Theory* (paper presented at the Eighth International Conference of Ethiopian Studies, Addis Ababa, 26-30 November 1984).

10. See the introductory section of NRDC-CPSC, *The Ten-Year Guiding Plan* (1984/85-1993/94), draft, 1: *General* [in Amharic] (Addis Ababa: NRDC-CPSC February 1984), hereafter cited as *TYGP.* The other volumes in this series, all in Amharic, are: 2: *Production and Construction* (Addis Ababa: NRDC-CPSC, February 1984); 3: *Economy and Social Services* (Addis Ababa: NRDC-CPSC, February 1984); 4: *The Ten-Year Development Guiding Plan* (Draft) (Addis Ababa: NRDC-CPSC, March 1984).

11. R. Sandbrook has tried to link basic needs development with socialist transition. See his *The Politics of Basic Needs* (London: Heinemann, 1982).

12. See NRDC-CPSC, *Ethiopia's Development Campaign* (Addis Ababa: NRDC-CPSC, September 1980) for a description of the early phase of the campaigns.

13. *TYGP,* 1, 14-15.

14. NRDC-CPSC, *Assessment of the Implementation of the Six Yearly Plans, 1978-1983* [Amharic] (Addis Ababa: NRDC-CPSC, December 1984), 114ff. Hereafter cited as *Assessment.*

15. ILO, *Socialism from the Grass Roots: Accumulation, Employment, and*

Equity in Ethiopia. (Addis Ababa: ILO/JASPA, 1982), 231.

16. *Assessment*, 61-68.

17. Ministry of Coffee and Tea Development, *Coffee Statistics Handbook 1961/62 to 1982/83.* (Addis Ababa: Ministry of Coffee and Tea Development, 1984), 30-32. Hereafter cited as *Coffee Statistics Handbook.*

18. ILO, *Socialism From the Grass Roots,* 16ff.

19. The discussion that follows is based on *TYGP*, vol. 1, 36ff.

20. Dessalegn Rahmato, *Agrarian Reform in Ethiopia* (Trenton, N.J.: Red Sea Press, 1984). For information on the performance of the rural sector, see CSO, *Time Series Data on Area, Production and Yield of Principal Crops by Regions 1979/80-1983/84* (Addis Ababa: CSO, 1984).

21. For an official history of the famine of 1974 and 1984, see RRC, *The Challenge of Drought, Ethiopia's Decade of Struggle in Relief and Rehabilitation* (Addis Ababa: RRC, 1985). For an independent view, see Mesfin Wolde Mariam, *Rural Vulnerability to Famine in Ethiopia, 1958-1977* (New Delhi: Vikas Publishing, 1984).

22. Ministry of Industry, *Statistical Bulletin* (Addis Ababa: Ministry of Industry, 1984), 4. For a survey of manufacturing industries for the years 1976 to 1982, see CSO, Results of the *Survey of Manufacturing Industries* (Addis Ababa: CSO, 1977, 1980, 1984).

23. HASIDA, *Report on a Survey of Handicraft Cooperatives,* 1978-1979 (Addis Ababa: HASIDA, 1982), esp. 161ff. For a survey of small-scale industry and handicraft, see the same agency's *Report on Handicraft Survey in Ten Towns, 1976-1977* (Addis Ababa: HASIDA, 1979). *Report on a Survey of Small-scale Industries in Eleven Towns, 1976-1977* (Addis Ababa: HASIDA, 1979).

24. ILO, *Patterns of Industrialization and Impact on Employment and Incomes in African Countries, The Case of Ethiopia* (Addis Ababa: ILO/JASPA, 1983), 11-12.

25. *TYGP*, 4, 992-996.

26. *Coffee Statistics Handbook,* 30-34.

27. G. White, R. Murray, and C. White, eds., *Revolutionary Socialist Development in the Third World* (Brighton: Wheat Sheaf Books, 1983). Other works that deal with the transition along the same lines are: K.P. Jameson and C. Wilbur, eds., *Socialist Models of Development* (Oxford: Pergamon Press, 1981); James Mittelman, *Underdevelopment and the Transition to Socialism, Mozambique and Tanzania* (New York: Academic Press, 1981); M. Palmberg, ed., *Problems of Socialist Orientation in Africa* (Uppsala: SIAS, 1978); John S. Saul, *The State and Revolution in Eastern Africa* (New York: MR Press, 1979).

chapter eight

The Angolan Economy:
A History of Contradictions

Gillian Gunn

Picture the scene. Two bikini-clad women arrive on the beach near Angolan President Eduardo dos Santos's residence on jet skis. As the machines, huge surfboards with 500-cc Kawasaki engines, roar onto the sand, a Land Rover filled with barbecue fixings and the women's friends, employees of Gulf Oil and a British diamond mining company, rolls along the beach to meet them. It's a typical expatriate outing.

Within five minutes, a military lorry stops at the temporary camp. Dozens of Cubans clamber down and peer at the group, their attention equally divided between the bikinis and the jet skis. They finally get up enough courage to ask if they can try the machines, and the Gulf Oil owner obliges, spending the next two hours teaching them, and rescuing the machines as the Cubans repeatedly fall off. The Cubans respond by sending back up to their barracks for rum, and a British-American-Cuban party gets started. The afternoon ends with a young Cuban helping the three-year-old daughter of one expatriate build a sand castle, while his colleagues construct larger mounds that uncannily resemble a naked reclining female form.

That Sunday afternoon was one of the most memorable events of my two-month stay in Angola in the summer of 1985. The ironic interplay of nationalities is more than just a good cocktail party story. By mirroring the paradox of Angola's economic dependence upon Western industrial skills and technology, and its political-military links with the Socialist Bloc, it illustrates the profound contradiction between Angolan politics and economics that has plagued the country since well before independence.

181

From Slavery to Independence

The divergence between economic and political integration dates back to the beginning of the slave trade in the sixteenth century, which strained political relations between the African population and the Portuguese. Intertribal raids for captives to sell, in particular Kongo attacks on the Kimbundu, contributed to ethnic resentments that are still visible today.[1]

From 1500 to 1850, Angola provided an estimated 30 percent of the world slave supply.[2] Slavery's adverse effects persisted longer than in non-Portuguese territories because Lisbon hung onto the slave trade decades after its European neighbors abandoned the practice. Lawrence Henderson has commented:

> England, France and Holland exploited the slave trade to transform feudalism into industrial capitalism, which demanded raw materials and markets more than slave labor or plantations. Therefore, by the middle of the eighteenth century, when they found the slave trade to be a brake on their economic development, they proceeded to abolish it. Portugal, on the other hand, resisted the abolition because the plantation-slave economy was compatible with its feudal system.[3]

Thus Portugal's attempts to integrate Angola into its own and the world economy only contributed to political alienation.

From final *de facto* abolition of slavery in 1850, until the 1930s, Portugal tried to reap economic benefits from its colony by "renting out" Angolan transport, diamond, and oil assets to other European powers through concession deals.[4] Portugal became a direct political colonizer but only an indirect economic colonizer. It was simply the semifeudal middleman for European capital and, again, political and economic trends ran against each other.

This was the situation António de Oliveira Salazar inherited in 1928, when he became Portugal's minister of finance, and in 1932, when he rose to the post of prime minister. He was determined to mobilize colonial resources to benefit the metropolitan economy, and instituted a series of policies collectively termed the Estado Novo, the "New State."

In 1928, Lisbon ruled that tax could no longer be paid in kind, but had to be paid in Portuguese currency. This was an attempt to force Africans to work as contract laborers, for that was one of the few ways to earn the cash. The policy was later refined with the *indigenato* statutes, which obligated all male *indigenas* ("uncivilized" Africans) to engage in paid employment or perform contract labor. Nonwhites could escape the forced labor laws by aquiring *assimilado* status. *Assimilados* had to be fluent in Portuguese, earn wages from a trade and follow

Portuguese social customs. By 1950, less than one percent of the African population qualified.[5]

In 19⁴⁸, Salazar also tried to force greater Angolan economic inte   with Portugal by ordering that one-half of any enterprise ope   in Angola had to be Portuguese-owned. This retarded Angolan ind .rial development, as there was simply not enough Portuguese capital available.

Salazar also sent increasing numbers of Portuguese bureaucrats, peasants, and convicts to the province. But, unlike the British and French colonies, the increase in the colonial presence did not lead to greater black employment and education. But, because the Portuguese settlers did not take to agriculture, congregated in towns, and were often not qualified for the higher responsibilities of colonial administration, they filled the lower rungs of the administrative apparatus, depriving Africans of the opportunity to learn office skills.

Salazar's policies paid off economically. From 1953 to 1962, Angola exported to the non-Portuguese world forty million dollars more than it imported. Thirty-four million of that trade surplus went to Lisbon in payment for Portuguese imports.[6] Because much of the foreign exchange flowed from the forced labor policies, Portuguese-African political relations were damaged. Eventually, the tactics Salazar used to promote economic integration spawned rebellion both among Africans and in a segment of the *mestiço* and white elite.

The party that finally came to power after independence, the Movimento popular de libertação de Angola (MPLA) was formed in 1956. It was urban-oriented; it pulled its membership from the Mbundu people around the capital, was led by educated *mestiços* and *assimilados*, and increasingly acquired a socialist outlook. A rival liberation movement, simultaneously formed by Holden Roberto, initially aimed to restore the ancient Kongo kingdom as an independent country, but later expanded its view to encompass Angola as a whole. The group, eventually titled Frente nacional de libertação de Angola (FNLA), had entirely African, mainly Bakongo, and largely *indigena* membership. It had an antiwhite tendency and a nationalist rather than a socialist outlook. Roberto's minister of foreign affairs, Jonas Savimbi, later split off, forming União nacional para a independência total de Angola (UNITA). It drew membership from the southern Ovimbundu people and had similar black nationalist views.

The division Portugal had created between the *indigenas* and the *assimilado-mestiço* group was mirrored in the formation of the liberation movements, as was ethnic resentment dating from the slaving days.

As the economic cost of guerrilla warfare escalated, Portuguese policy changed. In 1965, Salazar removed the prohibitions on foreign investment in an effort to raise more funds. This was basically a modified version of the earlier policy of renting out Angolan assets to foreign firms, and the country experienced a miniboom. In 1966, the U.S. company, Gulf Oil, found petroleum off the coast of Cabinda and was given a concession to exploit the province. By the end of 1972, Gulf was contributing 13 percent of Angola's budget and 60 percent of military expenditure.[7] Manufacturing grew by nearly a fifth per year in the decade ending in 1972 and five hundred "heavy" industries developed, mainly due to foreign investment.[8] Angola thus became increasingly integrated into the non-Portuguese Western industrial structure, requiring Western technology and spare parts to keep the factories running.

The boom petered out as the war intensified. Agriculture declined when one-sixth of the African population was forced into protected villages designed to cut them off from the guerrillas, and thousands fled to Zambia and Zaire. Coffee exports fell by more than half; diamond production by two-thirds. In the last year of colonialism, industrial production fell by 75 percent and GNP by at least 25 percent. Only oil exports continued unabated.[9]

Why, one may ask, did Portugal hang onto Angola when the war reached such intensity, long after other European powers relinquished their territories? One reason is that the British and French built up strong trading relationships with their colonies, and when independence movements exacted an increasing economic price, the metropoles were able to hand over political power to local leaders while maintaining the profitable exchange. In contrast, Portugal supplied its colonies not with industrial goods needed to build the economy, but with luxuries and raw materials such as wine and cork, which independent Angola could dispense with if it chose. Portugal also knew it could not collect rents from other nations for use of Angolan assets if it no longer had title to those assets. Thus Portugal hung on until the bitter end, which began on 25 April 1974, when the exhausted colonial army rebelled and culminated on 11 November the following year when the new Lisbon government gave Angola independence.

Clearly, the various methods by which Portugal had tried to reap economic benefits from Angola—slavery, forced labor, and renting out of Angolan assets to foreign firms, first through direct contract and later through investment—both strained political relations with the colony to the breaking point and led to greater Angolan economic ties with industrial Europe than with its main political partner, Portugal.

The First Half-Decade of Independence

This is not the place to outline the chaos surrounding the competition between the liberation movements on the eve of independence. Suffice it to say that the MPLA, with the help of Cuban troops and Soviet equipment, emerged victorious after defeating the U.S.-Chinese-Zairian-supported FNLA and U.S.-South African-aided UNITA initiatives.

The external political-economic dichotomy described above reappeared after independence, albeit in a different form. Political and military ties with the socialist countries grew because of ideological compatibility and military threats against the MPLA. Simultaneously, the integration of the Angolan economy with that of the industrialized West continued and, in some areas, even increased, despite intermittent attempts to turn the economy eastward.

The dichotomy also became evident in the internal sphere. The MPLA came to power believing in economic policies outlined in Marxist political theory, but as it applied those policies to Angolan conditions it increasingly became apparent that some aspects were not suited to Angola's existing economic structure. This problem was not evident during the first months of independence, when indeed it seemed the reverse was true, but it did become clearer toward the end of the decade.

The MPLA's external economic policy was initially outlined in September 1974, when a key "Interregional Conference of Militants" approved a program that included state control of foreign trade but permitted a role for those foreign enterprises "beneficial to the Angolan people."[10] The postindependence constitution added state ownership of national resources, which were then largely exploited by foreigners.

Clearly the MPLA had studied Angola's foreign economic links and decided it would be suicidal to immediately wrench the country away from the Western ties built up over hundreds of years. The MPLA wanted to acquire control of foreign investments, particularly in the diamond and oil industries, while still relying on the foreign firms for capital investment and expertise.

Following Algerian advice, the MPLA employed the accounting firm of Arthur D. Little as consultants, which encouraged the government's existing predisposition to not nationalize the oil sector aggressively. In June 1976, Angola formed a state oil company, Sonangol, but sought to transfer majority control of the existing oil activities through negotiation rather than nationalization. A new oil code was established in September 1978, and a few months later Angola signed its first accord with Gulf Oil. This transferred to Sonangol 51 percent of Cabinda Gulf's shares, management, and production. In a September 1979 deal with Texaco, Sonangol took over complete ownership of the concession, but signed a production-sharing agreement. The policy paid off. Both companies reinvested in Angola and, by 1980, Gulf was providing about 70 percent of Angola's foreign exchange revenue. Rules for future deals, as opposed to the renegotiations of the existing Texaco and Gulf investments, gave the Angolan state a monopoly on all natural hydrocarbon resources, with the right to enter into agreements with foreign companies for exploitation.[11]

The MPLA initially took the same line with the diamond industry. Production had fallen to 15 percent of preindependence levels, and some shareholders implied that they would welcome nationalization if it would liquefy their debts.[12] The MPLA at first refused, wanting the diamond company, Diamang, to continue to provide capital and technology as Gulf had. But, possibly because of lingering war resentment, the MPLA soon lost patience with Diamang's Portuguese shareholders. In August 1977, it nationalized all their holdings while leaving Diamang's European, U.S., and South African shares untouched.

The MPLA's appreciation of the need to remain on good terms with Western investors did not stop it from trying to expand economic relations with the socialist countries, but these initiatives were not entirely successful. In May 1976, Angola reached agreements with Moscow on trade, technical cooperation, fisheries, and merchant shipping. Subsequently, the Soviet Union aided in banking and electrification. However, by 1979, the Soviet Union's economic relations with Angola were still mainly military. It had supplied $410 million in arms, but Angola represented only 0.12 percent of its total nonarms trade.[13]

By the end of the decade, some Angolan managers were disillusioned with the fruits of economic cooperation with the socialist countries. Their technology was often incompatible with Western-installed manufacturing facilities inherited from the preindependence period, and the quality of their products was sometimes inferior as well.

Perhaps partially in response to this problem, in mid-1979 a new foreign investment law was introduced to encourage Western entrepreneurs. Although it prohibited investment in strategic areas and required the Angolan state to have a 51 percent stake in all enterprises, it did guarantee compensation for nationalization and permitted exceptions to the 51 percent rule when judged in the "national interest."

In the internal sphere, the situation started out somewhat differently. As mentioned above, the contradictions between internal politics and economics were at first not clear. Indeed, state takeover of private enterprise, as advocated by Marxist theory, seemed particularly appropriate for Angolan conditions. As one Angolan involved in the early postindependence decision making pointed out, "Who else was going to take over the shops and the farms the Portuguese abandoned? Few of us had any capital or experience to run the businesses. There was no one available to take over except the state."

The Portuguese exodus was massive. Over 300,000 left, taking two-thirds of the nation's 28,000 trucks, and abandoning 6,250 commercial farms.[14] Many technicians, managers, skilled workers, civil servants, and shopkeepers joined the exodus, often sabotaging their enterprises before leaving.

Although various MPLA economic documents mentioned that the private sector would continue in some form in Angola, shortly after independence the government set state ownership of 80 percent of the country's heavy industries by 1980 as a goal.[15] Nationalization was also an expression of war resentment. Property of FNLA and UNITA partisans, "saboteurs," and those (usually Portuguese) individuals absent from the country for more than forty-five days "without justification" was confiscated, with no compensation paid. Portuguese banks were also confiscated.[16]

In the agricultural sector, the MPLA was overwhelmed by the responsibility of running the over 6,000 farms abandoned by the Portuguese. The government believed that the easiest way to cope with these in the absence of large numbers of skilled farm managers was through centralization, and most properties went into state farms, which functioned poorly. Soviet, Bulgarian, and East German technicians came in to help, but to little avail. The shortage of experienced MPLA managers, the Portuguese habit of sabotaging equipment before departing, and the inappropriate equipment and agricultural techniques provided by some Socialist Bloc countries contributed to the low productivity of state farms. By mid-1978, only about a quarter of the abandoned farms were operating, and a year later only 12 percent of urban food needs were being met by state farms.[17]

Another problem was government policy on marketing agricultural produce. The network of Portuguese petty traders in the countryside was disrupted by the colonialists' postindependence exodus, and only a few private merchants remained. The MPLA then insisted that peasants sell to state buyers, provided no transport to market, offered low prices, and refused to barter produce for industrial goods. Naturally the farmers favored the few remaining private buyers, who did provide these services, and food started to disappear from the state markets, appearing only in the black market at inflated prices. A growing number of Angolans, attracted by the prospect of large black market profits, then took the risk of becoming illegal private traders. The growth of the black market produced industrial inefficiency because many workers spent a large part of their day chasing down food supplies.

As agricultural production plummeted, the MPLA became aware that the initial appearance of an ideal mesh between Angolan internal economic conditions and Marxist theory was illusory. In 1977 President Agostinho Neto said,

...[I]f we now, in the name of socialism, start expropriating our peasants, our people will feel at once that this socialism only means making more sacrifices. The way to transform the peasant private property into a special kind of property is through production co-operatives....[18]

Neto was trying to take account of existing conditions, without abandoning the socialist theory. His compromise cooperatives solution largely failed, however, because the government did not deliver, as promised, supplies of seeds, equipment, and credit. More loosely organized peasant associations did not work much better.

Angolan internal economic policy was further complicated by ideological differences. Worker committees associated with MPLA factions opposed to President Neto insisted on worker control and collective management of enterprises, in line with classical Marxist theory. These tensions contributed to an attempted coup in 1977, which Neto, supported by Cuban troops, put down. In the MPLA's First Congress in December 1977, Neto consolidated his power and awarded authority in enterprises to state-appointed managers rather than worker committees.

As in the preindependence period, the pattern of conflicting economic and political trends reemerged in the first half-decade of independence. In the external sphere, Angola was economically locked into the Western market as a result of Portugal's decision to rent out assets to foreign firms, and yet military and ideological imperatives made the MPLA align itself politically with the East. In the internal sphere, the initial appearance of economic and political compatibility soon dissipated, as Marxist collectivization led to collapsing agricultural production.

From Neto's Death to the Second Congress

From Neto's death in September 1979 until the Second Party Congress at the end of 1985, the contradictions between politics and economics continued.

In the early 1980s, Neto's successor, José Eduardo dos Santos, focused on the internal economy, seeking to come to terms with the fact that policies mandated by Marxist political theory were not producing the desired economic results.

At a 1980 Special Party Congress, directors of state enterprises were criticized for inefficiency, peasant cooperatives were given higher priority (although state farms were not abandoned), and new economic targets were selected to cover the period through 1985.

However, while the 1980 congress realized economic policy was not working, it failed to lay down a clear new mandate. In addition, it made economic forecasts on the mistaken assumption that hostilities in the south caused by UNITA and South Africa would end soon.

The inadequacy of the modest economic reforms was highlighted in the 1981-1982 slump. Until then, declining coffee and diamond production and stagnant oil exports had been offset by rising world commodity prices. But in 1981, a 50 percent fall in coffee prices, the slackening of the oil market, and a drop in diamond revenue triggered a foreign exchange crisis. Angola's international reserves dropped by two-thirds from 1980 to 1982, while the current account deficit grew by a factor of twenty in 1981 alone.[19]

The MPLA responded in December 1982 by giving dos Santos emergency powers, scrapping the First Congress's economic guidelines and severely curbing imports. In addition, the government stopped paying cash for imports and started to use credit facilities offered by trading partners. The debt service ratio therefore rose from 9 percent in 1980 to 17 percent in 1983, still a manageable figure.[20]

Another attempt to shore up the economy was the 1983 decision to introduce a series of emergency plans. These have never been published, but they reportedly make defense the top priority, followed by provisions of basic foodstuffs, increased material support for "family sector" farming, rehabilitation of the coffee industry, and the expansion of the supply of consumer goods to the countryside.

Finally, Angola was fortunate that just at the time of the crisis, the effects of growing oil company confidence in the MPLA's stability and the consequent doubling of oil exploration investment from 1981 to 1982 began to be felt. Gulf, Texaco, Elf Aquitaine, Cities Services, and Agip all put funds in, and oil production increased from the 1978-1982 average of 130,000 barrels per day to 179,000 barrels per day in 1983.[21]

The combination of new measures and the oil revenue began to turn the economy around. By the end of 1983, the current accounts deficit had recovered to the 1980 level and, by 1984, international reserves were up to about half the 1980 mark.[22]

However, Angola was still not out of the economic woods. UNITA scattered mines in many of the richest agricultural areas, and peasants stopped cultivating. Continued South African cross-border activity meant that a whole section of the south remained a "no-go" area. An estimated 600,000 peasants became refugees and a consequent drain on government resources. Despite government efforts, peasants still had no consumer goods or market transport to encourage their production. These problems in food production, combined with the new import curbs, triggered an explosion in the already vigorous black market, or *candonga*. The parallel markets received colorful names, such as "Bikini Strip," presumably because you had to sell even your underwear to buy there, and "Shut Up," referring to the need to keep black market transactions hidden from the authorities. A kilogram of potatoes came to cost half a month's pay. So while the government's accounts looked better, those of the average household went deeply into the red.

In late 1983, dos Santos responded to the deteriorating security situation and the continuing economic dislocation by establishing a new Defense and Security Council (DSC). This gave party figures close to him direct responsibility for a wide range of economic and political sectors, and virtually superseded the Council of Ministers. Regional Military Councils (RMCs) were established for all areas affected by the war and given responsibility for economic decisions in their respective territories. The RMCs reported directly to the DSC, bypassing the normal government structure. Clearly, the military was taking a growing role in both political and economic decision making, and dos Santos's personal power was increasing.

The president then used this new clout to follow up initiatives started earlier which were bogged down in internal debate. The January 1985 First National Conference, held to start preparations for the Second Congress due eleven months later, invigorated the reform campaign.

Dos Santos's opening speech at the conference laid out the foundation for future internal economic policy in the following terms: "One—giving absolute priority to defense needs; two—improving supplies to the population and attaining greater efficiency at work and in production as a precondition for guaranteeing the process of economic and social stabilization; [see below for three]; four—perfecting the methods of stabilizing the economy; and five—applying in a more efficient manner the evaluation of worth."[23]

This last statement was particularly important, for it implied a market rather than a bureaucratic approach to pricing. Already this policy had been unofficially followed, as the government increasingly winked at the black market, or *"candonga."* (Apparently, the authorities came to understand that the candonga was becoming the only source for many staple products, and was therefore impossible to repress efficiently.) The final conference resolution approved dos Santos's recommendations, and the MPLA's above-mentioned process of adjusting classical Marxist political theory to fit with existing economic realities moved forward.

However, during the same period, contradictions between external political and economic relationships intensified. Repeated South African invasions, and increasing UNITA activities gave the MPLA additional reasons to maintain good political relations with the socialist countries. At the same time, economic ties with the West became stronger than ever.

The 1981-1982 financial difficulties and the resultant emphasis on credit tied Angola even closer to Western suppliers. One government official commented, "The socialist countries offer better credit terms, but the total volume is limited. The West gives tougher terms, but can provide the volume we need."[24] As Angola increasingly bought from whoever could supply credit, Western goods gained a competitive edge.

In the above-mentioned First National Conference, dos Santos listed as the third item "giving priority and dynamism to economic relations with other countries to provide equilibrium to the economy," although he did not make it clear if this meant relations with Eastern or Western nations.[25] However, in April 1985, Angola announced that it would join the EEC's Lomé Convention, implying that the latter hemisphere had gained the upper hand in its economic priorities. This was significant because the treaty is viewed by some as involving recognition of Berlin as a part of West Germany, a gesture Angola's socialist allies would resent. Angola had long been an observer member of COMECON, and, in the final weeks before the announcement, numerous socialist country delegations arrived in Luanda hoping to forestall the Lomé decision. However, while not implying that this was COMECON's fault, Angolan officials privately remarked that COMECON could not offer Angola the same terms it gave Vietnam and Cuba.[26]

Angola probably joined the Lomé Convention less because it needed the aid on offer than because it wanted to make a good impression on Western bankers. The negotiations for a $350 million loan to finance the expansion of Gulf's Takula field were at hand, and the political climate in the United States meant the U.S. export credit, which had helped previous deals, would probably not be extended. The Takula financing went through smoothly. Paradoxically, the U.S. Bankers Trust led the syndication at the same time that the United States lifted the Clark Amendment prohibiting United States aid to UNITA, and Luanda-Washington relations strained to near breaking point.

Dos Santos continued to court Western business through 1985, taking time out during his visit to New York for the United Nation's anniversary celebrations to meet with businessmen, and later sending an economic team on a long tour of the United States. The political-economic contradictions continued, with the U.S. Congress proposing aid to UNITA while the Angolan delegation was reporting the advantages of economic cooperation with the United States back in Luanda.

The Angolan Central Bank also reportedly advised that the country would benefit economically from joining that bastion of the free market theory, the International Monetary Fund, although the idea awaited ratification by other government departments.[27]

Angola's desire to balance East with West was also highlighted in

1985 by the start up of the huge Kapanda dam project. The Soviet Union is experienced in the construction of such dams, and hoped to win both the management and construction contracts. According to unconfirmed sources, initially the Soviet Union received the contract for turbine supply and for overall accounting, while Brazilian firms won the rest of the execution contracts. However, the MPLA then reportedly decided to give the Brazilians the accounting responsibility as well, putting Brazilian managers in charge of monitoring Soviet billing.[28]

As 1985 drew to a close, economic ties with the West were stronger than ever. Angolan nonarms trade with the Eastern Bloc still only accounted for about 2 percent of total Angolan trade. Portugal, the United States, and France were the country's major suppliers, while the United States, the Bahamas, and Brazil remained the main buyers of Angolan goods.[29]

However, just as increased economic cooperation with the United States coincided with deteriorating political relations, the stagnating economic relations with COMECON countries were accompanied by an increase in political-military contacts. The MPLA September 1985 offensive did Savimbi more damage than any previous attack, and South Africa responded with air strikes that decimated MPLA equipment. Luanda concluded that South Africa would back Savimbi more vigorously than before, and the need for replacement arms from the Soviet Union became apparent. The United States congressional threat to fund UNITA no doubt also heightened MPLA concern to maintain this supply route.

By the end of the second half-decade of Angolan independence, the MPLA was on better economic terms and worse political terms with the West than ever before, while political-military relations with the East remained strong even as economic links stagnated.

The Second Congress and Beyond

The contradictory trends between Angola's economic and political life became more pronounced as the country entered its second decade of independence in November 1985.

The period started off with the party's Second Congress. Held in December 1985, it consolidated and expanded many of the pragmatic internal economic reforms discussed earlier in the year. The following were among the most important decisions:

1. Economic management was officially decentralized. Enterprise managers were given more autonomy, and told to make day-to-day decisions on their own, without having to constantly refer back to the central authority. Provincial officials were given similar decision making autonomy.

2. The congress deemphasized, but did not abandon, state farms. More emphasis was given to the peasant, private, and loosely structured cooperative sector, which produces most of Angola's food.

3. To stimulate peasant production the congress instructed that consumer goods be sent to the rural areas, to give the farmer something to buy with the local currency he receives in payment for his crop.

4. The congress favorably reviewed the suggestion that peasants be given foreign exchange payments in reward for high production. The scheme will take a while to implement, but is officially welcomed. If it works well, it may be extended to reward firms producing for export.

5. The overvaluation of the local currency, the kwanza, was debated. The party promised to "create conditions [for] stabilizing the purchasing power of the national currency by establishing rigorous controls over increased amounts of money in circulation and ensuring supplies of goods and services to satisfy the solvent demands of the population, while creating the appropriate mechanisms for fighting...black marketeering." After the congress, Angolan economic experts remarked that a modest devaluation of the kwanza may eventually occur.

6. Foreign-exchange-saving measures were outlined. The congress particularly focused on the cost of Western technical advisors, and concluded that they should increasingly be replaced with Angolans.

7. Development priorities were adjusted to favor completion of existing projects and rehabilitation of installations that had fallen into disrepair.

8. The congress suggested that the code governing foreign investment be rewritten to make it easier to understand and more attractive to potential investors.[30]

Although still espousing socialist rhetoric, the Second Congress resolutions clearly represented another step in the MPLA's efforts to adjust Marxist political theory to Angola's specific conditions.

However, no sooner was the ink dry on the resolutions than international oil prices collapsed, disrupting the government's budgetary planning and reducing the foreign exchange available to implement the reforms. This had interesting implications for Angola's external economic alignments.

The 1986 budget was drafted on the assumption that oil prices would remain at about twenty-five dollars per barrel. When the price hit eighteen dollars in February 1986, President dos Santos announced that the government would lose a third of its budget, about $600 million. The price then continued its downward spiral, eventually dipping below ten dollars a barrel before starting to modestly recover.

Rising oil production offset some of the price drop, however, and Angola did not suffer as much as the price fall would suggest. Production, estimated a 285,000 barrels per day in 1985, was scheduled to rise to at least 300,000 in 1986, keeping the country on target for its goal of 500,000 by 1990. In mid-1986, oil experts predicted that that year's production would earn Angola between one-half and two-thirds of the previous year's revenue.

As in the 1981-1982 foreign exchange shortfall, the economic problems encouraged Angola to solidify economic relations with the West to aid the credit search. Angola sent financial delegations to Europe in search of additional finance, and finally approved an investment and trade roundtable with Western businesses, which had been awaiting a decision for three years. Organized by the Geneva-based consultancy and publishing firm Business International, the June 1986 gathering in Luanda was attended by over forty companies.

Political relations, however, veered off in the other direction. After much debate, the United States decided to permit Savimbi to visit Washington in early 1986. By March, Pentagon officials were leaking stories to the press that the United States had decided to provide Savimbi with surface-to-air Stinger missiles.

The underlying contradiction between Angola's external economic and political relations therefore became starkly obvious. The United States was funding the MPLA's rival while United States companies traded with and lent money to the same government. Not surprisingly, congressional and private sector Savimbi supporters introduced measures designed to make economic relations as hostile as the political ones. The process started in January 1986, when Assistant Secretary of State for African Affairs Chester Crocker, apparently responding to pressure from the Right, said Chevron and other companies operating in Angola "should be thinking about U.S. national interests as well as their own corporate interests when making their decisions."[31] In March a State Department spokesman added, "U.S. economic policy toward Angola is: (1) to deny, pending an achievement of a negotiated settlement, all U.S. exports to Angola with a military use, and (2) to not support Angola's ability to earn foreign currency and thus fund its war against UNITA until the government of Angola demonstrates clear intent to reach a negotiated settlement on Namibian independence and in that context Cuban troop withdrawal."[32]

The Commerce Department then prevented the sale of a Lockheed aircraft on the grounds that it might be used to transport Cuban troops.

The United States Export-Import Bank (EXIM)also adopted a new policy of refusing to finance any sale that would help the MPLA earn foreign exchange with which to fight the war against UNITA, and faced congressional pressure to suspend all dealings with Angola. A "Chevron out of Angola" campaign was launched by the Conservative Caucus Foundation, using shareholder resolutions and boycotts of Chevron service stations. In addition, the Department of Defense announced it would review Chevron's military contracts in light of its operations in Angola. Eventually, the Department of Defense decided against punishing Chevron by cancelling its military contracts, but in late 1986 did rule that the U.S. military would not purchase any oil that originated in Angola.

So far, anti-MPLA initiatives in Washington have not resulted in significant reduction of U.S. business activities in Angola. And even if the United States were to cease all economic contacts with Angola, this would not reduce the level of Angolan links with the West, as European firms will be happy to fill any shoes the United States might vacate. France's Elf Aquitaine has expressed interest in buying Chevron's oil interests, as have Italian firms. If EXIM cuts Angolan credit, Britain's Export Credit Guarantee Department (ECGD) and France's Compagnie Française d'Assurance pour le Commerce Extérieur (COFACE) have a good opinion of Luanda's payment record, and would probably continue cover. Indeed, economic relations with Britain have recently hit a new high, with the May 1986 signing of a new general cooperation agreement.

By late 1986, Angola was on track to continue contradictory external economic and political relationships. As of that date, it seemed likely that the country would appeal for more Western credit and rewrite its investment code to attract more Western investment, while political relations with its major trading partner, the United States, deteriorated to a state characterized by the MPLA as undeclared war. However, in the internal sphere, the Second Congress brought some progress in adjusting Marxist political theory to fit Angolan economic realities.

Some European diplomats draw a conclusion from these facts that may not be warranted, but at least bears a hearing. They say that by adjusting internal economic policy, albeit agonizingly slowly, the MPLA has shown its willingness to modify political ideology to suit circumstances. They add that, if South Africa were to halt attacks on Angola and if the United States were to suspend Savimbi aid, removing the security motivation for maintaining links with Soviet Union, this pragmatism could extend to the external sphere, permitting the existing good economic relations Angola enjoys with the West to mature into better political relations. This idea hinges on the assumption that once cut off from South African and U.S. support, UNITA would no longer be such a threat that the MPLA would need Eastern Bloc security help, an assumption that is unproven. Whether such U.S. and South African moves really would change the contradictory character of Angola's external relations is therefore open to debate. But, under current circumstances, it seems unlikely the theory will be tested in practice.

Notes

1. Lawrence W. Henderson, *Angola, Five Centuries of Conflict* (Ithaca, N.Y.: Cornell University Press, 1979), 81.

2. Ibid., 94.

3. Ibid., 93.

4. Slavery was actually legally ended earlier, but the Portuguese continued to practice it until 1850 when a British naval squadron off the coast of Brazil forced its suspension.

5. Gerald Bender, *Angola Under the Portuguese* (London: Heineman Educational Books, 1978), 28.

6. Henderson, *Angola, Five Centuries*, 144.

7. Ibid., 210.

8. David and Marina Ottaway, *Afrocommunism* (New York: Africana Publishing Company, 1981), 110.

9. Ibid.

10. Michael Wolfers and Jane Bergerol, *Angola in the Frontline* (London: Zed Press, 1983), 131.

11. Ottaway, *Afrocommunism*, 118; and Wolfers and Bergerol, *Angola in the Frontline*, 134-136.

12. Ottaway, *Afrocommunism*, 119.

13. Michael Clough, ed., *Changing Realities in Southern Africa* (Berkley: Institute of International Studies, University of California, 1982), 211.

14. Ottaway, *Afrocommunism*, 111-112.

15. Ibid., 118.

16. Ibid., 117.

17. Wolfers and Bergerol, *Angola in the Frontier*, 141.

18. Second Congress of Angolan Trades Unions, 1977.

19. Figures drawn from the Economist Intelligence Unit (EIU) Quarterly Economic Review of Angola, 1985 Annual Supplement and QER, no. 3, 1985.

20. Ibid.

21. Ibid.

22. Ibid.

23. First National Conference Documents, ANGOP.

24. Author's interviews in Luanda, 1985.

25. First National Conference Documents.

26. Author's interviews in Luanda, 1985.

27. Author's interviews in Luanda, June 1986.

28. Author's interviews in Luanda, 1985.

29. EIU

30. "Second Congress of the MPLA-Workers Party," ANGOP; and author's interviews in February and June 1986.

31. Chester Crocker: quoted in "Crocker States Type of Support Needed for UNITA", *Africa Wire File*, 29 January 1986.

32. Charles Redman, *State Department Report*, 25 March 1986.

Afro-Marxism in a Market Economy: Public Policy in Zimbabwe

Michael Bratton
Stephen Burgess

In April 1980, the apparatus of the state in the settler colony of Rhodesia passed to the Zimbabwe African National Union (Patriotic Front), led by Robert Mugabe. The transfer of formal authority culminated a bitter political and military struggle in which two guerrilla armies, the dominant one avowedly Marxist-Leninist, wrested control of the countryside from a racial oligarchy of white landowners, industrialists, and public officials. The scene appeared to be set for a classic confrontation between zealous revolutionaries committed to the transformation of property relations and domestic capitalists with entrenched interests in industry and agriculture.

The drama that has since unfolded has been less polarized and more intricate than the initial scenario might have suggested. Confrontation has in some instances given way to accommodation, and social change has been measured rather than momentous. Zimbabwe's road to socialism has, so far, involved the preservation of a capitalist system of production in order to fuel the redistributive expenses of an African welfare state.

Against a backdrop of racial and class accommodation, fundamental antagonisms remain in postcolonial politics in Zimbabwe. These antagonisms are expressed in political competition over access to and control of the state. The institutions of the state comprise a focal arena for political activity, and the policies of the state constitute the substance over which different social actors compete. At the same time, the political elite endeavors to promote its own projects through the instrumentality of the state, but its capacity to do so depends crucially on the health of the national economy. This, in turn, is dependent on international and environmental factors and on the viability of the public budget.

Within the general conditions set by macroeconomic performance, the

199

Mugabe government's attempts to initiate redistributive public policies in the period from 1980 to 1985 can be explained in political terms. The new revolutionary elite enjoyed considerable popular legitimacy, won as a result of its leadership in the liberation war. The existence of a broad base of political support allowed the regime, on some occasions, to create an autonomous realm for state action and to fulfill promises of redistribution in favor of popular classes. On other occasions, the regime found the autonomy of the state to be impaired and opted for policies that favored the dominant classes. The ruling party had difficulty resisting a technically sophisticated bureaucracy, strong private sector lobbies, and concerted pressure from international donors and bankers. Against such pressures, the party leadership lacked ideological clarity and organizational cohesion.

The redistributive role of the state in the Zimbabwe case indicates that state autonomy and power are not "all or nothing" phenomena. Left-of-center regimes are sometimes able to sustain their programs and at other times they are not. In order to conceptualize this relationship between state and society, however, there is no need to resort to vague incantations about the "relativity" of autonomy. Instead, it is possible to be more specific by asking: In relation to what policy issues, and in relation to what social groups, is the state more or less autonomous? The answer to this question is likely to reveal the pragmatic core of a regime's development strategy and to determine the "openings" in the social structure (i.e., specific points of autonomy from dominant classes) that provide a regime with opportunities to maneuver.

It is desirable to develop and apply comparative concepts to the analysis of public policy. Policies of redistribution will be classified according to whether the resources at stake are public services, private incomes, or private assets. It is expected that a reformist regime will face a progressively higher intensity of political opposition as it attempts to move its redistributive efforts up this scale. As the case of Zimbabwe will show, the Mugabe government has been aggressive in distributing social services to the populace at large, but distinctly wary of dispossessing capitalist classes of their assets in private property.

Class analysis offers the most promising framework for understanding social competition over the largesse of the state, providing that this perspective does not ignore the salience of racial, ethnic, and regional identities in allocation decisions. In the case of Zimbabwe, the aspirant socialist regime has fabricated an unconventional alliance that cuts across lines of class conflict. The regime favors the agrarian sector, which includes both black smallholders in the Shona-speaking parts of the country and white, large-scale, commercial farmers. The relationship of the regime with the urban and industrial sectors—in this case, with both multinational and domestic firms, and with black trade unions—is more strained and problematic. The argument will be made in this chapter that the choice of allies by an "Afro-Marxist" state leadership in a market economy depends as much on the strategic economic position encountered by key political actors as upon the solidarities of class consciousness.

Market Economy
With the exception of South Africa, Zimbabwe has the most advanced market economy on the African subcontinent. Basic infrastructure—a modern road and rail network, highly capitalized farms and factories, and sophisticated financial institutions—has already been laid down. By African standards, economic activity is commercialized not only in the towns, but also in the outlying rural areas. By 1985, Zimbabwe had more people in wage employment (about 12 percent of the population) than in any other black-ruled neighbor in Southern Africa, and within Zimbabwe more than 30 percent of rural households received wage remissions from family members working in town. The most common economic activity—peasant farming—is increasingly oriented toward the market. Almost all peasant households purchase modern inputs (95 percent buy seed, 61 percent buy fertilizer), and one out of every two households is registered to sell agricultural commodities to an official marketing board.[1]

According to aggregate national accounts, the Zimbabwe economy is highly diversified. Industry (defined here as mining, manufacturing, and construction) makes up 32 percent of gross domestic product, with agriculture accounting for a mere 11 percent.[2] Yet agriculture is strategic: it guarantees national food self-sufficiency and leads to the provision of employment and foreign exchange earnings. In all but the worst drought years, Zimbabwe produces enough corn to satisfy national requirements, an exceptional success story in a continent wracked by declining per capita food production. At independence, the commercial farms and estates provided 33 percent of formal wage employment, compared with 26 percent for industry. Moreover, agricultural export crops (tobacco, sugar, and cotton) consistently earn the largest proportion of the nation's foreign exchange—around 40 percent of total export revenues in the early 1980s, rising to an estimated 65 percent in 1984.

The strength of agriculture contrasts with the recent anemic performance of mining and manufacturing. Prices for gold, nickel, and copper have declined steadily in the 1980s, and demand for asbestos has slumped. Mines have been closed and mineworkers have been laid off. The manufacturing sector, developed to substitute for imports during the period of international sanctions against Rhodesia, is unsuited for competition in export markets and, far from contributing to export revenues, remains a net user of foreign exchange. The relative advantage of agriculture over manufacturing in generating employment and export earnings explains the strategic nature of that sector and, in turn, helps to explain the pattern of relations between the regime and dominant classes in Zimbabwe.

Overall, the structure of Zimbabwe's market economy is basically sound, and the prospects for future growth are promising. The economy nonetheless remains "open," with growth heavily dependent upon international trade. To the extent that international recession reduces demand for exports and inhibits capacity to import, Zimbabwe finds itself in the familiar Third World plight of having to turn to the international financial community for development capital. The fiscal crisis of the state, in the form of debt burden and budget deficits, is not as advanced in Zimbabwe as in other African countries, but, as we will show, external dependence for budgetary resources reduces the capacity for autonomous state action.

"Afro-Marxist" Regime

During the colonial period in Zimbabwe, African political leaders, Robert Mugabe included, came to associate free enterprise capitalism with racial discrimination and unequal access to opportunity. From this analysis, a deduction was made that attainment of political and economic equity required a commitment to some form of socialism. The present regime in Zimbabwe is by its own description committed "to establish and sustain a socialist state in Zimbabwe based on Marxist-Leninist principles."[3] Robert Mugabe publicly declares that capitalism is "immoral" because it is based on the usurpation of property rights.[4]

Mugabe and the ZANU-PF leadership have sought to ensure that ideological development will not be based on the uncritical importation of foreign concepts, but must be guided by the distinctive conditions prevailing in Zimbabwe. Insofar as it has been spelled out, the "Zimbabwean road to socialism" is an intriguing variant of "Afro-Marxism." The national ideology is more gradualist, nationalist, and democratic when compared, for example, with that of Ethiopia, and bears some resemblance to the Marxism that guided European social democratic parties at the turn of the century. There is an explicit recognition that Zimbabwe inherited a thoroughly capitalist economic structure that "cannot be changed overnight" and that the construction of socialism is a multistage project that will take decades, if not generations.[5]

Against this moderate thrust, "radical populists" within the party have imprinted their preferences on national ideology, for example through resolutions passed at the ZANU-PF Second Party Congress of August 1984. Party policy now requires that "government must intensify socialization of the economy" through state ownership of the means of production, worker education and self-management, cooperative ventures in industry, commerce and trade, control of banking and insurance, and public sector economic activity through parastatal bodies. In the agricultural sector, resolutions recommitted the party to land reform, cooperative development, and the creation of state farms. In order to ensure party control of government, a Politburo was established with five standing committees for policy formulation and supervision. A leadership code was also launched to encourage ideological purity, for example by barring ZANU-PF leaders from serving as company directors, profiting from nepotism, and owning more than fifty acres of land. Mugabe commented that, in order to secure political independence, ZANU had let capitalists into the leadership, but they would now be forced to choose between remaining in the leadership or leaving to continue with the private accumulation of capital.

The practice of the Mugabe government to date belies much of its own populist rhetoric. The regime has endorsed a program for socialist change without committing itself to full or rapid implementation. The achievement of objectives has been sought through reformist rather than revolutionary means. The path of expropriation and collectivization of property that Mozambique and Ethiopia chose to follow was bypassed in the years 1979-1980 when the Lancaster House agreement brought about a nonrevolutionary transfer of power. For the period discussed here, 1980-1985, the clearest ideological point in the Mugabe platform is the determination of the leadership to keep the nationalist and social welfare promises made during the 1980 and 1985 election campaigns: to provide the social services, educational opportunities, and rural development so long denied to the country's black majority. It is from this point that any analysis of "socialist" political economy and public policy in Zimbabwe must begin.

Policy Overview: 1980-1985

At independence, the government of Zimbabwe embarked on a program that it described as "growth with equity." The objective of this strategy was to generate substantial economic expansion which, in turn, would permit redistribution. A good example of the intended approach was in agriculture: the government simultaneously aimed to sustain high levels of output from the commercial farm industry while it sought to redirect resources into the promotion of the long-neglected smallholder sector.

In the first six years of independence, perturbations in the domestic and international environments forced a realignment of the balance away from expansionism and toward austerity. At first, in 1980 and 1981, the economy grew rapidly in response to the lifting of sanctions and improvements in the international terms of trade, notably for gold. The government contributed to this buoyant climate with increased foreign borrowing, expanded allocations of foreign exchange for imports, and liberal fiscal, monetary, and income policies. The economy grew by a remarkable 14 percent in 1980. These favorable conditions provided the government with the fiscal capacity to respond quickly and generously to popular demand from both rural and urban masses for improvements in living standards and access to services. It was in this early period that the principal pillars of Zimbabwe's welfare socialism were erected.

In 1982, however, the boom came to an abrupt end. Export earnings subsided in the face of an international economic recession, and overland trade routes were disrupted by a regional campaign of economic destabilization conducted by South Africa. Nor did Zimbabwe escape the effects of the devastating three-year drought that shriveled agricultural output throughout Southern Africa. Far from reaching the ambitious plan target of 8 percent annual growth, gross domestic product fell in real terms in 1982 and 1983 and stagnated in 1984. In addition, the new leaders of Zimbabwe began to live with the consequences of their own policy choices. The public budget ballooned both in response to the government's redistributive policies and to the provision of emergency drought relief. The outcome was a budget deficit that grew to 10 percent of GDP.

As the recession deepened, the government was forced in late 1982 to turn to the International Monetary Fund for an infusion of capital. The conditions imposed by the IMF included a devaluation of the Zimbabwe dollar and limitations on the size of balance-of-payments and budget deficits. In practice, the government was unable to adhere to a deflationary program and, with the publication of supplementary public expenditure estimates in February 1984, the IMF standby collapsed.

In the negotiations to reconstruct Zimbabwe's eligibility, many of the government's strategic policy objectives had to be temporarily shelved, and ad hoc decisions were made in an effort to sustain output and employment. Policy choices thus came to reflect a compromise between a conventional economic stabilization program and a political commitment to redistribution in the form of subsidies, transfer payments, and expenditures on social services. This dissonant combination led one commentator to dub Zimbabwe a "tropical paradox."[6]

Mugabe's Redistributive Regime

We now discuss the redistributive measures undertaken by the Mugabe government within the conceptual framework outlined in the introduction to this chapter. Our discussion begins with the type of policy that is relatively "easy" to implement, namely the reallocation of public services, because its costs are diffuse and deferrable. We subsequently move on to the more "difficult" types of policy, culminating in a discussion of the acquisition by government of private assets, the consequences of which are immediate and specifically aimed at dominant classes. In between, the intermediate case of private incomes is considered.

Public Services

The Mugabe government has used the public budget as its principal instrument of social redistribution by making substantial outlays for mass social services.

One of the government's first acts was to abolish fees for primary education and to introduce a massive expansion program for rural schools. Free universal education had broad popular appeal. Every family in Zimbabwe aspires to educate at least one of its sons to become a breadwinner and, with half the population under the age of fifteen, it was a rare family that did not stand to benefit. An innovative in-service training program was introduced to meet the sudden demand for rural schoolteachers. The government also undertook to improve access to secondary, vocational, and university education.

As a result of the government's policy commitment, Zimbabwe has achieved a level of progress in the first five years of independence that has taken poorer developing countries decades to achieve. The number of schools has been increased by 73 percent and the number of school places by 205 percent. By 1985, nearly all children of primary school age were in school, in contrast to about half in 1980. Expansion at the secondary level was even more dramatic, with 82 percent of primary school leavers entering secondary school in 1983 compared with 12 percent before independence. Although figures are not yet available, adult literacy is expected to have made discernable progress.

The government also reformed health policy to emphasize primary care and preventive medicine, especially for rural dwellers. Within a year of independence, almost all the rural clinics destroyed or damaged in the war had been rebuilt, and medical fees for low-income patients were abolished. Special programs were introduced for maternal and child health education and for the supplementary feeding of children diagnosed to be at risk of malnutrition. Together, these programs led to a rapid increase in outpatient attendance.

The benefits of the preventive health policy quickly became evident. A 1984 government survey found that the proportion of children fully immunized against common childhood diseases had risen from 25 percent to 42 percent.[7] The minister of health was able to make a landmark announcement in June 1985 that the infant mortality rate for Zimbabwe had been halved from 120 to 60 per 1,000 live births.[8] In addition, maternal health education has led to an estimated contraceptive prevalence rate in Zimbabwe of 15 to 20 percent of women of child-bearing age, possibly the highest rate in Africa.[9]

The redistribution of public services has raised the quality of life for the population of Zimbabwe and built a base for a more equitable pattern of economic growth in the future. But the attainment of equity objectives has come at a high price, most notably in terms of pressure on the public treasury. After peaking at 25 percent of the national budget in 1981, combined education and health spending had to be cut back to the present level of 19 percent. It is worth noting, however, that the proportion of gross domestic product going to education in Zimbabwe is still almost double that of other African countries.[10]

Fiscal austerity has led to qualitative as well as quantitative changes in government policy. Fees have been reintroduced for certain medical and educational services. The government has called upon parents to shoulder responsibility for the construction of school buildings, the hiring of supplementary teachers, and the provision of extracurricular programs. While encouraging community self-reliance, this policy tends to undercut the drive for equity between high-income, suburban communities and marginal communities in town and countryside. One of the factors in the exodus of skilled professionals from the country has been the perceived decline in the quality of medical and educational services. As a result, the government has already softened its initially hostile stance toward private, fee-paying schools and hospitals, even to the extent of turning a blind eye to the fact that these institutions have been slow to integrate racially.

Private Incomes

The second leg in the government's redistributive strategy was to reduce income differentials, principally by raising the wages of the lowest-paid and by introducing progressive taxes.

In September 1980, minimum wages were introduced for the first time for workers in the agricultural, industrial, and domestic service sectors. The levels of minimum wages were subsequently raised over the next two years, resulting in real gains of 63 percent for farmworkers and 22 percent gains for urban workers, At the inception of the campaign for the July 1985 elections, a further 15 percent bonus was awarded. Upper-level salaries, pegged at first at Z$20,000 and later Z$36,000, were frozen. In addition to income legislation, job security was improved with regulations preventing employers from dismissing workers without first applying for permission from the Ministry of Labour.

The government introduced a number of measures between 1980 and 1985 to enhance its revenue base. Marginal taxes were raised to 53 percent on personal incomes above Z$15,000. The flat rate on corporate income was pegged at the same level, with few exemptions available. In addition, individuals and companies were expected to pay a tax surcharge in 1984 to help the government offset the expense of drought relief. The tax base is extremely narrow: in a country of eight million people, only 100,000 bear the entire personal tax burden. Because the scope for further increases in government revenues seemed limited, the minister of finance in 1984 announced the introduction of a nominal 2 percent tax on low-income wage earners.

Most adults in Zimbabwe do not enjoy paid employment in the formal sector and thus are beyond the redistributive reach of wage and tax policies. The majority of self-employed people live off the land, and family farming is the main source of income opportunity. In the first five years of independence, agricultural policies were realigned away from the large-scale commercial farmer and toward the smallholder. The government raised official producer prices for most crops at a rate ahead of inflation in the costs of production. New crops, including the millets and sorghums produced by small farmers, were added to the list of controlled commodities for which the government provides a guaranteed market. A network of supply and collection points was established in the "communal" farming areas with the aim of improving the access of the smallholder to the market.

The Muzorewa regime (1978-1979) had introduced consumer subsidies on basic food items in a bid to retain urban political loyalties in the closing stages of the liberation war. The Mugabe government inherited this cheap food policy but abandoned it in 1983. Despite subsidy reduction, agriculture still accounts for the largest share of subsidies in the budget, but government has made clear its intention ultimately to allow the market to determine food prices. The government has, therefore, refused to subsidize urban consumers at the expense of rural producers. Instead, the farming community enjoys attractive incentives to earn income from agricultural production, thereby guaranteeing the government with supplies to satisfy demand for food from the cities.

Since independence, there has most probably been a modicum of income redistribution away from higher-income urban households toward the rural poor. The policy of opening up market opportunities to small agricultural producers has been a notable success. Between 1980 and 1985, smallholders moved from producing less than 10 percent of total marketed output of maize and cotton to an estimated 45 percent. Although detailed and comprehensive figures are not available on rural household incomes, this shift has undoubtedly had a positive effect on incomes where these crops are produced.

For urban dwellers, however, the positive effect of redistribution was offset by the unanticipated consequences of wage policies, namely the rise in consumer prices and the decline in employment opportunities. Despite measures to reallocate incomes, workers experienced a decline in purchasing power in the first five years of independence. The price of foodstuffs for lower-income urban families more than doubled (107 percent) in the period 1980 to 1984. Urban workers spend about half their income on food. Yet urban minimum wages rose only 42 percent over the same period, with a freeze imposed in 1983 and 1984. The current level of real per capita income (approximately Z$430) is estimated to be no higher in 1985 than it was in 1965.[11]

Another worrisome long-term trend in the economy is the declining availability of jobs. Whereas in 1974, 18 percent of the population had employment in the formal sector, by 1985 the proportion had fallen to an estimated 12 percent.[12] This shift was partly attributed to population growth, but also was due to low levels of investment and a subsequent decline in the demand for labor. There was a real loss of employment opportunities (from 1.05 million to 0.99 million between 1980 and 1985), mostly in commercial agriculture and domestic service.

Redistributive policies do not always produce the intended result. One inadvertent effect of the introduction of regulations on minimum wages and job security in Zimbabwe has been to contribute to the loss of jobs. Because of the rising cost of labor, industrialists and commercial farmers shifted resources into capital-intensive operations; because of the ban on worker dismissals, employers have been reluctant to commit themselves to hiring for fear of being saddled with excess labor capacity during downturns in the business cycle.[13]

The decline in job prospects illustrates not only the unintended effects of policy, but also the potential for contradiction between different redistributory policies. In the Zimbabwe case, education policy can be seen to work at cross-purposes with employment policy. The loss of jobs is occurring against a backdrop of a rapidly expanding pool of entrants into the job market. In order to keep pace with the number of secondary school graduates, the economy must currently generate 80,000 new jobs annually.

Private Assets

Of the three levels of redistributive policy, the Zimbabwe government has been least active in restructuring property relations. Predictions that wholesale nationalization of land and factories would follow in the wake of independence have not come to pass.

A cautious resettlement program was launched in September 1980 to acquire land from commercial farmers for redistribution to the landless. All land acquisition has been made by the government in transactions on the open market without resort to seizure or confiscation. Most of the places in resettlement schemes have been made available to individual households and only a minority have taken the form of a production collective. Government ministers have emphasized that, although resettlement can relieve land pressure in the peasant farming areas and lead to a more equitable distribution of natural resources, it is also essential that an adequate economic return from the program be achieved for both the individual households and the economy as a whole.

The government's plan, including both intensive and accelerated resettlement programs, was to relocate 162,000 households by July 1985. However, by the target date, just 35,000 households had been resettled on an area that accounted for 11 percent of the commercial land area. Land reform was slowed by drought and by planning and financial constraints. In the face of the high cost of land acquisition and improvement, and given limited state capacity to administer resettlement, the government altered course. Land reform bore the brunt of austerity measures introduced at the height of the economic recession. In 1983, the budget of the Ministry of Lands was slashed by 52 percent, the largest cut for any ministry, a measure that put an effective end to new resettlement.

The beneficiaries of the program have also changed. At first, the emphasis in settler selection was upon the assetless and dispossessed—former combatants, refugees, and farmworkers—but, in time, this broadened to include experienced smallholders. At Karoi, north of Harare, there is a new individual scheme for 106 plots, the smallest of which is 100 hectares. The lack of finance appears to have had its harshest effect on the collective cooperatives, many of which constitute the livelihood of the ex-combatants from the liberation war. This is a potentially explosive issue because unemployed ex-guerrillas are no longer even eligible for demobilization pay. Unexpectedly for a leadership that once enjoyed their fervent loyalty, this group is now becoming a disaffected and volatile minority.

On the industrial front, the Zimbabwe government has given mixed messages to investors. On some occasions, promises have been made that the private sector will be left intact; at other times, the regime has indulged in strident rhetoric about capturing the commanding heights of the economy. On the one hand, the government has promulgated a clear policy document on the terms for foreign investment; on the other hand, it has declined to sign an agreement with the Overseas Private Investment Corporation (OPIC), a step that would let U.S. firms insure their property against government seizure. Moreover, in March 1984, in a measure to conserve scarce foreign exchange, the government imposed currency controls, including a temporary ban on the remission of profits and dividends abroad. The government accepts the need for a fair return on investment, but the minister of finance has stated that "we have to negotiate what we mean by this."[14]

In practice, the Zimbabwe government has not been active in extending state ownership of the economy. The government was satisfied with the battery of instruments for public regulation of the economy—price and exchange controls, an extensive parastatal sector—which were inherited from the colonial regime. Also, Zimbabwe presently cannot afford to buy out private concerns on a large scale. And given the government's acknowledged reliance on the private sector to generate employment and public revenues during the transition to socialism, forced acquisition seems unlikely.

The major move since 1980 has been the establishment of a Minerals Marketing Board to oversee the disposition of Zimbabwe's trade in minerals. Public investment has also occurred in the mining sector (Hwange Colliery and MTD Mangula) and in the following subsectors: banking (Zimbank, Bank of Credit and Commerce), pharmaceuticals (CAPS Holdings), food processing (Olivine Industries), hotels (Sheraton, Holiday Inn) and publishing (Zimbabwe Newspapers, Kingstons). In addition, the government-owned Industrial Development Corporation has been used as a vehicle to rescue domestic companies in financial distress or to relieve foreigners willing to divest of their minority interests in Zimbabwe. To date, the government's approach to industrial acquisition appears to be guided more by opportunism than by a coherent underlying strategy. Nor has the government always secured a sound investment, either by paying too much for its shares or, in a bid to preserve employment, by assuming control of declining enterprises.

Foreign investment has been disappointing. The Reserve Bank of Zimbabwe reports that a mere Z$60m ($102 million U.S.) was invested between 1980 and 1985, far short of the hundreds of millions required to make a significant impact on unemployment.[15] The business community at large faces an acute shortage of foreign exchange needed to import machinery and raw materials. Since 1980, the government's allocations of foreign exchange to commerce and industry have declined by more than 60 percent in real terms. Investor confidence, foreign and domestic, is at a low ebb. The World Bank speaks of "the highly depressed state of the private sector."[16]

The Organization of the State
To what extent can the policy choices and performance of the Mugabe government be explained in terms of politics and the state? It is

inconceivable that a radical reorientation of social services or a moderate land reform program would have been undertaken in Zimbabwe without a change of political regime in 1980. Given the relative economic powerlessness of the beneficiaries of the redistributive reforms outlined above, it is clear that an instrument of political power, namely the state, was wielded on their behalf by a political elite. By the same token, the regime did not have everything its own way. Fundamental objectives in its redistributive program remain unmet, and fiscal constraints will continue to compromise the drive for equity for the foreseeable future. While some would criticize the regime's postcolonial performance as "a revolution betrayed" by an unreliable elite, we tend rather to see it as a combined result of prevailing economic conditions and limited political capacity.[17]

It is difficult to disentangle the political and economic determinants of any development trajectory. In the Zimbabwe case, the economic recession and conditions set by international bankers were central to the change of policy direction. As for politics, a common sense analysis would suggest that, as an elite consolidates its hold on state power, so its capacity to act autonomously is enhanced. Yet the Zimbabwe case does not support this view. We will argue that the Mugabe regime has been able to entrench its political position, principally through the centralization of decision making in the office of the party leader and chief executive. At the same time, however, there has been no corresponding forward movement in the cohesion of the political elite and in the effectiveness of the state bureaucracy. Since 1980, there has been a decline in political momentum, generated in the liberation war, which has helped to inhibit the Mugabe regime from carrying through more radical reforms in accordance with its Marxist ideology. In sum, political factors have worked to undermine the efficacy of political initiatives and to reinforce the effects of austerity experienced from the economic sphere.

The Centralization of Power

Theda Skocpol has argued that "political leaderships involved in revolutions must be regarded as actors struggling to make good their claims to state sovereignty."[18] The argument applies nicely to Zimbabwe where a revolutionary elite came to power without a formally structured political party and without previous experience of public management. A harrowing transition occurred under threat of a military coup from the Rhodesian armed forces, intervention from South Africa, and assassination attempts on Mugabe. A prominent preoccupation of the first five years of independence, therefore, was the institutionalization of popular rule and the assertion of control over the apparatus of the colonial state.

In Zimbabwe, the first and most crucial step in the consolidation and centralization of power clearly involved the dismantling of the Rhodesian armed forces and the building of a national army. The restrictions imposed on the Mugabe regime by the Lancaster House agreement meant that the new leadership was forced to build a conventional army on the core of the Rhodesian colonial army. For the first six months of independence, the armed forces remained under the control of General Walls and his staff. On the opposite end of the spectrum, thousands of guerrillas were confined to camps while the new government engaged in the process of demobilizing them. Subsequently, Mugabe demonstrated his leadership skills by easing out Walls and Rhodesian commanders, while drawing on their expertise. The use of former Rhodesian forces in quelling disturbances around Bulawayo in 1981 and 1982 by ex-ZIPRA forces is a prime example. At the same time, the government rapidly promoted former ZANLA commanders to top positions and provided for the formation of the Fifth Brigade, which would be unshakeably loyal to the leadership. By 1982, the army was firmly in the hands of the Mugabe regime.

The party enjoyed considerable legitimacy not only because it had provided the political leadership for the armed struggle, but because it had won a landslide victory in a multiparty election on the eve of independence in March 1980. Unlike Marxist parties in Ethiopia, Angola and Mozambique, ZANU-PF chose not to rely on unconstitutional methods for the assumption of state leadership in March 1980. Despite the party's popularity, ZANU-PF was nonetheless weakly organized, particularly at the provincial and district levels that linked the top leadership to village cells. The first years of independence were spent attempting to ensure that party organization was uniformly firm everywhere and that pliable leadership was installed in areas of suspect loyalty, such as Manicaland and Matabeleland. This process culminated in the Second Party Congress of August 1984, when ZANU-PF adopted the trappings of a Leninist organization.

The most significant outcome of the party congress was the concentration of power in the hands of the first secretary-general, a post to which Mugabe was elected. The new party constitution granted effective carte blanche to the ZANU-PF leader to appoint the membership of the fifteen-member Politburo and to influence the Central Committee, which was expanded from thirty to ninety members. Mugabe took this opportunity to promote loyalists and to sideline rivals whom he considered to be too ambitious, corrupt, or unpredictable. In addition to the centralization of power in the party, decision making in the executive branch has been gradually shifted into the office of the prime minister. As prime minister, Mugabe retained direct oversight of defense affairs from the outset, and by 1985 intelligence, provincial administration, and cooperatives were also supervised directly. Mugabe has freely used the device of the cabinet reshuffle to reassign ministers and has asserted intellectual leadership in the formulation of government policy. The way has been cleared for a transition to an executive presidency once the current constitution expires in 1990.

The fact that Mugabe and ZANU-PF have no viable rivals has strengthened the hand of the political leaders to make bold tactical decisions. From the limited information available, it appears that Mugabe has final say on issues such as minimum wage increases and the acquisition of particular industrial properties. It also appears that the decision to accept IMF conditionality in 1982 was made within a very small circle of advisers and that the majority of the Central Committee and Cabinet was not informed.

There is a danger that, within the inner circle of loyalties, a leader could become increasingly isolated and lack the objective information necessary to make sound judgements on social and economic policy. Interestingly enough, the centralization of power appears to have made Mugabe and his colleagues more cautious. The boldest redistributive strokes were made in the first heady days of independence before the party's position was completely secure and before the hardships of national economic management hit home. The momentum enjoyed by radical reformers in 1980 has since been lost. The regime's principal initiatives are now political rather than economic, most notably the determination to introduce a one-party state.

The one-party state can be regarded as the capstone in the ZANU-PF program to centralize political power. It has been pursued vigorously, but not at the expense of constitutional procedures. A bill of rights embedded in the 1979 constitution provides for freedom of association. Diverse political views have found a degree of institutional expression through political parties and an active array of formal interest groups. The judiciary has been allowed to function independently, even to the extent of handing down judgments embarrassing to the regime.[19] The leadership has declared a preference for a voluntary transition to a one-party state in which opponents cross the floor and give voluntary support to ZANU-PF. To the extent that the centralization of power is incomplete, opportunities will remain for nonstate actors to influence the decision-making process.

Bureaucratic Capacity
Evans and Reuschemeyer remind us that "the State must have at its disposal a well-developed bureaucratic apparatus...and that this depends on a more delicate, long-term process of institution-building."[20] In this regard, Zimbabwe enjoyed a couple of advantages over neighboring

territories. It inherited from the settler regime a set of public institutions infused with norms of efficiency and probity and with substantial capacity to "get things done." A related benefit of the delayed political transition was that Zimbabwe was able to build up a pool of skilled manpower trained in overseas institutions much larger than those existing in any other African countries at the time of independence. After 1980, Zimbabwe gained a favorable reputation among foreign aid administrators as having a high "absorptive capacity" to apply resources to development.

There has been substantial growth in the public bureaucracy, with the number of employees rising from 71,000 to 92,000 between 1980 and 1985. The public sector wage bill went up by 65 percent between 1981 and 1984 alone. These changes were accompanied by localization of staff with 86 percent of established positions being occupied by blacks by 1983, compared with only 32 percent at independence. Almost without exceptions, the top administrative positions of permanent secretary are now filled by black Zimbabweans.

But expansion in the size of the state and the democratization and Africanization of hiring are not necessarily synonymous with enhanced state capacity. There are still significant shortages of skilled manpower due to the inadequate education and training of blacks and the emigration of whites before independence. The cadres trained overseas or newly established vocational programs after independence are only now becoming available to government ministries. At the same time, there is a persistent "brain drain" of top talent away from the bureaucracy and toward the higher-paying private sector. For those who remain, conditions of work are deteriorating as government departments suffer budget cuts because of fiscal stringency. Of most concern is the creeping cancer of corruption that is coming to light at all levels of public administration.

The shortage of skilled and reliable managers poses problems for a state-led option of economic development and more so for any program of socialist transformation. Certain redistributive programs have already been hit hard by the difficulty of recruiting and retaining staff, most notably agricultural extension workers and rural schoolteachers. The implementation of the land reform program has been slowed by inadequate planning capacity for resettlement schemes and a shortage of budgetary resources to provide for the day-to-day needs of newly settled farmers. Farms and factories offered to the government by willing sellers have been refused because of the shortage of liquid capital with which to pay for them. In these respects, the capacity of the bureaucracy is declining, a factor that contributes to the difficulty of meeting the development objectives mandated by the politicians.

Elite Cohesion

Alfred Stepan has hypothesized that "the greater a State elite's combination of organizational strength and ideological unity, the greater the possibility of installing [a] new regime."[21] As with organizational strength, the cohesion of the elite in Zimbabwe has been imperfect.

From the inception of ZANU-PF, the leadership was a coalition of diverse elements: old guard nationalists (with experience in political agitation and international diplomacy), ZANLA guerrillas (with experience in warfare and political education), and technocrats (with professional training and experience). The fact that the independence war was curtailed by the Lancaster House negotiations, before the guerrillas were able to consummate a military victory, prevented the revolutionary process from playing itself out to the full. Consequently, the Marxist-Leninist leadership of the guerillas was caught in midstream without a clear strategy for socialist transformation that could put their revolutionary slogans into practice. In contrast, the technocrats had prepared their own ground well at a conference held in 1979 in Tanzania to map out the basic lineaments of the postindependence economic strategy.

Although acceptance of the Lancaster House constitution provided ZANU-PF with the means to prove its legitimacy, it also imposed constraints on the socialist development strategy that the radical leadership wished to pursue. The option of expropriation without compensation was firmly barred. In addition, the guerilla leaders were stripped of their organization and cadres in the field when ZANLA fighters were confined to camps and then absorbed into the national army. Finally, the demands of the transition directed attention away from the mobilization of the peasantry and toward the assumption of administrative control of an existing state. Because of all these factors, the balance of power within ZANU-PF shifted decisively in 1980 away from the radical populists who had fought the war and toward the pragmatic technocrats who had to run the state machinery.

This is not to say that factional skirmishes within the political elite did not persist. The leadership of the more radical group came to be centered in the armed forces and in new government ministries established to oversee land reform and manpower development. The military men were too preoccupied with security concerns, however, to become deeply involved in the debates over redistribution, and the radicals within the bureaucracy lacked managerial experience. The technocrats held the crucial purse strings in the Ministry of Finance and controlled the strategic portfolios of planning and agriculture. They also fitted in comfortably with the prevailing technocratic culture of the inherited bureaucracy and foreign assistance community.

Indications are that when a clash occurred between the two factions, the technocrats prevailed, presumably by persuading Mugabe of the correctness of their position. Ideologues and populists in the top leadership have suffered demotions from central party organs (Edgar Tekere) and the cabinet (Herbert Ushewokunze), whereas technocrats have been brought in (Bernard Chidzero and Nathan Shamuyarira). Perhaps the best evidence of the demise of the radical populists is the abolition of the new ministries (for land reform and manpower planning) created at independence and their reabsorption within the inherited bureaucratic structure.

State-Society Relations

The character of state institutions through which public policies are formed and implemented do not provide the sole influence exerted on policy outcomes. These outcomes also reflect the political elite's alliances and relations with social classes in society at large.

Relations with Dominant Classes

In relations with dominant class interests, the regime generally proved more accommodating to domestic than international capital. While it has been unsuccessful in attracting multinational corporations to invest in Zimbabwe, the regime has nonetheless built a state investment program around flows of grants and concessional loans from bilateral and multilateral aid agencies. Within the domestic sphere, government has been more accommodating with agrarian than industrial capital, partly because the ownership of agricultural assets is largely in the hands of Zimbabwean citizens, whereas the industrial sector, especially mining, is foreign-dominated.

One of the interesting features of development policy in Zimbabwe is the extent to which the government has permitted foreign aid donors to channel resources to the private sector. The largest component of USAID assistance, itself the largest bilateral program in Zimbabwe, is a commodity import scheme that provides foreign exchange to commercial agricultural and manufacturing enterprises. The scheme is credited with keeping numerous industries functioning, easing employment cutbacks, and creating as many as 5,000 new industrial jobs. In addition, aid donors have solidly supported the government's effort to improve the access of the poor to production and social services. The World Bank has financed smallholder credit, agricultural extension, and urban self-help housing, while other donors have provided the wherewithal for health and education reforms. Although the major donors have contributed heavily to rural development projects, it is notable that they have been unwilling to provide funds for land acquisition. Future aid plans call for a diversification of training and institutional development programs that stress private sector versus government involvement. The availability of donor funding for some issue areas and not for others clearly has a formative effect on the redistributive policies that a recipient government is able to pursue.

The state's relations with domestic capital appears to depend upon the relative strategic importance of different class factions to national economic production. We demonstrated earlier that the agricultural sector in Zimbabwe is the leading nationally owned provider of basic commodities, employment, and foreign exchange. This dominant position has provided agrarian capital with leverage to influence the formulation of state policy. The white-run Commercial Farmers Union (CFU) has preserved much of the influence that it enjoyed before independence. White commercial farmers continue to control the management committees of agricultural parastatals, and, up until 1985, a former CFU President served as minister of agriculture.

By contrast, the industrial sector lobbies—like the Zimbabwe National Chambers of Commerce, the Confederation of Zimbabwe Industries, and the Chamber of Mines—have become less influential. Whites in this sector were represented in government only at the deputy minister level, and then only from 1983 to 1985. Industrialists have been late in demonstrating that manufacturing is strategic to Zimbabwe's economic growth, and have found themselves more often in the position of having to apply to the government for foreign exchange than being able to demonstrate a capacity to generate it. A further factor in poor state-industry relations is the slowness of inexperienced government bureaucrats in processing the exchange control and other regulations that must be traversed in order to trade across Zimbabwe's borders. From a business point of view, the policy regime is heavy on regulation and short on incentive.

The issue of prices and incomes demonstrates the different degrees of autonomy of the state vis-à-vis agrarian and industrial capital. Whereas producer prices in agriculture have been revised upwards, and farmers' profit margins protected, the food processing industry has seen its profits reduced by the need to pay higher acquisition costs for raw materials. A crisis point was reached in late 1983 when shortages of maize meal arose and the prime minister angrily threatened to nationalize the milling companies. With regard to wages, the minister of finance rejected complaints from manufacturers that the July 1985 minimum wage increases would be an undue burden at a moment when returns were just beginning to pick up after the two-year recession. Not much later, however, the prime minister reversed a decision by the minister of labour that minimum wages on agricultural estates (tea, sugar, coffee) be reclassified from the agricultural rate to the higher industrial rate when faced with representations from growers that the tea, coffee, and sugar industries might be forced to close down. Within the dominant class, agricultural producers have clearly been more effective in achieving policy responses favorable to their interests.

Relations with Regime Supporters
The base of support upon which ZANU-PF came to power was predominantly rural and predominantly Shona-speaking. While the party also enjoyed a following in the towns, it was unable to wrest complete control of urban areas during the liberation war from the Smith and Muzorewa regimes. Joshua Nkomo's ZAPU further complicated this picture with its popular support in the industrial city of Bulawayo and in the rural hinterland of Matabeleland. Since 1980, the government has not succeeded in building a coalition that would have facilitated a peaceful transition to a one-party state. Instead, the government has used the coercive power of the state in an attempt to crush opposition forces and to selectively deny elements of Zimbabwe's popular classes access to Zimbabwe's redistributive revolution.

For a putatively Marxist movement with a "proletarian" ideology, ZANU-PF has had difficulty in establishing rapport with the working class, as represented by the trade union movement. Immediately after independence, workers throughout industry went on wildcat strikes in support of improved wages and conditions. The government sent them back to work with appeals to national loyalty and promises of workers' participation in management. Since then, the regime has endeavored to bring the workers and the trade unions under corporatist control and to limit their autonomy, most recently through the introduction into parliament of a Labour Relations Bill that would ban strikes by "essential" workers and restrict the rights of other workers. In 1985, the membership of the Zimbabwe Congress of Trade Unions attempted to remove their own leaders for failing to oppose the bill, but the government intervened to reinstate them.

The government has imposed an umbrella body on workers' organizations, a situation that contrasts with its attitude toward farmer organizations. While the government has urged the two existing peasant farmer unions to amalgamate with the commercial farmers' union, it has taken no steps to enforce a merger or to influence the selection of leaders. The government evidently feels less of a threat from an independent and organized peasantry than from an autonomous movement among workers.

The first test of popular support for the Mugabe government's performance came in the July 1985 elections. The governing party won a modest boost to its mandate by increasing its share of the popular vote to 67 percent as compared with 63 percent in 1980. ZANU-PF won sixty-four seats out of eighty, six more than in 1980, mostly at the expense of the minority United African National Congress (UANC) party of Abel Muzorewa.

The striking result of the election, however, was the governing party's inability to overcome regional loyalties. Despite active campaigning in Matabeleland by the prime minister and party youth wing pressure on the populace to buy party cards, every seat in the region was won by Joshua Nkomo's ZAPU. In Matabeleland South, ZAPU received the same proportion of the vote (86.5 percent) as it had in 1980; in Matabeleland North, ZAPU actually increased its popular share (from 79 percent to 82.5 percent). Only in the marginal zones between Shona and Ndebele-speaking parts of the country, that is in Midlands and Mashonaland West, was ZANU-PF able to increase its share of the vote at the expense of ZAPU.

The failure of the governing party to penetrate the south and west of the country is attributable not only to traditional political loyalties, but to the contemporary performance of the ZANU-PF government. Although the government was generally successful in restoring peace to the countryside in the aftermath of the independence war, a wide variety of "dissident" elements in Matabeleland, bandits, soldiers, and agitators, refused to reconcile themselves to the new political order. A low-level insurgency was mounted to destroy rural development projects; local government officials were intimidated and, in an internationally publicized incident, six tourists were kidnapped and killed. The government reacted harshly. In 1983 it unleashed the ill-disciplined Fifth Brigade on a campaign of indiscriminate reprisals that resulted in perhaps 3,000 civilian deaths; in 1984 it suspended food aid and closed trading outlets in Matabeleland South at the height of the worst sustained drought of the century; and in 1985, the party youth wing and the security police were implicated in the "disappearances" of approximately fifty local ZAPU officials. Elected ZAPU councils in the rural areas could no longer operate. The net development effect was to worsen living conditions in that part of rural Zimbabwe, an area already saddled with the lowest natural potential for development.

The decision to crack down on Nkomo and ZAPU appears to have been a major tactical error. It reinforced, if not actually created, a legacy of distrust between the citizens in Matabeleland and the central government that will be difficult to erase and that offers opportunities for interference by neighboring South Africa. The election result also led to the removal of the last ZAPU ministers from the cabinet and an effective end to the coalition government that had prevailed through the first five years of independence. According to Mugabe, "only when there is one Zimbabwean people with one leader—the party—will a scientific reorganization of society along socialist lines be possible."[22]

Conclusions and Propositions

A remarkable amount of progress was achieved in the first five years of independence in Zimbabwe. The basic resiliency of the economy was demonstrated under trying conditions of recession and drought. At the same time, the dignity and life chances of most Zimbabweans were enhanced by access to basic political rights and social services.

The regime was nonetheless confronted with the classic dilemmas of a reformist regime in a market economy, namely how to reconcile growth with equity, change with stability. When forced to make hard choices about who would win and who would lose in a context of diminishing resources, the regime showed itself to be fiscally conservative and respectful of property rights. The reaffirmation of ZANU-PF at the polls indicated that the leadership had managed to avoid the potential delegitimating effects of economic stagnation. Opposition to the regime arose more as a response to clumsy use of the coercive powers of the state than to popular disagreements over the allocation of economic benefits.

The Zimbabwe case demonstrates the limited choices and ambiguous strategies of a regime that attempts to achieve socialism in a market economy. We think that the following generalizations may apply elsewhere under similar circumstances:

1. The capacity of a regime to redistribute resources is indissolubly linked to the fiscal viability of the state. In an "open" economy in a global market system, this in turn depends on (a) the business cycle in the world economy and (b) flows of concessional development assistance. The autonomy of the state to pursue the program of the political elite will be highest in periods of international economic expansion and lowest in periods when the government spending program is dependent upon infusions of scarce international public capital.

2. In a market economy, the autonomy of the state from different factions of capital depends upon (a) whether the capital is domestic or international and (b) whether domestic capital makes a strategic contribution to national production. It is to be expected that reformist regimes will be most able to confront international and nonstrategic domestic interests. In a market economy, the outcome of policy remains unpredictable in the degree that private interests retain control over resources and are able to make independent allocation decisions. Redistribution in

one issue area (e.g., wages) is likely to prompt measures from actors in the market that counteract redistribution in another (e.g., employment).

3. The concept of "redistribution" embraces a wide range of resources. These can be usefully classified as public services, private incomes, and private assets. The success of a "socialist" strategy depends upon which resources are targeted for redistribution. In a market economy, the least resistance will be felt from dominant classes in relation to the redistribution of public services and most resistance in relation to private assets in property.

4. In a market economy, the outcome of policy remains unpredictable to the degree that private interests retain control over resources and are able to make independent allocation decisions. Redistribution in one issue area (e.g., wages) is likely to prompt measures from actors in the market that counteract redistribution in another (e.g., employment).

5. If the organization of the state is restructured in an effort to enhance state autonomy and power, these changes must be mutually reinforcing. It is possible, for example, that the centralization of decision making may be neutralized by failure to develop cohesion of the ruling elite and efficacy of the bureaucracy.

Given our mixed assessment of the regime's performance in Zimbabwe, what can be said to summarily characterize the type of socialism espoused by Mugabe and ZANU-PF? The regime undoubtedly holds a Marxist vision, but in the economic sphere policy decisions are tempered with pragmatism. Marxism in Zimbabwe has not been enshrined as an "absolute truth" or an "unchallengeable guide" for social engineering. The current absence of a state-imposed Marxist orthodoxy is the best hope that a Zimbabwean road to socialism will be defined from concrete local practice in socioeconomic development. Whether this form of socialism is also humane and democratic depends to a large extent on how the regime resolves the problem of political opposition. It remains to be seen whether pragmatism will also prevail in the political sphere. A key indicator will be whether the centralization of power in a single-party state is ultimately effected by force or by negotiation.

Notes and References

1. Michael Bratton, "Farmer Organizations and Food Production in Zimbabwe," *World Development*, 14, 3 (1986): 378.

2. World Bank, *Zimbabwe: Country Economic Memorandum: Performance,*

Policies and Prospects (Washington: IBRD, October 1985), 178.

3. Zimbabwe African National Union-Patriotic Front, *Draft Constitution,* (Harare: ZANU-PF, July 1984), clause 5e.

4. Robert Mugabe, "An Overview of the Construction of Socialism in Zimbabwe," Harare, *The Herald,* 10 July 1984.

5. Robert Mugabe, "Speech to the Second Party Congress," Harare, September 1984.

6. Robert I. Rotberg, *Christian Science Monitor,* 1 March 1985.

7. Ministry of Health, Government of Zimbabwe, *Report on a Joint Mission to Evaluate Primary Health Care in Zimbabwe* (Harare: Ministry of Health with SCF, SIDA, UNICEF, WHO, July 1982).

8. *Sunday Mail,* 23 June 1985.

9. United States Agency for International Development, *Zimbabwe: Country Development Strategy Statement, FY 1987* (Washington: USAID, February 1985), 38.

10. Tony Hawkins, "Public Policy and the Zimbabwe Economy" (unpublished paper, Harare: University of Zimbabwe, Department of Economics, January 1985), 9.

11. Ibid., 2.

12. Ibid., 2.

13. Kay Muir, Malcolm Blackie, Louis de Swardt, and Bill Kinsey, "The Effect of Minimum Wage Increases on Commercial Agricultural Production in Zimbabwe," *African Affairs,* vol. 81, no. 322 (January 1982): 71-85.

14. Bernard Chidzero, *The Herald,* 11 July 1985.

15. *The Wall Street Journal,* 26 September 1985.

16. World Bank, *Zimbabwe: Country Economic Memorandum.*

17. Andre Astrow, *Zimbabwe: A Revolution That Lost Its Way* (London: Zed Press, 1983); and Christine Sylvester, "Zimbabwe's 1985 Election and the Search for Ideology" (paper presented at the national meetings of the African Studies Association, New Orleans, 23-26 November 1985).

18. Theda Skocpol, *States and Social Revolutions* (Cambridge: Cambridge University Press, 1979), 164.

19. Richard Sklar, "Reds and Rights: Zimbabwe's Experiment," in *Issue: A Journal of Africanist Opinion,* 14 (1985): 29-31.

20. Peter Evans and Dieter Rueschemeyer, "The State and Economic Transformation" in Peter Evans et al., eds., *Bringing the State Back In* (New York: Cambridge University Press, 1985), 48-49.

21. Alfred Stepan, *The State and Society* (Princeton: Princeton University Press, 1978), 83.

22. David Caute, "Zimbabwe's Elections: Mugabe Brooks No Opposition," *The Nation,* 31 August 1985, 141.

part three

International Influences on the Policymaking of Afro-Marxist Regimes

Soviet Influence on Afro-Marxist Regimes: Ethiopia and Mozambique

L. Adele Jinadu

The emergence of the Afro-Marxist regimes in the 1970s was enthusiastically received by the Soviet Union for several reasons. Soviet policy makers and scholars viewed it dialectically as presaging long-term structural changes in global trade relations. The emergence of these regimes was therefore seen as critical to the internalization of the class struggle and the eventual success of socialism on a global scale. Anatoli Gromyko expressed this positive response to the emergence of the Afro-Marxist regimes when he observed that: "The socialist orientation in Africa is a continuation of the cause of the October Revolution under the specific conditions of its carrying out the high mission of preparing the way for the victory of scientific socialism...."[1]

The geopolitical significance of the Afro-Marxist regimes was not lost on the Soviet Union, given the critical role that it played in Angola in 1975-1976. Their existence provided the Soviet Union with an opportunity for renewed challenge to the hegemonic position of the West in Africa, as well as the chance to reinforce its declining influence on the continent. The importance of these regimes in Soviet geopolitical calculations was further underscored by the fact that some of them were strategically located in Southern Africa (Mozambique and Angola) and the Horn of Africa (Ethiopia). The coastal states in these regions can, for example, provide the Soviet Union with naval facilities for maneuvers in the Indian Ocean.

The political and ideological orientation of the Afro-Marxist regimes also provided the framework around which the Soviet Union could develop military, economic, political, and sociocultural relations. The Soviet expectation was, therefore, that special relations between Afro-Marxist regimes and the Soviet Union would develop and grow. The decisions of the twenty-fourth and twenty-fifth Congresses of the

Communist Party of the Soviet Union (CPSU) emphasized this point. In a similar vein, the famous Brezhnev Doctrine, advanced in Leonid Brezhnev's report to the twenty-fifth Congress of the CPSU, asserted that the cultivation of special relations with the Afro-Marxist states would be a central element in the African policy of the Soviet Union.[2]

The Afro-Marxist states were equally enthusiastic about cultivating and developing special relations with the Soviet Union and Eastern Europe. For them, as for the Soviet Union, such relations were a structural and historical necessity, reflecting the dialectics of the global conflict between the forces of imperialism and anti-imperialism. Angola and Mozambique, for example, characterized the incipient relations as a natural alliance, arising out of and consolidating relations already established during the wars of national liberation in both countries. Samora Machel underlined this point of view by declaring that "the socialist countries were and are at all times our safe rearguard."[3]

The ideology of proletarian internationalism also provided a cornerstone for a relationship that both sides characterized as symbiotic, "...a new type of equitable and mutually beneficial international relations...."[4] The ideological formulation of this proletarian internationalism is concretely conceptualized in terms of opposition to neocolonialism and the pursuit of the noncapitalist path of development.

The Soviet Union's characterization of the relationship was part of a reassessment of its African and Third World policies. This reassessment took account of fluctuations and vagaries in African and Third World politics and of the need to be discriminating in developing close relations with regimes in Africa. The Soviet Union became more realistic about prospects for the socialist transformation of Africa and opted for selectivity and concentration in its relations with African countries. It is therefore useful to view Soviet relations with the Afro-Marxist regimes in the wider context of this reassessment of its African and Third World policies.

This is an important point to emphasize. However, behind the ideological rhetoric of proletarian internationalism lies the awareness that the nature of Africa's political economy poses an overwhelming obstacle to the transition to socialism for the Afro-Marxist regime. Soviet characterization of "the socialist orientation in Africa" is clear on this point. Thus, according to Gromyko:

> In Africa the socialist orientation arose and is developing in countries that have not yet broken away completely from the world capitalist economic system, that still have many economic ties with it. Social and economic transformations being effected in African countries with socialist orientation do not take place so far under the hegemony of the working class.... It should be stressed that in Africa, the socialist orien-

tation is advancing in countries with a multistructural economy, where ethnic hostilities are still left, where the level of development of productive forces is low, and where pre-capitalist and often prefeudal forms of society predominate.[5]

The establishment, cultivation, and consolidation of special relations between the Soviet Union and the Afro-Marxist regimes would, in this view, be necessarily complex and complicated. Yet the Soviet notion of socialist orientation contains the seeds of potential disagreement with the Afro-Marxist regimes over, for example, how Marxism-Leninism is to be conceptualized and concretely applied to specific situations. This is not unrelated to the strategic question of the policy options available to these regimes as they seek to structure their domestic and external environments in ways that are fundamentally (i.e., ideologically) different from those of neighboring countries.

The interlocking connection between domestic and external environments in structuring the options open to the Afro-Marxist states as they pursue efforts to democratize productive and political relations provides an important dimension to the dynamics of their relations with the Soviet Union. There is little doubt that these regimes viewed the cultivation of special relations with the Soviet Union as crucial to their development strategies. It is, of course, difficult to assess whether the expectations on which they sought to build these special relations were, in fact, realized by the programmatic or sectoral forms those relations have since taken.

In concrete terms, special relations are pursued within the following sectors: political, economic, ideological, scientific, cultural, and military. For example, within the political sector, cooperation is needed to build a Marxist-Leninist vanguard party and in the democratization of political structures. Cooperation is necessary within the economic sector to strengthen and broaden the role of the state in the economy on an anti-capitalist basis.

In what follows, the focus is on the forms and modalities of bilateral relations between the Soviet Union and two Afro-Marxist states—Ethiopia and Mozambique. As previously indicated, the theoretical and ideological formulation of the character of these bilateral relations is sometimes couched in terms of the Marxist-Leninist theory of the historical process in its transition from capitalism to socialism. Two closely related interpretations of Soviet objectives in the Afro-Marxist regimes have generally been deduced from this theoretical/ideological formulation.

First, is the thesis that Soviet cultivation of these relations is part of its general global strategy of confrontation with the West in general and the United States in particular. It is argued that "Soviet strategic motives in Africa differ substantially from region to region but are shaped by global rivalry with the United States."[6] In this way, the practical nature of the relations—utilization of Marxism-Leninism as a strategic development option for the Afro-Marxist regimes is neglected and replaced by Cold War explanations of Soviet motives. As Bhabani Sen Gupta has observed, "the presence of the Soviet Union anywhere in the Third World was seen as an overt...threat to the ramparts of the West's worldwide interests....Soviet policies were therefore analyzed in terms of the cold war."[7]

Second, some analysts see the consolidation of Soviet empire building in the cultivation and development of these bilateral relations. In fact, as far back as 1961, Hugh Seton-Watson had claimed that the Soviet Union was an "imperialist power" in the sense that it was seeking "by a series of weapons and tactics, to impose its doctrines and institutions on the other nations of the world."[8] Recently, Richard Bissell made much the same point, claiming that "the Soviet empire builders are leaving their tracks in Africa, and recent years have provided abundant evidence of their existence."[9] Ethiopia, Mozambique, and the other Afro-Marxist regimes are thus viewed as "client" or "satellite" states of the Soviet Union. The implication is that ideology is irrelevant or epiphenomenal in explaining relations between these countries and the Soviet Union. In this way, the high premium placed on Marxism-Leninism as a development option by the Afro-Marxist regimes is overlooked. But, more seriously, contradictions that have emerged from the dialectics of these bilateral relations are hardly considered; nor can they be explained within the framework of the Cold War or patron-client relationships.

What is required is, therefore, a conceptual framework that avoids Cold War or imperialistic explanations of relations between the Soviet Union and Ethiopia, Mozambique, and the other Afro-Marxist states. This can be done by situating the relations in the wider context of the conditions of the contemporary world system, characterized by asymmetries between central and peripheral states. These asymmetries fundamentally arise from the global capitalist economy, the class system it has created and which in turn sustains it, and the consequent income inequalities and other contradictions between developed and developing countries that it has generated.

A useful conceptual schema in this respect is Claude Ake's distinction between bourgeois and proletarian states.[10] This is also a distinction between developed and developing countries. Such categorization reflects the division of the global capitalist production system "into those countries which relate to it as owners of capital and technology. This distribution is the class division of the global system."[11] What does this mean in empirical terms?

A country's place within this division is based on its share of the world's capital and technology, "the two fundamental instruments of labour in the global capitalist system...."[12] Global class division, in other words, is based on a distinction between those countries that monopolize these fundamental instruments of labor and those who do not possess them and are, therefore, subject to exploitation. Another operational indicator of this global class division is the income gap or inequality between the bourgeois (i.e., developed) and the proletarian (i.e., developing) countries.

Given this objective criteria, Ake argues that "even internally progressive countries such as the Soviet Union must be regarded as bourgeois countries. To classify a country as bourgeois does not mean that it is unprogressive or that its internal economy is capitalist...but rather we are saying something about its share of the world's capital and technology."[13] This then suggests that bilateral relations between the Soviet Union and the Afro-Marxist regimes will not be immune to contradictions created by their different positions in the global production system. Ake has hypothesized that

...irrespective of the ideology of a country, its place in this classification is a matter of great importance which affects its behavior and creates contradictions between it and other countries with a similar ideology which are on the other side of the classification....[14]

This does not mean that contradictions do not exist between, for example, the Soviet Union and the other bourgeois nations or that these contradictions will tend to bring the Soviet Union closer to the Afro-Marxist regimes. By placing the relationship between the Soviet Union and Afro-Marxist regimes in the context of this primary contradiction between bourgeois and proletarian countries, explanations can be generated for a number of apparent paradoxes that conceptual frameworks based on Cold War or patron-client presuppositions fail to provide.

What role does ideology play then as an explanatory variable, in view of the conceptual schema suggested here? Much has been said about the limitations of ideology as an explanatory variable in discussing relations between the Soviet Union and the Afro-Marxist regimes. Crawford Young has argued that, "While ideology is indisputably a significant vector, it is powerfully cross-cut by other determinants, both for the great powers and the African states.... Both the Soviet Union and the United States define African strategy in a global perspective; broader strategic considerations may well override regional ideological factors."[15]

However, the problematic nature of the connection between ideology and policy outcomes, implied in Young's argument, may be symptomatic of an inherent problem in the very notion of "ideology." The problem can

230   L. Adele Jinadu

be placed in clearer perspective if ideology is viewed as a cognitive map or operational code in relation to objectives that are structurally determined in the sense of reflecting a nation's determination to consolidate or alter its position in the global production system. In this view, ideology need not be as determinist or as incorrigible a guide to policy choices as is sometimes assumed.

The antithesis that is thus often drawn between ideology and pragmatism is an overdrawn one if the instrumental or interest view of ideology is accepted. Indeed, the notion of pragmatism tends to give the impression of ideological inconsistency when, in fact, the connection between ideology and policy is dialectical and much more complicated than the antithesis usually drawn tends to suggest.

What are the specific forms and modalities of bilateral relations between the Soviet Union and Ethiopia and Mozambique, respectively? These Afro-Marxist countries are strategically located in regions that have experienced and are still experiencing intense regional conflict—the Horn of Africa and Southern Africa—and that additionally have attracted a great deal of international interest, partly because of their strategic importance and partly because of the ethical-practical issue of public policy raised by the conflict. Pertinent questions to raise include the following: What are the policy aims or goals of both sides for bilateral relations? What forms have the relations that have been established assumed? How have both sides characterized the relations? What are some of the internal and external environmental factors that have affected the direction taken?

Ethiopian-Soviet Relations

The genesis of modern-day Ethiopian-Soviet relations dates back to 1924 when the Soviet Union initiated discussion on the establishment of diplomatic relations between the two countries. In 1931, the two countries signed an agreement for "the delivery of a consignment of oil products and other Soviet commodities to Ethiopia."[16] The Soviet Union supported Ethiopia during the Italo-Ethiopian war for basically anti-fascist and anti-colonialist reasons, although there were also strategic considerations underlying its support. For example, Harry Brind contends that the Soviet position in the Italo-Ethiopian war arose out of a desire "to limit the influence of Western European states—particularly Britain" in the region.[17]

The Soviet Union opened its embassy in Addis Ababa in 1956, and in 1959 Emperor Haile Selassie paid the first visit by an African head of state to the Soviet Union. But the relations developed were never close, and much closer relations began to develop only after the overthrow of

Haile Selassie in November 1974. A basic reason for this was the strong relationship that Emperor Haile Selassie had cultivated with the West, particularly the United States in military, economic, and sociocultural matters. This was reflected, for example, in the 1953 treaty between Ethiopia and the United States that gave the United States a twenty-five-year lease on a communications center near Asmara. The United States experienced a reversal of its fortunes with the accession to power of a military government in Ethiopia that later committed itself to the radical project of socialist transformation along Marxist-Leninist lines.

Much has been written about the diplomatic realignment that has occurred in the Horn since the overthrow of Haile Selassie in 1974. The realignment has revolved around relations between the Soviet Union and the United States, and between these countries and Ethiopia and Somalia as well.[18] It has, moreover, underlined the significant effect that regional developments in Africa can have on the strategic calculations of the superpowers and their subsequent policy shifts and choice of allies. The sources of these regional developments lie deep in the contradictions unleashed as part of the dialectics of the process of conflict and change in Ethiopia and Somalia—the spillover effects of changes in one country on the other, and the specific form these contradictions have assumed with the outbreak of the Ethiopian-Somali War.

An important aspect of the realignment was the development of closer ties between Ethiopia and the Soviet Union. The two countries issued a declaration of basic principles, in May 1977, to provide the framework for their friendly relations and cooperation. This framework for bilateral relations was further strengthened with other agreements in 1977 and 1978, the highpoint of which was the initiation of a treaty of friendship and cooperation in November 1978. Somalia, having concluded a treaty of friendship with the Soviet Union in 1974, viewed this development in the context of its own deteriorating and confrontational relations with Ethiopia; it abrogated the treaty and began to seek better and closer relations with the United States.

The realignment was not an easy one for the Soviet Union to decide upon. Since the option before it was to choose between Ethiopia and Somalia, the Soviet Union tried to avoid this option and sought, instead, to steer a middle course that would enable it to retain the goodwill of Somalia while taking advantage of the new political situation in Ethiopia to strengthen the Soviet position there. This was the calculation behind the Soviet Union's attempt to act as a broker with Cuba to arrange a political solution to the Ogaden problem, and could have involved the creation of a loose federation in which substantial autonomy would be granted to Eritrea and the Ogaden, two critical issues in the Ethiopian-

Somali dispute. A result of this invasion was that the Soviet Union was compelled to commit itself militarily on the side of Ethiopia.

A number of other considerations could have influenced the Soviet Union's decision to commit itself to Ethiopia. Ethiopia provides a base from which the Soviet Union can expand its political and diplomatic influence in Africa. This is due to the political importance of Ethiopia in Africa: its key strategic position in the Horn, its economic and natural resource endowment, its large population of forty-two million (the second largest in Black Africa), and its huge physical landmass. There was also an ideological consideration: the desire to support the "progressive" forces that were increasingly gaining the upper hand in Ethiopia and particularly within the Derg, although there was in 1978 and still is much confusion and incoherence surrounding the evolving Marxist-Leninist ideology in the country. The threat posed to the Soviet Union's naval interests by the plan to convert the Red Sea into an "Arab lake" under the aegis of Saudi Arabia is another consideration. The seriousness of the threat to Soviet interests in the area was further underlined by Arab support for Somalia in its conflict with Ethiopia. Under the circumstances, Ethiopia assumed even more strategic importance to the Soviet Union because of its geopolitical location in the region.

If Soviet support was crucial to keeping the Derg in power and in preventing the disintegration of the Ethiopian state into anarchy, such support was, nonetheless, predicated on Soviet calculations of its own national interests and of advantages it would derive from establishing a foothold in Ethiopia. What, then, have been the forms and modalities of the relations?

The special character of evolving bilateral relations between Ethiopia and the Soviet Union was underscored by the twenty-year treaty of friendship and cooperation the two countries concluded in Moscow on November 20, 1978. The treaty covered such diverse but interrelated fields as political, economic, cultural and military relations. The special character of the relations has also been underscored by the frequency of visits between countries by high-powered delegations. These visits provide the occasion for negotiating, concluding, and reviewing the various areas of bilateral relations and cooperation between the two countries. The visits also provide a forum for the ventilation of mutual reservations and critical observations about each other's commitment to the treaty.

Let me illustrate with some examples.[19] In July 1980, Admiral Sergei Gorshkov, the deputy defense minister of the Soviet Union and commander-in chief of the Soviet navy, visited Ethiopia. Admiral Gorshkov visited the naval base in Maswa, Asmara, Ethiopia's command headquarters and the Dahlak Islands. It seems, however, that the primary purpose of the visit was to discuss the establishment of an anchorage in the Dahlak Islands, astride the sea lanes carrying most of Europe's oil, in compensation for the loss of the use of Berbera in Somalia, which the Soviet Union suffered with the abrogation of its friendship treaty with Somalia. What lends credence to this supposition is the fact that Admiral Gorshkov is allegedly the brain behind the policy of projecting Soviet naval power well beyond its adjacent sea lanes as a deterrence to subversion of Soviet interests.

As early as May 1980 the military-strategic factor in Ethiopian-Soviet relations had been underscored by the visit of an Ethiopian delegation to Moscow. The delegation held discussions with Marshall Dimitri Ustinov, the Soviet defense minister and Marshal Nikolai Ogarkov, the Soviet chief of general staff. In 1981, two top-ranking Soviet military delegations visited Ethiopia—one, in April headed by General A.A. Yenishev, chief of the Soviet army and navy's main Political Directorate and another in June, headed by Marshal S. L. Solokov, the Soviet Union's first deputy minister of defense.

Leonid Brezhnev used the occasion of the visit of Ethiopia's head of state, Mengistu Haile Meriam, in October 1980 to urge Ethiopia to negotiate political solutions to its problems in Eritrea and with Somalia. The Soviet Union was reluctant to get militarily entangled in those problems, and, for military-strategic reasons, preferred a peaceful solution in Eritrea. This was partly because the naval facilities that it was keen on securing were in Eritrea.

The Soviet Union, understandably, encouraged political solution of the Eritrean problem, and use the Italian Communist party as a proxy to encourage the Eritrean Liberation Front (ELF) to enter into negotiations with the Ethiopian government. As Richard Remneck has surmised, "in what appears to have been a counter initiative to the Saudi/Sudanese efforts to forge an Arab bloc of the Red Sea states, the Soviets following close on the heels of of the Cubans, proposed... that Ethiopia and Somalia join South Yemen and independent Djibouti in a federation of Marxist states, in which Eritrea and the Ogaden would receive substantial autonomy."[20] As indicated earlier, this option was scuttled by the Somali invasion of Ethiopian territory.

What has been the cost of the military-strategic factor in Ethiopian-Soviet relations? Much of this is shrouded in secrecy, making it difficult to assess the final cost. But it has been estimated that the Soviet Union supplied about $1.5 billion worth of equipment to Ethiopia during the war in the Ogaden, and, that further substantial financial costs were incurred in air-sea-lifting material to Ethiopia from the Soviet Union.[21] Military aid is easily the single largest item in the Soviet aid to Ethiopia, and this has meant a heavy debt burden for Ethiopia.

In 1981, for example, Ethiopia was paying off a $2,000 million arms debt to the Soviet Union. The annual repayment interests on the debt were about $328 million. This was being repaid in cash or by barter exchanges of such valuable Ethiopian commodities as coffee and hides and skins. Ethiopia also incurred the additional economic burden of maintaining Cuban and Soviet troops in the country. It has been estimated that there were between 1,200 and 1,500 Soviet military personal in Ethiopia in 1981. The economic burden, particularly that of repaying the arms debt, was aggravated by the precipitous fall in Ethiopia's foreign exchange earnings as a result of the downturn in world commodity prices for coffee and the fall in demand on the world market for hides and skins.

The Soviet response to Ethiopia's foreign and economic crisis was to enter into an agreement with Ethiopia, in 1981, to sell crude oil to her at about $10 a barrel less than world market prices. Another agreement provided for an increase in Soviet purchases of Ethiopian coffee, sesame oil, harricot beans, and other agricultural goods by about 50 percent. But this was conditional on an equivalent increase in the value of Ethiopian purchases of Soviet machinery, vehicles, and petroleum products. In spite of this, the Soviet Union was so worried about Ethiopia's unpaid debt of $2 billion for Soviet arms that, during the visit of Wollie Chiol, Ethiopia's minister of foreign trade, to Moscow in December 1981 the Soviet Union said that it was willing to provide Ethiopia with preferential prices for fuel imports only on a short-term basis.

By 1981, therefore Ethiopian-Soviet relations had begun to show signs of strain and stress. Ethiopian concern with the heavy arms burden it has had to carry was further exacerbated by disenchantment and disappointment with what Ethiopians regard as the paucity and inappropriateness of Soviet nonmilitary aid, particularly economic assistance and food aid. The strain created was further underscored by the precipitous fall in Ethiopian foreign exchange earnings because of declining world prices for its main export, coffee, and a dramatic fall in the demand for hides and skins, its second foreign currency earner. The urgent need to increase its foreign income earnings provides a context in which to consider Ethiopia's overtures to the West in 1981. But what have been the modalities and forms of Ethiopian-Soviet economic relations? The following is a representative illustration of the economic transactions between the two countries.

In March 1981, as part of its contribution to the drought and famine relief efforts, the Soviet Union donated 12,000 tons of wheat, fifty trucks, fifty water tankers, and ten water pumps of a total value of twelve million Ethiopian birr ($4.8 million U.S. dollars) to Ethiopia. In August 1981, S. A. Skachkov, the chairman of the Soviet Committee on Foreign Economic Relations, visited Addis Ababa to sign an economic cooperation agreement that provided for Soviet assistance in consolidating construction organizations in the state sector. The agreement also provided increased trade credits for Ethiopia.

In October of the same year, at the Third Session of the joint Ethiopian-Soviet Intergovernmental Commission on Economic and Technical Cooperation and Trade in Addis Ababa, the Soviet Union agreed to provide technical assistance for the construction in Ethiopia of a hydroelectric power station and the opening up of the land and water resources in the Gambela region. A major Soviet agricultural project was also begun in the Baabbi River valley, involving the construction of a dam to allow for irrigation and electric power supply.

Perhaps the most important industrial project undertaken by the Soviet Union in Ethiopia was the construction of an oil refinery at Assab at a cost of seven million birr. This refinery is made up of oil tanks capable of storing eighteen million liters of oil. The Soviet Union also helped to build Ethiopia's first tractor station. In April 1984, the Soviet Union agreed to provide the necessary technical assistance for the construction of a hydroelectric power station on the Webbe Shebbele

Table 10.1   Principal Trading Partners of Ethiopia
('000 birr; 1 birr = US$.40)

Imports	1979	1980	1982
China, People's Republic	13,355	30,742	8,210
France	19,486	32,634	52,111
German Democratic Republic	36,752	34,666	31,848
Germany, Federal Republic of	118,585	142,387	157,877
India	14,111	13,156	n.a.
Israel	15,925	21,317	n.a.
Italy	117,244	161,477	185,504
Japan	124,399	129,715	145,431
Kenya	15,779	15,596	n.a.
Korea, Republic of	22,347	14,557	n.a.
Kuwait	181,515	69,225	n.a.
Netherlands	23,870	33,986	30,424
Saudi Arabia	1,386	1,811	17,957
Sweden	36,741	22,249	n.a.
Switzerland	22,068	52,736	n.a.
Taiwan	13,734	11,494	n.a.
USSR	22,857	287,746	441,821
United Kingdom	77,871	97,930	122,810
USA	137,492	114,885	63,568
TOTAL (incl. others)	1,175,053	1,494,703	1,652,829

Source: National Bank of Ethiopia, Quarterly Bulletin (1979, 1980, 1982).
Figures for 1981 are not available.

Table 10.2   Principal Trading Partners of Ethiopia ('000 birr)

Exports	1979	1980	1982
Belgium	10,946	10,506	n.a.
Djibouti	50,923	100,351	77,519
France	30,342	58,399	44,311
German Democratic Republic	764	3,925	15,422
Germany, Federal Republic of	61,969	74,593	133,571
Israel	3,330	3,368	n.a.
Italy	97,820	89,150	43,913
Japan	53,419	56,649	62,172
Netherlands	32,007	17,884	10,564
Saudi Arabia	75,744	66,420	56,015
Spain	12,932	7,680	n.a.
Switzerland	3,325	1,107	n.a.
USSR	58,353	81,193	5,042
United Kingdom	19,503	18,451	16,922
USA	246,134	59,621	216,045
Yemen, People's Democratic Republic	11,374	11,437	n.a.
Yugoslavia	34,469	34,169	15,154
TOTAL	864,327	878,750	836,295

Source: National Bank of Ethiopia, Quarterly Bulletin.

Figures for 1981 not available.

River. In September 1984, the two countries signed a long-term economic cooperation agreement on Soviet participation in Ethiopia's ten-year plan. This also included provisions for Soviet help in oil and gold exploration in the country.

Ethiopia has been unhappy with the quantity and quality of Soviet development assistance and trade, and as a result has had no choice but to turn to the West for economic assistance. Soviet economic assistance has clearly failed to reduce the dependence of Ethiopia's economy on the West. Ethiopian-Soviet relations have not substantially diverted the direction of Ethiopian foreign trade from the West to the Eastern Bloc countries. In 1979, for example, over 46 percent of Ethiopian imports came from Western industrialized countries. This dropped to 45 percent in 1980, but in 1982 it had risen to about 63 percent (see Tables 10.1 and 10.2). The West, particularly the EEC, remains Ethiopia's main trading partner.

The Ethiopian disappointment with Soviet economic assistance and aid was reflected in a number of policy decisions and overtures beginning in 1981. In that year, Ethiopia began to look for loans in Western capital markets. For example, the Ethiopian government took measures to restore its eligibility for loans and assistance from the World Bank. The ten-year program of economic strategy, introduced in July 1981, shifted emphasis from collectivization and nationalization. It also outlined the role that Western bilateral and multinational economic assistance was expected to play in the implementation of the plan.

The liberalization reflected in these policy measures was due partly to disappointment with the record of the Soviet Union in the trade and aid area, and partly to Ethiopia's heavy arms debt. The regime felt compelled to find solutions to the conjecture of a number of interlocking, structurally induced problems that were buffeting the Ethiopian state: the debilitating impact of the drought and the world recession on the country's fragile economy; political insecurity and its attendant instability arising not only from dissention within the Derg over ideology and public policy, but also from the unsettled ethnic problem posed by irredentist and secessionist movements in the Ogaden, Eritrea, and Oromo.

As a result of liberalization, Western aid began to flow into Ethiopia late in 1981 for the first time since the Derg came to power. As was indicated earlier on, Ethiopia began the negotiations that led to the restoration of its eligibility to receive loans and assistance from the World Bank. The highpoint of the liberalization measures was the introduction in February 1983 of a new law on joint ventures in all but a few sectors of Ethiopia's economy. The law provided for transfer of shares and repatriation of profits by multinationals. By mid-1983 Ethiopia had agreed, as part of an agreement with the World Bank, to compensate British, Japanese, French, Italian, Dutch, and U.S. companies that had been nationalized in 1978.

A final area of Ethiopian-Soviet relations to be illustrated is the political aspect. The major Soviet concern here is the creation in Ethiopia of a Marxist-Leninist vanguard party to replace the Derg. The Soviet Union saw within party organization an area in which its own experience could serve as a model for Ethiopia. But there was another dimension to the Soviet Union's interest in party organization. Soviet ideologues considered the creation of a Marxist-Leninist vanguard party as essential for the transition to socialism and for the progressive democratization of political structures and institutions in Ethiopia.

The Soviet Union pressed for the creation of a vanguard party for a number of other reasons. First, based on its experience elsewhere in Africa (e.g., Egypt, the Sudan, Ghana, Guinea, and Mali), the Soviet Union had come to question the ability and even commitment of bourgeois African nationalist leaders, be they civilian or military, to effect a socialist transformation of their respective countries along Marxist-Leninist lines. Second, they assumed it was important to create durable Marxist-Leninist party structures that could survive the political misfortunes of particular leaders.[22]

The Soviet Union, after 1979, stepped up pressures on the Derg to set in motion the machinery to create a Communist party in Ethiopia. To facilitate this, various Ethiopian delegations visited Moscow between 1980 and 1984 to study the structure and organization of the Communist party of the Soviet Union (CPSU). For example, no less than twelve major delegations from the Commission for the Organization of the Party of the Workers of Ethiopia (COPWE) visited Moscow in 1983 to study the CPSU's structures. In addition, two delegations visited Ethiopia to oversee and help with efforts to build a Marxist-Leninist vanguard party in the country. An important development in the Ethiopian adoption of Marxism-Leninism was the First Congress of COPWE, which was held in 1980. COPWE had been formed in December 1979 to pave the way for the creation in Ethiopia of a proletarian party.[23] The Second Congress of COPWE decided in January 1983 to establish a full-fledged Marxist-Leninist party by September 1984, when the Third Congress was scheduled to take place. COPWE, which since its inception acted like a political party, was replaced in September 1984 by the Worker's Party of Ethiopia (WPE).

In spite of these developments, the Soviet Union is still apprehensive about the military composition of the Ethiopian government and has kept up pressures for demilitarization of party and bureaucratic structures in the country. The prolonged nature of the process of creating a Marxist-Leninist party in Ethiopia and the difficulties that still remain are not unrelated to the pertinent observation made by Marina Ottaway that the attempts of the military "to create a political party in order to break out of its isolation and establish a wider base of power were frustrated repeatedly by the very fact that many strata of the population were already mobilized politically."[24]

Some concluding remarks can now be made about the nature of Ethiopian-Soviet relations. For example, what does the foregoing discussion suggest about the hypothesis that the primary contradiction between bourgeois (i.e., developed) and proletarian (i.e., developing) nations provides a useful explanatory schema for looking at some aspects of Soviet bilateral relations with the Afro-Marxist states?

The problems created for Ethiopian-Soviet relations by this primary contradiction are largely reflected in their economic relations. In this area, the Soviet Union has done little that would indicate a determination to alter the global division of labor and the class system that underpins it. Nor has it shown any interest in bridging the income gap between it and Ethiopia. Indeed, the Soviet Union has been blatantly nationalistic in protecting its own economic interests and in taking advantage of its position in the capitalist global production system. For example, as was illustrated above, the Soviet Union has used the export of machinery to

Ethiopia to cover the costs of imports of primary commodities like coffee, hides, and skins from the country and to stockpile them in order to guarantee its access to them in the future.

An underlying consideration in Soviet economic relations with Ethiopia is, therefore, the exportation of hard currency exports like military hardware, petroleum products, machinery, and equipment that would bring benefits to the Soviet economy since such exports are tied to the import of raw materials needed by the Soviet economy. This has been the general trend of Soviet trade policy with developing countries.[25]

Soviet economic assistance has also not helped to bridge or narrow the income inequality gap between the Soviet Union and the rest of the industrialized world. The Ethiopian complaint about the meager nature of Soviet aid and technical assistance has already been detailed above. Nor has the Soviet Union offered substantial sources of investment capital to Ethiopia. Here again, the Soviet performance in Ethiopia can be generalized for its performance in the developing world in this area.[26]

Ideological considerations in Ethiopian-Soviet relations have not, however, been irrelevant. They have played, and are still playing, an important role in a number of policy areas: in efforts to create a proletarian-based vanguard party and in the training of party cadres; in the visible role played by Soviet military and technical assistance personnel in the highly sensitive area of the organization of logistics for the distribution of drought relief by the Ethiopian government; in Ethiopian support of the Soviet Union on critical world issues in the UN and elsewhere; and in the Ethiopian rebuff of overtures from the West, especially Western attempts to normalize relations.

Mozambican-Soviet Relations

The foundations of current Mozambican-Soviet relations lie deep in the Soviet military and political support of national liberation movements in the former Portuguese colonies of Angola, Guinea-Bassau, and Mozambique. This support found theoretical justification in Lenin's position on the Soviet support of oppressed colonial peoples.

The Soviet presence in the Southern African region dates back to the 1920s, when the Soviet Union established links with the South African Communist party and, through it, with a number of black South African nationalists. As was the case in Ethiopia and the Horn of Africa, the Soviet role and presence in Mozambique and Southern Africa took on a much more dramatic turn in the mid-1970s. The Angolan civil war of 1975-1976, was critical in this respect. Soviet military support of the MPLA against its rivals, UNITA and FNLA, certainly contributed to the eventual success of the MPLA and its accession to power in independent Angola. The direct Soviet military intervention, which was in response to direct South African and U.S. involvement in support of UNITA and the FNLA, was on a large scale and marked the first such Soviet involvement in sub-Saharan Africa.

Christopher Stevens has calculated that, in the latter half of 1975, the Soviet Union "sent the MPLA military equipment worth over $200 million and several hundred military advisors, while at the same time it provided the logistical and economic support indispensable to the Cuban provision of some fifteen thousand troops."[27] One effect of this was that in the West "fears were expressed that the Soviet Union would support revolution elsewhere in the region..." on a similar scale and "the 1977 Soviet intervention in Ethiopia reemphasized these fears."[28]

Another effect of Soviet intervention in Angola was that it brought the Soviet Union closer to Mozambique. This development eventually led to a diplomatic realignment in which China, the major communist ally and supporter of Frelimo during the national liberation war in Mozambique, saw its influence in the country wane while that of the Soviet Union waxed stronger. This also reflected a general decline of Chinese influence in Africa in the 1970s—a decline that was due, among other reasons, to "a series of diplomatic blunders that put them on the side of the losing causes," including support of the CIA-backed FNLA in Angola, of Mobutu in Zaire, and of Somalia after its invasion.

More needs to be said about the internal and external contexts in which Mozambican-Soviet relations should be placed and understood. One factor linking the internal and external contexts, which highlights the sometimes tenuous nature of the distinction in the case of Mozambique, is the structural factor arising from the political economy of Portuguese colonialism in Mozambique. The relative backwardness and under-development of Portugal in comparison to the other imperial powers resulted in the transformation of Mozambique into a labor reserve and plantation to serve the needs of expatriate non-Portuguese capital.

Portuguese colonial rule in Mozambique, therefore, played the role of an intermediary for South African capital, making the Mozambican economy a fragile and dependent one. As Hanlon puts it, "the poorest and most underdeveloped of Europe's colonial powers left behind one of the poorest countries in Africa."[29] This colonial inheritance has made the Mozambican economy susceptible to political, military, and economic blackmail and sabotage from South Africa. This heritage has also had a major impact on the Frelimo government in Mozambique as it considers and chooses options to pursue in trying to unlink from South Africa. The success of South Africa and international finance capital in undermining those options must be viewed in the context of the historically determined structural fragility of the Mozambican economy and its peripheral integration into the South African economy.

Other factors that provide the internal and external nexus for Mozambican-Soviet relations include the following: the hegemonic role of South Africa as a proxy for international finance capital in Southern Africa; the wars of national liberation in the region, and the special dimension given to those wars by the racist philosophies of white minority regimes in the region; and great power interests and involvement in the region. The interconnectedness of all these factors provides the background against which cooperation and tension in Mozambican-Soviet relations should be examined. What are the modalities and forms that these relations have taken? What have the expectations of both countries in forging relations been based upon?

As in the case of Ethiopian-Soviet relations, these relations are based on "a certain community of ideas and a desire to advance along the road of social progress."[30] A central objective is to advance the progress of proletarian internationalism in the Southern African region. In concrete terms, this has meant that both countries would support liberation movements in South Africa, Namibia, and Rhodesia/Zimbabwe, although as the case of Zimbabwe showed, both countries did not support the same liberation movement. The role of Mozambique in providing a rear base for the liberation movements in Rhodesia (Zimbabwe) and South Africa was a critical dimension in advancing the prospects for proletarian internationalism in the region.

The support of proletarian internationalism has also been defined in terms of reducing dependence on the West and of constructing socialist economies within the region. The aim, in the words of Leonid Brezhnev, is "to establish totally new relations of production, change the psychology of the people and set up a new administrative apparatus relying on the support of the masses."[31] This rationalization puts relations between the two countries in the wider perspective of Soviet global interests and the hegemonic competition between capitalism and socialism as ideologies of development.

Mozambique views the Soviet Union as a "natural ally" and a "safe rearguard" in the socialist project that Frelimo has undertaken. The Mozambican expectation was based on its acceptance of Marxism-Leninism as providing a terrain of choice in transforming Mozambican society and overcoming the legacy of Portugese colonial rule in the country. The choice of Marxism-Leninism and the projected vanguard nature of Frelimo were decisions that grew out of the dialectics of the war of national liberation.

In a way, the Soviet Union was important in the conceptualization of socialism in Mozambique. The Mozambican expectation was that Soviet assistance would be substantial and critical enough in the twin areas of social reconstruction and military and security assistance to withstand South African political and military aggression, as well as economic sabotage against Mozambique. This is concretely or operationally what the phrases "natural ally" and "safe rearguard" refer to. The "image" that "the Soviet Union brought from Angola...of an ally prepared to back its friends to the hilt," reinforced this expectation in the late 1970s.[32]

As will be shown, however, Mozambique has been disappointed with the amount and substance of Soviet economic and military aid. With the country virtually besieged by South Africa, its economy paralyzed and its political control of the state shaky, the Mozambican government has had little room to maneuver. It had no choice but to reach the détente with South Africa that the Nkomati Accord represented. Disappointed with its "natural ally" and with its "safe rearguard" exposed, Mozambique was forced to reassess its international relations and attitude toward the role of Western capital in the country's development.

What are the forms of Mozambican-Soviet relations? As in the case of Ethiopian-Soviet relations, these have typically been expressed in the frequency of exchange visits by top party and government functionaries of the two countries. The framework of these relations is provided by a treaty of friendship and cooperation initiated in March 1977, which covers military, strategic, political, economic, and social-cultural bilateral relations.

An observation which should be made about the forms of Mozambican-Soviet relations when compared with Ethiopian-Soviet ones is the close working relation in the former case between the Soviet Union and the German Democratic Republic (GDR), so much so that there has been talk of a "quasi-alliance" or "quasi-coalition" of the Soviet Union, Cuba, and the GDR in the Southern African region.[33] Much more so than in Ethiopia, the GDR role in Mozambique has been as active as, if not more active than, that of the Soviet Union. Christopher Coker sees Southern Africa as offering a good illustration of "how East European interests have forced the Soviet Union to confront the responsibilities as well as the limitations of its power."[34] Indeed, it is Coker's argument that "fundamental differences between the East Europeans and Moscow have been reflected in disputes over three main issues" of which "the wisdom of admitting Mozambique into the Council for Mutual Economic Assistance (COMECON)" is "perhaps more than any other" the one about which "the divergence of opinion is most clear."[35]

Some illustration of the modalities of Mozambican-Soviet relations can now be given. As in the case of Ethiopian-Soviet relations, a most prominent feature has been Soviet military aid to Mozambique. Their treaty of friendship and cooperation provides for mutual consultations and military aid, "in the case of situations tending to threaten or disturb the peace...." The precarious military and security situation of Mozambique as a target for Rhodesian and South African attacks and sabotage was obvious enough to underscore the importance of the military clauses of the treaty, especially since Mozambique provided a rear base for liberation movements in Rhodesia (Zimbabwe) and South Africa. The clauses are perhaps intended to underscore Soviet transfer and deployment of military arms, equipment, and personnel to progressive regimes and liberation movements in Southern Africa.

Soviet military aid has not been substantial enough, however, to provide Mozambique with security against South Africa. Nor was it enough to deter Rhodesian incursions into Mozambique and support of the MNR. In the aftermath of the treaty of friendship and cooperation, Soviet arms and military equipment that were transferred to Mozambique included what has been described as "outmoded" T-34 tanks, MiG-17s and 122-mm rockets. According to this same observer, "the Soviets did not see fit to provide Mozambique with the sophisticated air defense that would be necessary to deter the intermittent and destructive raids by the Rhodesian air force." Daniel Papp makes much the same observation: "In the years since the treaty was signed, Rhodesia has launched positive air strikes and ground operations into Mozambique primarily against ZANU guerrilla bases. These attacks have been carried out with impunity."[36]

What then has been the nature of Soviet military aid and assistance to Mozambique? The total value of Soviet arms transfers to Mozambique in 1982 was about $250 million. Much of this was made up of thirty-five tanks (T-34s, T-54s, and T-55s), eight MiG-21 fighters, a number of SAM-7 missiles, and 122-mm howitzers.[37] But this aid has also been generally symbolic and feeble. In February 1981, for example, the Soviet Union deployed warships from its Indian Ocean fleet to Maputo and Beira as an expression of solidarity with Mozambique. The aim was to deter South Africa from future attacks such as those carried out when it bombed houses occupied by members of the African National Congress (ANC) in Maputo. In October-November 1981, the Soviet minister of defense, Dimitri Ustinov, held discussions in Maputo with his Mozambican counterpart, Alberto Chipande. This was followed by a visit in mid-December 1981 by a Soviet naval squadron. As a result of these naval movements, the South African minister of defense accused the Soviet Union of a military design to open up "a second front against South Africa" and of having deployed 250 Soviet tanks, 400 armored cars, a number of MiG-21 fighters, and antiaircraft missiles to Mozambique.[38]

Another illustration of Soviet solidarity was provided by the visit of two Soviet warships to Maputo in April 1983. When two Soviet technicians were murdered and twenty-four others kidnapped by MNR bandits in Mozambique's Zambesia Province in August 1983, the Soviet Union sent four warships, including an aircraft carrier, on an eight-day visit to Maputo. This was intended as a strong signal of the seriousness with which the Soviet Union viewed South African-inspired aggression against Mozambique. But, as was indicated above, such demonstration of naval power and solidarity with Mozambique has been ineffective in deterring or curbing South African and South African-inspired aggression against Mozambique, which has itself been reticent about granting "Soviet warships basing rights in the country's harbors. Soviet military vessels are granted only restricted access to certain facilities on an occasional basis. To make the message very clear...the principle of not allowing any foreign military bases [with no exception] is enshrined in the 1978 constitution."[39] This is partly because of Mozambican attempts to strike a delicate balance between commitment to proletarian internationalism and nonalignment.

The overall picture that emerges is that Soviet military assistance was ineffective in providing the badly needed guarantee against South African and South African-inspired military and subversive activities against the Mozambican state. The militarily exposed and insecure position of Mozambique compounded and exacerbated the dependent and fragile economic situation of the country. The Nkomati Accord, entered into by Mozambique and South Africa on 16 March 1984, was part of the Mozambican attempt to come to terms with its fragile military and economic position and the political problems that this position was creating domestically for the Frelimo government.

The Nkomati Accord highlighted the failure of the Mozambican-Soviet treaty of friendship and cooperation in helping to build and ensure a militarily and economically strong Mozambique, able to stand up to the overpowering regional power of South Africa. It had become increasingly clear to Mozambicans that the Soviet Union was not prepared to commit its forces to the defense of their country. Leonid Brezhnev's comments that "the Soviet-Mozambique treaty was non-military in nature" underlined the Soviet reluctance to commit its forces in defense of Mozambique.[40] Colin Legum has asserted that "it can be stated for a fact that Samora Machel was counselled on at least three different occasions by Soviet leaders to do everything possible to avoid an open military confrontation with South Africa; the first was by Brezhnev, the second by President Podgorny, when he paid a state visit to Maputo, and the third was by Andropov when Machel visited Moscow in 1983."[41]

There had been, prior to the Nkomati Accord, a number of signals of Mozambican disenchantment with the nature of Soviet military and economic assistance. In April 1982, Mozambique entered into a treaty of military cooperation with Portugal, and shortly thereafter the idea of

Mozambican military cooperation with France and Great Britain was rumored as well. Also in 1982, there was a marked improvement in Mozambican relations with the United States. An earlier signal contained in Samora Machel's description of his meeting with President Jimmy Carter, in October 1977, as marking the beginning of a new era in their bilateral relations was now being seriously and vigorously pursued.[42] Sometime in 1982, as Winrich Kuhne claims, "Mozambique signalled to the State Department in Washington that it would welcome U.S. assistance in reaching a fundamental accommodation with South Africa on questions of mutual security."[43]

How was the Nkomati Accord viewed by the Soviet Union? In a sense, it was a setback for the Soviets in their pursuit of the mission of proletarian internationalism in Southern Africa. This partly explains their failure to provide military security to Mozambique and their private prodding of Mozambique not to provoke South Africa militarily; the Soviet Union did not want to offend Mozambique and the Front-line states by publicly condemning the Accord. On the other hand, the Soviet Union was sensitive to the sense of betrayal felt by the African National Congress of South Africa (ANC) as a result of the accord. It therefore privately had to reassure the ANC of its continuing support of the liberation struggle in South Africa. The statement credited to President Ceausescu of Romania that the Nkomati Accord was a positive factor that would help Mozambique consolidate its revolutionary gains was a view also probably shared by the Soviet Union.[44] What the accord also underscores is a credibility problem for the Soviet Union. As Legum has argued, "developments in 1983 and especially in 1984 showed up the Soviet role of strategic ally as being so weak as to be almost derisory."[45]

Why has the Soviet Union been unable to meet the security and military needs of Mozambique? One explanation is that, in view of the hard choices it has had to make in pursuit of its global interests, particularly because of its limited resources, the Soviet Union has tended to relegate Mozambique, and indeed the entire Southern African region, to a back seat in its geopolitical and strategic considerations.[46] A similar explanation is that the Soviet Union is playing a "low-key regional role" in Southern Africa because it accepts the region as essentially being in the sphere of influence of the West. A Soviet challenge to the hegemony of the West in the region might encourage the West to exert "deterrent pressure" and to challenge Soviet hegemony elsewhere.[47]

While there is some merit in these explanations, the active military presence of the Soviet Union in Angola suggests the need to look for another explanation. One such explanation is that Mozambique, unlike Angola, which earns substantial foreign exchange from the sale of petroleum, lacks the hard currency to pay for modern and sophisticated

Soviet weaponry. Another is that the Soviet Union is unprepared to deploy its troops or those of Cuba, for example, in Mozambique because the risks of direct military confrontation with South African troops is much higher than in Angola.[48]

Another important area of Mozambican-Soviet relations is the socioeconomic sphere. An agreement between the two countries was signed in November 1980 to cover agriculture, fishing, and mining. There were also discussions on Soviet-assisted projects in Mozambique. These developments were followed in May 1981, when the first session of the Soviet-Mozambique Intergovernmental Commission for Economic Cooperation and Trade was held in Moscow. A result of the session was an agreement on economic and trade cooperation to cover the period 1981-1990. Among other provisions, there was a protocol for Soviet aid and assistance in the creation of three state cotton-growing farms, a polytechnic school, and four vocational and technical schools. The importance attached to these relations by both countries translated into increased trade and commercial transaction flows between them.

For example Tass, in September 1981, reported that the volume of Mozambican-Soviet trade had increased from $8 million to $80 million between 1977 and 1980. The growing trade and economic links were further consolidated in April 1982 when Prakash Ratilal, the governor of the Bank of Mozambique signed an agreement in Moscow for a loan of 40 million rubles on "favorable terms" to finance geological and cotton projects.[49]

In March 1983, a Soviet agricultural delegation visited Mozambique to discuss methods of improving cotton production in Manpula Province. That same month, a delegation from the Soviet Central Consumer's Cooperative Union visited Maputo to discuss ways to implement a three-year cooperation agreement that both countries had signed in 1982. In 1983, a three-year bilateral trade agreement was the highlight of a visit to Maputo by G. K. Zhuravlev, the Soviet Union's first deputy minister of foreign trade, with the expectation that trade turnover between the two countries during the period would be about $300 million. This was followed by a number of further developments in 1983. A delegation from the Soviet Union, headed by Yuri Minayer, deputy chief of the Soviet Foreign Ministry's Department of Trade with African Countries, met with Mozambican officials in mid-November to consider precise items to include in Soviet-Mozambican trade in 1984. It was agreed that the Soviet Union would supply raw materials, chemical products, animal feed, and consumer goods; Mozambique would export sisal, cashew nuts, and prawns. The delegation also announced the Soviet donation of clothes, textiles, and other articles worth about $13 million to Mozambique to aid victims of drought. This was in addition to an earlier donation in

October 1983 of 10,000 tons of rice and 700 tons of frozen fish. In December 1983, the Soviet ambassador to Mozambique, Yuri Sepelez, indicated that the Soviet Union was sending shiploads of rice and oil to Mozambique, in addition to a recently signed $300 million trade agreement.[50] Late in 1984, the Soviet Union again donated 3,000 tons of fish and consumer goods valued at about $12,000,000 as a contribution to Mozambique's agricultural marketing campaign.

These transactions suggest that great importance is attached to bilateral economic relations in fostering the economic and sociopolitical development of Mozambique. Bilateral economic relations are intended to strengthen the state productive sector, assure state control of the national economy, and diminish economic dependence on South Africa in particular and on the world capitalist economy in general. But, as in the case of Ethiopian-Soviet economic bilateral relations, this hope has generally not been achieved. South Africa and the West remain the major sources of foreign exchange earnings and imports for Mozambique. In other words, these countries are still Mozambique's trading partners, although there has been some decline in the volume of trade between Mozambique and the West relative to that between Mozambique and the centrally planned economies between 1977 and 1982. Table 10.3 shows that, between 1977 and 1982, the percentage share of Mozambican exports to OECD countries dropped from 76 percent to 40 percent, while imports dropped from about 59 percent to 39 percent. On the other hand, during the same period,

Table 10.3   Trade Balance by Groups of Countries (million pounds)

	1973	1975	1977	1979	1981	1982
OECD countries						
Exports to	66	51	59	93	82	55
Imports from	125	104	102	121	197	196
Countries with centrally planned economies						
Exports to	0	0	0	12	32	18
Imports from	0	1	2	53	63	114
Other countries						
Exports to	22	29	19	27	43	18
Imports from	56	65	68	120	190	191
Total						
Exports to	88	80	78	132	158	136
Imports from	181	171	172	295	449	501

Data published by the National Planning Commission as a part of request to reschedule debts. Extracted from Hanlon, 1984.

Mozambican exports to countries with centrally planned economies rose from zero to 13 percent while imports grew from zero to 23 percent.

In spite of its trade links with the OECD countries, Mozambique was reluctant to accede to the Lomé Convention. The Berlin Clause in Annex 35 of the Lomé treaty would have created tension in Mozambican-East German relations since it makes recognition of Berlin as part of the Federal Republic of Germany mandatory. When Edgar Pisani, the EEC development commissioner, visited Maputo in February 1982, President Samora Machel informed him that Mozambique was interested in forms of economic cooperation and aid outside the framework of Lomé. Refusal to join the convention deprived Mozambique of considerable development cooperation assistance, the loss of which was not offset or compensated for by assistance coming from the Soviet Union and Eastern Europe. Disappointment on this score, as in the case of Ethiopia, led Mozambique to seek closer trade ties with the West, to whom it turned for more development assistance.

The sacrifice that nonaccession had meant for Mozambique was compounded by the failure of its efforts to join COMECON, to which it was granted an observer status in 1979. The issue of Mozambique's application for full membership in COMECON, especially the need to secure Soviet support, was a major reason for Samora Machel's visit to Moscow in November 1980. The Mozambicans placed a high premium on COMECON membership for ideological and developmental reasons. According to Machel, Mozambique regarded "cooperation between the developed socialist states and the socialist states whose economies are still developing as a decisive factor in strengthening the position of socialism on four continents."[51] But Soviet support was not forthcoming and has been, at best, lukewarm for reasons discussed below.

The issue of Mozambique's full membership in COMECON raised a number of issues. First, it highlighted contradictions between developed and developing economies within the socialist world, and especially the reluctance of the developed ones to "level up" with the developing ones. As Coker sums it up, "for many European economists, 'levelling up' has become an increasingly transparent smokescreen for unjust or inequitable development in contravention of their ideological posture."[52] Second, there is, according to Peter Wiles and Alan Smith, the emerging concensus within the Soviet Bloc "since the early 1960s...that the [new Communist Third World] should remain attached to the capitalist world market [although] under effective state control."[53]

The reason for this is partly the Soviet Bloc realization that the kind of capital assistance and transfers needed for development in Africa and Third World countries are much more ready and available in the West. Related to this is the refusal of the Soviet Union to subsidize

Mozambique to the extent that it has committed itself in Cuba and Vietnam. In this respect, East Germany and Bulgaria have provided Mozambique the most generous credit terms of the Soviet Bloc countries. The two countries were also the most active supporters of Mozambique's application for membership in COMECON.

A third issue concerns the criteria for admission to full membership status in COMECON. This is an important issue in view of the fact that none of the Afro-Marxist states or "African countries of socialist orientation" has achieved that status. One explanation for this state of affairs is that offered by Charles Lawson:

> Within the communist Third World, what distinguishes the full CMEA ememebers from the "candidate" members is partly their degree of effective planning, and partly the degree of their attachment to Soviet policy, but mainly, as Singleton has argued, the assurance that their transition to a Marxist-Leninist state is irreversible. Soviet commentators are quite clear on this point. They admit that a change of ruling elite can alter relations with any African country very rapidly, whether or not it is of socialist orientation.[54]

The critical criterion, therefore, is ideological reliability. In the view of the Soviet Union, this can best be assured by the development of a bona fide Marxist-Leninist party. This is why so much importance is attached to the political, especially party-building, dimensions of its bilateral relations with the Afro-Marxist regimes. Only the creation of a Marxist-Leninist party will create conditions that will not tie the prospects for socialist transformation to the political fortunes or misfortunes of particular leaders of ruling cliques.

As indicated earlier on, and as happened in the case of Ethiopian-Soviet bilateral economic relations, disappointment with the record of the Soviet Union in the economic and development assistance field led Mozambique to adopt a more open policy toward the West and Western capitalist financial institutions. It began to consider liberalization measures more seriously than it had earlier in 1980, when it returned some concerns in the public sector to private enterprise. Talks with the International Monetary Fund (IMF) began late in 1983. The IMF, in endorsement of the liberalization that had been initiated in the country, approved a $45 million loan for Mozambique. The need to gain access to Western capital markets also led Mozambique to make other concessions. Giving up its objections to the Berlin Clause, Mozambique accepted aid from West Germany. This was a signal that it was reconsidering its stand on the Lomé Convention. It eventually acceded to the convention in 1984.

There were probably strategic security considerations in Mozambique's decision to seek improved economic relations with the

West. For example, Hanlon has speculated that these "improved links...are also to be seen in the light of growing South African aggression. Frelimo hopes that if it increases Western investment and involvement in Mozambique then these countries will stop South Africa from attacking their new property."[55] Again it is clear how military, political, and economic factors converge and lead to radical policy changes.

What this also underscores is the way in which domestic and external factors interrelate to shape the government's policy options and narrow its range of choice. While the adoption of socialist development options and the pursuit of closer ties with the Soviet bloc has been designed to remove the economic and security weaknesses of the Mozambican state, these same weaknesses now impelled Mozambique to reconsider its options domestically and externally. While this might suggest the limited value of ideology as an indicator of economic policy choices and foreign policy behavior in the Afro-Marxist regimes, the point should, however, not be overdrawn.

Economic and trade relations with the Soviet Bloc are still important and, although limited and inadequate to deter South African aggression, Soviet Bloc economic, technical, and military assistance has nonetheless been useful in preventing the total collapse of the Mozambican state. As the debate during Frelimo's Fourth Congress in April 1983 made clear, bad management, leading to serious mistakes in a number of critical sectors, was also partly responsible for the anemic state of the national economy. Ideology is nonetheless important, and this is underscored by the distinction that is given in the report of the Frelimo Central Committee to the Fourth Congress to the party "which establishes relations with all countries on the basis of respect for national sovereignty and territorial integrity, noninterference in internal affairs...and peaceful resolution of conflicts."

Let us now turn to Mozambican-Soviet bilateral relations in the political and sociocultural spheres since, in addition to economic and military relations, these form the core around which the parties in both Mozambique and Ethiopia are centered. President Machel's visit to Moscow in November 1981 had, among other objectives, the development of strong interparty links between Frelimo and the CPSU. Frelimo, following the logic of its revolutionary tradition, had declared itself a Marxist-Leninist vanguard party in 1977 at its Third Congress. The links that President Machel sought were therefore intended to consolidate Frelimo as a vanguard party by enabling it to learn from the experience of the CPSU.

What form have the links assumed? As in the case of Ethiopian-Soviet relations in this particular area, officials of Frelimo and the CPSU have exchanged annual visits to each other's country. For example, in March 1981, a parliamentary delegation from the Soviet Union visited Maputo. This was followed in mid-November 1981 by the visit of a CPSU delegation to Maputo. Since February 1981, Frelimo has been sending a delegation at the invitation of the CPSU to the latter's annual congress in Moscow. In addition, the two parties have discussed expanding cooperation in education to include the training of Frelimo cadres in the Soviet Union.

The vanguard role of Frelimo is still defined as that of moving the party from a popular mass movement into a vehicle for socialist transformation, under the alliance of workers, peasants, and progressive petit bourgeois elements. It was in pursuit of this task, under the ideology Marxist-Leninism, that Frelimo looked up to the Soviet Bloc for continued organizational and other strategic support in much the same way as it had supported the liberation struggle. But if Frelimo saw in the Soviet Bloc a model for its theoretical-practical formulation of Marxism-Leninism, it did not intend to emulate or copy that model slavishly, regardless of Mozambican realities. President Machel has been quoted as affirming that "Africans must use Marxism but Marxism cannot be allowed to use Africans."[56]

The Soviet Union has had a considerable impact on the definition and conceptualization of Mozambican Marxism. That impact must, however, not be overemphasized. Many people, including Frelimo's top functionaries, have always insisted that Frelimo's adoption of Marxism-Leninism has its deep roots in the party's revolutionary tradition. Oscar Monteiro has been quoted as saying, "It is our experience which led us to Marxism-Leninism. We have spontaneously demonstrated its universal character. We have, on the basis of our practice, drawn theoretical lessons."

In spite of this close affinity between Frelimo's revolutionary tradition and Marxism-Leninism, it is the chronic shortage of trained and educated party cadres within its rank and file that led Frelimo to turn to and depend on the Soviet Bloc for experts, *cooperantes,* as it set out to build durable party structures and train Mozambican cadres. This was an important reason why President Machel and other Frelimo leaders placed such a premium on establishing strong and close interparty links with the CPSU. That way, links that had been forged during the liberation struggle against Portuguese colonial rule would be further consolidated. The Soviet influence on the conceptualization and concretization of the party's role in Mozambique has, therefore, been substantial. This was evident in efforts in the period 1980-1981 to strengthen the role of the party by giving it a grass roots presence throughout the country, a task that two important ministers, Marcelino dos Santos and Jorge Rebelo, left the cabinet to pursue.

But this effort was itself the result of another development that could be attributed to the influence of Soviet Marxism. This is the trend toward centralization and bureaucratization. The tension between centralization and populist democracy and between leadership and mass action is a constantly recurring one in the Mozambican debate over Marxism-Leninism. It was an issue that dominated public debates in the period leading up to and during Frelimo's Fourth Congress in April 1983. The emphasis in the debates was on participation and decentralization if the party was to maintain contact with the base and encourage cell members to be self-reliant and to direct and manage affairs in their local communities. The determination to strengthen links between the party and the base was underscored by the increase in the composition of the Central Committee from about sixty-five to 130. This was done to allow for the infusion of new blood from the peasantry.

Recent developments in Mozambique have generated serious questioning of orthodox Marxism-Leninism as an ideological formulation for ordering the processes of change and transformation in the country. These developments, which have pitted a number of Frelimo cadres and officials against their Soviet Bloc counterparts, have highlighted problems concerning the type of theoretical training party cadres should be given. At issue was the question whether and, if so, how Marxist-Leninism should be adapted and applied to the concrete and historically specific situation of Mozambique. The issue arose because it was becoming increasingly clear to a number of Frelimo leaders and Mozambican intellectuals that *cooperantes* from the Soviet Bloc, and particularly from the German Democratic Republic, were not relating their Marxist-Leninist theoretical formulations to Mozambican realities. Their formulations appeared abstract and unreal to the Mozambican students and Frelimo cadres they were training. As a result, the teaching of Marxism-Leninism was suspended at Edouardo Mondlane University in 1983 and the Faculty of Marxism-Leninism closed down, pending curricula review to design more relevant courses.

There are other dimensions to these developments. First, the issue of an appropriate or relevant Marxism-Leninism touched on the issue of indigenization and self-reliance in the area of ideological training. Second, at issue, albeit implicitly, was the viability of Marxist internationalism as a guide to policy making. In this respect, the debate over an appropriate Marxism-Leninism could be viewed as part of a wider debate within Frelimo's hierarchy over Mozambique's future and its role in internationalizing its own struggle in the larger context of furthering a proletarian revolution in Southern Africa.

What seems to have emerged, and is perhaps underlined by the Nkomati Accord, is the notion of potentially divergent paths to socialism. In Mozambique, a fixed line has not emerged, but what is becoming more and more apparent is that the party and state seem to be moving on a contingency plan that is influenced as much by the superordinate position of South Africa as a proxy for finance capital in the region as by disappointment with the Soviet Bloc.

Conclusion

How much influence has the Soviet Union exerted over Ethiopia and Mozambique? Neither country is a client state or satellite of the Soviet Union. This, in itself, suggests that there are strong limitations on the extent of the Soviet influence over their domestic and external policies. In other words, both Ethiopia and Mozambique have much room for maneuvering and for pursuing independent foreign and domestic policy options. No doubt this is also partly due to the extent to which the Soviet Union is prepared and willing to invest to maintain and consolidate its bilateral relations with each country. The overtures of both countries to the West and the limited but important concessions they have made to market forces by encouraging private enterprise in some sectors of their economies are attributable, in part, to the low level of Soviet development assistance and aid.

The fragile political economies of both countries have, therefore, been a powerful factor in shaping and moving the course of their domestic and foreign policies in directions which might appear to belie and undermine their ideological affinities with the Soviet Union. Does this point to the irrelevance of ideology? Not necessarily. As I noted earlier, ideology admits to flexibility. This is why it is sometimes characterized as a cognitive map to guide policy options and choices and to define objectives, while it is itself subject to modifications, reinterpretations, and reexaminations in the light of historical conjectures and specifics.

Therefore, what may appear as ideological deviations or heresies, like the adoption of essentially monetarist policies and the introduction of liberalization measures by Ethiopia and Mozambique, are often viewed as short-term responses to domestic and external constraints, which are structurally determined. Indeed, these short-term responses must be viewed alongside the fact that the regimes in both countries are also captives of their ideological preferences. This is reflected in the continuing debates in both countries about the best road to socialism, in the self-critical assessment of progress toward socialism, and in the socioeconomic structures that are being gradually created. The road is tortuous, precisely because of the constraints already mentioned. The character of these constraints is such that the political control of the state by the Afro-Marxist regimes in Mozambique and Ethiopia has not been translated into control of their economies. Yet ideology still matters in that it has served the instrumental role of defining and structuring the developmental options chosen.

The Soviet influence can be seen in the adoption of Marxism-Leninism by both countries. In the case of Mozambique, the choice of Marxism-Leninism grew out of Frelimo's revolutionary tradition, whereas in Ethiopia the military regime had no socialist project when it took over power, although Marxist-Leninist-oriented groups played a prominent role in the overthrow of Haile Selassie. But the Soviet model or version of Marxism-Leninism has not been dogmatically followed. Here again, the combination of domestic and external factors has given rise to nationalism.

The Soviet Union itself has been conscious of the limitations of ideology as a basis for sustaining its bilateral relations with each country. It has taken advantage of its position in the global division of labor to secure better terms of trade in its economic relations with both countries. As its lukewarm attitude toward COMECON membership for Mozambique demonstrated, the Soviet Union is still skeptical of the depth of the commitment to Marxism-Leninism and its durability in both countries.

To say all this is to illuminate the nature of the contradictions that have characterized the relations between the Soviet Union and each of the two countries. It is not, however, to deny the positive elements in those relations. It is to look at them dialectically. Although Soviet support has not been all that it should have been in terms of the military and economic aspects of Soviet relations, it has nevertheless been a critical sustaining force in both countries. This fact is well-captured in President Machel's statement, quoted earlier on, that "the socialist countries were and are at all times our safe rearguard."

Notes

1. Anatoli Gromyko, *Africa: Progress, Problems and Prospects* (Moscow: Progress Publishers, 1983), 82-83.

2. E. A. Tarabrian, ed., *USSR and Countries of Africa* (Moscow: Progress Publishers, 1980), 12.

3. David and Marina Ottaway, *Afrocommunism* (New York: Africana Publishing Co., 1981), 30.

4. Tarabrian, *USSR and Countries of Africa.*

5. Gromyko, *Africa: Progress,* 81.

6. R. Craig Nation and Mark V. Kauppi, *The Soviet Impact in Africa*

(Lexington Mass: D. C. Heath, 1984), 36.

7. Bhabani Sen Gupta, "An Approach to the Study of Soviet Policies for the Third World," 20-37 in Roger E. Kanet and Donna Bahry, eds., *Soviet Economic and Political Relations with the Developing World* (New York: Praeger, 1974), 20.

8. Hugh Seton-Watson, *The New Imperialists* (London: The Bodley Head, 1961), 120.

9. Richard E. Bissell, "Soviet Interests in Africa," 1-15 in W. Weinstein and T. H. Henricksen, *Soviet and Chinese Aid to African Nations* (New York: Praeger, 1980), 6.

10. Claude Ake, *Revolutionary Pressures in Africa* (London: Zed Press, 1978), 17-18.

11. Ibid.

12. Ibid.

13. Ibid.

14. Ibid.

15. Crawford Young, *Ideology and Development in Africa* (New Haven: Yale University Press, 1982), 294.

16. Tarabrian, *USSR and Countries of Africa,* 42.

17. Harry Brind, "Soviet Policy in the Horn of Africa," *International Affairs,* 60:1 (1983/84):92.

18. Harry Brind, "Soviet Policy in the Horn of Africa," *International Affairs,* 60:1 (1983/84); Richard B. Remneck, "Soviet Policy in the Horn of Africa: The Decision to Intervene," in Robert H. Donaldson, ed., *The Soviet Union and the Third World: Successes and Failures* (Boulder: Westview Press, 1981); Marina Ottaway, "Superpower Competition and Regional Conflict in the Horn of Africa," in R. Craig Nation and Mark V. Kauppi, eds., *The Soviet Impact in Africa,* 165-195.

19. Much of the information that follows is drawn from the annual issue of *Africa Contemporary Record,* beginning in 1979.

20. Richard B. Remneck, "Soviet Policy in the Horn of Africa: The Decision to Intervene," 125-149 in Donaldson, ed., *The Soviet Union and the Third World,* 136.

21. Remneck, "Soviet Policy," 141; Brind, "Soviet Policy," 93.

22. Colin Legum, "The Continuing Crisis in Southern Africa: Pax Praetoriana or Pax Africana?" *Africa Contemporary Record,* (1983/84): 24.

23. Ottaway and Ottaway, *Afrocommunism,* 148.

24. Marina Ottaway, "Superpower Conflict and Regional Conflict in the Horn of Africa," in Nation and Kauppi, eds., *The Soviet Impact in Africa,* 13.

25. Roger E. Kanet, "Soviet Policy Toward the Developing World: The Role of Economic Assistance and Trade," 331-357, in Donaldson, ed., *The Soviet Union and the Third World,* 347-353.

26. Kanet, "Soviet Policy," 337; Legum, "The Continuing Crisis," 25-26.

27. Christopher Stevens, "The Soviet Role in Southern Africa," in John Seiler, ed., *Southern Africa Since the Portuguese Coup* (Boulder: Westview Press, 1980), 48.

28. Stevens, "The Soviet Role," 45.

29. Joseph Hanlon, *Mozambique: The Revolution Under Fire* (London: Zed Press, 1984), 15.

30. Tarabrian, *USSR and Countries of Africa*, 122.

31. Gromyko, *Africa: Progress*, 82.

32. Stevens, "The Soviet Role," 51.

33. David E. Albright, "The Communist States and Southern Africa," 3-44, in G. Carter and P. O'Meara, eds., *International Politics in Southern Africa* (Bloomington, Indiana: Indiana University Press, 1982), 4.

34. Christopher Coker, "Adventurism and Pragmatism: The Soviet Union, COMECON, and Relations With African States," *International Affairs*, 57:4 (1981):619.

35. Ibid.

36. Daniel S. Papp, "The Soviet Union and Southern Africa," 69-96, in Donaldson, ed., *The Soviet Union and the Third World*.

37. Stevens, "The Soviet Role," 51.

38. Colin Legum, ed., *Africa Contemporary Record*, 13 (1980-1981): 1418-1419.

39. Winrich Kuhne, "What Does the Case of Mozambique Tell Us About Soviet Ambivalence Toward Africa?" *CSIS Africa Notes*, 46 (30 August 1985):2.

40. Papp, "The Soviet Union and Southern Africa," 81.

41. Colin Legum, "The Continuing Crisis in Southern Africa: Pax Praetoriana or Pax Africana?" *Africa Contemporary Record*, 16 (1983-1984):A47-A48.

42. Papp, "The Soviet Union and Southern Africa," 81.

43. Kuhne, "What Does the Case of Mozambique Tell Us," 2.

44. Colin Legum, ed., *Africa Contemporary Record*, 16 (1983/84): V673.

45. Colin Legum, "The Continuing Crisis in Southern Africa: Pax Praetoriana or Pax Africana?" A48.

46. Albright, "The Communist States," 16; Legum, "The Continuing Crisis," A48.

47. Stevens, "The Soviet Role," 52-53.

48. Kuhne, "What Does the Case of Mozambique Tell Us," 4.

49. Colin Legum, ed., *Africa Contemporary Record*, 14 (1981/82): V659.

50. Kuhne, "What Does the Case of Mozambique Tell Us," 1.

51. Charles W. Lawson, "The Soviet Union and Eastern Europe in Southern Africa, Is There a Conflict of Interest?" *International Affairs*, 59:1 (1982/83): 37.

52. Coker, "Adventurous and Pragmatism," 630.

53. Lawson, "The Soviet Union," 35-36.

54. Lawson, "The Soviet Union," 38.

55. Hanlon, "Mozambique: The Revolution," 236.

56. John S. Saul, ed., *A Difficult Road Ahead: The Transition to Socialism in Mozambique* (New York: Monthly Review Press, 1985), 138.

57. Saul, "A Difficult Road," 136.

chapter eleven

South Africa and Afro-Marxism: Pretoria's Relations with Mozambique and Angola in Regional Perspective

Robert M. Price

To understand South Africa's policies toward Angola and Mozambique two dimensions in the relationship between the erstwhile Portuguese colonies and their white minority-ruled neighbor must be taken into account. First, and most obvious, is the nature of Angola and Mozambique as "Marxist regimes." Official spokesmen for Pretoria claim that South Africa is the victim of a "total onslaught" orchestrated by the Soviet Union and conducted through the states of southern Africa. Thus, Mozambique and Angola, with their *Marxist* ideological orientation, their ties to the Soviet Union, China, Cuba, and the countries of Eastern Europe, and their long-standing fraternal relations with the South African liberation movement in exile, ought to constitute a "special project" for Pretoria's foreign policymakers. But it would be a mistake to focus exclusively, or even predominately, on the Marxist aspect of Angola and Mozambique in order to adequately comprehend the evolution of Pretoria's policies toward them. These two countries are part of a Southern African subregional system toward which Pretoria has adopted a general strategy. It is only when viewed as an aspect of this strategy that the logic and dynamic of Pretoria's policies toward its two Marxist neighbors is revealed.

Pretoria's International Goals and Regional Strategy

In its pursuit of security for white rule, the government of South Africa has, at least since the end of World War II, been challenged by a fundamental contradiction between its international and domestic requirements. Internationally, South Africa requires access to markets for capital and technology and to export markets for its minerals and manufactured goods. These are prerequisites for the growth and development of its modern industrial economy. But those policies Pretoria pursues at home in order to ensure continued political domination of the black majority produce international reactions that threaten access to global markets, thus directly placing economic growth and development in jeopardy, and indirectly raising the cost of security by interfering with the flow of advanced technology and weaponry to South Africa's security agencies. This contradiction between domestic and international requirements is a dynamic one: the greater the government's use of overt repression against the black majority, the greater its problems with its international environment. Active political pressure by the majority and its counterpoint, repressive action by the minority government, render the nature of the South African system visible to the world, and thus serve as a catalyst for international reactions.

Conversely, in periods of political quiescence, Pretoria's international problem remains largely hypothetical. It is when the majority makes its political opposition felt and visible and when the need of the white government to make its domination manifest is greatest, that the international threat becomes real. The empirical manifestation of this dynamic security contradiction is found, on the one hand, in the costly international economic repercussions that followed the Sharpeville shootings of 1960, the "Soweto Uprising of 1976-1977," and have accompanied the prolonged township "unrest" of 1984-1986. On the other hand, it is found in the periods of open access to international markets that separate these events.

One can comprehend the internal logic of South African foreign policy as an effort to resolve, or break out of, its security contradiction. Pretoria seeks to maintain white control by decoupling its domestic actions from international repercussions, and so gain greater freedom for governmental efforts to deal with the "threat" from the black majority. In regional terms, this has meant that since the collapse, in the mid-1970s, of the buffer of white-ruled states that had previously surrounded it, South Africa has sought ways to render its African-ruled neighboring states neutral in respect to its domestic sociopolitical system.

Neutralization can be thought of as Pretoria's strategic goal for the Southern African region. It can be understood to involve the pursuit of three specific objectives: First, the prevention of a conventional military attack on South Africa by one, or a combination, of its African neighbors. Given the vastly superior capability of Pretoria's military forces relative to those of its neighbors, this must be viewed as a long-term, rather than immediate concern. Nevertheless, the gradual development of organizationally capable and technically sophisticated militaries in African countries hostile to a continuation of white control represents a medium- to long-term security concern for Pretoria. It is in this respect—the potential development of local military capability—that the role of the Soviet Union, Cuba, and other "Eastern Bloc" countries constitutes a genuine threat to white South African security interests.

Second, neutralization involves denying the territory of Southern African states to the main black opposition and liberation movement, the African National Congress (ANC). Pretoria seeks to eliminate the ANC from its Southern African neighbors, forcing the liberation movement to operate in exile far from the borders of the republic.

Third, Pretoria seeks to render its neighboring African countries neutral in respect to the international campaign for economic and diplomatic pressure against white rule. Most important, South Africa would like to prevent the governments of neighboring states from focusing international attention on its domestic system of racial rule and from mobilizing African and global opinion against it. Looked at from another, "positive" angle, Pretoria seeks to use its neighbors in an effort to end its pariah status—i.e., to help achieve international acquiescence in a reformed system of white rule.

In pursuit of the objective of neutralization, Pretoria has, since the late 1970s, pursued a conscious strategy of creating a system, or regime, of regional hegemony.[1] Utilizing instruments of destabilization (i.e., support for antigovernment insurgents), direct military attack, and economic leverage—or by threatening these—the South African government has sought to impose on the Southern African region a set of rules of interstate behavior that are consistent with Pretoria's neutralization objectives.[2] By actively demonstrating its predominant military and economic position in the region, Pretoria has worked to create a "regional regime" that will render its neighbors neutral in respect to its domestic arrangements and foreign policy interests. This regime of regional hegemony can be seen to have three distinct modes, with each successive mode representing a more complete achievement of neutralization.

De Facto Hegemony

De facto hegemony exists when Southern African states, in recognition of South Africa's superior power resources, adopt self-imposed limitations on the activities of the ANC. South Africa's relations with Botswana and Zimbabwe represent a regime of de facto hegemony. Without any formal diplomatic accord, African states restrict the number and activities of ANC cadres within their borders, limiting the liberation movement's ability to use their territory for actions directed at South Africa.

De Jure Hegemony

The relationship of Swaziland and Mozambique with South Africa is characteristic of this mode of hegemony. A formal treaty relationship of "good neighborliness and non-aggression" details the specific limitations that these African-ruled states agree to impose on the South African insurgent movement.[3] These limitations are extremely broad, as well as detailed. In addition to a prohibition on ANC military installations and arms depots, Mozambique and Swaziland are under treaty obligation to forbid within their territories, among other things, the shelter or accommodation of individual cadres, the recruitment of new personnel, the transit of cadres into South Africa, and "acts of propaganda" that might incite "terrorism or civil war."[4]

A particularly important aspect of these treaties is the commitment by African governments to active cooperation and coordination with the South African Defense Forces in eliminating the activities, organizational presence, and cadres of the ANC. The Nkomati Accord between Mozambique and South Africa, for example, established a Joint Security Commission composed of high-ranking political and security officials from both countries to ensure that the prohibitions agreed upon are enforced.[5]

The significance of *de jure* hegemony should be understood as going well beyond logistical and organizational losses it imposes upon the ANC. By drawing African governments into formally recognized diplomatic exchanges and joint security efforts, Pretoria seeks to breach the united front of African opposition, and in so doing to render European and U.S. hostility less likely. At the time of its signing, the Nkomati Accord with Mozambique was hailed in South Africa as a triumph for Pretoria not just regionally, but more important, at the global level.[6] The South African *Sunday Times* declared, "The new alliances in Southern Africa will have a valuable spin-off benefit in the international arena by making the prospect of economic sanctions against South Africa—ever present for two decades—more remote."[7] *De jure* hegemony is seen to offer Pretoria not only security in respect to conventional and guerrilla military attack, but also protection against isolation and pressure from its main trading partners in the industrial world.[8]

Institutional Hegemony
An intermittent but recurring theme of South African foreign policy has been the desire to establish a constellation of Southern African states. The idea is to create a formal multilateral institution, based on the core South African economy, whose members would include, along with South Africa and the African-ruled states of the Southern African region, the nominally independent "national states" created under Pretoria's separate development policy. It is this last membership feature that makes the notion of a constellation so attractive to the South African policymakers.

Such a formal institutional arrangement would not only lock the region more firmly into the South African economic orbit, but, more important, it would constitute African recognition of the sovereignty of the Pretoria-created "homelands-cum-states." For the very first time, the political goal of separate development would achieve diplomatic acceptance. The importance of this goal has not been lessened by the orientation toward reform that has characterized the South African government in the 1980s. As Pretoria searches for a formula that will allow the sharing of power without the loss of control, the "national states" figure prominently as distinct units within some complex confederal/federal arrangement.[9]

The creation of institutional hegemony through some form of constellation should be seen as a long-term project from Pretoria's vantage point. Nevertheless, the South African government has, for the past several years, been creating the constellation's institutional infrastructure. In 1983, Pretoria launched two new "multilateral" agencies—the South African Development Bank (SADB) and the Multilateral Development Council (MDC).[10] It is intended that public and private South African economic assistance to the "TBCV countries" (Transkei, Bophuthatswana, Ciskei, and Venda) will be channeled through these organizations. Although initial membership involves only Pretoria and its own homeland creations, South African officials have made it clear that membership is open to any state in Southern Africa that wishes to join.[11] It is likely that Pretoria will seek to utilize its predominant economic position in the region to draw its African neighbors into these new structures of institutional hegemony. At the same time, Pretoria has been attempting to extend the membership definition of the sixteen-year-old Southern African Customs Union (SACU) to include the TBVC countries. Since 1982, Pretoria has pressed the other member states (the BLS countries of Botswana, Lesotho, and Swaziland) to accept this redefinition, but they have resisted.[12]

In 1986, the South African government proposed the creation of yet another institutional component of its regime of regional hegemony. In his "Rubicon II" speech opening the South African Parliament, State President Botha called upon the governments of Southern Africa to "give urgent and serious consideration to the establishment of a permanent joint mechanism for dealing with matters of security." He identified the task of this proposed regional organization as establishing "the specific *rules of the game* regulating the conduct of neighbors toward one another." This proposal by the state president was immediately followed by a threat: "Should this offer by the Republic of South Africa be ignored or rejected, we would have no choice but to take effective measures in self-defence to protect our country and population against threats."[13]

How does South Africa's relationship with Mozambique and Angola fit into this general regional strategy of achieving neutralization through hegemony? As viewed from Pretoria, the problem is clear—how to neutralize states whose governing regimes have a strong ideological antipathy toward its domestic system; whose ruling parties have long-standing and close fraternal ties with the ANC; and whose governments have significant links with Leninist countries that have a record of providing military assistance to national liberation movements in general, and ANC in particular. Two tactical approaches to this problem have developed within the South African government. Each approach has its proponents within officialdom, and is associated with different agencies of government. At times, the two lines conflict and compete, creating confusion, contradiction, and incoherence at the tactical level of Pretoria's regional strategy. The two tactical approaches can be termed *regime reconstitution* and *cooptive domination*.

Regime reconstitution involves using the instruments of destabilization, direct military attack, and economic leverage so as to destroy and dislodge the "Marxist-oriented" regimes in Angola and Mozambique. In this approach, the strategic goal of neutralization is sought through replacement of the MPLA and FRELIMO governments with insurgent movements that Pretoria has supported with financing, equipment, logistics, and technical assistance.[14] The assumption underlying this tactic is that UNITA in Angola and Renamo in Mozambique, being supported by and presumably beholden to Pretoria, would be willing and full participants in South Africa's regional hegemonal regime.

The second tactical approach, cooptive domination, seeks to use the same policy instruments to so weaken the Angolan and Mozambique governments that out of desperation, and an instinct for political self-preservation, they will accept South Africa's hegemonic rule and cooperate in its neutralization objectives. In contrast to regime reconstitution, this tactical line, while pursing a weakening of Southern Africa's Marxist governments, does not seek their replacement.

The cooptive domination tactical approach was developed within South Africa's foreign policy establishment during 1983, and became manifest with the signing of the South African Mozambique Nkomati Accord in early 1984. At the time of the signing, Pretoria publicly committed itself to ending its support for Renamo, ceasing its commando raids into Mozambique, and extending its economic relations with the Marxist government in Maputo. Broad hints were dropped that South Africa also was prepared to cut a deal with Luanda, with similar implications for Angola's military security, political stability, and economic health.

But from the outset, strong objections to Nkomati, and to its implications for relations with Mozambique and possibly Angola, were voiced by conservative Afrikaner factions,[15] and were reported to exist within the military establishment.[16] Particularly strong exception to the new policy line was apparently taken by the military intelligence agencies that had been charged with aiding Renamo and UNITA, and which were being asked to cut off their assistance and to watch, even participate in, the defeat of their erstwhile protégés.[17]

Evidence of the conflict between military and foreign policy establishments over how to deal with Marxist states in Southern Africa is provided in documents captured from Renamo in August of 1985.[18] Notebooks containing minutes of meetings between senior South African military officers and Renamo leaders reveal a virtual conspiracy to continue the insurgency in Mozambique, despite the Nkomati Accord. They also show senior military personnel displaying deep animosity toward Pretoria's Foreign Minister Pik Botha and antipathy toward his policies. A diary entry for 6 September 1984 has General Viljoen, chief of staff of the South African armed forces, recommending to Renamo officials that they "not be fooled by the schemes of Pick [sic] Botha because he is a traitor."[19] Instead, the head of the South African military recommends "a joint strategy [South African-Renamo] for putting Machel out." "Because we want to remove the Russians from our region of South Africa, we have to employ a joint strategy to be able to defeat communism."[20] In a pointed reference to the policy difference between the military and foreign affairs establishments, General Viljoen tells the Renamo officials, "South African politicians too,...have their way of fighting communism. And we soldiers have our way of fighting the Russians."[21] Three other senior South African officers were present at the meeting at which General Viljoen made these statements. These were Brigadier Van Tonder, chief of secret operations, General Van Der West Huisen and Colonel Vanikerke, both of military intelligence.

The statements of General Viljoen suggest that, in addition to the organizational and professional interests that tie the military to the insurgent movements, there exists an important ideological basis to the military's preference for regime reconstitution. The anti-communist ideology that has been at the core of the National Party rhetoric since 1948 provides a fertile attitudinal environment for the regime reconstitution approach, and thus an advantage for its proponents in the political infighting over appropriate tactics. Indeed, regime reconstitution can be seen as a logical extension of that ideology. For almost four decades, the South African government has depicted "communism" as the chief domestic threat to the stability of its racial order. The omnibus security law introduced in 1950 to deal with the political threat from the black majority was thus "appropriately" titled "The Suppression of Communism Act." After 1975, with the emergence of Marxist Angola and Mozambique, an external communist threat was joined to the domestic threat, and South Africa was depicted by government officials, political leaders, and the Afrikaner media as the subject of a "total onslaught" by the forces of international communism. According to minister of defense, General Magnus Malan, there exists a "communist-inspired onslaught" that intends the "overthrow of the present constitutional order and its replacement by a subject communist-oriented black government."[22] To the extent that the notion of a "total onslaught" is taken seriously, the elimination of key actors in that onslaught, the governments of Angola and Mozambique, becomes a strategic necessity. Even if the total onslaught doctrine is viewed by officialdom primarily as political rhetoric, it still serves to generate support for the tactic of regime reconstitution within the white mass public.

As noted earlier, set against the tactical approach of reconstituting the political systems of Angola and Mozambique is the approach that seeks to coopt the existing Marxist governments into Pretoria's regime of regional hegemony. Proponents of this latter approach have supported the same regional policies of destabilization, forward military attack, and economic leverage as do those in Pretoria that advocate regime reconstitution. The difference between the two tactical approaches lies in how far these policies ought to be pushed. In the cooptation approach, regional policy serves the purpose of forcing neighboring states into accepting formal agreements of "cooperation" with Pretoria, rather than changing the form of their governments.

The primary attractiveness to Pretoria of the cooptive domination approach lies in the potential international benefits that it can generate. These lie in four areas:

International Acceptability
As discussed at the outset of this chapter, white-ruled South Africa is caught in a fundamental contradiction between its domestic security needs in preserving its political control on the one hand, and its requirements for access to international capital, technology, and export markets on the other. Attending to the former undermines the latter. The debilitating effects of this dynamic have never been clearer than over the past ten years. The "diplomatic deep freeze" into which Pretoria was thrust after the Soweto Uprising of 1976-1977 has rendered South Africa's foreign economic relations insecure and unstable. The governments of the industrial countries have been unwilling and/or unable to resist taking direct and indirect steps that limit the South African economy's access to international capital and technology markets, and private firms have come

to recognize significant costs in an expanded, or even continued, presence in South Africa. Difficulty in obtaining new direct investment from abroad, in importing the latest technology, and in gaining access to international bank loans, threatens South Africa's long-term economic growth. Without economic growth, the prospects for domestic tranquility and security decline. Unemployment and downward pressure on wages serve to increase black anger and to make militant political responses more likely. A violent and seemingly unstable domestic situation, in circumstances of diplomatic isolation and hostility, serves to further undermine South Africa's foreign economic relations, by increasing the likelihood of embargoes and sanctions, and by reducing the attractiveness of her "investment climate." All of which, in turn, threaten economic growth, jobs, and income, producing more alienation and threats to domestic security in a continuing cycle of economic decline and political unrest.

Pretoria seeks to break this cycle by achieving some measure of international acceptability. By shedding its status as an international pariah it could, in theory, decouple its domestic problems from its prospects for economic growth. If it were dealt with as a "normal" country, efforts to maintain domestic "security" would not immediately have a negative impact on international economic and political relations. In pursuit of this "normalcy," or acceptability, cooptive domination offers several benefits that cannot be realized through regional efforts at regime reconstitution.

The policies of direct and indirect military assault and of economic pressure that Pretoria adopted toward her neighbors after 1978 had the effect of further undermining South Africa's international position by casting it as an aggressor and bully. By substituting for these policies a public commitment to "negotiated" agreements of "nonaggression," Pretoria was able, in early 1984, to project an image of moderation and flexibility. Of course, the shift from regime reconstitution to cooptive domination, which was marked by the signing of the Nkomati Accord and the Lusaka Agreement in spring 1984, was prepared by these same policies of destabilization, direct military attack, and economic pressure as Mozambique and Angola were bludgeoned into submitting to Pretoria's terms. Nevertheless, liberal observers[23] and Western governments praised Pretoria for its willingness to pursue "moderation" and "diplomatic solutions."[24] In the diplomatic atmosphere created by the switch from tactics of regime reconstitution to cooptive domination, Prime Minister P. W. Botha was able to undertake a six-nation European tour, the first such official trip undertaken by a South African head of government since the National Party achieved its parliamentary majority in 1948.

The shift by South Africa to cooptive domination had particular importance to Pretoria-Washington relations. Pretoria's policies of destabilization, military attack, and economic pressure escalated after the Reagan election victory of 1980. Some within the new U.S. administration had concerns regarding the effect of Pretoria's policies on the U.S. interest in containing Soviet influence in Southern Africa.[25] In May 1981, Chester Crocker, assistant secretary for African affairs, warned Secretary of State Alexander Haig that "SAG [South African government] intransigence and violent adventures will expand Soviet opportunities and reduce Western leverage."[26] By mid-1983, this concern had greatly intensified. With the Machel government under increasingly effective assault from Renamo, it appeared that Mozambique might receive a major increase in Soviet Bloc assistance. Under these circumstances, U.S. officials clearly warned South Africa "that a continuation of destabilization could damage U.S.-South African relations" and suggested "that South African cooperation would make it easier for the West to deal with Pretoria more openly."[27]

In the regional and global circumstances of late 1983, a tactical shift toward cooptive domination held out immediate diplomatic benefits not only for Pretoria's relations with its most important trading partners, but also for sustaining the improved relations with the United States that had been made possible by the election of Ronald Reagan. By throwing its weight behind "negotiated nonaggression agreements," Washington provided a momentary advantage to those in Pretoria most sensitive to South Africa's diplomatic posture: the members of the foreign affairs bureaucracy.

These direct and immediate benefits derived by Pretoria from a shift to cooptive domination are only part of the potential gains offered by this tactical approach. A switch away from regime reconstitution also enhances Pretoria's ability to achieve the international aims of its regional strategy of hegemonial rule. A major purpose of establishing *de jure* hegemony has been to obtain the active and public cooperation of African states in the repression of the ANC. If the South African security forces and the military of other African countries are seen to be jointly engaged in operations against the ANC, then a sharp break will have been achieved in the Africa-wide consensus on the need to ostracize Pretoria. With Africa divided on the issue of cooperative engagement with Pretoria, the way would presumably be open for Western countries to reduce their pressure on, and improve their relations with, South Africa. It is in this sense that the South African media interpreted the Nkomati Accord of 1984 as "the beginning of a new road which could, if followed...lead South Africa back into Africa and through Africa back into the world."[28]

This "road back into the world" will, however, vary in its utility depending upon the type of African state with which cooperation is established. Pretoria's diplomatic mileage is likely to be greatest if the cooperating African government is one that is ideologically radical and has bona fide credentials as an opponent of apartheid. The diplomatic gains are likely to be smallest, or even nonexistent, if the cooperating African state is perceived as ruled by a quisling government. This would likely be the case if that government's rise to power had been financially and militarily supported by Pretoria. This is the dilemma posed by Pretoria's support for the Renamo and UNITA insurgencies. A Nkomati Accord signed with a victorious Renamo might eliminate the ANC from Mozambique but could be expected to be relatively worthless internationally, compared to the same accord entered into with the Marxist Frelimo government. A similar situation would arise if a security pact were entered into with a UNITA government in Angola.

The dilemma of the regime reconstitution approach, in other words, is that success in respect to the ANC brings with it a loss of international benefits. A regime of *de jure* hegemony with reconstituted governments may achieve certain regional aims, but render the road back into the world a "dead end." The tactic of cooptive domination can be viewed as a means out of this dilemma. Stopping short of the actual overthrow of Marxist governments, while forcing them into publicly acknowledged joint security efforts, preserves the international benefits of destabilization policy. The attractiveness of cooptive domination for Pretoria lies in its potential for simultaneously realizing both regional and international objectives.

Propaganda

In an attempt to limit the international pressure on it for rapid sociopolitical change, Pretoria has in recent years focused its international propaganda effort on contrasting the dire economic plight of Black African countries in the 1980s ("Africa is dying" is a refrain heard repeatedly from Pretoria) with the supposed strength of the South African economy. The message to those who would pressure Pretoria is that, by supporting the cause of majority rule, they may be dooming all South Africans—black as well as white—to the same bleak economic future now enjoyed by the rest of the African continent. Economic collapse in Angola and Mozambique, with their Marxist-oriented governments and "socialist" economic policies, provides dramatic "corroboration" of this propaganda thesis, and a pointed reminder to those "foolish" enough to believe that the ANC might have a legitimate and viable role in the future of South Africa. This message serves to instruct a domestic as well as an international audience. It has taken on special significance in the mid-1980s, as a variety of individuals associated with different elements of white society—opposition politicians, industrialists, clergymen, and Afrikaner student leaders—have taken it upon themselves to seek meetings with the ANC leadership-in-exile. The contribution that Marxist Mozambique and Angola make to Pretoria's propaganda campaign would be lost should regime reconstitution be pushed to its logical conclusion.

There is an important corollary that follows from the propaganda "benefits" of cooptive domination. It is essential that Pretoria's Marxist neighbors should be economically faltering and politically insecure. Otherwise, the tactic would backfire, and a South African future in which the ANC plays a major role would come to appear less threatening. Consequently, there are likely to be very real limits on the extent to which Pretoria will permit South African economic resources to be utilized for the economic development of regional states. The acceptance by her neighbors of even a regime of *de jure* hegemony is not going to obviate Pretoria's need to maintain the destabilization policy option. The willingness on the part of proponents of cooptive domination to accept the continued existence of Marxist neighbors and the need, at the same time, to keep them weak are likely to continually blur, at the policy level, the line between them and the proponents of regime reconstitution.

Strategic Importance
The existence of neighboring states that profess a commitment to Marxism-Leninism, and have close ties to the Soviet Union and other "Eastern Bloc" countries appears, on the surface, to pose a strategic threat to South Africa. Ironically, however, the actual situation may be just the opposite.

In policy circles in the United States much is made of U.S. dependency on access to South Africa's critical minerals and of the vulnerability of Western shipping to interdiction of the Cape Sea Route.[29] However unless mineral access and sea lanes are perceived as threatened, these are interests that have little salience for U.S. policymakers.[30] Marxist Angola and Mozambique, with their ties to the Soviet Union and reliance on Cuban military personnel, raise the perception of threat to these interests, and thus dramatically increase the salience of developments in Southern Africa for U.S. policymakers.

Since the end of World War II, the doctrine of containment has guided U.S. foreign policy. Top priority has been given to countering the expansion of Soviet influence. For a significant and influential political faction within the United States, the emergence of Marxist regimes in Mozambique and Angola, after the collapse of Portuguese colonialism, represented a trend toward such expansion in sub-Saharan Africa. Secretary of State Henry Kissinger told a Senate committee in 1976, for example: "Last year the situation in Africa took on a new and serious dimension.... The Soviets and Cubans had imposed their solution on Angola. Their forces were entrenched there, and fresh opportunities lay before them....We saw ahead a process of radicalization which would place severe strains on our allies in Europe and Japan."[31] Implicit in the secretary's comment is the notion that radical destabilization of the South African regime would involve a continuation of the trend toward increased Soviet influence, with dire consequences for Western access to minerals and sea lanes. In this manner, stability within South Africa, or at least the avoidance of radical change, comes to be seen by those concerned with stemming the flow of Soviet influence, as important for the United States.[32] The key point for our discussion is that it is the existence of *Marxist* Angola and Mozambique that stimulates and sustains this perception. Cooptive domination serves the strategic interests of South Africa because it permits the continued existence of these Marxist governments. It facilitates a tacit acceptance by Washington that Pretoria should control the pace and direction of change.

The main benefits of the cooptive domination approach, in comparison to regime reconstitution, lie in the area of Pretoria's international relations. The financial implications of the competing tactical approaches however, add to the attractiveness of the former. The financial risks attendant upon reconstituting the governments of Angola and Mozambique are severe. These go beyond the direct and indirect costs of supporting insurgencies in both countries. Should the insurgent movements be successful in overthrowing and replacing their Marxist opponents, Pretoria would find itself with a major interest in the new regimes' domestic political stability. That stability would significantly rest upon rebuilding the shattered Angolan and Mozambique economies. Pretoria, as patron of the new regimes, would thus find its interest in the political survival of its clients requiring the outlay of significant financial and other economic resources. For a South African government, struggling to stimulate its own economic recovery, and financially strapped by the requirements of its domestic reform program, this prospect serves to devalue the goal of reconstituting the regimes of neighboring states. At the same time too, it creates the context for a coalition in support of cooptive domination that is broader than just those with direct responsibility for Pretoria's international relations.

Cooptation versus Reconstitution: Which Approach Prevails?
In the foregoing, it has been argued that each of the tactics employed by Pretoria in order to establish a regime of regional hegemony has proponents that coalesce in a different segment of the government bureaucracy. The military, as a result of its decade-long association with the insurgencies in Mozambique and Angola, pushes for regime

reconstitution while the foreign affairs bureaucracy, because of its mission, is sensitive to the international advantages of pursing a tactic of cooptive domination. Each group of proponents, moreover, can call on a different type of "resource" to generate support for its position both in and outside of government. Ideology of long-standing within the Afrikaner community assists the proponents of regime reconstitution, while the fiscal exigencies in which South Africa finds itself assists the proponents of cooptive domination. In the final analysis, however, the extent of domestic political unrest in South Africa may create the decisive context for determining whether the concerns of the foreign affairs or military bureaucracies prevail in shaping regional policy.

As was pointed out earlier, South Africa's international relations are a hostage to its peculiar domestic political, economic, and social arrangements. When political confrontation and state repression render these arrangements visible and salient to the international community, the impact of Pretoria's foreign policy on its international and diplomatic position is marginalized. South Africa's internal situation becomes far more important in the decisions made by external actors than do Pretoria's actions abroad. Consequently, the potential benefits to Pretoria of the regional strategy of cooptive domination—the promise of gaining international acceptability—disappear when the South African domestic scene is characterized by large-scale and violent confrontations between the black opposition and the South African military and police.

Moreover, a rise in domestic violence, especially when it involves attacks on civilian targets by the ANC, creates internal political pressure for retaliation. Military assaults upon regional neighbors accused of harboring ANC cadres allow Pretoria to demonstrate to its white constituents that it is not impotent in the face of attacks on their security. When such a retaliatory impulse coincides with a situation in which Pretoria's regional actions cease to have a significant impact on the policies of foreign countries, the major factor inhibiting cross-border military attacks is eliminated.

During the period from mid-1977 through the first half of 1984, South Africa was characterized by a surface tranquility; the large-scale township unrest associated with the Soweto rebellion had seemingly run its course. These circumstances created a context in which Pretoria could, in 1984, dramatically improve its diplomatic posture vis-à-vis the West by shifting the tactical emphasis of its regional strategy from regime reconstitution to cooptive domination. The position of the ministry of foreign affairs was strengthened in the intrabureaucratic struggle by a situation in which the continuation of regime reconstitution contained very apparent international costs while its alternative, cooptation, had equally apparent benefits.

The ascendancy of the foreign affairs point of view and the shift to cooptive domination was manifest in the Nkomati and Lusaka agreements and in the reduction, by Pretoria, of military pressure on its neighbors. After almost six years of military occupation and intermittent invasions, Pretoria began to withdraw its military forces from Angolan territory, and announced that it would end its occupation of Angola's southernmost province of Cunene. As already noted, there were almost immediate diplomatic gains realized by this shift, and South African observers believed that a major breakthrough had been achieved in relations with the West.

The ascendancy of the Foreign Affairs perspective was short-lived. When large-scale urban unrest erupted once again in the latter part of 1984, the benefits of the cooptive domination approach were quickly eroded. The determining factor in the posture of Western governments toward Pretoria shifted rapidly to South Africa's domestic situation, rather than its regional policy. Reacting to escalating township unrest and police repression, the anti-apartheid movement in the United States was, by spring of 1985, successfully pressuring large institutional investors to reduce their holdings in companies with ties to South Africa. By summer, the Congress of the United States was poised to enact a law mandating a series of economic sanctions against Pretoria. In early August, international banks, following the lead of Chase Manhattan, called in their short-term loans to South Africa. On 9 September 1985, President Reagan announced limited economic sanctions; the European Economic Community followed suit one day later.

Throughout the remainder of 1985 and continuing through 1986, the actions of both private and governmental actors served to rachet up the economic pressure in both symbolic and real terms. Disinvestment, the selling off of South African assets by private business, which had been a phenomenon largely confined to smaller firms, became in 1986 an option exercised by some of the major multinational corporations—General Motors, IBM, Coca Cola, Eastman Kodak, Barclay's Bank, and Exxon. In fall 1986, the European Economic Community and the government of Japan adopted new economic sanctions. The U.S. Congress overrode President Reagan's veto of the Comprehensive Anti-Apartheid Act of 1986, the legislative package of new economic sanctions. This represented not just an intensification of U.S. economic pressures, but also served as an indication to Pretoria of the direction in which the dynamics of U.S. politics was pushing U.S. policy on South Africa.

Under these circumstances, the tactical preference of the foreign affairs bureaucracy lost much of what had made it an attractive option. The reality, as opposed to the threat, of economic sanctions significantly altered the calculus of policy for Pretoria. A commentary in *The Citizen*, an English-language newspaper with close ties to the government, offers an unambiguous statement of this change:

> Now that severe sanctions are our lot...there are some things we don't have to do any longer. We don't have to look over our shoulders to see whether what we do pleases or displeases the United States or other Western governments. Doves in the Government have cautioned, "Don't do this or that because the Americans will think we're cruel, nasty, oppressive, and will impose stiff sanctions against us." Sanctions...have freed us from the restraints imposed by those who wished to placate the United States, to placate the West, to buy more time, to avoid tough actions against us.[33]

As the concerns of the foreign affairs bureaucracy were rendered increasingly marginal by the combination of domestic and international circumstances, the proponents of the more aggressive regional policy associated with regime reconstitution found themselves in a strengthened position. Pretoria returned to the types of policies it had followed prior to Nkomati. In June of 1985, South African commandos raided the houses of ANC members in the Botswana capital of Gaborone, killing an estimated fourteen people. In mid-September, Pretoria's air and ground forces reentered Angola in a major action in support of UNITA. In December, South African commandos struck at Lesotho, killing nine ANC cadres in the capital city, Maseru. In January 1986, South African border guards blockaded landlocked Lesotho. After three weeks of economic squeeze, the Lesotho army staged a coup d'état. Five days later, after a meeting between Lesotho and South African officials in Cape Town, ninety ANC personnel were expelled from Lesotho, and the South African blockade of the Lesotho border was simultaneously lifted. Four months later, Pretoria's commandos struck at alleged ANC targets in Botswana, Zimbabwe, and Zambia, with the attack on the latter accompanied by air strikes.

As the momentum for increased economic sanctions intensified in fall 1986, Pretoria escalated its campaign of destabilization and economic pressure on Mozambique. Exactly one week after the U.S. Congress's override of President Reagan's sanctions veto, Pretoria announced that it was ending, immediately, further recruitment of Mozambican labor for South African mines, and that it would not permit those Mozambican workers already in South Africa to return once their permits had expired.[34] Given that worker remittances from South Africa are one of Mozambique's few sources of foreign exchange, and that new jobs for displaced workers are exceedingly scarce in an already depressed Mozambican economy, Pretoria's move must be seen as a calculated step to further undermine the Frelimo government both economically and politically. It represents a reversal of the cooptive domination strategy associated with Nkomati.

Along with the new economic measures, Pretoria stepped up the pressure militarily as well. The Renamo insurgency escalated its attacks in the fall of 1986. The environment of impending economic sanctions provides the important context for this as well. As the landlocked states of Southern Africa look to protect themselves from economic retaliation by Pretoria, the transport route from Zimbabwe to the Mozambican port of Beira looms as central to both the security of African states and the maintenance of Pretoria's regional hegemony. If, with international assistance, the Beira corridor can be rendered a viable transportation route for cargoes to and from Zimbabwe, Zambia, Zaire, Botswana, and Malawi, then Pretoria's means for dominating the South African region and making African states pay a heavy price for international sanctions will be dealt a severe blow. Conversely, one can expect Pretoria to adapt its regional strategy so as to prevent such a development. A renewed and expanded commitment to Renamo in order to reconstitute the Mozambican regime would be the obvious means to that end. Renamo officials make no secret about their role in Pretoria's Southern African strategy. Thus, Mr. Thomas Schaff, a spokesman for the Washington office of Renamo, discussing the increased fighting in Mozambique, stated:

> The fighting has intensified because Zimbabwe has said its survival depends on securing the Beira corridor. All the stops are pulled out.[35]

The policy shift of 1984-1985 offers a clear lesson in the dynamics of Pretoria's regional strategy. We can expect the tactical balance to shift, depending upon the condition of South Africa's domestic affairs as those relate to Pretoria's international situation. In periods of domestic tranquility, the foreign affairs establishment will probably have the upper hand. But, when domestic conflict and violence erode the significance of regional policy in determining the posture adopted by foreign governments toward Pretoria, the military's preference for regime reconstitution as a means to regional hegemony is likely to prevail.

All of this takes on special significance in the context of the imposition of economic sanctions against Pretoria. Pretoria's control of the Southern African transport network gives it significant assets in the fight against international economic pressure—providing the means for "sanction busting" via transshipments and relabeling. It also places South Africa in a position to impose such economic pain on her African neighbors that they may be induced to call on the international community to cease the sanctions effort. Thus, the Beira corridor initiative, whereby Southern African states, with foreign assistance, would establish a viable transportation route to the sea independent of South Africa's railroads and harbors looms as a matter of vital concern both for the African states and for Pretoria. Discussions of the international financial and technical effort needed to upgrade the Beira corridor ignore what is probably the greatest obstacle to the viability of such a project. It threatens to undermine South Africa's entire regional strategy, and thus it will most likely be the target of the South African military, both directly and indirectly.

The Angolan Exception

Angola represents a special case for Pretoria's tactical options. Certain features of the Angolan case increase the likelihood that regime reconstitution will be Pretoria's preferred approach in its relations with Luanda. Angola can be distinguished by its economic independence from South Africa. Unlike other Southern African countries, Angola is not dependent on Pretoria's transportation network or mining employment. Angola's petroleum reserves provide a source of considerable financial strength. Consequently, Pretoria is unable easily to squeeze Luanda economically to force it to expel the ANC, as it has done to Mozambique and Lesotho. Without significant economic leverage over Angola, it is unlikely that Pretoria can get the MPLA government to accept South Africa's hegemony. Neutralization of Angola thus requires a new government in Luanda that will accept Pretoria's hegemonic role.

The role of the UNITA leader Jonas Savimbi also strongly inclines Pretoria to maintain its regime reconstitution approach toward Angola. Savimbi combines three elements that give him special significance for Pretoria. First, he is an African leader with a genuine mass base. Unlike Renamo in Mozambique, which appears to have undermined the government by sowing chaos and terror in the rural areas, UNITA and Savimbi's successes have been built upon a popular following among the Ovimbundu-speaking people of Southern Angola. Second, also in contrast to Renamo, which has not put forward any recognizable leader, UNITA has a leader in Savimbi who has attained international prominence. More significantly, he has drawn attention and support to himself from powerful circles within Western countries, especially the United States. Third, Jonas Savimbi has been willing to lend himself to Pretoria's rituals of African legitimation. Thus, for example, he attended the inauguration of P. W. Botha as state president in 1984, an event that simultaneously celebrated the implementation of the reformed South African constitution.

When one recalls the importance of African acceptability in Pretoria's efforts to break out of its diplomatic isolation, the great attraction of

Savimbi to South Africa can be understood. He has the potential to play the legitimating role for Pretoria and its policies that the homeland leaders were intended to play domestically. With his ethnically based popular following, his powerful international supporters, and his willingness to participate in Pretoria's legitimation rituals, Savimbi appears, from Pretoria's vantage point, as a regional Buthelezi (the chief minister of the Kwa Zulu homeland and leader of the conservative Zulu-based Inkatha movement). The commitment of the South African military to Savimbi, then, should not be viewed as some quixotic quest, but rather as a reflection of real interests that are served by his success. Getting him into the Angolan government is something that is important to Pretoria; therefore, switching between the goals of regime reconstitution and cooptive domination is more difficult in Luanda than it is in Maputo.

Notes

1. A hegemonic system exists when one state is powerful enough to create and maintain the rules that govern interstate behavior. The dominant state, or hegemon, must be willing to expend resources in maintaining the system. Its dominant position allows it to "write" new rules, and prevent the adoption of new rules that it perceives as contrary to its interests. The set of essential rules governing interstate relations is what is referred to as a "regime." On the concepts of hegemony and regime in international relations, see Robert O. Keohane and Joseph S. Nye, *Power and Interdependence* (Boston: Little Brown, 1977), 42-46.

2. See Robert M. Price, "Pretoria's Southern African Strategy," *African Affairs* 83: 330 (January 1984):11-32.

3. See "South Africa and Mozambique Sign Nkomati Accord," *South African Digest*, 23 March 1984, 3-7; and "SA, Swaziland Sign Security Agreement," *South African Digest*, 6 April 1984, 3.

4. See "Full Text of SA, Mozambique Accord," *South African Digest*, 23 March 1984, 6-7.

5. See Article Nine of the Nkomati Accord, ibid., 7.

6. See *Sunday Times* (Johannesburg), 18 March 1984.

7. "Hurtful Ripple," *Sunday Times*, 18 March 1984.

8. In this respect, at least, the "benefits" of *de jure* hegemony have not materialized to the extent expected. After a brief period of apparent diplomatic "breakthrough," South Africa found itself more isolated and subject to greater international economic pressure than ever before in its history. The reasons for this rapid turnabout will be developed later.

9. Commenting on constitutional options under discussion by officialdom, *The Citizen*, a newspaper with close ties to the government declared: "All signs point to a confederation between South Africa and the TBCV countries [Transkei, Bophuthatswana, Ciskei, and Venda] and a federal system in a 'common' South Africa...," *The Citizen*, 2 December 1985.

10. See *Africa Confidential*,24, 15 (20 July 1983):6.

11. See "South Africa's Development Offensive," *African Business,* December 1982, 11.

12. See "Between SA and SADCC: Squaring the Circle," *African Business,* September 1984, 63.

13. *South African Digest,* 7 February 1986, 100. (Emphasis added.)

14. In addition, in Angola the insurgents have received direct combat support from South African air and ground forces.

15. See "Nkomati," *Frontline,* April 1984, 11.

16. According to *African Confidential,* "For two years all but a handful of verlighte senior officers have been profoundly sceptical of foreign minister Pik Botha's efforts to reach political accommodation with South Africa's neighbors...," 26,1,2 (January 1985):8.

17. See, ibid.

18. See *Africa News,* 66 (4 November 1985).

19. Ibid.

20. Ibid.

21. Ibid.

22. Magnus Malan, quoted in Deon Geldenhuys, "Some Foreign Policy Implications of South Africa's 'Total National Strategy'" (The South African Institute for International Affairs, March 1981), 3.

23. See, for example, Flora Lewis, "South African Watershed,: *New York Times,* 22 March 1984; see, also, Stephen S. Rosenfeld, "Clark Kent in Africa," *Washington Post,* 23 March 1984.

24. See, for example, Chester A. Crocker, testimony before the Subcommittee on African Affairs of the Senate Foreign Relations Committee, reprinted in *Current Policy,* 619 (27 September 1984), Department of State, Bureau of Public Affairs, 4.

25. See Michael Clough, "Beyond Constructive Engagement," *Foreign Policy,* no. 61, (Winter 1985-86):7-8.

26. Memorandum on meeting with South African Foreign Minister Botha, from Crocker to Haig, reprinted in *CounterSpy* (August-October 1981):55.

27. See Clough, "Beyond Constructive Engagement," 9.

28. *Sunday Times* (Johannesburg), 18 March 1984. (Emphasis added.)

29. See U. S. House of Representatives, Subcommittee on Africa, *U. S. Interests in Africa* (hearings, October-November 1979); see, also, Subcommittee on Africa, *Is There a Resources War in Southern Africa?* (hearings, July 1981); and U.S. Senate, Subcommittee on African Affairs, *Imports of Minerals from South Africa by the United States and the OECD Countries* (September 1980); and U.S. House of Representatives, Subcommittee on Mines and Mining, *Sub-Saharan Africa: Its Role in Critical Mineral Needs of the Western World* (July 1980).

30. For a discussion of the policy implications of U. S. interests in Southern Africa, see Robert M. Price, *U.S. Foreign Policy in Sub-Saharan Africa: National Interest and Global Strategy* (Berkeley:Institute of International Studies, 1978), 6-29.

31. U. S. Congress, Senate, Committee on Foreign Relations, Subcommittee on African Affairs, *U. S. Policy Toward Africa* (hearings, 5 March 1976), 193.

32. See, for example, Patrick Wall, ed., *The Southern Oceans and the Security of the Free World* (London, 1977), passim; see also, David Rees, "Soviet Penetration in Africa," *Conflict Studies* 77 (November 1976):1.

33. Reprinted in *South African Digest,* 10 October 1986, 937.

34. See *South African Digest,* 17 October 1986, 948.

35. Reported in James Morrison, "Mozambique Rebels Claim Government Offensive Foiled," *The Washington Times,* 3 September 1986, 1.

part four

Conclusion

Ideology and Policy in Afro-Marxist Regimes: The Effort to Cope with Domestic and International Constraints

Donald Rothchild
Michael Foley

Two questions perplex analysts of ideology in general and of ideology in Afro-Marxist regimes in particular, and they continue to preoccupy the authors of this book. The first is quite straightforward: Does ideology count? Or, to put the matter another way, what does ideology explain that cannot be better explained by the international environment, economic conditions, and political networking and constraints? The second is both more complex and more prone to be heavily weighted with normative considerations, but it is closely related to the first: What makes a regime "Afro-Marxist," and what justifies the designation?

In this concluding chapter, we draw together some of the threads of argument on both questions. We consider first what the term "Marxist-Leninist" entails in Africa. Second, we review more closely the policy choices of the Angolan, Mozambican, Ethiopian, and Zimbabwean regimes and the relations of these policy choices to domestic and international constraints and to ideological preferences. Third, we take up the question of policy choice and performance to uncover the extent to which Afro-Marxist regimes cope with constraints. Finally, given their limited ability to translate their policy preferences into actions, we ask: What are the implications of current policy adjustments for the future course of these regimes?

In doing so, we advance not so much an answer but an approach to our first question, "Does ideology count?" We argue that ideology, whether explicit or implicit, both identifies and legitimates the principles and purposes around which policies are determined. It also sets the parameters of choice in terms of which salient constraints are recognized and dealt with. The center of our inquiry, accordingly, is ideology, interpreted as the set of understandings that policy makers bring to their situation. After taking full account of ideology's role in setting out the parameters of choice, we consider the ways in which policy is intended to shape the environment and is itself reformulated as a political necessity in terms of that environment. Our view is essentially that of Crawford Young, who argues that

> the texture of the policy making of a Houphouet-Boigny is simply not the same as that of a Nyerere; nor [did] Samora Machel of Mozambique view the world through the same prism as Daniel arap Moi of Kenya. Overriding political or economic imperatives may force upon a regime choices that appear to be inconsistent with ideological preference. Such dissonance may be rationalized as either not truly inconsistent with ideology correctly understood or as a conscious and temporary departure from rectitude; it does not annul the world view with which it is in tension.[1]

But lest this suggest that we allow such "rationalizations" to obscure the question with which we started, we should be clear that analysis must deal constantly with the relation between rhetoric and reality, between "understanding,""prisms," "views of the world," and actual behavior. This chapter begins, then, with an examination of what "Afro-Marxism" entails, in an effort to set the stage for just such an investigation.

Ideology: What Makes a State Afro-Marxist?

Edmond Keller, in his introduction to this book, has described the shift, over the last two decades, to explicit avowal of "scientific socialism" and "Marxism-Leninism" on the part of some African leaders. These avowals were greeted at first with considerable (and occasionally justifiable) scepticism, but in the cases, especially, of Angola, Mozambique, and Ethiopia they have been taken increasingly seriously by Western observers.[2] David and Marina Ottaway's volume *Afrocommunism* set out a number of arguments for treating these regimes as genuinely different from the "Afro-socialist" experiments of the 1960s.[3] Keller argues that they represent relatively unique hybrids of Leninist and populist strains, and that Angola, Mozambique, and Ethiopia are qualitatively different from other African regimes that claim the Marxist-Leninist label in their ideological sophistication and the seriousness with which they have pursued ideologically determined policies. Following both Keller and the Ottaways, we can discern at least seven elements of an ideology that can properly be called "Marxist-Leninist" in the African setting:

1. *Profession of a unitary "scientific socialism," adapted to African circumstances, but true in its main outlines and institutional i mperatives to a supposedly orthodox Marxist-Leninist doctrine.* In the words of Soviet academician Anatoli Gromyko, such a

blueprint distinguishes between those countries with a socialist orientation that "adhere to revolutionary, but at the same time petty-bourgeois ideology" (Tanzania, Guinea, Algeria) and those countries that are "characterized by a wider and more profound range of revolutionary transformations embracing all or almost all spheres of social life" (Angola, Mozambique, Ethiopia).[4] For Gromyko, the emergence of the second subgroup of countries in Africa "shows a new qualitative leap in the development of national liberation struggles and the manifestation of a major law of socialist orientation at the current stage."[5]

2. *Analysis of the political, social, and economic situation facing the regime in class terms, in contrast to the populist regime's e emphasis on "the people" as an undifferentiated whole:* While the populist rhetoric of the "national democratic revolution" persists, and "revolutionary democrats" may include a diverse range of allies, there is a persistent effort to cast policy choices in terms of the class struggle.[6] Such a view has an international dimension as well, since "scientific socialism" involves a recognition of the principle of proletarian internationalism.[7]

3. *A determination that society and the state be led by a vanguard party representing (but not necessarily consisting of) the " working class":* Along with this determination comes the necessity of democratic centralism, implying both mass mobilization and party (and state) control of mass organizations.

4. *A commitment to strengthening the state and state institutions:* From the Soviet point of view, according to Seth Singleton, "the major and primary task of the African vanguard on which later success depends is strengthening the state."[8] But this has economic as well as political implications. Thus Karen Brutents comments on the "progressive role" played by the state in socialist-oriented countries "as an active factor in national consolidation and moulding national consciousness, as an effective lever for promoting public education and educating the people in an anti-imperialist spirit...."[9]

5. *An open acceptance of revolutionary transformation, involving, if necessary, the use of coercion to establish a new social order:* Not only will the state nationalize the commanding heights of the former colonial economy, but it will take steps, wherever possible, to reduce the penetration of foreign-based capitalism. In the words of an official government pamphlet, "the oppressed masses of Ethiopia have been conducting a revolutionary struggle for the last three years, in order to wipe out the system of oppression and exploitation and to build a new social order."[10]

6. *A commitment to create the "social and economic conditions" for the redistribution of wealth and the triumph of socialism:* The latter implies the creation of class structures and economic institutions appropriate to a genuine "proletarian" democracy. As Barry Munslow put it, "The aim of the vanguard party, by controlling the state, is to create not only the conditions for the development of class consciousness, but also to create the classes necessary for effective socialist development. A working class must be built up as a conscious strategy to provide an essential material foundation for the transition to socialism."[11] The ideology, as Keller observes, recognizes clearly the complex and amorphous character of African social and economic structures; but Afro-Marxist theoreticians insist that the economic transformation underway throughout the Third World will be accompanied, in regimes with a "socialist orientation," by a social transformation that secures a steady accretion of power in the hands of emerging working and peasant classes.

7. *The conviction that "socialist orientation" entails finding "natural allies" in the Socialist Bloc is the basis for foreign policy decisions among these regimes:* The Soviet Communist party, for its part, in its 1985 Program, devoted a whole section to the strengthening of its relations with the newly free countries and emphasizing its solidarity with the socialist-oriented countries.[12]

There are those, of course, who would dispute this characterization on ideological grounds. In this volume, for instance, Dessalegn Rahmato suggests that the statist position outlined above (the fourth element) is a betrayal of the genuine Marxian heritage, interpreted as the participatory politics and vehement antistatism of Marx's own *Civil War in France.* John Saul, similarly, has found reason to be concerned with certain interpretations of democratic centralism and certain uses of coercion in Mozambique today. (He stresses, however, that the tensions between "leadership and mass actions" "have at least been kept alive and that there is some ongoing effort to resolve them, rather than merely to suppress them.")[13] These are differences, widely recognized even in Soviet theory, between what we might call the overt institutional and operational ideology and the ideals or putative goals that that ideology is supposed to serve. Among those goals are: popular sovereignty over the market and, more broadly, over the economic conditions of life; meaningful popular participation, therefore, in decisions that affect people's lives; rapid economic growth to enhance the quality of life; and relatively egalitarian distribution of the fruits of production.[14]

Judged in these terms, the gap between ideology and performance widens considerably, and it is this gap that some critics have in mind when they question the seriousness of the Afro-Marxist leaders. But, while such criticisms direct our attention to important questions and are often justified, they can be answered with the response that these states, like a great many others, are still attempting, under very difficult circumstances, to achieve their goals. Our examination of the relation of ideology and policy must start with a look at the sorts of policies which the Leninist operational ideology outlined above might be expected to generate. Only then can we go on to consider policy performance, longer-term goals (the ideal), and the possibility that those goals may stand in contradiction to the organizing principles of the regime.

Before we do so, however, it is important to note that a great deal of debate about the possibility of genuinely socialist regimes in Africa hinges on misunderstandings about what a "scientific socialist orientation" might entail. There are those who argue, for instance, that there is simply no social or economic basis for a socialist society in Africa, and particularly in Angola and Mozambique. African leaders, however, are aware of this. So, too, are Soviet theorists.[15] In their eyes the task, as we have seen, is to transform both economy and society, to create the working class basis for a socialist state. So far from suggesting a paradox, this view of socialist development (or the development of socialism) represents the norm: no socialist transformation in the past has been able to depend upon a fully developed working class. In fact, a review of Soviet experience only confirms what has been the rule throughout the socialist world: "state-building," Singleton shows, "preceded the push toward a fully modern society."[16] This explains why Marxism-Leninism in Ethiopia can be seen by Marina Ottaway "primarily as a blueprint for state power organization and consolidation"[17] and by Dessalegn Rahmato as nothing more than "a formula for capital accumulation and rapid growth."[18] It is both, of course, because the two are distinctively intertwined in Marxist-Leninist ideology. But this also explains the relative indifference on the part of Soviet and Afro-Marxist thinkers toward the origins of the state apparatus they are strengthening. Indeed, in the African situation, where class stratification is still more rudimentary and amorphous than it was in Czarist Russia, any regime might provide the basis for socialist transformation, whatever the social origins of its leaders, so long as they commit themselves to the ideology and the operating rules of Marxism-Leninism.[19]

Finally, this helps us to understand, without clearing up completely, the paradox of a growing dependence of Afro-Marxist states upon the West coupled with their continued ideological, diplomatic, and military alliance with the Soviet Bloc. How do we explain such a situation? There are obvious pragmatic considerations: the Soviet Bloc does not have the economic resources to support rapid development in these states; the West provides markets for their products and financial and other resources for expanding production or meeting economic difficulties; meanwhile, the Soviets provide some protection against outside interference in the pursuit of socialist construction. Yet it would be a misunderstanding to see the policy choices manifest here as wholly externally determined. Angola, Mozambique, and Ethiopia courted and won Soviet protection, such that it is, precisely *because* their ideological preferences put them in jeopardy from their neighbors and/or the West. Soviet support was also indispensable to Joshua Nkomo's Zimbabwe African People's Union (ZAPU). By the same token, although economic dependence on the West is a paradoxical outcome of the option for rapid development, it is a choice founded on the dominant ideology and taken within the terms of an assurance, to quote Singleton once more, "that if political consolidation is assured, socialism has nothing to fear from expanded or continued economic contacts with the West."[20] This may or may not be true, but it represents, as David and Marina Ottaway put it, a pragmatism "more akin to that of the Soviet New Economic Policy (NEP) of the early 1920s than to the American meaning of the term."[21] It is a pragmatism, in other words, within the terms of the goals and parameters prescribed by ideology.

Ideology, and in particular the operational ideology outlined here, provides important parameters of choice within which regimes assess constraints, formulate policy choices, and pursue certain outcomes over others. Choices are rarely unconstrained, but ideology delineates the goals and many of the means that take shape in policy. We turn next, then, to a more detailed examination of the policy choices, pragmatic and not so pragmatic, dictated by this operational ideology.

Ideology, Policy, and International Linkage

As is the case with virtually all African regimes, the Afro-Marxist regimes in Angola, Mozambique, and Ethiopia must cope with a number of inherited constraints that greatly limit their political choices. Largely poor, malintegrated, dependent, and militarily exposed, these states are gravely hampered in their ability to transform their societies along socialist lines. Ethiopia's imperial government and Angola's and Mozambique's colonial administrations failed badly in educating their local populations, in providing the necessary industrial and agricultural base for self-sustaining growth and development, and in giving an experience in the practices of political governance. These previous administrations (and here one can include the one in "self-governing" Rhodesia) also left behind societies deeply divided and stratified in terms of race, ethnicity, region, and socioeconomic class. As a consequence of this inheritance, these regimes are like their capitalist and populist socialist counterparts in being "soft": that is, they are limited in their capacity to implement their policy preferences throughout the domains nominally under their control. To their dismay, pockets of power remain substantially outside of their authority, representing a kind of *de facto* autonomy that mocks their claims to full "sovereignty" and ability to regulate their societies. Moreover, the export-oriented nature of their commodity- and minerals- producing economies perpetuates their dependence, much as in the rest of Africa, upon the powerful industrial economies of Western Europe and North America. Despite a dramatic change of regime goals and values, the newly emergent Afro-Marxist regimes find themselves no more capable of breaking out of a structure of dependency and unequal exchange than other regimes the continent over.

The Afro-Marxist regimes also face a number of constraints special to their revolutionary experiences. The devastation, which can be likened in the cases of Mozambique and Angola to a scorched earth policy on the part of the retreating Portuguese settlers, has been compounded by the broad-scale destruction wrought by opposition guerrilla units, backed by the South Africans, who are intent upon a continued destabilization of the region. The result is to thwart reconstruction along socialist lines and, as John Marcum shows in the case of Angola, to create heavy military costs in purchasing equipment and paying for a foreign military presence. Moreover, as Forrest Colburn puts it when discussing Third World revolutionary regimes: "As laudable as the intentions of post-revolutionary regimes may be, their policies tend to produce severe economic problems that undermine the welfare of their citizens."[22] Thus the Afro-Marxist regime finds itself caught in a vise partly of its own making. To gain support for its claim to power and its vision of the future, it necessarily heightened expectations among the citizenry about the good life that would follow after colonialism.[23] However, with foreign exchange sources drying up, spare parts unavailable, skilled personnel emigrating, and transportation in short supply, the Afro-Marxist leadership inevitably found it most difficult to deliver on its promises of redistribution and a general upgrading in the quality of life. Programs of nationalization, collectivization, and self-reliance quickly gave way to pragmatic policies, made in the spirit of tactical adjustment, which allowed greater opportunity in certain sectors for foreign initiative, private business and commercial activities, and an opening to Western private voluntary organizations and lending agencies. As James Mittelman concludes, "The transition to socialism is traumatic under any circumstances."[24] In poor states, struggling under past neglect and exploitation, Western opposition, the devastation of the current insurgencies, and ideological commitments frustrated by a lack of capacity, the cumulative consequence is likely to be public disappointment and cynicism, a headlong retreat from the state and its formal economy, and forced policy adjustments on the part of state administrators.

To some extent, on the other hand, Marxist ideology and practice has appeal precisely because it is perceived as strengthening the new regimes in their effort to overcome these heavy domestic and international constraints. Marxism-Leninism, declared Frelimo's Third Congress, "is a powerful beacon which lights the way that the laboring classes must follow in the process of constructing the new society."[25] Not only does Marxism have appeal to the downtrodden because of its rejection of past domination and inequality of opportunities, but also because it is perceived as a means of reorganizing the society "scientifically" to achieve the economic and social objectives of socialism. Marxist theory and practice gain legitimacy in the Afro-Marxist countries, then, because they hold out a promise of salvation in contemporary times.

At another level, Marxism also has appeal to ruling elites in these "soft" Afro-Marxist states because it sanctions the consolidation of party and state power at the political center to achieve its self-proclaimed ends. The Marxist-Leninist emphasis upon vanguard parties, democratic centralism, nationalization and collectivization, planned economies, and popular mobilization follows logically from its certainty of truth regarding the objective laws of history. It is but a short leap from a certainty of historical laws to the suppression of organized dissent, an opposition that would distract and possibly undermine popular support for the regime and its program. As Marcum shows in his chapter in this book, Angola's MPLA did in fact reject political pluralism as "reactionary," and thereupon set about crushing any autonomous groups viewed as challenging the supremacy of its authority: labor unions, peasant and women's associations, religious organizations, the mass media, and so forth. Power consolidation became the means to achieve ends which the dominant political elites of these countries could regard as historical necessities.

Party and State

Given this general ideological predilection for centralized decision making, it becomes important for us to examine the way this preference has been put into effect by Afro-Marxist regimes. It seems appropriate in this regard to start with regime determination to establish a vanguard party, one of the distinguishing characteristics of a genuine Marxist regime. Marxist-Leninist theory itself is quite explicit as to the primacy of party over state. Following conventional practice, Angola's MPLA leadership committed itself to creating a vanguard party prior to assuming political power, and at its First Party Congress in 1977 delivered on this promise by reconstituting itself formally as a vanguard party of the working class.[26] Similarly in Mozambique, Frelimo made the party's leading role explicit, a fact that accounts in no small part, according to Herbert Howe and Marina Ottaway in their chapter, for the capacity of the regime to survive the unanticipated succession problems that followed President Samora Machel's untimely death in October 1986. Ethiopia is clearly the exception among the Afro-Marxist states in this regard. In this case, the normal roles were reversed, because in Ethiopia it was the state that created the party. Even so, the Ethiopian experience has, in time, largely conformed to Marxist-Leninist tenets on the principle of party primacy over all other institutions in the society, for after its formation, the vanguard party is in the process of reconstituting the state machinery and firmly establishing its supremacy over the state.

By Soviet standards, the Afro-Marxist parties were "not yet fully formed proletarian parties—in their composition, structure, experience, political consciousness." Soviet analysts nonetheless described these ruling parties in the socialist-oriented states as "parties completing the transition from revolutionary-democratic to Marxist-Leninist."[27] What constitutes a vanguard party in the African context? Clearly, the vanguard party idea, which grew out of the need for a decisive expression of the leaderships' doctrinal preferences and strategies in the period after the assumption of political power, embodies Marxist-Leninist preferences for central leadership, high selectivity of membership, and discipline, combined with popular mobilization. The historical process is not to be left to chance, to spontaneous action; instead, the most committed members of the working class and other progressive groups must seize the initiative and offer leadership to the society as a whole. "The party's historic mission," declared Frelimo's *Central Committee Report to the Third Congress*, "is to lead, organize, orientate and educate the masses, thus transforming the popular mass movement into a powerful instrument for the destruction of capitalism and the construction of socialism."[28] In practice, this disciplined leadership was secured by creating a hierarchical system of control and participation, running from the party cells at its base to the ruling Politburo or Central Executive Committee at its apex. In principle,"democratic centralism" ensures a flow of messages from the bottom to the top and an authoritative statement of preferences, to be implemented at the middle and lower levels by those in leading positions in the party.

However, the relationship among different party strata has not always worked smoothly. In Angola, just before the MPLA became a vanguard party, internal party differences and the breakdown of discipline and message flow came publicly into view when, in May 1977, Nito

Alves and Jose van Dunem, allegedly with radical and pro-Soviet support within the ranks of the MPLA, launched an abortive coup.[29] Subsequently, the MPLA has been described as the least effective of our three core cases in meeting the expected requirements of a vanguard party. Certainly, discipline in the vanguard parties in the revolutionary African countries is remarkable by African standards and certainly lends a very considerable coherence and stability to these regimes, but it is by no means comparable with that prevailing in the well-entrenched communist countries.

The achievements and problems involved in instituting vanguard parties points to another challenge confronting Afro-Marxist regimes as they go about the task of consolidation their power: that is, preserving the distinction between party and state. If the party is in theory supreme and responsible for formulating policy guidelines, in practice overlaps occur and the distinction between the two is not nearly so self-evident. Given the historical context, such overlaps are not surprising. Bureaucratic institutions—both civil and military—were operating on the scene before party control was firmly established over these societies. With bureaucracies in place at the time of the changeover, the parties faced something of a dilemma between their desire for a full reorganization and reconstitution of the administrative apparatus and a need to "facilitate" the expansion of these administrative activities to cope with new functions.[30] For the most part, the Afro-Marxist parties have found satisfactory formulas, insisting upon their own supremacy and the need for a revamping of the administrative structure while accepting, for the time being, the reality of continuity in state norms and values.

The extent of this accommodation with earlier administrative imperatives has varied from regime to regime. It has entailed the least conflict for those in authority in Mozambique, for as Howe and Ottaway show, a relatively strong and legitimate regime has encountered minimal difficulties in its relations with weak, resource-poor state institutions. Even here, there are conflicts of orientation and of what Saul refers to as "possible class interest[s];" in this instance, a bureaucratic arm "overvalu[es] the merits of the top-down, big-project, heavy investment line of thinking."[31] But these differences are less intense than in Angola, where the continuance of a somewhat more entrenched colonial state administrative structure has frustrated the organization of a "revolutionary state apparatus" as desired by the MPLA officials.[32] In the case of Ethiopia, the vanguard party was a long time in coming, giving the postimperial military and state bureaucracy an opportunity to play a significant role in shaping the lines of socialism in that country. By the early 1980s, what Dessalegn Rahmato describes as a political anomaly had emerged, for Ethiopia espoused Marxism-Leninism but lacked a vanguard party. Without a party, it was difficult to inspire the public and to exercise legitimate control over the society at large. Hence, the vanguard party was "formed because of need," as Marina Ottaway argues—need perceived through Marxist-Leninist lenses.[33] Established by the provisional military administrative council in 1984, the Workers' party of Ethiopia became a new, strong center of regime power consolidation in its own right. Yet it still seems too early to determine with any precision the extent of its control over other facets of life in the society; consequently, doubts remain as to the party's capacity to dominate the state and its military arm in such a way as to bring state officials fully in line with party preferences.[34] Finally, in Zimbabwe, the continuity between colonial and postcolonial public service norms and values has placed strict limits on the capacity of President Mugabe's ZANU to consolidate political power in its own hand. In part, this was intended by the Lancaster House Conference agreement that restrained, at least for temporarily, ZANU's ability to restructure its society and state institutions along socialist lines. It is also a reflection of the more complex character of Zimbabwean society and of the administrative apparatus developed to serve it.

The result is four very different experiences in regime power consolidation, ranging across a continuum from Mozambique, with its relatively successful effort to bring Marxist ideology on party supremacy in line with practice, to that of Zimbabwe where, in accordance with the negotiated formula at Lancaster House, the divergence of party and state remains most pronounced. Clearly, the nature and extent of this cleavage is of enormous practical significance as the various one-party regimes go about the task of implementing a Marxist-Leninist program.

Economic Transformation

The complex relationship between ideological imperatives and environmental constraints is particularly clear when we turn to the efforts these regimes have made to transform their economies along socialist lines. Again, a desire to strengthen the regime converged with state-centric objectives on central planning, collectivization, industrialization and self-reliance. The Afro-Marxist regimes, initially at least, regarded socialism as an effective means of coping with their hostile environments, not, as Westerners would have it, as a blind attack on the mechanisms of economic growth in favor of pure equity and social welfare objectives.[35]

Although the policy preferences of the Afro-Marxist regimes seem largely similar, the extent and timing of their programs differed, in part at least reflecting variations in environmental contexts. Mozambique's Frelimo, seizing the initiative after its bitter war of independence and the precipitous flight of the Portuguese, moved swiftly to begin the restructuring of the country's economy along socialist lines. Starting with the abolition of private schools, legal assistance, and medical services, Frelimo went on to take over unused housing and abandoned estates, and subsequently to nationalize the commanding heights of the economy (i.e., the main industrial, financial, and agribusiness enterprises), as well as land. Despite a heavy emphasis on state farms and communal villages, actual progress toward transforming the rural economy proved slow. The Isaacmans report, for example, that despite a substantial investment in state farms and the establishment of 1,352 communal villages with a population of 1,806,447 persons by 1982, peasant smallholders still farmed 94 percent of cultivated land and produced 80 percent of total agricultural output.[36] As we shall note later, central planners, faced with drought, international recession, Renamo banditry, and a lack of capital, inevitably became cautious about their ambitious rural program, as well as their commitment to the development of heavy industry and the proposed involvement of the state in retail trading, particularly the "people's stores." This caution represented an adjustment born partly of political and economic necessity; clearly, Frelimo's long-term policy preferences remained firmly oriented toward a restructuring of the economy along Marxist-Leninist lines.

In Angola, the emphasis on the objectives of nationalization, centralization, and state planning was equally strong from the outset. In part, this emphasis on state action reflected the harsh realities facing the country's new rulers at independence, in particular, the difficulties caused by the massive exodus of skilled Portuguese in a brief period of time. As Crawford Young observes, the flight of some 440,000 Portuguese "left no other possible manager than the state."[37] These difficulties also followed from the strong preferences of many MPLA leaders for a state-centric policy orientation. Guided generally by Marxist-Leninist theory and practice, these new rulers quickly moved to transform their economy along socialist lines. The Angolan state nationalized heavy industries, established publicly run agencies to purchase locally grown commodities, and organized thousands of state farms, partly as an emergency program for keeping in operation the private estates left behind by the Portuguese. Even so, MPLA practices evidenced a pragmatic side from the very outset. For example, certain long-standing linkages with Western capitalism (most prominently, the tie with Gulf—now Chevron—Oil Company) were allowed to remain in place. Such tactical adjustments were not discouraged by the Soviets, and represented an obvious effort on the part of the new state to deal with the constraints of the Portuguese exodus, an insurgency, and external destabilization.[38] But they also represented an ideologically sanctioned commitment to economic growth. Nevertheless, adjustments of this sort are not likely to prove cost-free, for Marxism-Leninism might lose some of its credibility as an explanatory force, once the black-and-white opposition of capitalism and socialism familiar in Marxist-Leninist rhetoric is abandoned for a more pragmatic practice. Such accommodation might lead, over time, to a questioning of faith in the regime's vision of the future.

In the case of Ethiopia, Marxist-Leninist economic programs were implemented more slowly. Following the assumption of political power in February 1974, the Derg was under strong pressure from the intelligentsia and the articulate public to transform the old order of Emperor Haile Selassie. At the outset, however, the new ruling elite lacked a clear sense of direction. The Derg was an institution of the state, the top army officials, and not a political party—much less a vanguard party with a clear program of action to put into effect. In John Harbeson's words, "The demise of the structures of the old imperial order has meant . . . both that the Derg has been faced with the creation of a new political order . . . and that the Derg has not been able to depart completely from the political style of the old order being replaced."[39] New structures were formed and a new ideology was introduced, but the bureaucratic institutions remained much as before. The consequence of this party vacuum and lack of ideological commitment was evident in the Derg's initial caution in developing and implementing a program of economic transformation. At first, the Derg's statements called in general terms for an end to feudalism and discrimination and for the implementation of a socialist program. Then, in early 1975, the state moved decisively to define its socialist economic program. It nationalized the "commanding heights" of the Ethiopian economy (the banks, insurance companies, and some seventy manufacturing and commercial firms); placed all land under state control; terminated tenancy and allowed peasants usufructary rights to a maximum of ten hectares of land; and created peasant associations throughout the rural areas.

In July 1975, these reforms were followed up by a sweeping decree that nationalized urban land and rental properties and established urban associations *(kebeles)* with extensive authority over local affairs in the urban areas. Such reforms had at least two main purposes: to consolidate the power of the new Ethiopian rulers and to achieve regime goals on creating a socialist society, thereby easing pressure on them from an articulate body of urban supporters intent upon extensive change. "The hope of the new authorities," writes Dessalegn Rahmato, "was that these far-reaching reforms would not only meet what was believed to be the general expectations of the majority of the people, but also usher in a period of stability and growth."[40] But the public's expectations were not to be met so easily. Central control over the new economic organizations proved difficult to maintain, and new conflicts and disappointments, in particular over the extent and pace of collectivization, emerged. Soviet advisers, seeking to enhance the stability of agricultural operations, counseled against overburdening the state and called for giving commercial farms, as well as producers' cooperatives and state farms, a significant role in the development of new lands and crops.[41] Thus the Marxist-Leninist approach to economic transformation, as interpreted by the Mengistu regime, no doubt contributed to regime legitimacy and sense of purpose; however, it became the source of new constraints while enabling the regime to deal with others.

Zimbabwe's leadership has been the most cautious of all the Afro-Marxist cases dealt with here in designing and implementing its socialist program. Such caution is less a commentary on Mugabe's preferences than on the country's historical experiences and institutional continuities. The process of negotiating an independence agreement created ongoing bargaining obligations and institutional continuities in the period after independence.[42] Dependence on external skills and capital, as well as access to indispensable transportation routes through white-dominated South Africa, also predisposed the new regime toward a market economy and the maintenance of links with Western capitalism. The imperative of maintaining such links in Zimbabwe was apparently evident to Mozambique's Machel, who reportedly advised his Zimbabwean counterpart, Robert Mugabe, at the time of independence, to learn from Mozambique's current difficulties and to go slowly in implementing a socialist program; an overly hasty socialist transformation, he contended, might endanger Zimbabwe's more developed and sophisticated economy.[43] Whether accurate or not, it seems doubtful that Mugabe, despite his clearly articulated Marxist-Leninist preferences, ever seriously considered unsettling his smoothly operating market economy in the short term for a radical transformation along Marxist-Leninist lines. Soon after independence, the ZANU regime set forth its values very explicitly in its Transitional National Development Plan. Declaring its long-term commitment to the goal of "building a national economy founded on socialist and egalitarian principles," it also stressed making each move prudently and pragmatically, taking "the requirements of time, circumstances, and actual conditions obtaining in Zimbabwe" into account. In stating the case for reconciling change with continuity, the plan read as follows:

> While the inherited economy, with its institutions and infrastructure, has in the past served a minority, it would be simplistic and, indeed, naive to suggest that it should,therefore, be destroyed in order to make a fresh start. The challenge lies in building upon and developing on what

was inherited, modifying, expanding and, where necessary, radically changing structures and institutions in order to maximize benefits from economic growth and development to Zimbabweans as a whole.[44]

In light of such prudence, what role does a Marxist-Leninist commitment play? It seems obvious that even here ideology can set parameters of choice, helping to guide decisions about the country's future along certain predetermined paths. Moreover, coming out of a long and bitter war of independence, a commitment to Marxism-Leninism may act to legitimate the regime at a time of public frustration and continuing high expectations. Paradoxically, ideology may both raise expectations and satisfy the doubts of the frustrated when these expectations are not fulfilled, for it can explain accommodations while promising fulfillment in the long run. Ideology, then, represents an important political resource which, when used carefully, acts to strengthen a regime committed to a Marxist-Leninist transformation at a difficult time of transition. In the Zimbabwean case, Mugabe's apparent sincerity on the issues of equality and socialism underscores the impact of his basic ideological message, giving the regime a much needed breathing space to achieve, in Mugabe's words, "the delicate balance that exists in the process" of changing the old social order.[45]

If the Afro-Marxist regimes are able to mobilize the domestic political and economic resources at their disposal to promote their objectives under conditions of scarcity and military harassment, they are not without external support as well. The intersection between domestic and international capabilities in contemporary Africa is critical to an understanding of the survival abilities of these soft and vulnerable states. From the standpoint of the leaders in Angola, Mozambique, and Ethiopia, the Soviet Union and its allies represent a reserve asset, a "firm rearguard" as one Mozambican publication put it, for coping with the constraints of the environment.[46] For the Afro-Marxist states, as for the Soviet Union, notes L. Adele Jinadu, their special relations "were a structural and historical necessity, reflecting the dialectics of the global conflict between the forces of imperialism, and anti-imperialism. Angola and Mozambique, for example, characterized the incipient relations as a natural alliance, arising out of and consolidating relations already established during the wars of national liberation in both countries."[47] The Soviets had gained trust in Afro-Marxist circles through their military support of the struggle against the old social order. Now, with the signing of treaties of friendship and cooperation, and their provision of indispensable military arms and advisers for use against insurgencies and external attacks, they again were viewed as a reliable ally in times of need. Thus, "proletarian internationalism," characterized by Singleton as "meaning the duty of all socialists everywhere to cooperate toward defending the gains of socialism," created links among socialist countries.[48] The result was to strengthen the Afro-Marxist regimes, enabling them to cope with perceived threats at home and abroad.

Certainly, the main evidence of Soviet backing for their Afro-Marxist allies has been in the military area. Such assistance has taken a variety of forms: the provision of military advisers, active military engagements by Soviet bloc forces, the extension of materiel and equipment, and the training of local personnel in the use of this equipment. In their dealings with Ethiopia and Angola, the Soviet Bloc countries (the Soviet Union, Eastern Europe, and Cuba) have gained considerable credibility in African eyes for their speedy actions in dispatching combat troops, advisers, and some $2 billion to $4 billion in military equipment to meet the initial crises encountered by these regimes. Commenting on the extent of the Soviet assistance for Ethiopia, David A. Korn, the former American chargé d'affaires in Ethiopia, notes as follows:

> Even the figure of $4b. probably does not cover everything supplied by the Soviet Union, for it appears that substantial amounts have been delivered gratis. One has only to look at the size of the Ethiopian military establishment to realize what an enormous amount of weaponry and other equipment the Soviets must have had to supply. Ethiopia's armed forces stood at 45,000 in 1974 at the time Haile Selassie was deposed. Ten years later, reliable Western estimates put the army at 306,000 with another 5,000 for the airforce and navy, and para-military forces of 169,000....[49]

The massive arms buildup in Ethiopia, combined with the dispatch in 1977 of Cuban combat troops and of Soviet and Eastern European advisers, turned the tide at the critical moment in the Somali invasion, enabling the Ethiopian-backed force to gain the initiative and, by the following year, the victory. In the case of Angola, the outcome was not nearly so decisive. To be sure, the Soviets gave the MPLA generous support, estimated, by one observer, at some $500 million in military supplies, training, and the transportation of Cuban combat forces to the area.[50] Although this backing did enable the MPLA to gain a firm hold over the administrative capital of Luanda and its environs, it did not prove sufficient to end the internal fighting permanently. This can be explained in part by the survival powers of Jonas Savimbi's UNITA and in part by the intervention of external adversaries, South Africa and, to a lesser extent, the United States.

In the years following this initial arms buildup and military support in Ethiopia and Angola, the Soviets have not wavered in their commitments to these fraternal allies. Available data indicate that $500 million of Angola's $890 million in arms purchases from 1975 to 1979 came from the Soviet Union, and $1.5 billion of Ethiopia's $1.8 billion came from this source.[51] This heavy dependence on Soviet military supplies and, in the case of Angola, on Cuban combat troops has continued into the 1980s. This is not to say that either the Ethiopians or the Angolans are entirely pleased with the relationship. They express misgivings over the low levels of Soviet economic assistance and the insistence of Soviet bureaucrats on the repair of aircraft and tank engines back in the Soviet Union. Nevertheless, their options remain limited, and "proletarian internationalism" still seems more of a benefit than a cost and clearly in line with their ideological commitments.

In the case of Mozambique, the Soviets can still be viewed as a rearguard, but with less of a sense of commitment than was true for Ethiopia and Angola. Between 1975 and 1979, $170 million of Mozambique's $240 million in arms purchases came from the Soviet Union.[52] Throughout this period and afterwards, as Frelimo appealed to the Soviet Union for arms and advisers to help prevent the incursions of Rhodesian forces and then Renamo, the Soviets responded quickly and generously. In the 1980s, in the face of an intense Renamo challenge, the Soviets not only supplied sophisticated (but soon outdated) weaponry such as MiG-21s, Mi-24 helicopter gunships, tanks, armored vehicles, and surface-to-air missiles (SAM-7s), but their pilots reportedly were actively engaged in the defense of the port of Beira.[53] However, for a variety of reason—donor fatigue, the desire to avoid a direct confrontation with South African forces, the independence shown by Mozambican leaders regarding military basing rights, and a wider opening to Western economic trade and assistance—some observers detect a slight shift in Soviet policy toward Mozambique in the 1980s.[54] What is true for Mozambique is even more the case for Zimbabwe, where Mugabe seemed to distance himself from the Soviet Union after independence and where no formal friendship treaty has been signed. While Mugabe's reasons may also be important, it appears that the Soviets have stepped back of their own accord. Moscow seems to have little propensity for further risking confrontation with South Africa at this time. As Winrich Kuhne observes:

> Quite a number of Soviet experts are rather worried about the problems such an escalation of violence might create. One prominent official, when asked why Moscow is so hesitant about responding to Zimbabwe's quest for closer and substantial military cooperation, put it bluntly: "We have enough problems!"
> ....In the mid-eighties Soviet awareness about the differences between short-term opportunities and stable long-term gains in Africa is much

greater than it was a decade ago. The catastrophic developments—above all in Mozambique, but also Angola and Ethiopia—have had their effect. Moscow now takes a hard and critical look at the costs and risks of a substantial involvement in the further escalation of violence in South Africa.[55]

In brief, the Afro-Marxists of Mozambique continue to count on the Soviets to recognize their fraternal obligations toward them, but with a somewhat greater ambivalence in the years after the signing of the Nkomati Accord. In the case of Mozambique, the Soviets showed ambivalence about being drawn too closely into the center of violence. Perhaps Moscow is in the process of redefining the Brezhnev doctrine, which holds that once included in the Soviet orbit, always included. Now the emphasis would appear to be on the polycentric aspects of the communist world. As Mikhail Gorbachev, the secretary general of the CPSU Central Committee, asserted: "The communist movement's immense diversity and the tasks that it encounters are . . . a reality. In some cases this leads to disagreements and divergencies. The CPSU is not dramatizing the fact that complete unanimity among communist parties exists not always and not in everything."[56] In this view, a new ambiguity appears in Soviet-Mozambican relations, for the Soviet Union remains a rearguard while watching from the sidelines as the weaker partner experiments with new relations with the capitalist powers. In any event, this contraction of Soviet commitment, if that is what it proves to be, further undermines the ability of Afro-Marxist regimes, especially in Southern Africa, to cope with a threatening external environment. We turn next, then, to persisting constraints on the Afro-Marxist states and to their effects on the leaders' abilities to implement their policies.

Persisting Constraints on State Capacity

Even though Afro-Marxist regimes make relentless efforts to consolidate their power—through ideological exhortation, institution building, and alliances with fraternal socialist parties—their efforts in strengthening their state institutions so as to cope more effectively with their domestic and international environment are only partially successful. To utilize the thesis so effectively argued by Howe and Ottaway in this book, they build firmly entrenched regimes without establishing equally strong states. Thus the succession from Machel to Chissano in Mozambique could take place, outwardly at least, in a relatively smooth manner, but the state could neither rebuild its war-devastated economy nor protect its citizens from Renamo's guerrilla activities. Persisting state softness tends to undercut the strength of the ideological vision and its promises of a good life, forcing responsible leaders, albeit most reluctantly, to improvise and adjust the tenets of Marxism-Leninism to local circumstances. Such an adjustment process no doubt goes further than what Gorbachev had in mind in his reference to polycentrism noted above, but it is necessitated by the perilous conditions in which the Afro-Marxist regime finds itself.

Given the state-centric orientation of a Marxist-Leninist worldview, the reality of the "soft" state, with its inability to regulate and to implement public policy, comes as a continuing reminder of grave disappointment. For all their remarkable cohesion and sense of purpose, these regimes are limited in an organizational sense, unable fully to translate their strongly held socialist preferences into public policies. In appearance, these regimes seem centralized and unitary; in practice, however, they lack the capacity to penetrate the rural areas and to exercise the kind of leadership normally associated with a socialist transformation. In Ethiopia, the administrative structures have been expanded greatly under the Mengistu regime, but they are not always effective in the provinces because of peasant unrest and national rebellions. Similarly, in Angola and Mozambique the continuing ravages of insurgency and South Africa's regional destabilization makes a mockery of the principle of regime control over its sovereign territory, not to mention the regimes' efforts to effect a fundamental change in their modes of production. In the three countries under consideration here, the weakening of regime control is most apparent for all to see in Mozambique, where Gillian Gunn writes in another context of the possibility of an "approaching collapse." "It is an objective fact," she continues, "that Mozambique is approaching mass starvation and financial bankruptcy; that the country's military...is in danger of losing control of several central provinces and vital regional transport routes to antigovernment guerrillas of the Resistencia Nacional Mocambicana, known as Renamo or MNR; and that rhetorical, economic, and military pressures by its powerful neighbor, South Africa, are increasing."[57] Although Mozambique represents the extreme case, it is nevertheless clear that, for the time being at least, the picture for all three Afro-Marxist regimes is indeed one of very considerable frustration.

But why these particular regimes? Like many African regimes with different ideological perspectives, these Afro-Marxist regimes have inherited weak economies and infrastructures, their state institutions are fragile, and they have suffered from drought and international dependency. Yet these factors do not represent the complete explanation for their difficulties. Hence we must go further and distinguish between problems intrinsic to these particular regimes and other constraints of an extrinsic nature. Only when we have this full range of constraints in mind will we be able to appreciate the reasons for the policy shifts that have marked the Afro-Marxist experience in contemporary Africa.

In poor, neglected, predominantly peasant-based societies such as Ethiopia, Mozambique, and Angola, it is not surprising that Afro-Marxism, with its state-centric orientation, creates state-building difficulties of its own despite its ability to resolve other problems related to regime building. As already noted, the onset of an Afro-Marxist regime heightens public demands and expectations beyond the new regime's powers to deliver. To be sure, the new regime may reorganize its political and economic structures, exert control over the mass media, bring civil court proceedings closer to the people, and initiate successful literacy campaigns; but its commitments to economic centralization, agricultural collectivization, economic planning, and party discipline tend to lead to a sharp dichotomy between the formal state sector and the ineffectively regimented informal sector. As the Afro-Marxist state superstructure reaches out to redefine its relations with rural society, it crosses the boundary between the preferences it holds and a pragmatism founded on mere survival needs. This creates conflicts that expose the state's limited capabilities and that further undermine its ability to promote economic growth and development.

Such contradictions differ in degree and kind from regime to regime, but it is important to examine a few of these regime-generated constraints to understand the impact on performance. First, in the political area, Marxism-Leninism has appeal to some leaders because it legitimates the concentration of state power in the hands of the revolutionary leadership. This can lead to the abuse of political power where the state elite becomes insulated from the articulate public and where there is little scope for public participation in the decision-making process. Among the states under review here, the problem of power has so far been limited to the case of Ethiopia, where the leader, Mengistu Haile Mariam, exerts a dominating presence and appears to brook no opposition. In his handling of groups such as MEISON and student factions that have voiced criticism of his regime, Mengistu has shown cunning and a capacity for survival.[58] Commenting that "A Marxist-Leninist system [or more accurately, a perverted one] can give him power to do whatever he likes," Dawit Wolde Georgis, the former commissioner of relief and rehabilitation in Ethiopia, describes in another context what this means in practice:[59]

> The 10th anniversary celebration, which took four days, was a most disgusting, unforgiveable and irresponsible act. At the time the ceremonies were being conducted thousands were dying every day, and thousands had abandoned their homes, trekking across the desert and

mountain tops in search of food and shelter. Thousands of people had walked all the way from the northern part of Ethiopia and were at the gates of Addis Ababa. The police were sent to form [a] human fence around the capital to make sure none of these people would enter the city and spoil the show.[60]

By the way that it channels and organizes power, then, a Marxist-Leninist system can lead either to collective leadership that abides by the system's organizing principles regarding effective public participation or, in a most devastating way, as under Mengistu, it can build up "callous" authority figures who accept no limits on their exercise of power. Where the latter occurs, it inevitably leads to alienation and intense political opposition to the regime. Second, in the social arena, the Afro-Marxist regime tends needlessly to antagonize society by its evident disdain for religious and ethnic identity groupings. Dismissing such identities as evidence of a so-called "false consciousness," these regimes often exacerbate conflict with a peasantry they do not control. In this, Frelimo is somewhat of an exception, as it has displayed considerable tolerance toward religion, albeit somewhat less so toward the "institutional role of the Catholic Church," a role that Saul depicts as having been "so important within the armory of colonial domination."[61] More aggressively, the MPLA has conducted "strident campaigns against religion" (even attempting to exclude Christians from the formal political process); and the Workers' party of Ethiopia has attempted to discourage the activities of missionaries, especially the Lutherans and members of the Pentacostal churches, fearing that they will have a conservative impact on society. In addition, party regulations forbid members to attend church functions or be buried on church-affiliated lands.[62] Such anti-religious initiatives apparently have had little overall success, indicating the limited capacity of the state, even an Afro-Marxist one, to impose cultural values on a resistant society.

A distaste for the politicization of ethnicity, even a tendency at times to deny its "objective reality," leads to an insensitive and somewhat heavy-handed relationship with the representatives for these interests. In some respects, the Ethiopian leadership has gone the furthest in formulating a policy for dealing with nationality groups. At the end of 1982, the Ethiopian regime sanctioned the formation of an Institute of Nationalities, both to conduct scholarly research on the composition of nationalities in the country and to incorporate these groups as the basis for a new state structure. The first project has shown some progress, but the second remains stillborn, as the new constitution was not based upon the ethnic group but rather on the administrative unit. In practice, the Mengistu regime has shown itself to have little tolerance for ethnic

302   Donald Rothchild & Michael Foley

autonomy. It has ruled out any political accommodation with the Eritreans and Tigreans, waging bitter military campaigns against these and any other ethnic challengers making political demands for what these movements describe as national liberation. In Angola, the MPLA regime has been quite open about its rejection of ethnicity as a legitimate basis for political action. Significantly, however, the MPLA has gone beyond voicing its disapproval to actions, most specifically underrepresenting the Ovimbundu in high political and party offices. This has the effect of fueling ethnoregional grievances and contributing to UNITA's capacity to survive over the years as an effective guerrilla movement.

Ethnicity has not been as significant a concern for the Mozambican leaders, in part because of the relatively greater heterogeneity of their society; yet, even here, ethnicity is not a factor to be discounted, for Renamo reportedly directs its appeal primarily to the Shona-speaking peoples and plays on resentment toward mestiço influence in the decision-making process at the political center (a resentment that has also manifested itself within the MPLA in Angola).[63] To the extent, then, that a Marxist-Leninist ideology causes the African leadership to refuse to develop effective relations with ethnic intermediaries and their supporters, these regimes, with their state-centric orientations, will be ineffective in negotiating the kinds of political solutions essential to their society's stability and development. The fact that each of them lacks the capacity for effective control over their domains leads to the emergence of powerful separatist movements that have managed to secure a kind of *de facto* autonomy for themselves. Paradoxically, regime insistence on centralization has helped to promote its antithesis in the form of determined separatist movements. Ideological inflexibility has acted to weaken the already soft state.

Third, Afro-Marxism, with its emphasis on central planning and regulation, collectivization, industrialization, and large projects, has an economic vision that surpasses regime capabilities. "Centralization and rigidity became the hallmark of the economy," Howe and Ottaway write about Mozambique, "because of a fatal flaw that appears to afflict socialist economies in all Third World countries: a desire for control, coupled with scarcity of personnel leading to the formation of giant farms nobody can manage."[64] The three core Afro-Marxist states, like many of those across the continent, are scarcity-prone, neglected, dependent peasant-based societies. Their state institutions lack the skilled cadres and administrative infrastructure so necessary for effective planning and management; they are superstructures isolated from the many rural producers upon whom they rely for resource extractions and compliance. But, beyond the normal constraints of poverty and external dependence, are the added complications of their ideology. On assuming power, these regimes hold out a promise of equality and abundance, raising public expectations to unsustainable heights. Disappointment and frustration soon spread among the public as the impact of emigration, loss of capital, and the misallocation of scarce public resources takes it toll. Rahmato shows, for example, that in Ethiopia some 60 percent of total budgetary allocations for agriculture was spent on the state farms in the late 1970s and early 1980s, a practice he describes as "a costly experiment."[65] Total agricultural production declined, partly because of the difficulty of managing the state farms efficiently and partly because collectivization of agriculture, although very limited, antagonized the peasants who felt that they had lost control over the land. Nationalization of industry also occurred rapidly after the new Afro-Marxist regime took power, but again the results were disappointing, partly because of ineffective management, overstaffing, poor recruitment, price controls, and the difficulty of securing foreign exchange and spare parts.

Afro-Marxist regimes, determined to transform their economies as swiftly as feasible, invoked policies on nationalization, collectivization, and redistribution; these policies had the effect of heightening expectations while reducing the incentives of managers, professionals, farmers, and skilled workers. Forrest Colburn notes that the resulting economic "crisis" is predictable: regimes institute price controls in order to protect the purchasing power of the less advantaged classes, especially those in the urban areas, causing declines in production and the misallocation of scarce resources.[66] The gap that emerges between regime goals and performance becomes plain for all to see, leading to frustration and opposition at the very time when the regime is most fragile and exposed.

Two main consequences seem to follow from efforts to press radical transformation in Africa under perilously soft state conditions. First, such policies place new and unanticipated constraints on state power consolidation. The Afro-Marxist regime may be reasonably strong, allowing for party discipline and centralized organization of affairs. Its reach into the hinterland is limited, but this is the case in much of Africa. Yet its rigid insistence on ideological commitment creates a sharp distinction between friends and foes, both internal and external. Internally, those excluded may find fulfillment in the unofficial economy, but others drift into insurgent ranks. Not surprisingly, then, all of the countries in our core sample are currently encountering internal guerrilla oppositions that are sufficiently strong to maintain a kind of *de facto* autonomy within the confines of the state. And to make matters worse, these movements are sustained and supported by external backers—various Middle Eastern supporters in the case of the Eritrean liberation movements, and South Africa in the cases of Angola, Mozambique and, reportedly, Zimbabwe.[67] To aggravate matters even further, South Africa complicates the process of state power consolidation by sending its own forces into Mozambique and Angola from time to time. The upshot is to weaken the political center gravely at its most urgent time of need.

Second, Afro-Marxist programs heightened expectations of redistributed wealth and new opportunity, often at a cost in terms of total productiveness. In Saul's terms, inherited backwardness and weaknesses in Frelimo's own projects were two of the major factors "in producing the present grim denouement to the Mozambican revolution."[68] Certainly each of the Afro-Marxist regimes discussed in this book has encountered unanticipated difficulties in production, Zimbabwe less than the others. Yet even here, with its relatively developed market-based economy, its food surpluses, and positive balance of payments, an overextended state has had to cut back on 1987 allocations to the industrial and commercial sectors. But Zimbabwe's problems pale by comparison with those of the more "command" type of economies of Ethiopia, Angola, and Mozambique. Nationalization of industry in Ethiopia is described by Rahmato as contributing to the country's economic malaise: in the rural areas, collectivization, combined with drought, low commodity prices, and the increasing role of state purchasing agents, led to a worsening food situation in the mid-1980s. Angola, for all its abundance of resources, has seen agricultural production decline, with only 20 or 30 percent of arable land currently under cultivation. It remains dependent for 90 percent of its foreign exchange earnings on the sale of petroleum products.[69] Coffee output declined precipitously, from 5.2 million sacks in 1974 to 283,000 sacks in 1983.[70] Mozambique, battered by South African-inspired destabilization and reprisals (for example, the South African announcement in 1986 that many Mozambican mineworkers would not have their contracts renewed), finds itself mired in $2.6 billion in foreign debts at a time when its 1986 exports fell to $83 million. Its main export earner, cashew nuts, has fared badly in recent years, declining in output from 90,000 tons in 1981 to 30,000 tons in 1986.[71]

As applied in African circumstances, then, the implementation of Afro-Marxist policies has resulted in new difficulties in the areas of state power consolidation and economic performance. Inevitably such difficulties have a feedback effect over time. We have to ask how policymakers in the regimes under review have responded, fine-tuning or altering their initial policies to cope with the increasing challenges of a hostile environment. In our next section, we examine the various reluctant adjustments made by the Afro-Marxist regimes to reduce the domestic and international constraints under which they operate.

The Reluctant Pragmatism of the Afro-Marxist Regimes

Given the magnitude of the internal and external constraints encountered by these regimes, a very hesitant shift in some policy areas from rigid orthodoxy to pragmatism has taken place. In this regard, the response of our sample of Afro-Marxist regimes has differed considerably. Whereas the current Ethiopian regime tends to make the fewest concessions to domestic or international capitalism, the regimes in Angola and Mozambique have shifted positions reluctantly on certain issues to allow for greater flexibility. No move to pragmatism was necessary after independence in Zimbabwe, since it had already decided in the preindependence period to retain its market economy. At another level, even within the regimes themselves, there are elements which favor new adjustments to reality. In Mengistu's Ethiopia, with its headlong rush to collectivization and military solutions to the nationalities question, elements in the cabinet, the diplomatic corps, and the military are known to seek a softening of the current militant line.

To examine the extent of Afro-Marxist pragmatism, it will be useful to look at regime policies in three major issue areas: the preparedness of the regime to enter into political negotiations with domestic insurgency movements to achieve the objective of state consolidation; the acceptance by the regime of a need to negotiate with hostile neighboring governments to reduce external pressures; and a willingness to step back, temporarily at least, from policy commitments on nationalization, socialism, and collectivization. If the Afro-Marxist regimes differ little regarding the first issue, they diverge in interesting ways on the latter two, especially with respect to economic transformation and the opening to the West.

Nowhere is the Afro-Marxist ideological inflexibility more apparent than on the issue of political negotiations with nationalist or ethnic separatist movements. These Afro-Marxist regimes, with their state-centric perspective, have all encountered domestic insurgencies. Although none of these regimes has achieved a total victory over these insurgencies, it does not follow that weariness with the continuing struggles will lead them to the bargaining table. Their inflexibility on the reconciliation of ethnic-based secessions through the negotiating process grows out of a long tradition of theoretical analyses that draw extensively on the writings of Lenin and Stalin. In a statement written on the national question in 1976, for example, Ethiopian intellectuals described proletarian internationalism and bourgeois nationalism as adopting fundamentally opposed positions on this question. Where the bourgeois nationalist was depicted as relying upon the ruling class to pursue a reformist path, the Marxist-Leninist, adopting a class perspective, would see the national question as rooted in class oppression and would conclude that "the national question can never be solved apart from revolution and class struggle." [72] Social forces are in direct contention; in the zero-sum struggle that ensues, one or the other must emerge a victor. From this, it is but a short leap to the Ethiopian regime's denial of the legitimacy of the insurgency movement and to its assertion of a determination to "smash" the counterrevolutionary opposition. Moreover, calling for proletarian solidarity on the issue of Eritrean "liberation" or "secession" (depending on one's perspective), the Addis Ababa regime dismisses any concession outside the framework of the state:

> The deepening of the revolution especially as regards organizing, politicising and arming of the masses will eventually decide the Eritrean issue and all other problems the revolution faces from imperialist-reactionary Arab alliance. In the final analysis, the forces that will have to confront each other will be all progressives and the Ethiopian masses on one side, and the die-hard lackeys of imperialism and reactionary Arab ruling classes on the other. Since the Ethiopian revolution has now broken the fetters of isolation imposed on it by imperialists and won the firm support and solidarity of the international socialist forces, the revolution can certainly count on the socialist camp in its struggle to crush counter-revolutionaries and all those lurking to dismember the Ethiopian state. [73]

For Mengistu, there will be no compromise with secessionist claims, a position questioned by other Ethiopians who fear being bogged down in an unwinnable war.

The regimes of Angola, Mozambique, and Zimbabwe also view political negotiations with present-day insurgent leaders as unacceptable, and they have waged costly wars against opposition elements in all three countries. Despite UNITA's continuing support from the relatively numerous Ovimbundu peoples in the central highlands of Angola, the MPLA regime has ruled out negotiations on the formation of a coalition government at the political center. The Luanda regime has declared Savimbi to be a "traitor," partly because of his very extensive reliance upon the South Africans for arms and critically important military backing in the field. Similarly, Frelimo dismisses the notion of political negotiations with Renamo, which, as noted above, makes ethnic (among other kinds) of appeals. This reflects a desire to avoid giving the movement any kind of legitimacy, as well as resentment over Renamo's identification with earlier Rhodesian purposes and, more currently, with South Africa's destabilization goals, even in the period after the signing of the Nkomati Accord. Finally, in Zimbabwe, the Mugabe-led ZANU regime rejects any appeals for autonomy or separatist goals on the part of the Ndebele-based guerrilla movement in Matabeleland, acting forcefully by sending the North Korean-trained Fifth Brigade to that province in 1983-84.[74]

In all cases, the Afro-Marxist regimes moved as decisively as they could to consolidate their political power at the center and to rule out any political accommodations with insurgent elements within their domains. It was only the ineffectiveness of state institutions that prevented them from eliminating these opposition movements, leading to varying degrees of stalemate and *de facto* autonomy. Clearly, ideology played an important role in the decision of each regime to soldier on against heavy odds, refusing any compromises on this issue out of a concern for such political necessities as order and economic development.

Second, if the Afro-Marxist regimes acted rather similarly in the way that they ruled out political negotiations with *domestic*-based insurgent movements, those in Angola and Mozambique, which have suffered the worst effects of South Africa's destabilization program, have shown themselves to be prepared, most reluctantly, to take a realistic posture on *international* negotiations with the powerful white-dominated state to their south. Such pragmatism comes despite their affinity with fraternal South African political movements and their general abhorrence of apartheid and white dominance. Nevertheless, at roughly the same time that the South African onslaught had forced a reluctant pragmatism upon Afro-Marxist leaders, the South Africans themselves were in the process of shifting from what Robert Price describes in this book as a tactic of "regime reconstitution" (i.e., the use of destabilization to destroy or dislodge the Frelimo and MPLA regimes) to the tactic of "cooptive domination" (the use of destabilization to force these Afro-Marxist regimes formally to accept South Africa's subregional hegemony, as well as its goals on the neutralization of the ANC and noninterference in South Africa's domestic politics).

What has this reluctant pragmatism regarding negotiations with South Africa meant in practice? For Mozambique's rulers, the difficulties of reconstruction in the face of a searing drought, declining production, and military instability meant that they had little choice but to search for some kind of a peace accord with South Africa, the main source of its difficulties. Contacts between the two sides started as early as 1982, but it was not until 16 March 1984 that the Nkomati Accord, brokered by the United States, was signed by President Samora Machel and Prime Minister P. W. Botha. To the dismay of the Soviet Bloc and much of

Africa, a proud Afro-Marxist regime was compelled, because of circumstances largely beyond its control, to accept a nonaggression pact with the South Africans. Botswana's President Quett Masire spoke for many across the continent when he described Mozambique as "bullied" into signing the agreement. Masire added: "This is not something freely entered into but more out of fear." [75]

In the Nkomati Accord, the two parties solemnly agreed to refrain from interfering in each other's internal affairs; to desist from the threat or use of force against the other's sovereignty or territorial integrity; to refuse to use their territory as a base for violence, terrorism, or aggression by other states, military forces, or organizations; to eliminate other irregular forces or armed bands and their training centers, depots, command posts, communication facilities, radio stations, and so forth from their territories; and to maintain periodic contacts to ensure the agreement was applied in an effective manner.[76] Machel made far-reaching concessions, particularly regarding the role of the ANC; yet it soon became apparent that elements high in the South African military had no intention of abiding by the promises that their prime minister had made at Nkomati.[77] As shown by the documents captured by Zimbabwean and Mozambican troops at Gorongosa in August 1985, Renamo continued to receive extensive amounts of military supplies from the South Africans after the signing at Nkomati, in full violation of the terms of the accord.[78] Realizing the gravity of the situation, Great Britain and the United States put pressure on the Botha regime to prevent the unraveling of the accord. Moreover, after warnings from the Mozambicans that a continuation of the current situation could seriously endanger the nonaggression pact, South African leaders took steps to salvage the deteriorating agreement and publicly conceded their responsibility for Renamo guerrilla activities and their role in the violation of Nkomati.[79] Despite these admissions, the Renamo insurgency continues as strong as ever, raising grave doubts as to the value of pragmatism, at least when it involves dealings with the Botha regime.

Afro-Marxist Angola's negotiations with its archenemy South Africa over a troop withdrawal agreement arose from a similar desire to reduce the effects of destabilization in its territory. Mediated by high U.S. officials as in the case of Nkomati, the Lusaka Agreement of 16 February 1984 provided for a ceasefire along the Angolan-Namibian border, the staged withdrawal of South African troops from Angolan territory, and a commitment by the Angolan government to prevent SWAPO (the Southwest Africa People's Organization) forces from infiltrating into Namibia. The Angolans also agreed, according to the South African foreign minister, Pik Botha, to reassert their authority as South African forces were withdrawn from their territory, and not to allow SWAPO or Cuban military elements into the vacated area.[80] In addition, the conferees agreed to set up a joint Angolan-South African commission, which allowed for the inclusion of U.S. officers, "to monitor the disengagement process in southern Angola and to detect, investigate and report any alleged violations of the commitments of the parties."[81] Although the Soviets implicitly accepted the agreement worked out at Lusaka, they expressed themselves as highly critical of the U.S. role in bypassing the procedure on Namibian independence as set out in the resolutions of the UN Security Council.[82]

At the time the Lusaka Agreement was signed, hopes were high that it would be the beginning of a wider settlement of outstanding issues in the subregion. In Luanda, Lieutenant Colonel Alexandre Rodrigues Kito, the minister of the interior, told a press conference that South Africa had begun the withdrawal of some of its troops, and the process leading to a rapid and peaceful settlement of the conflict in southern Angola and Namibia was under way.[83] Moreover, as provided in the agreement, the South African-Angolan Joint Military Commission was established to monitor the disengagement, and the United States, which participated in the activities of the commission, set up a temporary liaison office in Windhoek. Although the South Africans did pull a sizable contingent of their forces out of Angola around the time of the agreement, their disengagement was less than total, and it was followed, on subsequent occasions, by further deep probes by South African units into southeastern Angola. The pragmatism shown by Angola's leaders in signing the agreement proved a disappointment. Significantly for the future, it raised grave doubts in the minds of many Africans about the South Africans as reliable bargaining partners.

Third, as regards domestic economic policies and openings to the West, the Afro-Marxist regimes dealt with in this book diverged in important ways. Despite a decline in aggregate production and difficulties in restructuring the economy along socialist lines, the Ethiopians have shown the least inclination to modify Marxism-Leninism in terms of their circumstances. Their leaders are moving ahead with the collectivization of agriculture and gradually ending the role of the private sector in the grain trade. Ethiopians do trade extensively with Western countries, although here, as Rahmato shows, there has been a modest shift in the direction of the Soviet Bloc countries in the early 1980s. Ethiopia also relies heavily upon Western sources for economic aid and food assistance. Some administrative autonomy is accepted for such parastatals as Ethiopian Airways and for certain agencies involved in relief and rehabilitation, but, by and large, the regime's policy is to adhere strictly to Marxist-Leninist guidelines on nationalization, centralized administration and planning, and collectivization. If anything, the regime seems to be moving toward greater ideological inflexibility, tightening its control over all agencies and administrative bodies that retain any element of autonomy.

This trend contrasts markedly with the remaining countries in our sample. Zimbabwe has preserved intact many of the features of the colonial economy, maintaining a market system that allows a relatively free play to domestic capitalist interests and a relatively free access to foreign multinational firms. Certainly, one hears rousing appeals from the Zimbabwean left calling for a change toward a more egalitarian and socialist orientation, but so long as the benefits of the current tilt appear to outweigh the costs of altering the system, some form of compromise and adjustment with the Western-led capitalistic order seems likely to persist.

Nevertheless, for the moment as least, it is in Angola and Mozambique where cautious experiments with mixed economic systems are currently gaining the widest attention. Despite their continuing commitment to a Marxist-Leninist world view and their firm strategic and military assistance links with the Soviet Union, these regimes are exhibiting a new pragmatic interest in nonsocialist economic practices. On the domestic scene, these countries have responded to a falling output of goods and services with measures intended to overcome bureaucratic rigidity and stimulate greater productivity. In Angola, the MPLA's Second Congress held in December 1985 expressed dissatisfaction with the country's low production of such export crops as coffee and urged greater accommodations with "all types of enterprise in rural areas, notably family types of enterprise and private initiatives in farming and livestock."[84] The party congress, as Gillian Gunn notes in her chapter, also deemphasized the role of the state farms; while not abandoning these relatively costly enterprises, it sought to give a higher priority to smallholder production and the cooperatives. Excessive bureaucratic centralization was described as stifling initiative, leading to decisions to give the managers of the various enterprises greater autonomy. In subsequent moves, the regime has taken actions to raise producer prices and allow a greater scope for private trading. As Marcum notes:

> The small private enterprise that is "beginning to appear in agriculture," the MPLA now asserts, may be "to the country's advantage" and may even "develop in other sectors of low technology where the lack of initiative from the state as well as the private sector has often led [Angolans to resort] to foreign companies." It is hoped that regulated competition between private traders...and state outlets charging official prices will bring a fall in real prices. Such thinking contrasts sharply with the MPLA's earlier commitment to rigid state centralism.[85]

Similarly in Mozambique, internal and external constraints led to a new spirit of pragmatism. The 1980 decision to allow private traders to play an increased role in the commercial life of the country was an early sign of the regime's willingness to rethink previous beliefs. President Machel was quite clear that there were limits to the state's capacity to engage effectively in retail trading. "Marxism," he declared, "has nothing to do with selling eggs or tomatoes. The state cannot set up to sell cigarettes or run garages. It must simply supervise the economy's primary sectors."[86] In 1983, Frelimo's Fourth Congress gave a more systematic boost to the party's program of economic liberalization. It emphasized the need to make greater use of the market mechanism to revive the rural economy. In particular, it urged that producer prices be raised and that a broader array of goods be made available to the peasants, all with an eye to encouraging greater smallholder productivity. Recent visitors to Mozambique indicate that these reforms have had generally positive effects. A former research associate at Mozambique's National Institute of Physical Planning concludes that a freeing of the prices on many agricultural products and the turning over of some state farm lands to peasants and capitalist farmers has led to increased supplies of farm goods in the lower Limpopo Valley.[87] Faced with an overriding need to increase food production, the regime altered its position on the proper role of the market in the economic life of the society, but it was a shift of emphasis intended to strengthen the country to deal with a hostile environment, not a substantial retreat from basic Marxist-Leninist principles.

With respect to international economic openings to the West, a trend toward pragmatism in Angola and Mozambique has also been apparent. Frelimo's decisions on domestic economic liberalization discussed above were followed by moves to join the International Monetary Fund and the World Bank in 1984 and the Lomé Convention in 1985. Such a shift in ties brought a series of credit and aid agreements from these multilateral organizations, as well as an increasing flow of bilateral aid from Western donor agencies. Frelimo's more liberal investment code, with its guarantees on the transfer of profits and capital and on compensation in the event of nationalization, led to a renewed interest in Mozambique on the part of multinational companies. The British firm Lonrho invested $40 million in the revival of three agricultural plantations, and General Motors reportedly signed an agreement with the government to supply trucks and training to carry coal from Tete Province in the north to the port of Beira. Rebuffed in its appeals for full membership in the Soviet-led Council for Mutual Economic Assistance, a desperate Frelimo looked to the West. The new source of support was not to be cost-free, however. IMF backing in 1987 involved the usual accompanying package of devaluation, new taxes, increases in the cost of certain consumer goods, and a loosening of price controls.[88] But great need, combined with limited options, made this alternative seem indispensable.

Likewise, Angola's reluctant dealings with international capitalism and Western donor agencies largely reflects its lack of meaningful alternatives. The combined effect of a costly exodus of skilled Portuguese workers and a highly destructive insurgency and South African intervention has been the undermining of a number of promising economic sectors, such as the coffee, timber, diamond, and iron ore industries. As a consequence, the Luanda regime has become heavily dependent upon petroleum exports, from which it currently receives some 90 percent of its foreign exchange earnings. The upshot is a pragmatism that links an Afro-Marxist regime to international capitalism in a mutually beneficial arrangement. Although fully committed to Marxist-Leninist ideology, the regime nonetheless has excellent business relations with a wide array of prominent multinational firms. Angola's state oil corporation, Sonangol, in partnership with Chevron, Texaco, Elf Aquitaine, Conoco, and others, is actively exploring the country's rich offshore deposits, and prominent Western banks such as Chase Manhattan play an important role in financing the country's development. As a petroleum company executive told one of the authors in 1985: Angola is, in his experience, the easiest country in Africa in which to conduct the oil business; the people are efficient, supportive, punctual, and careful to live up to their contractual obligations. Not surprisingly, therefore, foreign firms have flocked to Angola, and this occurs despite the lack of formal political ties between Washington and Luanda. Petroleum production is rising rapidly, from 130,000 barrels per day in the late 1970s to an estimated 300,000 barrels per day in 1986.[89] Inevitably, however, politics has intruded into this business relationship between ideologically opposed partners. Private pressure groups in the United States have denounced business dealings with a "Marxist" regime at war with an ally, Savimbi's UNITA, and government officials have raised questions about the propriety of these burgeoning business links and about the prudence of U.S. Export-Import Bank credits under present circumstances. Ironically, U.S. policymakers appear increasingly inflexible at a time when Afro-Marxist Angola is committed to a course of pragmatism.[90]

Conclusion: Ideology, Policy, and the Afro-Marxist State

Ideology, we have seen, has played an important role in the consolidation of Afro-Marxist regimes in contemporary Africa and in the patterns of policymaking evident in Ethiopia, Angola, and Mozambique. On the one hand, the outlines of a fairly coherent Marxist-Leninist vision of economic, social, and political transformation can be discerned in the concrete programs undertaken by these three states: consolidation of a vanguard party with extensive control over the state apparatus, collectivization, nationalization, centralized planning, and close links with the Soviet Union, Cuba, and Eastern Europe. On the other hand, these same policy choices have created difficulties and constraints peculiar to Third World Marxist-Leninist regimes: possibilities for the abuse of authority under the cloak of "democratic centralism"; the exacerbation of ethnic conflict through principled refusal to acknowledge the legitimacy of ethic demands; economic dislocation as a result of attempts to restructure agriculture, commerce, and industry radically and rapidly; and rising discontent based both on ethnic, regional, and religious differences and on the disappointment of expectations raised by the rhetoric of the regimes themselves.

In these terms, it is proper to speak of Ethiopia, Angola, and Mozambique as Afro-Marxist regimes—regimes that despite their inherently "soft states," have consolidated regime power through their adoption of Marxist-Leninist organizational principles and ideology. In the case of Zimbabwe, on the other hand, a party that claims Marxist-Leninist inspiration has accepted the constraints imposed both by the Lancaster House agreements and by the more complex character of the country's bureaucratic apparatus and economy. Although maintaining the distant goals of socialist transformation, Mugabe has adapted both means and goals to accommodate the established parameters of a relatively "open," market-based economic system, whose state institutions are administered in the efficiency-oriented tradition of the professional civil service. Politically, despite lip service to Marxist-Leninist prescriptions, ZANU seems committed more to "Africanization" and the creation of a mass-based single-party system than to one based on the guiding role of a proletarian vanguard party. How do we explain such pragmatism?

"Pragmatism," however, often masks but another ideological position, in this case, an apparent accession to gradualism and to the relative "efficiency" of the market and of a professionalized state apparatus. Wedded to the goals of redistribution and democratization, such pragmatism, as Bratton and Burgess remark, "bears some resemblance to the Marxism that guided European social democratic parties at the turn of the century."[91] Nevertheless, it is important to press the question of why Mugabe and ZANU have taken this course rather than another.

Several historically related answers emerge. Most fundamentally, the conditions under which ZANU came to power differ markedly from those prevailing in Ethiopia, Mozambique, and Angola. As Bratton and Burgess argue, "The fact that the independence war was curtailed by the Lancaster House negotiations, before the guerrillas were able to consummate a military victory, prevented the revolutionary process from playing itself out to the full."[92] The political settlement, dominated not by the radicals of the military wing of ZANU, but by the politicians and technocrats of the insurgent coalition, set the parameters for subsequent events. In particular, this meant that both the military and bureaucratic arms of the settler state apparatus would become the core of the new state. While ZANLA fighters waited in camps, the army was reconstituted within the old command structure. In these circumstances, the military could not easily be used as a revolutionary force to effect fundamental social change, as was the Ethiopian army under the Derg. Similarly, the bureaucracy was simply Africanized under the terms of a professional civil service. So far from becoming an instrument of mobilization and reconstruction, as in Mozambique and Angola (where the ranks of the colonial administration were thoroughly depleted as the Portuguese fled), the bureaucracy resumed its role of technocratic administrator of a fundamentally market-oriented economic system and society. The resulting continuity obstructed the new leadership's capacity to orchestrate a thoroughgoing political, economic, and social transformation.

These self-imposed constraints, however, were backed by the powerful rationale of reconstruction and redistribution. Social justice would be attained not through further revolutionary dislocation, but via a policy of "growth with equity." The two terms of this difficult equation, the plague of social democracies everywhere, would naturally become unbalanced from time to time; but the equation both justifies and ensures moderation and pragmatism in regard to nationalization, foreign investment, incomes policy, land reform, and the like. Moreover, the importance of the peasantry to ZANU means a continued commitment to what traditional Marxism would label the "petit bourgeois" concerns of land to the tiller and fair prices for the small producer. In short, a regime anxious to live up to promises of redistribution could easily endorse national reconciliation and continued respect for private property as the price one had to pay for the social welfare all desired. This reasoning was all the more attractive to a party like ZANU, which lacked cohesion and ideological clarity and was faced with a powerful bureaucracy and a developed private sector.

The situation is quite otherwise in the cases of Ethiopia, Angola, and Mozambique, where the accession to power and regime consolidation took place in circumstances lending themselves to considerable autonomy for the ruling elites. Here pragmatism appears not at the outset of the regime as an alternative vision of socialist transformation, but in the course of consolidation as a necessity born of circumstance. In each case, we noted, Marxist-Leninist ideology provided legitimacy for the regime even as it created new hurdles and difficulties for the leadership. In each case, these difficulties were compounded by the weakness of the state itself, natural disaster, and international pressures and interference.

The pragmatism of these regimes, we have argued, is reluctant; and it varies from issue to issue. On strictly political issues, we saw, all three regimes have chosen to draw the line, going to considerable trouble, in the case of Ethiopia, to construct a vanguard party, attempting against considerable odds, in the case of Mozambique, to honor the "democratic" commitments of democratic centralism. More revealing, perhaps, all three regimes have put up determined resistance to ethnic claims, claims that are seen as threatening both to the cohesion of the regime and to the principles of class solidarity. This choice, as much as any other, demonstrates the seriousness of the claims of ideology, for it has brought enormous costs, especially in Angola and Ethiopia, and to date has resulted in the *de facto* autonomy of the contending regions. Calculations of power, whatever role they play in the long run, surely play a secondary role in this instance, for leaders have exchanged the effective power available in negotiated settlements for a protracted struggle with no end in sight. In this respect, even ZANU has sacrificed the possible fruits of accommodation for a difficult and sometimes brutal struggle over control.

If the Leninist prescriptions for maximum control over the revolutionary process make political pragmatism difficult on the home front, there remains considerable room for adaptation in economic matters and in international relations. In regard to South Africa, experiments with accommodation born of a desperate desire to halt that country's destabilizing activities have been severely disappointed. What lessons the leaders of Angola and Mozambique have drawn from this experience are not yet clear, but certainly there are no overwhelming ideological obstacles to a policy of "peaceful coexistence," particularly when the neighbor in question controls vastly superior military power. The reluctance of the Soviet Union to become deeply embroiled in the affairs of Southern Africa only underlines the necessity for pragmatic accommodation of some sort.

In economic matters, the flexibility of Marxist ideology provides considerable room for maneuver, despite the relatively recent endorsement by Soviet theoreticians of a strategy of rapid and massive transformation in the Third World. The Hungarian experiments with decentralization and markets, which Moscow has noticeably ceased to criticize of late, provide not so much a model as a justification for the pragmatic adjustment of policies initially cast in a virtually Stalinist mold. Heavy industrial development, centralization, nationalization, and collectivization remain the norms for Ethiopia, despite its substantial debt burdens, resettlement costs, and inadequate infrastructure development. But Mozambique and

316   Donald Rothchild & Michael Foley

Angola have reduced their emphasis on the immediate implementation of such goals, allowing considerable scope for market activities in commerce, farming, and artisanal industries. If, from an ideological point of view, this represents a backward step in the "socialization" of production, it can nevertheless be justified as an evolutionary necessity, one hedged moreover by socialist restrictions on individual accumulation and the exploitation of hired labor. Relations with multinational corporations can be justified in the same terms, and the line between ideology and a pragmatism founded on necessity thus blurs easily.

The opening of relations with the World Bank and the IMF, nevertheless, poses dilemmas that highlight the dangers of pragmatic accommodation, even when justified on soundly Marxist lines. IMF-imposed stabilization polices, in particular, represent a severe strain on the redistributive capacities of any regime proclaiming a commitment to the working population. Working-class incomes and welfare provisions are routinely downplayed in favor of accumulation, presumably on the part of entrepreneurs, both foreign and domestic. Societal aspirations are sacrificed to the logic of comparative advantage, a logic that too often favors First World producers over Third World development. But IMF conditions are part of the price one must pay for the foreign exchange and aid the Third World countries desperately crave. Accommodation at this level poses severe difficulties for the fragile Afro-Marxist regimes. China could experiment with market forces and an opening to the West within the socialist framework because in part it enjoyed an enormous foreign exchange surplus. Angola and Zimbabwe have some leeway in this respect, although the fluctuating price of oil makes Angola in particular highly vulnerable. Mozambique has no such advantage, and the opening to the West could end not simply in disappointment, as in the Nkomati Accord with South Africa, but in entanglement in a situation where Marxist-Leninist goals increasingly recede into the background as the costs of accommodation mount.

Zimbabwe's incipient social democracy is likely to grow more pragmatic over time, that is, more accommodating to capitalist interests. The Africanization of the bureaucracy was not accompanied by its ideological transformation; on the contrary, as Bratton and Burgess show, even the most progressive new agencies associated with the land reform have been reabsorbed into the preexisting structure. Growing pressure for the social peace necessary for economic growth may even force the regime to slacken its pressure on the dissidents in Matabeleland. There is nothing irreversible about the path ZANU has chosen, but there are powerful incentives for the party to maintain the parameters it has so far accepted.

Afro-Marxist leaders thus face difficult choices in the current situation. The Ethiopians appear to have opted for intransigence—

strengthening the newborn party and extending its power over the state apparatus; continuing emphasis on industrialization and collectivization; and taking a hard line toward secessionist movements. Within these rigid parameters, it has allowed a limited autonomy to certain relief agencies and parastatals, but accommodation stops there. Angola and Mozambique, by contrast, far weaker in terms of external military and economic constraints, have been forced to adapt to a difficult and often hostile environment. Those adaptations, especially in the case of Mozambique, although they appear not to have weakened the regime itself, may ultimately create considerable costs in regime legitimacy and capacity to act. Finally, Zimbabwe's ZANU, despite party claims of allegiance to Marxist-Leninist principles, appears much more committed to the sort of Marxism that Lenin despised in both the German Social Democrats and the later Narodniks, a Marxism committed more to social welfare (in this case, especially for the peasantry) than to revolutionary transformation and the socialization of production. Pragmatism, while it may find ideological justification within the parameters of Marxist-Leninist thought, entails the possibility for both "soft" states such as Angola and Mozambique and relatively more developed states like Zimbabwe of a long-run abandonment of the goals of socialist transformation in a world whose resources and economic and military power still largely reside in the hands of capitalist powers.

Notes

We wish to express our appreciation to Edmond Keller, Marina Ottaway, Dawit Wolde Giorgis, Roy Pateman, and Forrest Colburn for helpful comments on the first draft of this essay.

1. Crawford Young, *Ideology and Development in Africa* (New Haven: Yale University Press, 1980), 10. Compare the more conservative view, formulated specifically with respect to Soviet decision making, taken by Daniel S. Papp, *Soviet Perceptions of the Developing World in the 1980s: The Ideological Basis* (Lexington, Mass.: Lexington Books, 1985), xi: "First, Soviet-style Marxism-Leninism shapes the lenses through which Soviet leaders and decisionmakers view the external world; to a certain extent, then, the Soviet world outlook is a product of Marxism-Leninism. Second, Soviet-style Marxism-Leninism serves to legitimize foreign policy behavior; it rarely, if ever, serves as a motivating factor when other state interests and objectives are not at stake, but always must legitimate actions that are taken." As we shall see, there is considerable evidence that, in the case of the Afro-Marxist regimes at least, ideology often serves as a motivating factor.

2. See, especially, Kenneth Jowitt, "Scientific Socialist Regimes in Africa: Political Differentiation, Avoidance, and Unawareness," in Carl G. Rosberg and Thomas M. Callaghy, eds., *Socialism in Sub-Saharan Africa* (Berkeley: Institute of

318   Donald Rothchild & Michael Foley

Political Differentiation, Avoidance, and Unawareness," in Carl G. Rosberg and Thomas M. Callaghy, eds., *Socialism in Sub-Saharan Africa* (Berkeley: Institute of International Studies, 1979).

3. David and Marina Ottaway, *Afrocommunism* (New York: Africana/Holmes Meier, 1981).

4. Anatoli Gromyko, "Socialist Orientation in Africa," in Editorial Board, eds., *The Ideology of African Revolutionary Democracy* (Moscow: Social Sciences Today, USSR Academy of Sciences, 1984), 12-13.

5. Gromyko, "Socialist Orientation," 13.

6. See Jowitt, "Scientific Socialist Regimes," 156-159, for prescriptions similar to these first two for any genuinely "Leninist" regime, and Keller, Chapter 1, in this book, on the limited character of the language of class struggle in Afro-Marxist regimes.

7. Gromyko, "Socialist Orientation," 12.

8. Seth Singleton, "Building Vanguard Nations: Soviet Theory and Policy Toward State-Building in Africa" (unpublished paper, Ripon College, 1982).

9. Karen Brutents, *The Newly Free Countries in the Seventies* (Moscow: Progress Publishers, 1983), 76.

10. Government of Ethiopia, *Support the Just Cause of the Ethiopian Peoples* (Addis Ababa, n.d.), 6.

11. Quoted in John S. Saul, "The Content: A Transition to Socialism?" in John S. Saul, ed., *A Difficult Road: The Transition to Socialism in Mozambique,* (New York: Monthly Review Press), 97.

12. CPSU, *The (Draft) Programme of the Communist Party of the Soviet Union* (Moscow: Novosti Press Agency, 1985), 90-94.

13. Saul, "The Content," 103.

14. See David D. Laitin, "Somalia's Military Government and Scientific Socialism," in Rosberg and Calleaghy, *Socialism in Sub-Saharan Africa,* 174-177.

15. See Singleton, "Building Vanguard Nations," 7-11; Gromyko, "Socialist Orientation."

16. Singleton, "Building Vanguard Nations," 5.

17. Ottaway, Chapter 2 in this book.

18. Dessalegn Rahmato, Chapter 7 in this book.

19. Singleton, "Building Vanguard Nations," 10-11.

20. Singleton, "Building Vanguard Nations," 6.

21. Ottaway and Ottaway, *Afrocommunism,* 196-197.

22. Forrest D. Colburn, *Post-Revolutionary Nicaragua* (Berkeley: University of California Press, 1986), 16.

23. Interview, Dawit Wolde Giorgis, Princeton University, 10 February 1987; see also Allen Isaacman and Barbara Isaacman, *Mozambique: From Colonialism to Revolution, 1900-1982* (Boulder Co: Westview, 1983), 110.

24. James H. Mittelman, "The Dialectic of National Autonomy and Global Participation: Alternatives to Conventional Strategies of Development— Mozambique Experience," *Alternatives* 5 (November 1979):326.

25. Quoted in John S. Saul, "The Content," 137.

26. David and Marina Ottaway, *Afrocommunism,* 116.

27. Elizabeth Kridl Valkenier, "Revolutionary Change in the Third World: Recent Soviet Assessments," *World Politics* 38, 3 (April 1986):419.

28. Saul, "The Content," 78.

29. Correspondent, "Angola: Neto's Troubles," *Africa Confidential* 19, 2 (20 January 1978):1-3.

30. On the concepts of "facilitation" and "impedence" and their application in postcolonial state consolidation in Africa, see Donald Rothchild and Robert L. Curry, Jr., *Scarcity, Choice, and Public Policy in Middle Africa* (Berkeley: University of California Press, 1978), 61-77.

31. Saul, "The Content," 115.

32. David and Marina Ottaway, *Afrocommunism*, 123-124.

33. Ottaway, Chapter 2 in this book.

34. See, for example, Edmond J. Keller, "State, Party and Revolution in Ethiopia," *African Studies Review* 28, 1 (1985), 2.

35. On these trade-offs, see Donald Rothchild, "Kenya's Africanization Program: Priorities of Development and Equity," *American Political Science Review* 64, 3 (September 1970):737-753.

36. Isaacman and Isaacman, *Mozambique*, 155-157.

37. Young, Ideology and Development, 86.

38. Seth Singleton, "Soviet Policy and Socialist Expansion in Asia and Africa," *Armed Forces and Society* 6, 3 (Spring 1980):349.

39. John W. Harbeson, "Socialism, Traditions, and Revolutionary Politics in Contemporary Ethiopia," *Canadian Journal of African Studies*, 11, 2 (1977):219.

40. Rahmato, Chapter 7 in this book. Also see David and Marina Ottaway, *Afrocommunism*, 138.

41. *Considerations on the Economic Policy of Ethiopia for the Next Few Years*, report prepared by the team of Soviet consulting advisers attached to the NCCP of Socialist Ethiopia (Addis Ababa: September 1985), 15 (typescript).

42. On the promotion of reciprocity through exchange obligations around the time of the transfer of power, see Donald Rothchild, *Racial Bargaining in Independent Kenya* (London: Oxford University Press, 1973), especially 114, 145.

43. Robert Shaplen, "A Reporter at Large: Sanctions and Survival," *The New Yorker* (2 February 1987), 76.

44. Republic of Zimbabwe, *Transitional National Development Plan 1982/83-1984/85*, 1 (Harare: Government Printer, 1982):1-2. For similar priorities in the plan that followed, see the remarks of Prime Minister Mugabe in Republic of Zimbabwe, *First Five-Year National Development Plan 1986-1990*, 1 (Harare: Government Printer, 1986):i.

45. Quoted in *First Five-Year...Plan*, i.

46. Saul, "The Content," 135.

47. L. Adele Jinadu, Chapter 10 in this book.

48. Singleton, "Soviet Policy," 342.

49. David A. Korn, *Ethiopia, The United States and the Soviet Union* (London: Croom Helm, 1986), 91.

50. Robert I. Rotberg, "South Africa and the Soviet Union: A Struggle for Primacy," in R. Rotberg, H. Bienen, R. Legvold, and G. Maasdorp, *South Africa*

and Its Neighbors: Regional Security and Self-Interest (Lexington, Mass.: Lexington Books, 1986), 56.

51. Robert Legvold, "The Soviet Threat to Southern Africa," in Rotberg et al, *South Africa and Its Neighbors*, 37-38.

52. Legvold, "The Soviet Threat," 38.

53. Martin Lowenkopf, "Mozambique: The Nkomati Accord," in Michael Clough, ed., *Reassessing the Soviet Challenge in Africa* (Berkeley: Institute of International Studies, 1986), 55; and Peter Clement, "Moscow and Southern Africa," *Problems of Communism* 34 (March-April 1985):41.

54. Winrich Kuhne, "What does the Case of Mozambique Tell Us About Soviet Ambivalence Toward Africa?" *CSIS Africa Notes* no. 46 (30 August 1985):1-5.

55. Winrich Kuhne, "Moscow Scorns the 'Comrades' in South Africa's Black Townships," *Africa Analysis* (12 December 1986):1. Also see Francis Fukuyama, "Gorbachev and the Third World, "*Foreign Affairs* 64, 4 (Spring 1986):722-726.

56. Mikhail Gorbachev, *Political Report of the CPSU Central Committee to the 27th Congress of the Communist Party of the Soviet Union*, 25 February 1986 (Moscow: Novosti Press Agency Publishing House, 1986):93.

57. Gillian Gunn, "Mozambique After Machel," *CSIS Africa Notes* 67 (29 December 1986):1; Joseph Hanlon, *Mozambique: The Revolution Under Fire* (London: Zed Press, 1984).

58. René Lefort, *Ethiopia: An Heretical Revolution?* (London: Zed Press, 1983), 279.

59. Dawit Wolde Giorgis, "Power and Famine in Ethiopia," *Wall Street Journal*, 12 January 1987, 24.

60. Dawit Wolde Giorgis, "Starvation Became a Tool in Mengistu Experimentation," *San Diego Union*, 8 February 1987, C-4.

61. Saul, "The Content," 89.

62. Marcum, Chapter 4 in this book; and interview, Dawit Wolde Giorgis, 28 April 1987.

63. Allen F. Isaacman, "Mozambique: Tugging at the Chains of Dependency," in Gerald J. Bender, James S. Coleman and Richard L. Sklar, eds., *African Crisis Areas and U. S. Foreign Policy* (Berkeley: University of California Press, 1985), 143.

64. Howe and Ottaway, Chapter 3 in this book.

65. Rahmato, Chapter 7 in this book. Also see Dessalegn Rahmato, *Agrarian Reform in Ethiopia* (Trenton, N.J.: Red Sea Press, 1985), 68-73.

66. Colburn, Post-Revolutionary Nicaragua, 18-21. Also see Richard R. Fagen, "The Politics of Transition," in Richard R. Fagen, Carmen Diana Deere, and Jose Luis Caraggio, eds., *Transition and Development: Problems of Third World Socialism* (New York: Monthly Review, 1986), 254-258.

67. Robert I. Rotberg, "Introduction: South Africa in Its Region" in Rotberg, et al., *South Africa and Its Neighbors*, 5.

68. Saul, Chapter 6 in this book.

69. Gillian Gunn, "The Angolan Economy: A Status Report," *CSIS Africa Notes* 58 (30 May 1986):1, 6.

70. Marcum, Chapter 4 in this book.

71. Serge Schmemann, "Mozambique Rethinking its Dreams, "New York Times, 19 February 1987, A18.

72. Ethiopian Students Union in North America, The National Question in Ethiopia (Toronto: Norman Bethune Institute, 1976), 25.

73. Government of Ethiopia, The Ethiopian Revolution and the Problem in Eritrea (Addis Ababa: Ethiopian Revolution Information Center, 1977), 24.

74. On this, see the reports in the Observer (London), 7 August 1983, 10, and 15 April 1984, 1,9; also see Sunday Times (London), 6 May 1984, 1.

75. Allister Sparks, "How South Africa Beat the Marxist in a Rolls-Royce," Observer (London), 18 March 1984, 6.

76. The documents and accompanying statements appear in South Africa Digest, 23 March 1984, 3-7.

77. Michel Bole-Richard, "Guerrilla Raids Threaten Pretoria/Maputo Links," Manchester Guardian Weekly 133, 17 (27 October 1985):14.

78. See excerpts from the captured notebooks in Africa News 25, 9 (4 November 1985), 9-12.

79. New York Times, 20 September 1985, 6; and Allen Isaacman, "After the Nkomati Accord," Africa Report 30, 1 (January-February, 1985):12-13.

80. Africa Research Bulletin, 1-29 February 1984, 7151.

81. Ibid., 7150.

82. Clement, "Moscow and Southern Africa," 36.

83. Foreign Broadcast Information Service, Middle East and Africa, 5, 22 February 1984):U1.

84. John A. Marcum, "Angola: Twenty-Five Years of War," Current History 85, 511 (May 1986):194.

85. Ibid.

86. Saul, "The Content," 126.

87. Otto Roesch, "Mozambique's Agricultural Crisis: A Second Look," Southern Africa Report (Toronto) 2, 3 (December 1986):19.

88. New York Times, 19 February 1987, A18.

89. Gunn, "The Angolan Economy" 1.

90. For a similar view of recent U. S.-Latin American relations, see Albert O. Hirschman, "Out of Phase Again," New York Review of Books 33, 20 (18 December 1986): 53-57.

91. Bratton and Burgess, Chapter 9 in this book.

92. Ibid., 27.

The Contributors

Michael Bratton is currently program officer for the Ford Foundation in East Africa. He is also an associate professor in the Department of Political Science at Michigan State University. Professor Bratton has spent many years in central and southern Africa conducting research and contributing to development projects. Most recently, he has published several articles on rural development in Zimbabwe. He holds a doctorate in political science from Brandeis University.

Stephen Burgess is an advanced Ph.D. candidate in Michigan State University's Department of Political Science. He is currently engaged in dissertation research on the state and development in Zimbabwe. From 1980 to 1982, he was lecturer in the Department of African Development Studies at the University of Zambia. He has traveled extensively in East and southern Africa and has conducted research on liberation movements, conflict, and cooperation. He holds a masters degree in the social sciences from the Institute of Social Studies in The Hague, The Netherlands.

Michael W. Foley is assistant professor of political science at Texas A & M University, and a specialist in political development and the politics of agrarian change. He has written on peasant mobilization in contemporary Mexico and on Marxist theory, and is the coauthor, with Donald Rothchild, of two articles on political development in Africa.

Gillian Gunn is a 1986-1987 visiting fellow in the Washington-based Center for Strategic and International Studies' African Studies Program. She served as Africa editor of *Business International* (London) from 1981 until March 1984, when she was designated a Rockefeller Foundation International Relations fellow. Her two years as a Rockefeller fellow were devoted to in-country research on Angola's and Mozambique's relations with the West since independence.

Herbert Howe is acting chairperson of African Studies at Georgetown University. He travelled to Mozambique in January 1987 under a grant from the Edmund A. Walsh fund. He has published articles on U.S. policy toward Southern Africa and on Southern African security concerns.

L. Adele Jinadu is professor of political science at the University of Lagos in Nigeria and executive director of the African Association of Political Science. He is the author of *Fanon: In Search of the African Revolution; Social Science and Development in Africa;* several monographs; and numerous articles on African politics and political theory.

Edmond J. Keller, professor of political science at the University of California at Santa Barbara, received his M.A. and Ph.D. degrees from the Department of Political Science at the University of Wisconsin at Madison. His specialty is African politics and public policy. He has lived and worked in Kenya and Ethiopia. He is the author of numerous articles on African and Afro-American politics. He is the author of three books: *Education, Manpower, and Development: The Impact of Educational Policy in Kenya; Revolutionary Ethiopia;* and this volume, edited with Donald Rothchild, *Afro-Marxist Regimes.*

John A. Marcum is professor of politics and coordinator of international programs at the University of California, Santa Cruz. His work on Southern Africa includes a two-volume study of *The Angolan Revolution;* and *Education, Race and Social Change in South Africa.*

Marina Ottaway is associate professor in the School of International Service at the American University in Washington, D.C. She has written a number of books on problems of socialism in Africa, including *Afrocommunism,* co-authored with David Ottaway, and *Soviet and American Influence in the Horn of Africa.*

Robert M. Price is associate professor of political science at the University of California, Berkeley. He is the author of *Society and Bureaucracy in Contemporary Ghana; U. S. Foreign Policy in Sub-Saharan Africa: National Interest and Global Strategy;* and numerous journal articles and symposium volume contributions dealing with South African domestic and foreign policy, and U. S. policy toward Southern Africa. He is also coeditor of *The Apartheid Regime: Political Power and Racial Domination.*

Dessalegn Rahmato is a senior research fellow at the Institute of Development Research at Addis Ababa University. He is a political scientist by training, and his major research interests lie in problems of transition in agrarian societies and in political development. His publications include *Agrarian Reform in Ethiopia* and several articles on the food crises in Ethiopia and on food and dependency.

Donald Rothchild is professor of political science at the University of California at Davis, and visiting fellow at the Center of International Studies, Princeton University. In recent years, he has written or edited the following books: *Racial Bargaining in Independent Kenya; Scarcity, Choice, and Public Policy in Middle Africa; State Versus Ethnic Claims: African Policy Dilemmas; Eagle Entangled; Eagle Defiant;* and *Eagle Resurgent?* His contribution to this book was written under the auspices of the Center of International Studies at Princeton University.

John S. Saul is professor and chairperson of the Department of Social Science, Atkinson College, York University, and also professor in the Graduate Faculty in Political Science at York University. He taught for seven years at the University of Dar es Salaam and, on various occasions, at the University of Eduardo Mondlane and at the Frelimo Party School in Maputo, Mozambique. He is on the editorial working group of *Southern Africa Report* and a member of the Toronto Committee for the Liberation of Southern Africa (TCLSAC). His publications include *Essays on the Political Economy of Africa*, with Giovanni Arrighi; *The State and Revolution in Eastern Africa;* and *The Crisis in South Africa*, with Stephen Gelb. Among his edited works are *Socialism in Tanzania* (in two volumes) with Lionel Cliffe; and *A Difficult Road: The Transition to Socialism in Mozambique*. His forthcoming book is entitled *South Africa: Apartheid and After*.

Masipula Sithole is senior lecturer in the Department of Political and Administrative Studies at the University of Zimbabwe where he was dean of the Faculty of Social Studies from 1982 to 1985. He is author of *Zimbabwe: Struggles Within the Struggle*, and numerous articles on ethnicity and class in African politics.

Index

AEPA. *See* All-Ethiopian Peasant
Association
Africanization; Zimbabwe, 95-96, 98, 313,
316
African National Congress (ANC), 49, 79,
86, 110, 125, 142, 245; South Africa
and, 259, 260, 262, 266, 272; strength,
267-268
African National Council (UANC), 87
Afro-Marxism, 282-286, 317 (n1);
development of, 3-6, 12-13; economic
policy, 302-303; policy constraints,
286-288; pragmatism, 305-312;
regimes, 7-11; Soviet influence, 225-
230; state-building, 300-301
Agip, 189
AGRICOM, 148
Agricultural Marketing Corporation
(Ethiopia), 39
Agriculture, 29; Angola, 184, 187, 189,
304; Ethiopia, 39, 165, 169, 170, 171-
173, 303; Mozambique, 46, 47, 63
(n13), 118- 119, 246; Zimbabwe, 201,
202, 204, 207, 216, 217
Aid; Angola, 6, 70, 78-79, 186, 187, 194-
195; Ethiopia, 176, 233-234, 236-237,
239; Mozambique, 50, 54, 56-57, 143,
145, 153 (nn 57, 63), 242; Renamo, 52,
65 (n41); Soviet, 234-236, 239, 242,
296; Soviet Bloc, 248-249; Zimbabwe,
95, 216
Algeria, 1, 73, 283
All-Ethiopian Labor Union, 36

All-Ethiopian Peasant Association (AEPA),
31, 36, 41 (n18)
All-Ethiopian Socialist Movement
(MEISON), 33, 34, 41 (n13), 160-161
Alves, Nito, 71, 81 (n21), 289-290
ANC. *See* African National Congress
Angola, 10, 15, 80 (nn 2, 5), 181, 187, 190,
263, 286, 300, 302, 304, 305, 317;
Afro-Marxism, 8, 9, 11, 17, 282, 283,
285, 290, 314, 315, 316; budgetary
plans, 193-194; colonialism, 68-69,
182-184; Cuba, 78-79; development,
183-184, 188-193, 292-293, 310, 312,
316; economic reconstruction, 73, 76-
77, 185-186, 187-188, 189, 191-192;
factions, 67-68, 70-71; foreign
investment, 186, 189, 191, 194-195;
insurgency, 306, 307, 309; Marxism-
Leninism, 71-72; organization, 14, 82-
83 (n46); party consolidation, 289-290;
political education, 72-73; socialism, 5,
78-80; South Africa, 262, 264, 265,
267, 268, 271, 274-275, 299, 304, 308-
309; Soviet Union, 3, 226, 239-240,
286, 295, 296, 297. *See also*
Movimento popular de libertação de
Angola
Angolan Central Bank, 191
Angolan Writers' Union, 76
Arusha Declaration, 2-3
Assistance. *See* Aid
Atnafu (Colonel), 163

327

Bahamas, 192
Bakongo, 183
Bale, 27
Bank of Mozambique, 246
Bante, Tefferi, 163
Beira corridor, 273-274
Benin, 10, 17
Bindura, 129
Black market, 189-190
BLS countries, 261
Bophuthatswana, 261
Botha, Pik, 131, 263
Botha, P.W., 130, 261
Botswana, 259, 261
Brazil, 192
Brezhnev Doctrine, 226
Bulgaria, 249

Capitalism, 14-15
Cardoso, Alvaro, 128, 129
Carter, Jimmy, 4
Catholic Church, 74-75, 301
CELU. See Confederation of Ethiopian
    Labor Unions
CFU. See Commercial Farmers Union
Chevron, 194, 195, 312
Chidyausiku, Godfrey, 96
Chidzero, Bernard, 216
Chikerema, James, 88, 104 (n7)
China, 185, 240, 316
Chipande, Alberto, 59, 243
Chissano, Joaquim Alberto, 43, 50, 61 (n2),
    149
Chitepo, Herbert, 89, 90
Church of Christ, 75
Ciskei, 261
Cities Services, 189
Class consciousness; Zimbabwe, 200-201,
    215.
Collectivization; Angola, 188; Ethiopia, 29,
    31-32, 36; Marxism-Leninism, 300,
    301
Colonialism, 1; Angola, 182-184; ethnic
    problems, 99-100; Mozambique, 111-
    112, 240
COMECON. See Council for Mutual
    Economic Assistance
Commercial Farmers Union (CFU)
    (Zimbabwe), 217
Commission for the Organization of the
    Party of the Working People of

Ethiopia (COPWE), 13, 35, 164, 238
Communism; Soviet models, 10-11; U.S.
    concerns, 3-4
Communist Party of the Soviet Union
    (CPSU); Afro-Marxism and, 225-226;
    and Frelimo, 250-252
Comprehensive Anti-Apartheid Act (1986)
    (U.S.), 271
Confederation of Ethiopian Labor Unions
    (CELU), 161
Congo, 3, 10, 12, 17
Conoco, 312
Cooperatives; Ethiopia, 36, 39, 174
COPWE. See Commission for the
    Organization of the Party of the
    Working People of Ethiopia
Council for Mutual Economic Assistance,
    191, 311; Mozambique, 242, 248, 249
Counterinsurgency. See Insurgency
CPSU. See Communist Party of the Soviet
    Union
Cristina, Orlando, 128-129, 130-131
Cruz, Viriato da, 74
Cuba; Angola, 3, 71, 78-79, 185; Ethiopia,
    234

Dahlak Islands, 232, 233
Dare. See Dare re Chimurenga
Dare re Chimurenga (Rhodesia), 90, 104
    (n15)
Derg, 28-29, 39, 40, 158, 159, 232, 237;
    organization, 162-163, 178 (n6); party
    building, 32-34, 41 (n14); power
    centralization, 31, 37; reform, 156,
    293. See also Ethiopia
Destabilization; Mozambique, 128-129, 130-
    132, 133-134, 135, 138-139; southern
    Africa, 110-111, 123, 125, 132-133,
    262, 299; terrorism, 136-137; Zambia,
    127-128. See also Guerrilla war;
    Insurgency
Development; Angola, 292-293, 316;
    destabilization, 131-133; Ethiopia,
    165-166, 170-171, 173-175, 176, 293-
    294; Mozambique, 50, 57, 117-120,
    127, 129-130, 143, 146- 147, 291-292,
    311; reconstruction, 73, 76-77;
    Zimbabwe, 216-217, 294-295
Dhlakama, Alfonso, 129, 132
Diamang, 186
Diamond industry, 186

Disinvestment, 271
Dumbutchena, Enoc, 96
Dunem, Jose van, 290

East Germany. See German Democratic
    Republic
Economic development. See Development
Economic sanctions; South Africa, 271-272,
    273-274
Economy; Afro-Marxism, 302-303; Angola,
    188-193, 304; capitalism, 14-15;
    colonization, 182-183; dislocation,
    166-167; Ethiopia, 38-39, 164-165,
    168-169, 175, 304; Mozambique, 44,
    47, 48-49, 111, 113, 118-120, 131-132,
    143, 144-146, 246-248, 304; regional,
    110, 125; socialization, 15, 16; South
    Africa, 257-258, 264-265, 267, 271;
    Zimbabwe, 100-101, 106 (n47), 201-
    202, 203-204, 220-221. See also
    Development; Economic sanctions
EDU. See Ethiopian Democratic Union
Education; Angola, 72-73; in communism,
    13, 35; Mozambique, 52; Zimbabwe,
    205
EEC. See European Economic Community
ELF. See Eritrean Liberation Front
Elf Aquitaine, 189, 195, 312
Employment; Ethiopia, 174; Zimbabwe,
    201, 206, 207
EPLF. See Eritrean People's Liberation
    Forces
EPRP. See Ethiopian People's Revolutionary
    Party
Eritrea, 26-27, 303-304, 306; resistance
    movement, 37, 38; Soviet Union and,
    231, 233
Eritrean Liberation Front (ELF), 27, 37,
    233
Eritrean People's Liberation Forces (EPLF),
    37
ESP. See Ethiopian Senategnoch Party
Ethiopia, 5, 12, 13, 155, 228, 286, 304, 305,
    316-317; Afro-Marxism, 8, 9, 11, 17,
    282, 283, 285, 313, 314, 315;
    agriculture, 169, 171-173, 303;
    collectivization, 31-32; development,
    176, 293; economy, 164-167, 173-175;
    ethnicity, 301-302; famine aid, 234-
    235; ideology, 13-14, 305-306; land
    reform, 29, 30, 41 (n10); Marxism-

Leninism, 254, 290-291, 309-310, 315;
    military aid, 233-234; military rule,
    28-29; modernization, 25-28;
    opposition, 159-162; party
    organization, 32-36, 41 (nn 9, 13, 17),
    289; peasant associations, 29-30, 40-41
    (nn 7, 8); planning, 15, 168-169;
    political change, 156-164; populism,
    157-159; power consolidation, 25, 31,
    38-39, 40 (n8), 299, 300-301; power
    struggle, 159-162; resistance
    movements, 37-38; rural sector, 171-
    173; socialist reforms, 163-164;
    Somalia, 231-232; Soviet relations, 4,
    6, 230-231, 232, 245-236, 238-239,
    253, 286, 295, 296, 297; state
    organization, 14, 28-30, 161; Ten-Year
    Guiding Plan, 36, 39, 166, 169, 170-
    171; western relations, 236-237. See
    also Derg
Ethiopian Democratic Union (EDU), 160
Ethiopian People's Revolutionary Party
    (EPRP), 34, 41 (n13), 160
Ethiopian Senategnoch Party, 164
Ethiopian-Soviet Intergovernmental
    Commission on Economic and Technical
    Cooperation and Trade, 235
Ethiopia Tikdem, 157
Ethnicity; Angola, 75, 182, 183, 302;
    Ethiopia, 301-302; Mozambique, 302;
    party politics, 88-89, 90, 98, 99-100,
    219.
European Economic Community (EEC), 236,
    271
EXIM. See United States Export-Import
    Bank
Exports. See Trade

Fabian Colonial Bureau, 1-2
FAM. See Mozambican Armed Forces
Famine; Ethiopia, 173, 234-235;
    Mozambique, 138-139
Federal Republic of Germany (FRG), 249
FNLA. See Frente nacional de libertação de
    Angola
Ford administration, 3
France, 126, 192, 245
Frelimo. See Front for the Liberation of
    Mozambique
Frente nacional de libertação de Angola
    (FNLA), 70, 183, 185

FRG. *See* Federal Republic of Germany
Frolizi. *See* Front for the Liberation of
    Zimbabwe
Front for the Liberation of Mozambique
    (Frelimo), 12, 14, 61-62 (nn 1, 2, 3),
    88, 141-142, 262, 289, 301;
    counterinsurgency, 134-135; country
    control, 51-52; and CPSU, 250-252;
    economic development, 48-49, 291-292,
    311-312; ideology, 112, 115-117;
    influence, 109-110; insurgency, 44,
    306-307; leadership, 50-51, 115;
    military, 54, 56; organization, 115-
    116; peasantry, 118, 119-120; political
    view, 141-142; state consolidation, 45-
    46, 61; strength, 43, 44-45, 46-47, 48,
    57, 58, 59, 60, 61-62 (n3);
    urbanization, 47-48. *See also*
    Mozambique
Front for the Liberation of Zimbabwe
    (Frolizi), 87, 88, 89, 90, 97, 103 (n16)

GDR. *See* German Democratic Republic
General Motors, 311
German Democratic Republic (GDR), 35,
    52, 79, 242, 248, 249, 252
Ghana, 1, 5
Gojjam, 27
Gonder province, 160
Gorongosa, 129
Gorshkov, Sergei, 232-233
Great Britain, 56, 94-95, 195, 245, 311
Guerrilla war, 123, 128-129; Angola, 73,
    183-184; Mozambique, 43-44, 45, 54-
    55, 112, 124, 127, 136, 137-138, 139;
    Rhodesia, 89, 90. *See also*
    Destabilization; Insurgency; Low-
    intensity conflict
Guinea, 5, 283
Gulf Oil; in Angola, 184, 185, 189

Haile Selassie; personal power, 25-26, 27-
    68; Soviet Union and, 230-231
Health care; Zimbabwe, 205-206
Herbert Chitepo College of Marxism-
    Leninism, 13
Heritage Foundation, 143, 144

Ideology, 12, 97, 203; Afro-Marxism, 7-9,
    16-17, 229-230, 282- 286, 317;
    Ethiopia, 232, 305-306; flexibility,

253-254; Frelimo, 45, 112, 115-117;
    Mozambique, 250, 252-254; regime
    consolidation, 312-317; role, 281-282;
    South Africa, 263-264; ZANU, 96-99
IMF. *See* International Monetary Fund
Imports. *See* Trade
Income; Zimbabwe, 206-208, 217-218
Industry; Angola, 183, 184; Ethiopia, 169,
    170, 171, 174, 235- 236; Zimbabwe,
    201, 209-210, 216, 217
Insurgency, 121-122, 124, 162, 167, 219,
    307; Angola, 76-77; Ethiopia, 159-160;
    Mozambique, 54, 56; South Africa,
    121, 126-128, 299; U.S. tactics, 122,
    125-126
International Conference for Resistance in
    Occupied Countries, 143
International Monetary Fund (IMF);
    Angola, 191, 311, 316; Mozambique,
    110, 145, 249, 311; Zimbabwe, 204
Investment, 265; Angola, 186, 189, 191,
    194-195; Zimbabwe, 209-210, 216
Italo-Ethiopian war, 230

Japan, 271
Jardim, Jorge, 128

Kapanda dam project, 192
Karanga, 90, 91
Kebeles, 171; power, 30, 32, 34, 163-164
Korea, North, 95

Labor unions. *See* Unions
Lancaster House agreement, 212, 215, 291,
    313
Land reform; Ethiopia, 29, 30, 31, 32, 41
    (n10), 158, 167; Zimbabwe, 209, 214
Legitimacy, 5; Ethiopian government, 28,
    294, 306; Zimbabwe, 212, 215
Lesotho, 261
LIC. *See* Low-intensity conflict, 122-123
Lomé Convention; Angola, 191, 311;
    Mozambique, 64 (n24), 248, 249, 311
Lonrho, 102, 311
Low-intensity conflict (LIC), 122-123
Lusaka Agreement, 115, 265, 308-309

Machel, Samora, 8, 13, 43, 53, 55, 61 (n1),
    116, 148-149, 248, 251; foreign
    relations, 143-144
Madagascar, 10, 17

Malawi, 51, 57, 65 (n41), 138
Mali, 1, 5
Manica province, 129
Manufacturing. *See* Industry
Manyika, 90
Maputo, 47, 48, 132
Marxist-Leninist theory; state organization,
    12-13; in ZANU, 96, 97
Mashonaland, 88-89
Mass organizations; Ethiopia, 35-36, 163
Matebeleland, 219; ZAPU affiliation, 98,
    100, 102, 219
Matzangaissa, André, 129
MDC. *See* Multilateral Development
    Council
MEISON. *See* All-Ethiopian Socialist
    Movement
Mengistu Haile Mariam, 13-14, 161-162,
    163, 233, 300, 306
MESN. *See* All-Ethiopian Socialist
    Movement
Methodist Church, 75
Military; Angola, 186, 190; Mozambique,
    52-53, 54-56, 59, 62 (nn 34, 36), 147-
    148, 242-243, 244-245; South Africa,
    269-270, 271, 273; Soviet, 6, 186, 232-
    233, 234, 242-243, 244, 296-298;
    Zimbabwe, 94-95, 105 (nn 28, 29),
    212, 314. *See also* Military rule
Military rule; Ethiopia, 28-29, 31, 34, 35,
    155, 158-159. *See also* Military
Minayer, Yuri, 246
Minerals Marketing Board (Zimbabwe), 210
Mining, 186; Zimbabwe, 201, 210, 216
Ministry of Land Reform (Ethiopia), 29
MNR. *See* Mozambican National Resistance
Modernization, 6; political, 25-26
Movimento popular de libertação de Angola
    (MPLA), 3, 6, 12, 67-68, 78, 79, 80
    (n2), 81 (n16), 82 (n34), 185, 192,
    262, 302, 306, 310; anti-religious
    policies, 74-76; economic
    reconstruction, 76-77, 185, 186, 187,
    292; organization, 69-70, 74-75, 183;
    party consolidation, 14, 71-72, 288-
    290; Soviet Union, 239-240, 296. *See
    also* Angola
Mozambican Armed Forces (FAM);
    operations, 52-53; organization, 54-55
Mozambican National Resistance
    (MNR)(Renamo), 14, 43, 44, 51, 52,
65 (n41), 129-130, 273; costs, 58-59;
    counterinsurgency, 48, 49, 54-55, 56,
    123-124, 128, 129, 132-134, 135, 308;
    Frelimo, 306-307; Malawi, 57, 138;
    power, 51-52, 299; recruitment, 135-
    136, 151 (n28); Rhodesia, 128, 129;
    South Africa, 57-58, 130-131, 134,
    136, 137, 144, 262, 263, 267; Soviet
    Union and, 243-244, 297
Mozambique, 5, 12, 109, 228, 243, 248,
    252, 253, 286, 302, 305, 317; Afro-
    Marxism, 8, 9, 11, 17; agriculture, 63
    (nn 13, 15), 118-119; aid, 54, 153 (nn
    57, 63), 248-249; colonialism, 111-
    112; counterinsurgency, 124-125, 133;
    destabilization, 131-134, 138-139, 307;
    development strategy, 15, 117-120,
    129-130, 134-136, 146-147, 148-149,
    150 (n16), 291-292; economic policies,
    48-49, 50, 145, 250; economy, 16, 47,
    57, 64 (n24), 110, 113, 119-120, 144-
    146, 310; foreign relations, 49-50;
    Marxism-Leninism, 251-252, 254;
    military, 52-53, 54-57, 59, 64 (nn 34,
    36), 244-245; nationalism, 111, 112;
    Nkomati Accord, 51-52, 152 (n51),
    245; party organization, 43-44, 50-51,
    298-299, 300; people's armies, 147-148;
    population relocation, 48, 62 (nn 7,
    11), 63 (n15); reconstruction, 307-308;
    regime strength, 43-45, 59-60;
    Renamo, 58, 129-130, 138; socialism,
    113-114, 150 (n14); South Africa, 60-
    61, 63-64 (n23), 141-142, 243, 244,
    265, 266, 267, 268, 272-273, 290, 299,
    304, 314, 315; Soviet Union, 56, 226,
    242, 240-244, 245-246, 250-251, 286,
    295, 297, 298; state organization, 14,
    43, 45-46, 61; survival strategy, 140-
    142; trade, 246-248, 250; United
    States, 142-144, 245; warfare, 53-54;
    western relations, 249-250; ZANU in,
    88, 89. *See also* Front for the
    Liberation of Mozambique;
    Mozambican National Resistance
MPLA. *See* Movimento popular de
    libertação de Angola
MPLA-Partido do trabalho, 72-73, 75, 83
    (n47)
MPLA-PT. *See* MPLA-Partido do trabalho
Mugabe, Robert, 3, 10, 13, 15, 89, 92, 295;

power, 88, 212-213. *See also* Mugabe regime
Mugabe regime; Afro-Marxism, 17, 203; redistribution, 205, 207. *See also* Mugabe, Robert
Multilateral Development Council (MDC) (South Africa), 261
Muzenda, Simon, 92
Muzorewa, Abel, 87, 104 (n7)
Muzorewa regime, 207

Namibia, 73, 75, 308-309
National Democratic Party (NDP)(Rhodesia), 86
National Democratic Revolution (NDR), 165
National Institute of Physical Planning (Mozambique), 311
Nationalism; action against, 128-129; African, 68-69; Angola, 183; Mozambique, 111, 112; ZANU, 96, 97; Zimbabwe, 97-98, 99, 103
Nationalization; Angola, 185-186, 187; Ethiopia, 29, 158, 166-167, 173-174, 304; Zimbabwe, 210
Ndebele, 219; Shona and, 88, 99-100, 106 (n4)
NDP. *See* National Democratic Party
NDR. *See* National Democratic Revolution
NEP. *See* New Economic Policy
Neto, Angostinho, 8, 69-70, 71, 72, 82 (n36), 187-188
New Economic Policy (NEP), 119, 144-145
Ngouabi, Marien, 3
Nhari rebellion, 89
Nhongo, Rex, 95
Nigeria, 67
Nkala, Enos, 95
Nkomati Accord, 16, 49, 51-52, 110, 129, 131, 133, 136, 152 (n51), 245, 253, 263; Mozambique, 307-308; purpose, 139-140, 141, 244; South Africa, 260, 262, 265, 266, 308
Nkomo, Joshua, 86-87, 89
Nkrumah, Kwame, 1, 2, 11
Nonaligned Movement, 64-65 (n39)
Nyandoro, George, 88, 104 (n7)
Nyerere, Julius K., 1, 2

OAU. *See* Organization of African Unity
Ogaden war, 34, 231, 233

Ogarkov, Nikolai, 233
Oil production; Angola, 184, 185-186, 189, 312; Ethiopia, 235- 236; prices, 193-194
OLF. *See* Oromo Liberation Front
"Operation Production" (Mozambique), 48, 135-136
OPIC. *See* Overseas Private Investment Corporation
Organization of African Unity (OAU), 67
Oromo Liberation Front (OLF), 38, 41 (n13)
Overseas Private Investment Corporation (OPIC), 209
Ovimbundu, 75, 183, 306

Pan-Africanism, 96-97
Partido Comunista de Angola (PCA), 69
Patriotic Front (PF) (Rhodesia), 89, 102, 202-203. *See also* ZANU-PF
PCA. *See* Partido Comunista de Angola
PCP. *See* Portuguese Communist Party
Peasant associations, 29-30, 31, 32, 36, 40-41 (nn7, 8). *See also* Peasantry
Peasantry; Angola, 74, 76, 77, 189; Ethiopia, 156, 171, 172-173; Frelimo, 118, 119-120; Mozambique, 47, 118. *See also* Peasant associations
People's Republic of Angola (PRA). *See* Angola
People's Republic of China. *See* China
People's Republic of the Congo. *See* Congo
PF. *See* Patriotic Front
PMAC. *See* Provisional Military Government (Ethiopia)
Political Office for Mass Organizational Affairs (POMOA), 34
POMOA. *See* Political Office for Mass Organizational Affairs
Popular Movement for the Liberation of Angola. *See* Movimento popular de libertação de Angola
Populism, 1, 2, 8; Ethiopia, 157-159
Portugal; African destabilization, 127, 128; Angola, 182-184, 192; Mozambique, 240, 244; nationalism and, 68-69
Portuguese Communist Party (PCP), 70, 81 (n13)
PRA. *See* Angola
Private sector; Ethiopia, 165-166; Zimbabwe, 100-101

Provisional Military Government (Ethiopia) PMAC, 157, 161-162, 163
Public sector; Zimbabwe, 93-94, 205-206. *See also* Nationalization

Rassemblement Démocratique Africaine, 1
Reagan, Ronald, 130. *See also* Reagan administration
Reagan administration; Mozambique, 143-144; South Africa, 266, 271
Rebellion. *See* Guerrilla war; Insurgency
Rebelo, Jorge, 252
Redistribution, 209; private income, 206, 207-208; Zimbabwe, 200, 203, 211, 214, 220, 221
Reform, 156, 189; Ethiopia, 171, 293-294; socialist, 163-164. *See also* Land reform
Religion; Angola, 73, 74-76; Frelimo and, 301
Renamo. *See* Mozambican National Resistance
Reserve Bank of Zimbabwe, 210
Revolutionary Ethiopia Women's Association (REWA), 36
Revolutionary Ethiopia Youth Association (REYA), 36
Revolutions, 12; democratic, 20-21 (n38); party building, 33-34
REWA. *See* Revolutionary Ethiopia Women's Association
REYA. *See* Revolutionary Ethiopia Youth Association
Rhodesia, 44, 86; destabilization efforts, 111, 127, 128-129, 130; Mozambique, 54, 243. *See also* Zimbabwe
Rhodesia Front, 86
Roberto, Holden, 70, 183
Rowland, Tiny, 102
Rural areas, 36, 74; Ethiopia, 160, 165, 171-173; income redistribution, 207-208; land reform, 29-30; Mozambique, 48, 118-119; relocation, 48, 136. *See also* Peasantry

SACU. *See* Southern African Customs Union
SADB. *See* South African Development Bank
SADCC. *See* Southern African Development Coordination Conference
SADF. *See* South African Defense Forces
Salazar, António de Oliveira, 68, 182, 183

Santos, José Eduardo dos, 75, 188, 190, 191
Santos, Marcelino dos, 64 (n26), 252
Savimbi, Jonas, 70-71, 79, 183, 194, 274, 275
Shamuyarira, Nathan, 216
Shoa, 159
Shona, 106 (n40); ethnic tensions, 88, 90, 99-100; political affiliation, 90, 98, 219
Sithole, Ndabaningi, 86, 89, 104 (n13)
Socialism; in Africa, 1, 20 (n31), 28-29; populist, 2-3; scientific, 4-5, 6, 10, 13, 78, 96, 97
Social stratification. *See* Class consciousness; Ethnicity
Solokov, S.L., 233
Somalia, 3, 65 (n41), 162, 167; Ethiopia, 231-232; Soviet Union, 6, 233
Sonangol, 73, 185, 312
South Africa, 135; aggression, 110-111, 140; Angola, 71, 185, 190, 192, 262, 267, 268, 274-275, 308-309; anti-communism, 263-264; counterinsurgency, 121, 124-125, 126-127, 128, 307; destabilization, 299, 304; economic sanctions, 271-272, 273-274; hegemony, 241, 259-264, 275 (nn1, 8); ideology, 263-264; international relations, 264-267, 270; military, 269-270; Mozambique, 53, 60-61, 63-64 (n23), 110-111, 131-132, 141-142, 243-244, 262, 267, 268, 272-273; Nkomati Accord, 136, 140, 308; propaganda, 267-268; regional strategy, 257-260; Renamo and, 44, 49, 51, 52, 57-58, 130-131, 134, 136, 137, 144; United States, 265-266, 268-269
South African-Angolan Joint Military Commission, 309
South African Communist party, 239
South African Defense Forces (SADF), 75, 260
South African Development Bank (SADB), 261
Southern African Customs Union, 261
Southern African Development Coordination Conference (SADCC), 125, 132
South West Africa People's Organization (SWAPO), 73, 79, 308-309
Soviet-Mozambique Intergovernmental Commission for Economic Cooperation

and Trade, 246
Soviet Union (USSR), 4, 5-6, 10-11, 102,
    185, 186, 266, 317 (n1); African
    socialism, 226-230; Afro-Marxism,
    225-230; Angola, 3, 78, 79, 192, 195,
    226, 286; Ethiopia, 34-35, 41 (n14),
    230-236, 237-239, 253, 286, 295-296;
    famine aid, 234-235; military aid, 233-
    234, 245-246, 296-298; Mozambique,
    52, 54, 56, 226, 240, 244, 246-248,
    286, 298; Somalia, 231, 232, 233
SWAPO. See South West Africa People's
    Organization
Swaziland, 259-260, 261

Takawira, Leopold, 89
Tanzania, 283; Mozambique, 56-57, 147,
    153 (n6); populism, 2-3
TBCV countries, 261
Teixeira da Silva, Gilberto, 70
Tekere, Edgar, 101, 216
Ten-Year Guiding Plan (TYGP) (Ethiopia),
    166, 169-171, 172
Terrorism. See Guerrilla war
Tete province, 88, 129
Texaco, 185, 189, 312
Tigre, 26, 27, 37-38, 160
Tigre People's Liberation Front, 37
Trade; Angola, 183, 192; Ethiopia, 169, 236;
    Mozambique 246-248. See also
    Economy
Transitional National Development Plan
    (Zimbabwe), 294
Transkei, 261
Treaties of friendship and cooperation;
    Ethiopia, 231, 232, 242- 243;
    Mozambique, 244
Tungamirayi, Josiah, 95
TYGP. See Ten-Year Guiding Plan

UANC. See United African National
    Congress
União nacional dos trabalhadores angolanos
    (UNTA), 71
União nacional para a independência total de
    Angola (UNITA), 14, 58, 70- 71, 75,
    183, 189, 190, 195-196, 296, 306; as
    opposition force, 76-77; South Africa,
    262, 263, 267, 274; U.S. assistance, 79,
    191, 194, 195
Union of Marxist-Leninist Organizations

(Ethiopia), 35, 164
Unions; Ethiopia, 35, 36, 161; Zimbabwe,
    218
UNITA. See União nacional para a
    independência total de Angola
United African National Congress
    (UANC), 87, 219
United Nations; Eritrean problem, 26-27
United States, 209, 231, 307; African
    policy, 268-269; Angola, 79, 184, 185,
    191, 312; communist concerns, 3-4;
    counterinsurgency tactics, 121-123,
    125-126; Mozambique, 49-50, 56, 142-
    144, 245; South Africa, 266, 268-269,
    271, 272; Soviet Union, 227-228
United States Agency for International
    Development (USAID), 216
United States Export-Import Bank
    (EXIM), 195, 312
UNTA. See União nacional dos
    trabalhadores angolanos
Urban areas, 30, 74, 208; Ethiopia, 156, 160,
    173-175; Frelimo, 47-48. See also
    Urban associations
Urban associations, 30, 32, 34, 163-164,
    171, 293
USAID. See United States Agency for
    International Development
Ushewokunze, Herbert, 216
USSR. See Soviet Union
Ustinov, Dimitri, 233, 243

Vanguardism, 13-14
Venda, 261
Viljoen (General), 263
Voz da Africa livre, 129

Walls, Peter, 95, 212
Warfare. See Destabilization; Guerrilla war;
    Insurgency
West Germany. See Federal Republic of
    Germany
Wollo province, 160
Worker's Party of Ethiopia (WPE), 13, 35,
    41 (n18), 238, 291
World Anti-Communist League, 143
World Bank; Angola, 311, 316; Ethiopia,
    236, 237; Mozambique, 49-50, 64
    (n24), 110, 145, 311; Zimbabwe, 216
WPE. See Worker's Party of Ethiopia

Yenishev, A.A., 233
Youth League (Rhodesia), 86, 88

Zaire, 185
Zambia, 127-128
ZANLA. *See* Zimbabwe African National
  Liberation Army
ZANU. *See* Zimbabwe African National
  Union
ZANU-PF, 202-203, 212-213, 215, 218-219
ZAPU. *See* Zimbabwe African People's
  Union
Zezuru, 90, 91
Zimbabwe, 3, 10, 49, 101, 199, 305, 307,
  317; aid, 216-217; class competition,
  200-201; destabilization, 132-133;
  development, 216-217, 294-295;
  economy, 15, 100-101, 106 (n47), 201-
  202, 203-204, 220-221, 310; elites,
  215-216; income, 217-218; institution-
  building, 213-214; investment, 209-
  210, 216; justice system, 95-96; land
  reform, 209, 214; Marxism-Leninism,
  313-314, 316; military, 95, 105 (nn28,
  29); Mozambique, 54, 243;
  nationalism, 97-99, 103;
  nationalization, 208, 210; political
  ideology, 202-203; political power,
  100, 211-213, 218-220, 221, 291;
  public sector, 93-96, 105 (nn 21, 23),
  205-206; redistribution policies, 200,
  204, 211, 214; Soviet Union, 297-298.
  See also Zimbabwe African National
  Union
Zimbabwe African National Liberation
  Army (ZANLA), 89, 91, 98
Zimbabwe African National Union
  (ZANU), 3, 13, 14, 56, 104 (n19),
  294, 307; ethnic problems, 90-91, 99-
  100; ideology, 96-99; Marxism-
  Leninism, 313-314, 315; organizational
  changes, 90-93; power, 85, 86-89, 94-
  95, 100-101, 102, 291. *See also* ZANU-
  PF; Zimbabwe
Zimbabwe African People's Union (ZAPU),
  56, 86, 98, 103; 219; Soviet Union,
  102, 286; strength, 87-88, 89, 100;
  ZANU, 87, 102
Zimbabwe Congress of Trade Unions, 218
Zimbabwe National Army (ZNA), 95
Zimbabwe Republic Police (ZRP), 95
ZIPRA, 95, 105 (n28)
ZNA. *See* Zimbabwe National Army
ZRP. *See* Zimbabwe Republic Police
Zvobgo, Eddison, 101-102